MW01143210

Intercultural Dispute Resolution in Aboriginal Contexts

Edited by Catherine Bell and David Kahane

Intercultural Dispute Resolution in Aboriginal Contexts

UBCPress · Vancouver · Toronto

15   14   13   12   11   10   09   08   07   06   05   04   5   4   3   2   1

Printed in Canada on acid-free paper

National Library of Canada Cataloguing in Publication

Intercultural dispute resolution in aboriginal contexts / edited by Catherine Bell
and David Kahane.

   Includes bibliographical references and index.
   ISBN 0-7748-1026-2 (bound); ISBN 0-7748-1027-0 (pbk)

   1. Dispute resolution (Law). 2. Mediation. 3. Indigenous peoples – Legal status,
laws, etc. 4. Indigenous peoples – Government relations.
I. Bell, Catherine Edith, 1961- II. Kahane, David J. (David Joshua), 1962-

K2390.I57 2004   347'.09   C2003-907458-7

Canadä

UBC Press gratefully acknowledges the financial support for our publishing
program of the Government of Canada through the Book Publishing Industry
Development Program (BPIDP), and of the Canada Council for the Arts, and the
British Columbia Arts Council.

This book has been published with the help of a grant from the Canadian
Federation for the Humanities and Social Sciences, through the Aid to Scholarly
Publications Programme, using funds provided by the Social Sciences and
Humanities Research Council of Canada, and the Alberta Law Foundation.

UBC Press
The University of British Columbia
2029 West Mall
Vancouver, BC V6T 1Z2
604-822-5959 / Fax: 604-822-6083
www.ubcpress.ca

Contents

Foreword
Paul Chartrand

We are indebted to Catherine Bell and David Kahane for having produced this timely publication on a subject of growing scholarly and practical interest. I am honoured to have been asked to write a foreword, and am also privileged to have met many of the distinguished authors whose works grace this book, including those who have written on international perspectives.

Interest in alternative dispute resolution (ADR) is seen as a response to various sorts of perceived deficiencies in the adversarial court system. The application of ADR theory and practice to Aboriginal issues results from the recent emergence of Aboriginal peoples' rights, or the recognition that the interests of Aboriginal peoples must be considered in public and private decision making.

Once Aboriginal peoples are officially recognized as having a distinct existence, and, consequently, distinct group interests, the manifestation of conflicts between competing interests is inevitable. Justice and practical considerations raise a number of pertinent questions. How are such competing interests to be reconciled and disputes resolved? Who decides and how? This recent concern manifests itself in various ways, and in a wide context. It reflects shifts from the idea of colonial systems doing things *to* Aboriginal peoples, to doing things *for* Aboriginal peoples, and finally, to the imperative of doing things *with* Aboriginal peoples. In this regard, the editors have carefully selected their materials and authors to reflect the complexity and international breadth of ADR responses.

In modern nation states that emerged out of former European colonies, Aboriginal rights are being debated within a tradition of citizenship rights. This context generates specific conflict resolution issues that emerge from the more general questions previously raised: Where do the Aboriginal peoples fit within the state and its institutions? How is state sovereignty to be reconciled with substate functional sovereignty of Aboriginal peoples? What is the relationship between citizenship rights and Aboriginal rights? How are the group interests of the Aboriginal peoples to be articulated and defended against the interests of all citizens, and of their governments? These questions, and the multiplicity of subsidiary issues which they raise, are being debated and resolved in a variety of forums. Some of them are created especially for Aboriginal people's issues but are operated by others, some involve only Aboriginal people, and others are operated jointly by Aboriginal and non-Aboriginal people. Some prominent examples discussed in this book include, in Australia, the Council for Aboriginal Reconciliation and the National Native Title Tribunal; in Aotearoa/New Zealand, the Waitangi Tribunal; and in the United States, the Indian tribal courts. The Canadian experience negotiating these issues in modern treaties is unique. Dispute resolution mechanisms under these agreements also receive well-deserved and valuable attention.

Emerging international concern about indigenous issues manifests itself in many ways. At the United Nations, small and tentative steps are being taken in response to persistent efforts by representatives of indigenous peoples from around the world to create new institutions that at least provide a forum for articulation of indigenous rights and interests, if not their resolution. There is the Working Group on Indigenous Populations, which brings together indigenous people from around the world to Geneva annually. The Group drafted a Declaration on the Rights of Indigenous Peoples currently being elaborated in a working group of the Commission on Human Rights. A Permanent Forum on Indigenous Issues, comprising appointed indigenous people and elected state government representatives, also began operating in May 2002. Its mandate is to advise the Economic and Social Council (ECOSOC). Some regional institutions established by aggregations of states have also provided a forum where the interests of indigenous people have received juridical attention and recognition. Examples are the Organization of American States (OAS), the Inter-American Commission on Human Rights (IACHR), and the Inter-American Court of Human Rights.

So, in a sense, Aboriginal interests are now firmly entrenched in a wide variety of dispute resolution systems. However, there are some nagging problems which need to be addressed and are thoroughly canvassed in this work. If I tried to put my own gloss on the authors' works, I would succeed only in tarnishing them. Accordingly, I venture here some general observations that arise from my experience with Canadian processes designed to address Aboriginal issues.

In the early 1980s, Aboriginal representatives were able to take advantage of the conflicts between federal and provincial interests in a national process of constitutional reform to secure official recognition of all Aboriginal peoples of Canada and protection of their Aboriginal and treaty rights. This was done in the form of an amendment to the Constitution Act, 1982. The resulting constitutional text, however, did not define those rights, nor the people who have them. Instead, political expediency led to a constitutional guarantee of constitutional conferences involving government and Aboriginal leaders. An observer of the conferences might have characterized this provision as a constitutionalization of mistrust. After not just one but four national conferences on Aboriginal constitutional reform in the 1980s, and a final national round of constitutional reform negotiations in the early 1990s, a national agreement on Aboriginal rights was reached, but floundered in a national referendum. Throughout the process it was not easy, or even possible, on matters of significant concern, to overcome problems caused by differences in power between the negotiating parties.

The failure of the political process to reconcile Aboriginal interests with Canadian interests has resulted in courts being the main forum for the resolution of conflicts that have roots predating Canada itself. In these cases, the courts of Canada cannot easily render decisions that have moral and political legitimacy with Aboriginal people. Decisions are viewed as one-sided and the dominion of Canada over Aboriginal peoples continues. In the eyes of some critics, the courts are the government gizzard, which grinds up Aboriginal interests. Even the courts themselves have recently been at pains to emphasize that negotiation is better than adjudication to resolve disputes.

This view has been echoed elsewhere. During the 1990s I had the privilege to serve as a commissioner on the Royal Commission on Aboriginal Peoples (RCAP). In our 1996 final report, we recommended a new direction in Canadian Aboriginal policy. The Aboriginal peoples recognized by the Constitution must be formally recognized in new legislation. The legislation must reflect guidelines established in a national political process involving Aboriginal and government leaders. But any policy, the commission emphasized, must be developed and implemented only with the effective participation of its ostensible beneficiaries, the Aboriginal peoples. To date, the federal government has been silent on these basic recommendations for fundamental change, which included the establishment of a jointly appointed independent Aboriginal Land and Treaties Tribunal. Instead, the focus has been on reform of an existing legislative framework that dates back to the 1870s.

The most recent government initiatives include a reformed Indian Claims Commission with a narrow mandate restricted to particular types of claims, introduced as Bill C-6 in October 2002. Also introduced on the same date was Bill C-7, which deals with election reform on Indian reserves. Both bills apply only to those Aboriginal people recognized as Indians in pre-1982 legislation, the Indian Act. The constitutional recognition of all the Aboriginal peoples of Canada, not just Indian Act Indians, compels new recognition legislation, but this has not been forthcoming. It seems even constitutional imperatives cannot overcome significant power imbalances.

One of the most positive Canadian policy developments is the negotiation of new treaties that deal with a comprehensive range of Aboriginal interests, from land rights to political rights of self-government. But even here, RCAP recommendations have not been adopted. RCAP advocated for recognition of Aboriginal nations. We not only recommended that the Aboriginal Lands and Treaties Tribunal assist with the processes of treaty negotiations but also emphasized that the tribunal "must be only one of an array of dispute resolution mechanisms available to the treaty parties."

Despite lack of progress on a national level, innovative ADR mechanisms are finding their way into local and regional agreements. In this book the reader will be treated to an insightful and sobering treatment of ADR mechanisms in modern treaties, land claims agreements, and other contemporary indigenous contexts. The editors have avoided the role of advocates for ADR as an intellectual fad and have included a balance of positive and critical treatment of its ideological foundations and practical applications.

Even if one takes the view that the ideological inspiration for ADR is heavenly, actual dispute resolution happens on earth. It results from human actions motivated by human concerns. These concerns are manifested in the apparent reluctance of Canadian and Aboriginal governments to embrace national and provincial processes that affect diverse Aboriginal issues and communities. For example, there is little evidence of fervent support among Aboriginal political representatives for the RCAP national tribunal, although the report as a whole received their enthusiastic endorsement. Consider also the fate of one of the basic recommendations in the June 2001 final report of Manitoba's Aboriginal Justice Implementation Commission (AJIC), a body on which I was appointed as one of two independent commissioners.

Governments largely ignored the recommendations of the original Aboriginal Justice Inquiry Report (the Sinclair-Hamilton Inquiry) of 1991. The AJIC acknowledged this and proposed a permanent round table on Aboriginal issues involving Aboriginal people of Manitoba, the federal and provincial governments, and other parties. This forum was modelled on something that had already worked in Manitoba in another policy sphere. Although the provincial government agreed to implement this process, Metis and Indian organizations showed only passing interest. The provincial government ended up replacing the round table concept with a Cabinet committee.

Just as one will be reluctant to buy a dog that might bite its new owner, governments are reluctant to set up tribunals and other bodies that can embarrass them politically, and Aboriginal people are skittish about participating in forums where their interests may be drowned or eroded. Nevertheless, Aboriginal and Canadian governments have successfully negotiated and implemented dispute resolution mechanisms designed to better accommodate values and interests of specific Aboriginal groups. This book explores the opportunities, challenges, effectiveness, and limits of these processes. It also raises questions about appropriate mechanisms to promote and protect indigenous values.

The essays collected by Catherine Bell and David Kahane show, in a most compelling way, that Aboriginal issues are complex and cannot be ignored. Resolution of these issues requires constant vigilance and efforts to improve dispute resolution processes. Most importantly, the editors have brought together the voices of Aboriginal commentators and analysts who demonstrate, in persuasive and sometimes elegant language, that justice and practical reconciliation demand that Aboriginal people and their values be involved in setting the norms upon which social order and effective dispute resolution depend. Through not only its structure, including excellent introductions to sections and commentaries on chapters, but also its content, this book offers invaluable insights to the reader. It belongs on the shelf of every student, scholar, or practitioner with an interest in ADR and Aboriginal issues.

Acknowledgments

The idea for this volume, and many of its key themes, emerged from the national forum on Intercultural Dispute Resolution: Opportunities and Issues, held at the University of Alberta in July 1999. We owe a continuing debt of thanks to our co-organizers, David Elliot, Wendy Fayant, Tom Ghostkeeper, and Judge Leonard Mandamin, and to presenters at the conference, who included Phyllis Collins, Chester Cunningham, Elmer Ghostkeeper, Stein Lal, Steve Mills, Andrew Sims, Q.C., Rebecca Williams, and a number of contributors to this volume. We also thank the larger group of forum participants, who helped us to identify key issues to be explored in this volume, and strengthened our conviction that this book could contribute to both theories and practices of dispute resolution in Aboriginal contexts.

We are grateful for financial assistance received for the forum from the Alberta Arbitration and Mediation Society; the Faculty of Law, University of Alberta; the Alberta Metis Settlements Appeal Tribunal; the Sahtu Dene Metis Arbitration Panel; and the University of Alberta Conference Fund.

Special thanks to the Alberta Law Foundation, which provided funding for the forum and helped to cover some of the costs involved in preparing this manuscript.

This book has been several years in the making; it has been a labour of love, with lots of the emphasis on labour. We owe a debt to those who laboured with us. Special thanks to Kim Cordeiro for the endless hours she devoted to this manuscript, and to Dale Dewhurst for assiduous help with footnotes and copy-editing. Thanks as well to our contributors, who have borne with us through the long journey that took this manuscript from brainstorming to bound pages.

Most of all, we wish to express our love and gratitude to our partners, Darren Lesperance and Cressida Heyes, for their ongoing encouragement and support. We dedicate this volume to them.

Intercultural Dispute Resolution in Aboriginal Contexts

Introduction

David Kahane and Catherine Bell

The past two decades have seen a burgeoning of theoretical and popular interest in alternative dispute resolution (ADR). Given perceived deficiencies in adversarial, court-centred responses to conflict, there has been a search for forms of dispute resolution less costly in both social and economic terms. ADR denotes modes of problem solving, negotiation, conciliation, mediation, and arbitration less formalistic than conventional legal approaches to conflict, more attentive to underlying interests, and less likely to create winners and losers.

However, notwithstanding their growing appeal, alternative forms of dispute resolution raise serious questions of justice: Does a move away from formal legal processes threaten the impartiality of outcomes? Do the dynamics of ADR disadvantage those with less economic or social power? How are concepts of justice and approaches to dispute resolution inflected by culture, and how can approaches to ADR take seriously the challenges of intercultural justice, understanding, and negotiation?

These questions seem particularly pressing, as ADR processes are designed and implemented in the context of Aboriginal land claims, treaties, and self-government agreements, and in connection with court-based institutions in indigenous communities. On the one hand, ADR offers the prospect of resolving disputes involving Aboriginal communities more effectively than is possible through formal legal processes, and in ways potentially informed by indigenous knowledge, concepts of justice, and approaches to conflict resolution. On the other hand, there are uncertainties about how to write effective ADR mechanisms into new agreements or implement them under existing agreements; questions around the design of fair and culturally appropriate ADR processes and the interface between such processes and existing state legal mechanisms; concerns about whether the outcomes of such processes will approximate the rules of natural justice; and skepticism about the ability to design culturally appropriate mechanisms with sufficient delegated substantive and procedural authority, given limits imposed by Canadian law. Questions also arise concerning the impact of delegated forms of decision making on Aboriginal autonomy and the survival and promotion of separate Aboriginal justice systems. Underlying this concern is a fear that modification of conventional ADR mechanisms furthers the project of colonization by adopting only those aspects of indigenous knowledge, values, and processes that do not conflict with Western values and laws.

These hopes, uncertainties, and concerns around ADR in Aboriginal contexts are intensely practical, yet also have extensive theoretical connections. Indeed, they can only be fully addressed by bringing together indigenous and non-indigenous legal and political theorizations of justice, dialogue, culture, and power with detailed reflection on actual cases. This volume establishes such dialogue between theories and practices of dispute resolution in Aboriginal contexts, thereby focusing and developing existing scholarship on intercultural approaches to ADR, including mediation, negotiation, and arbitration. The volume also makes available reflections on how the establishment of effective intercultural processes may be constrained by the institutionalizations of problem solving with ADR by jointly appointed Aboriginal/government tribunals, and other hybrid and indigenous processes. It also offers examples of indigenous dispute resolution philosophies and systems and explores the critical issue of whether it is possible to design ADR processes that empower indigenous institutions given the impact of colonization.

Although significant progress has been made in developing intercultural processes and joint Aboriginal and non-Aboriginal dispute resolution bodies in Canada, lessons learned from the design and implementation of these processes have not been recorded in a comprehensive fashion, have yet to significantly inform scholarship, and are slowly filtering into the language and implementation of agreements. Further, negotiators, dispute resolution practitioners, lawyers, tribunal members, and others engaged in dispute resolution in Canada have never systematically shared their knowledge in person or in print, nor has there been a review of the extent to which existing mechanisms are serving community needs. And while other countries such as Australia, the United States, and New Zealand employ models of culturally based dispute resolution in connection with Aboriginal justice, few of these models have been canvassed in writing from the point of view of Canadian needs and practices.

The chapters that follow engage these issues in both theoretical and practical registers, from the perspective of Aboriginal and non-Aboriginal scholars and practitioners. It is our hope that by framing a discussion between theorists and practitioners of ADR in Aboriginal contexts, this volume advances debates within legal and political theory over intercultural dispute resolution, and offers much-needed guidance to scholars, lawyers, negotiators, dispute resolution practitioners, and representatives concerned with dispute resolution in Aboriginal contexts.

Part 1: Theoretical Perspectives

The first section of the volume offers theoretical explorations of cross-cultural communication and dispute resolution between Aboriginal and non-Aboriginal parties. In particular, it grapples with the question of how concepts such as culture, power, dialogue, constitutionalism, liberalism, and tradition play out in theories and practices of conflict resolution. Authors in this section help the reader to understand how concepts that appear to be value-neutral can operate to undermine intercultural understanding. These authors lay the groundwork for a deeper understanding of the opportunities and challenges of intercultural dispute resolution demonstrated in the case studies and practical proposals that follow in subsequent sections.

Michelle LeBaron describes how forms of domination are sedimented in established modes of conflict resolution, including ADR: communication skills central to ADR training may not translate well across cultures, standardized ADR processes mistakenly assume that "one size fits all," and mediators aren't sufficiently prone to recognize their own cultural horizons. She offers a historical sketch of how issues of culture have entered conflict resolution, and suggests that an emphasis on efficiency and cost-management has obscured key complexities, at the expense of intercultural appropriateness. She then suggests how dispute resolution could better adapt itself to intercultural challenges: intervenors could develop intercultural competencies, which would involve leadership, creativity, authenticity, and empathy; and process design could become more elicitive and open to multiple meanings, in part through the use of intercultural facilitation teams.

David Kahane lays out shortcomings with conventional understandings of legal processes as potentially neutral between cultures, showing how these tend to favour dominant groups; he then explores how incorporating cultural sensitivity into theories and practices of dispute resolution may provoke legitimate worries about the potentially confining or oppressive effects of generalizations about specific cultures. Having characterized the complex "politics of cultural generalization" necessary within alternative dispute resolution, he explores its implications for ADR training and system design.

Dale Turner focuses on how differences between Aboriginal and non-Aboriginal worldviews have played out legally, especially around issues of sovereignty and land ownership. Taking up the work of Canadian political philosopher Will Kymlicka, Turner shows how even "diversity-friendly" accounts of intercultural negotiation inadvertently privilege dominant languages of law and justice, with the result that Aboriginal understandings become unjustly distorted when presented within these frames. He argues that Aboriginal perspectives on ownership of and relationship to land have been distorted by the requirement of translation into discourses of Aboriginal title and sovereignty; he then considers how Aboriginal voices might achieve equal dignity and influence within processes of dispute resolution, and the distinctive role for Aboriginal intellectuals in bringing this about.

Natalie Oman lays out a continuum of approaches to intercultural relations, from egregious misrecognition (denying moral status to the other), to solely instrumental recognition (assimilating the other to you), to fuller recognition of the other in her own terms. She then focuses on two complementary approaches to intercultural understanding, one associated with the Gitxsan-Wet'suwet'en model of intercultural relations and the other developed in the recent work of the Canadian philosopher, Charles Taylor: each of these associates dialogue with actual participation in others' cultural practices, and each preserves a place for moral judgment as part of intercultural understanding.

In her commentary on Part 1, Julie Macfarlane weaves together and extends the arguments of the four chapters to explore appeals to shared meanings in dispute resolution, and then charts a number of forms taken on by collisions between "cultures of conflict resolution."

Part 2: International Contexts
In this second section, authors discuss indigenous and hybrid forms of dispute resolution in the United States, Australia, and New Zealand. Values informing design and implementation and dispute resolution procedures and outcomes are elaborated for comparative purposes and to offer lessons from a wider range of ADR models than those found within the Canadian context. The chapters in this section also discuss the limitations of the ADR processes described and raise important questions about how indigenous processes can, and whether they should, fit into non-indigenous systems of law.

Robert Yazzie, chief justice of the Navajo Court, discusses the historical marginalization of Indian law and the rise of contemporary Navajo courts. He considers whether and how Navajo peacemaking can be transposed to other communities as a form of dispute resolution. He doubts that there are culture-transcending "principles" to be found beneath particularities of the practice, suggesting that any community wanting to learn from the Navajo must go through the same process as gave rise to Navajo peacemaking: plumbing their own indigenous values and understandings of leadership and wisdom. Yazzie discusses two particular dangers of legal indigenization: the reiteration of current legal and political pathologies when dominant systems incorporate traditional practices, then use them "on" indigenous peoples; and the setting up of mainstream courts as "gatekeepers" empowered to ignore or initiate peacekeeping.

Larissa Behrendt sketches struggles over Indigenous dispossession in Australia as these have played out in the legal system as well as in public debates over reconciliation. She shows how Indigenous cultural values conflict with those of the legal system, and characterizes a rival Aboriginal approach to conflict resolution. Against this background, she describes the limitations of existing approaches to intercultural mediation in the Australian context and describes changes that might make dispute resolution processes genuinely empowering for Aboriginal communities.

Morris Te Whiti Love, director of the Waitangi Tribunal in New Zealand, describes the historical bases for grievances and disputes between the Maori and the Crown. He then describes the structure and procedures of the tribunal in addressing inter- and intratribal disputes, bringing out the distinctiveness of its approaches to researching claims, mandating tribal representation, and mediating settlements. Through this account, he presents approaches to culturally appropriate dispute resolution that highlight its complex challenges, but also its promise.

Jeremy Webber's commentary on Part 2 shows how all three chapters point to features of successful mechanisms and to specific challenges of indigenous dispute settlement in the shadow of the colonial experience. He points in particular to the importance of incorporating indigenous standards of authority and wisdom, and of recognizing dispute resolution as a genuinely deliberative and collective process. Webber suggests that the fashioning of mechanisms of dispute resolution by Aboriginal communities represents a new generation of theory and practice of Aboriginal rights, one that moves beyond equality within dominant institutions to challenge existing institutional forms; he then shows how such modes of adjustment and accommodation have a hidden history within courts and governments, and considers how non-indigenous jurists can best foster culturally responsive means of dispute resolution.

Part 3: Canadian Contexts

This section offers four perspectives on efforts within Aboriginal communities to return to traditional models of dispute resolution, and sharpens the reader's sense of the challenges of accommodating these models within contemporary contexts and established systems of law. Each chapter demonstrates the tensions that arise in attempts to reconcile Aboriginal knowledge and processes with Canadian law and legal process but also offers a vision for intercultural dispute resolution that more adequately addresses Aboriginal justice issues.

Elmer Ghostkeeper argues that dispute resolution in Aboriginal contexts calls for more than good mediation skills: it requires an engagement with different knowledge systems. He articulates his conception of *Weche,* a partnership of Aboriginal wisdom and Western scientific knowledge; in doing so he characterizes a holistic Aboriginal worldview focusing on balance, and a Western scientific search for underlying laws. Ghostkeeper describes how these worldviews encounter one another at negotiation tables, using examples from forestry disputes and from Metis settlements legislation. He then suggests ways that translation across cultures and languages can enable just accommodations.

Val Napoleon begins from the context of reconciliation agreements between the Gitxsan Nation and the province of British Columbia, turning to broader questions of trust, forgiveness, and the construction of narratives of reconciliation. Napoleon draws lessons from modes of reconciliation in the following contexts: practices of restorative justice, reconciling Aboriginal and Crown sovereignty, the Australian council for Aboriginal Reconciliation, and ceremonies of reconciliation in British Columbia. She then articulates a Gitxsan perspective first on external reconciliation, insisting on the prerogative of Aboriginal peoples to define the standards of success and decide how they are willing to forgive; and then on internal reconciliation, wherein the Gitxsan must grapple with changes to their society and culture under the pressures of colonialism and the Indian Act.

Richard Overstall suggests that the legal device of the trust can help us conceptualize a just interface between Aboriginal legal orders and those of the state. He describes challenges of external reconciliation between these orders, internal reconciliation for Aboriginal communities based on kinship institutions, and future-use reconciliation whereby land is preserved for future generations. Overstall suggests that the cultural and political requirements of these diverse areas of reconciliation might be met through the legal device of the trust, exploring the strengths of this model using the example of a fishery co-management trust; such a model "shifts the locus of power from the nation state to the community and shifts the focus of change and experiment from positivist legal rules to equitable legal structures."

Dale Dewhurst discusses the shortcomings of incorporating indigenous models of dispute resolution into authoritative state systems. The Tsuu T'ina First Nation Court is a provincial court with jurisdiction limited to on-reserve offences; First Nations judges and prosecutors work with peacemakers to resolve conflicts, the emphasis being on the restoration of healthy relationships by addressing underlying causes of conflict. Dewhurst offers an illuminating parallel between the development of hybrid and indigenous justice mechanisms within the state system, and the development of the courts of common law and equity in English law; this parallel suggests that the expectations of Aboriginal people for their cultural norms and spiritual laws to be incorporated into the justice system are neither unreasonable nor unique. He considers the main objections to granting greater authority to Aboriginal courts – that Aboriginal spiritual values are not shared by all Canadians, that there is no monolithic "Aboriginal spirituality," and that a parallel system of justice invites too much conflict with adversarial standards of law – concluding that Aboriginal courts, to be legitimate, need far greater authority relative to the established adversarial system.

In his commentary on the four chapters, N. Bruce Duthu draws out their common emphasis on the challenges of reconciling Aboriginal and non-Aboriginal institutions: there are not only struggles over power and jurisdiction but deeply divergent conceptions of power and conflict, and distinctive "negotiating postures" cultivated by Aboriginal and non-Aboriginal mechanisms of conflict resolution. The goal of institutionalizing culturally diverse forms of dispute resolution may first require clarity and even consensus between parties about the substantive content, language, and conventions at stake.

Part 4: Issues of Design and Implementation

This section explores in greater detail issues of design and implementation. In particular it considers how issues of intercultural understanding and accommodation explored in previous chapters have played out on the broad landscape of Canadian legal institutions. Through a detailed review of emerging intercultural legal institutions and agreements, the authors provide examples of methods designed to reconcile justice goals and tensions identified in this and earlier sections.

Catherine Bell surveys a broad array of "indigenized" legal forms and agreements in Canada, drawing in part on presentations to the national forum on Intercultural Dispute Resolution: Opportunities and Issues. She highlights a number of questions about indigenized forms of dispute resolution, including concerns about their tendency to adopt only those aspects of indigenous ways that are congruent with dominant legal forms, and then explores how diverse Canadian experiments with Aboriginal forms in conven-tional legal contexts help to bear out the risks and also the promise of alternative dispute resolution. Drawing on examples such as the Metis Settlements Appeal Tribunal, the Nisga'a youth justice initiative, the Tsuu T'ina court, and the Nunavut justice system, Bell brings out not only the deep challenges of intercultural negotiation faced in establishing such programs but also the overlaps between conventional ADR rationales and the values of indigenous communities. She goes on to explore aspects of institutionalization that have enabled hybrid and bicultural legal institutions to meet challenges posed by particular cultural, social, and legal contexts.

Diana Lowe and Jonathan H. Davidson focus on innovations within the Canadian civil justice system and consider the extent to which such innovations may make space for traditional Aboriginal modes of dispute resolution. Lowe and Davidson survey indigenous approaches to justice, as well as fusions of traditional dispute resolution with contemporary legal systems in the Canadian context. Against this background they discuss the impetus toward court-annexed dispute resolution models and suggest that such models offer significant openings to Aboriginal attempts to have indigenous values reflected in at least some aspects of the civil justice system.

Nigel Bankes surveys dispute settlement provisions in three northern land claims agreements, offering a detailed picture of how quasi-judicial forms of dispute resolution and arbitration may be accommodated within existing regimes of law. Whereas Bell, and Lowe and Davidson see promise in the incremental incorporation of alternative dispute resolution into established legal forms, Bankes shows the variety and complexity of mechanisms that result from this piecemeal approach to change. He also reveals the forlornness of dispute resolution mechanisms, given the availability of recourse to known, adversarial mechanisms. Articulating and comparing features of particular land claims agreements, Bankes draws lessons for the incorporation of dispute resolution mechanisms into broader systems of law.

Commenting on the three chapters of this section, Andrew Pirie points out the extent to which all the authors invest hope in the proper design of institutions so as to be sensitive to or reflect Aboriginal values, while also acknowledging the asymmetries of power that shape the design of institutions. Pirie sees troubling tensions here: while the authors evince optimism about the openness of ADR to Aboriginal perspectives and aspirations, they may not fully credit the susceptibility of ADR to more conservative appropriations, especially given the deep challenge to existing distributions implicit in many Aboriginal claims.

Conclusion

In the concluding chapter, John Borrows argues for recognition of separate indigenous justice systems, weaving in observations and examples offered by other authors in this volume. Responding to six common objections to separate justice, he persuades the reader that indigenous separatism is not detrimental to intercultural harmony or Western democratic notions of citizenship, fairness, equality, and justice. Integral to his analysis is an understanding that "intercultural dispute resolution is best facilitated through separate systems because they most strongly promote answers to questions guided by indigenous traditions." However, Borrows does not advocate separate justice at the expense of developing appropriate intercultural dispute resolution processes. Rather, he argues that these activities must proceed together to address the injustices and disadvantages suffered by indigenous peoples in postcolonial states.

Part 1:
Theoretical Perspectives

How should we understand and address conflicts between Aboriginal and non-Aboriginal communities? What sorts of cultural gaps and power differentials are typical of these conflicts, and how well are they dealt with by mainstream and alternative approaches to dispute resolution? The chapters in Part 1 grapple with these issues, in part by asking how notions such as culture, power, and dialogue play out in theories and practices of conflict resolution, and how we should understand connections between these concepts, especially in struggles for Aboriginal justice. The theoretical reflections in this section lay the groundwork for the case studies and practical proposals ahead.

1

Learning New Dances: Finding Effective Ways to Address Intercultural Disputes[1]

Michelle LeBaron

Parallel Dances: First Nations and Dominant Culture Patterns of Conflict and Resolution

In Canada, intercultural conflict is a part of life. A society of diverse immigrant and First Nations cultures, we conceive of and resolve conflict differently. Our histories and cultures have brought us into conflict as we have struggled to compose systems to bring order to our lives and the resources on which we depend. Conflict can be addressed well only with awareness of our historical context that includes oppression, subjugation, and misunderstanding, along with the development of social consensus.[2] As we talk and write about communication and conflict resolution, it is important to acknowledge that our history is marked by occasions of not understanding and not listening. To address First Nations and dominant culture communication and conflict, it is therefore essential to identify our standpoints, our experience, and our blind spots.

I was raised as a white, middle-class girl in southern Alberta. The city where I grew up is near two reserves, the Peigan and the Blood. I had no First Nations friends, knew little of their history except from the perspective of white interpreters, experienced no crossed paths. It was years later at a Virginia university that I had occasion to meet Madeleine Dion Stout, originally from the Peigan reserve, when she came to give a presentation on violence against women. I was struck with the realization that there had been violence between us, also. It was the kind of violence that keeps people apart, that bestows privileges on some and not others, that marks as different (and often as less than) cultural styles that deviate from the dominant culture. This violence has deep roots in Canada, taking hold when European settlements followed the demise of the fur trade.[3]

While I have worked to unpack the conditioning that was a part of my upbringing, I realize that I continue to be a member of a society that struggles with issues of equity, fairness, and access. It is with this awareness that I present some observations and questions related to bridging conflict involving First Nations and other cultural groups in Canada.

Many resources for intercultural conflict target improving communication skills and enhancing information about specific First Nations and other ethnocultural groups. While communication skills are essential to effective conflict resolution, they cannot transcend the barriers posed by systems and processes that reflect dominant culture values. Assumptions underlying our processes and our way of engaging in them must be examined if we are to develop ways to truly create deep change and durable solutions.

The need to look below the surface was reinforced for me when I attended a negotiation training for First Nations and representatives from the federal and provincial governments. The session began with a prayer and acknowledgment of the First Nation on whose land the training was held. Each group then had time to introduce themselves to others and to talk briefly about their approach to the upcoming negotiations. The First Nations representatives spoke about the stories of their people for seven generations, as these issues related to the land and the resources that would be the focus of the negotiations. Government representatives listened without interrupting; the expressions on their faces suggested that they had heard all this before. When it was their turn, these government representatives projected flowcharts showing the process for consultation and ratification within various ministries related to the negotiations. First Nations listeners received this in silence.

In this instance, First Nations and government representatives were involved in parallel activities. They were engaged in a dance that each has come to expect from the other. The material that they were presenting to each other had little meaning for those outside their own group. I suspect that rituals like these have been repeated often and have done little to advance genuine communication or dialogue among those who need to come to negotiated conclusions on important issues.

This chapter is about moving beyond these unsatisfactory dances. It identifies limitations of current approaches in the field of conflict resolution and suggests ways to enhance intercultural competence in training and practice. These ideas will be useful only to the extent that they are combined with a meaningful acknowledgment of ways that racism and privilege have shaped Canadian institutions, including courts, bureaucracies, and the laws themselves. Unless they are confronted, these values will continue to influence alternatives to our court system, including negotiation, mediation, and other conflict resolution processes. One way of confronting the privilege implicit in designing and implementing conflict resolution processes is to examine what is missing from our approaches.

My observations suggest that contemporary conflict resolution training and practice tend to be limited in three respects:

- Conflict resolution training tends to focus on culturally shaped communication skills that may not translate well across cultural boundaries. Little emphasis is placed on the development of intercultural competence as a core qualification for practitioners.
- Culturally embedded conflict resolution processes are becoming standardized as we move to increased institutionalization. Prescriptive approaches purport to be "one size fits all," but they actually fit those whose culture is similar to that of the designers.
- Our training and practice norms do not encourage third-party mediators and facilitators to assess their own cultural frames of reference in ongoing ways, nor to question how these frames may limit access, understanding, progress, or engagement in conflict processes.

I will discuss each of these issues in turn, suggesting steps to improve third-party training and practice to meet the challenges of intervening in intercultural conflicts. These suggestions are predicated on a dynamic understanding of culture as a source of differences, but also as a bridge that can connect peoples when it is understood and put at the centre of practice.

It is challenging to develop and apply a complex understanding of culture. We are necessarily drawn to generalizations that may or may not hold true within and among cultural groups (as David Kahane will address in the next chapter). Addressing intercultural conflict between First Nations and dominant culture peoples in Canada means trying to understand patterns that divide and keep us from resolving old issues that play out in new disputes. Even as I describe patterns, I acknowledge that change is constant and diversity everywhere within First Nations and dominant culture communities. I hope the reader will forgive me if I choose generalizations over denial of differences, even as exceptions exist for every generalization.

Generalizations at least raise awareness, and awareness stimulates our curiosity about each other. As we learn genuine information about each other, culture becomes a resource for increased understanding and cooperation between First Nations and other ethnocultural groups in Canada. Relationships will improve and conflicts transform as intercultural competence is woven into training and intervention along with sensitivity to ever present issues of power and structural barriers. But before we can move forward to improvement, it is important to understand from whence we have come.

Context and History: Culture Meets Conflict Resolution
Arising out of labour relations and dissatisfaction with costs and delays of courts, conflict resolution processes were never developed nor promoted

for their cultural adaptability. They have been touted as processes that make conflict resolution more accessible to more people; processes that give a more human, relational face to problem solving. These processes live up to that promise only when they take cultural issues into account, as these issues inform both process design and participation in processes. If processes carry unexamined cultural assumptions that fit better for some than others, then the human face of problem solving will not be universally accessible.

In the mid-1980s, the conflict resolution field began to recognize the importance of cultural issues in conferences, research, and pedagogy. One of the most comprehensive projects was the Multiculturalism and Dispute Resolution Project at the University of Victoria. The Multiculturalism Project yielded over a hundred interviews from diverse cultural communities related to conflict resolution. One of the chief findings of the project was that many conflicts involving individuals from outside the dominant culture and institutions (banks, government agencies, schools, and so on) were simply falling through the cracks. There were no existing mechanisms to address them, and there were a variety of visible and invisible barriers to their resolution.

Two other research contributions came from the University of Alberta. Carol Murray wrote a doctoral dissertation called *Transforming Environmental Dispute Resolution in Jasper National Park* in which she used an ethnographic approach to evaluate a multiparty decision-making process.[4] Murray's work emphasized that because the approach taken did not invite a focus on values, emotions, and relations, it did not fit well for all participants. Virginia Gibson wrote a master's thesis on the dispute between the Lubicon Cree Nation and Unocal Canada over a sour gas plant.[5] Her work emphasized the shortcomings of a process that did not take First Nations values, relations, and history into account.

These projects and other studies like them have been helpful in generating interest in culture as an important variable in conflict resolution. Culture has come to be understood as a broad construct, extending far beyond the ethnocultural group association that often limits it. Attention has been directed to the multiple cultural influences that shape individual behaviour and conflict processes, as well as to the centrality of power to understanding cultural dynamics. Power is always a factor that shapes whose cultural values are seen as legitimate, whose values are accommodated and how.

Awareness has grown of the truism that conflict resolution processes reflect the cultural assumptions of those who design them, especially in the absence of culturally sensitive assessment processes. For example, a process designed to focus on "the facts" may reflect a cultural bias against the expression of emotions. For members of highly expressive cultures, participating in a process where emotions are contained and viewed with suspicion is difficult and inhibiting. Similarly, a process designed with the values of cost savings and efficiency in mind may screen out what some participants see as critical relationship-building steps. Given a high value on individualism in Canadian and American dominant cultures, First Nations peoples' collectivistic focus on relationship may seem superfluous and unnecessary.[6]

First Nations cultures exist as permeable islands, collectivistic clusters surrounded by seas of individualism. Viewed from this perspective, it is not surprising that dominant culture legal processes and systems have been experienced by First Nations people as exclusionary, disempowering, and unfair. Bringing different cultural assumptions, values, and behaviours, they have not accepted procedures and structures that reflected dominant cultural "common sense." When conflict resolution programs multiplied, providing a revolutionary alternative to court handling of conflicts, a new opportunity to incorporate a wide range of values emerged.

In the last ten years, more and more conflict resolution programs have been launched. Mediation became institutionalized in the court system, schools, and administrative tribunals. The numbers of Canadian programs grew from a small list to too many to count. More and more mediators were trained. The alternative dispute resolution section of the American Bar Association in the United States changed its name to the "dispute resolution section." The adjective "alternative" no longer fit, since dispute resolution was becoming institutionalized. Ministries, departments, and communities began to get training, and law firms established dispute resolution departments. Everywhere, activity was directed at setting up dispute resolution systems designed to be less adversarial, have a human face, save costs, and minimize the destructive effects of adversarial processes. But not all this activity was responsive to cultural pluralism.

Integrating Culture with Conflict Resolution

As institutionalization of conflict resolution continues, it is important to pause and observe the processes and programs that have been adopted. Questions like these arise: Has theory and research on culture and conflict resolution been integrated into the systems that have been developed? Are trainers and programs including cultural perspectives in their curricula? When they are, is cultural diversity seen as an important aspect of awareness, as a module disconnected to other facets of conflict processing, or as an integral part of the conflict resolution process from initial assessments to final implementation of solutions? Are skills presented as generic or identified for the cultural frames from which they originate? Is process design done with an awareness of the cultural factors at the centre of the conflict and the parties' sense of how they should be accommodated? In conflict involving First Nations and dominant culture peoples, how is the history between them playing out, and is it being addressed meaningfully through conflict processes?

While there is much work to do to uncover answers to these questions, it is clear that limitations in our systems and practices exist. On one hand, we are constantly developing more sophisticated understandings of complex conflicts and how to approach them. Yet institutionalization has brought a push for ever increasing efficiency and cost-management that militate against a complex conceptualization of culture in many settings. This tension plays out at all levels, from process design to discourses within processes. Concerns related to this tension are not specific to any one group but are relevant generally for those in the process of incorporating dispute resolution into their structures or organizational settings. They apply to interactions between the dominant culture and First Nations, but they extend beyond this to intercultural settings from the interpersonal to the international.

In much conflict resolution training, culture is treated as a distinct module or topic, without being fully integrated into all aspects of skill acquisition, process design, and implementation. It is conceptualized as something external that divides us, without recognition that culture is everywhere, including within us; it is a set of lenses through which we see all human interaction and information. When communication and process design skills are taught without reference to the cultural assumptions underlying them, processes are more likely to mirror bureaucratic, legal culture than the culture of any particular ethnocultural group. Non-dominant culture values may be pushed to the sidelines in the interests of efficiency, cost savings, and even the laudable goal of fairness.

Challenging the Communication Skills Basis of Conflict Resolution Training

Most conflict resolution training courses focus on improving communication skills and learning a process. These skills tend to be presented as generic and pan-cultural. They are practiced diligently without regard to fit or transferability across cultural boundaries. We do not think to ask these questions: For whom are the skills taught comfortable? For whom are they awkward, too confrontational, or too focused on outcome?

For example, the ubiquitous skill of active listening appears in most dispute resolution training programs. Active listening involves attending carefully to the speaker and then paraphrasing back in a way that reflects both content and affect. It is a two-way process, involving confirmation from the original speaker of the paraphrase, followed by incremental turn taking – and sharing of information and perspectives.

While listening well is certainly an important feature of all communication, the skill of active listening has cultural assumptions built into it. It assumes relative parity in the status of speakers and a rhythm and cadence involving a frequent give and take in conversation. It also involves a relatively high level of directness. If elders are part of the dialogue, it may be seen as disrespectful to interject or paraphrase. If community norms favour hierarchy and deference to authority, active listening may seem assumptive or disruptive. If indirect communication is the norm among the parties, active listening may seem unduly confrontational. Indirectness, non-interference, not showing anger, and choosing carefully the time to talk are all part of some First Nations' communication norms.[7] Active listening may have limited usefulness in these contexts.

This example could be applied to many other communication skills that tend to appear in conflict resolution training, including paraphrasing, summarizing, and "appropriate" non-verbal behaviour such as maintaining eye contact. It is important to question the values underpinning skills taught and to include intercultural competence as a desirable goal for third parties. Intercultural theorists are divided on how intercultural competence should be cultivated and measured. Generally, there is agreement that intercultural competence is evidenced by relational empathy,[8] respect, tolerance for ambiguity, a spirit of inquiry, flexibility, and adaptability in being able to correct or adjust communication style to keep a process running smoothly.[9]

Intercultural Effectiveness as a Core Competency for Conflict Resolvers

My work suggests that it is as important to focus on developing capacities for intercultural effectiveness as on communication microskills, yet the latter receive far more attention in training and practice. Capacities most needed by effective intervenors in intercultural conflict include leadership, creativity, authenticity, empathy, and cultural sensitivity.

Leadership is central to effective assessment and intervention in conflict. Effective leaders achieve meaningful collaboration in process design, tapping the strengths and addressing the needs of all parties. They set a positive, appropriate tone, monitor the dynamics of processes for constructive engagement, and adjust to changing situations. Cultural sensitivity to the parties' cultural "common sense" is essential, as is attention to the fit between the parties' perspectives and those of the third party. A good leader checks back frequently to be certain that her or his "common sense" about the process is something all the parties can relate to.

The use of healing circles and family group conferencing in Aboriginal settings is an example of leadership responsive to cultural beliefs. It has been long understood that dominant culture justice does not fit well with Aboriginal worldviews. Ross quotes a justice proposal from the Sandy Lake First Nations: "Probably one of the most serious gaps in the system is the different perception of wrongdoing and how to best treat it. In the non-Indian community, committing a crime seems to mean that the individual is a *bad person* and therefore must be punished ... The Indian communities view a wrongdoing as *a misbehaviour which requires teaching or an illness which requires healing.*"[10] Circles in which community members witness and support a plan for reintegration of offenders respond to these cultural views. Implementing them involves a willingness to step outside "the way we've always done it" to find the most appropriate way of resolving conflicts. Healing circles, conferencing, and other approaches consistent with First Nations traditions have flourished, drawing on another core capacity for intercultural third parties: creativity.

Creativity involves a spirit of curiosity and innovation as well as access to a variety of modalities. When confronted with a culturally complex conflict, a third party may feel overwhelmed with competing information and dynamics. This may fuel an impetus to narrow issues, parties, and tasks as soon as possible. Experienced third parties may sometimes believe that they have insight into a good outcome, making it possible to "cut to the chase."

Creative third parties resist the impulse to short circuit the process. Instead, they cultivate ongoing curiosity about issues, parties, forms of intervention, and possible outcomes as these fit with cultural values, needs, and understandings of parties. Creativity is central to Aboriginal teachings that emphasize the human capacity to dream and bring dreams forth into reality, to receive inspiration from spiritual sources, and to recognize inspiration as an invitation to do or be something different than we have done or been in the past.[11] Creativity means being open to a wide range of resources for handling conflict – not just rational, analytic tools, but symbolic, relational tools as well. It means using all of ourselves in resolving conflict. To do this, authenticity is essential.

Authenticity is a measure of the congruence between our inner selves (and our perceptions, knowledge, and beliefs) and what we project to the outside. All of our communication skills are effective only to the extent that we use them authentically. This is not to suggest that well-intentioned and sincere third parties are always successful. Rather, third parties who have high levels of self-awareness, sensitivity to others, and good intercultural skills are likely to be experienced as more authentic by the parties in conflict. Authenticity is the mark of someone who has insight into her or his own set of lenses and patterns and is thus able to help others find ways through knots and complex conflicts.

Conflict between First Nations and dominant culture peoples has been marred by lack of authenticity and damage to trust. Denial through legislation and ignorance of the simple historical fact that First Nations peoples were present in established societies of high attainment before the

Europeans arrived has been a source of grief and betrayal for many indigenous peoples.[12] Attempts to reclaim lost rights have been resisted in many cases by governments that suggest that entitlements to land and cultural preservation have been extinguished by First Nations peoples' adaptation to dominant culture society. In disputing the Gitxsan-Wet'suwet'en land claims in court, government lawyers were at pains to establish that Indians "eat pizza, watch television, and drive motor cars."[13] With this legacy, it is understandable that First Nations people bring suspicion and a desire for authenticity to the table. Also missing from our history is empathy.

Empathy is an essential capacity for the intercultural third party: it means the experience of thinking and feeling with another. Empathy is a powerful way to build a working relationship and is surely essential to a lasting one. The literature on empathy is extensive, spanning psychology, communication studies, and intercultural relations. While there is no single agreed definition, many writers refer to it as the attempt to enter the frame of mind or worldview of another to the extent possible. To empathize is not to agree, nor does it require the listener to have had an identical experience in the past. Instead, it means to become the "I" in the other's story for a moment, feeling, sensing, and thinking from their perspective. True empathy is always interactive and may lead to the creation of a third shared culture.[14]

We cannot empathize unless we have a core of respect for another. Deep respect means a willingness to examine our assumptions about processes and the ways things get done. Within First Nations communities, respect may mean dealing with conflict indirectly rather than stating recommendations and fighting for them. Efforts may be directed to avoiding an aftermath of conflict where there are winners and others who feel left out or put down. Ross reports that, "to traditional eyes, few decisions are worth such kinds of unhealthy developments in the relationships between people."[15]

Parties to conflict impede themselves in empathizing with others by creating enemy images of them, as when the other is seen as chronically unreasonable or irresponsible. Dominant culture peoples in Canada have responded to First Nations communities by isolating them, denying their existence and their rights, stereotyping them, and adopting a paternalistic attitude toward them. These actions operate to justify a feeling of distance and foreclose the opportunity to make sense of the world from the perspective of First Nations people. Some theorists maintain that most cultures habitually identify "an other" on whom to project negative or unacceptable parts of themselves.[16] Conflict resolution must be concerned with the challenge of moving beyond the unconscious but deeply disrespectful practice of seeing another group as "less than" our own. Doing so draws on all the capacities we have discussed.

Leadership, creativity, authenticity, empathy, and sensitivity to culture are important resources in moving beyond long-erected fences that protect narrow-minded cultural habits from new ways of relating. Together with process design, structuring skills, and political will, they are critical to the resolution of intercultural conflicts involving First Nations and dominant culture parties.

Cultural Competence in Process Design

Conflict resolution systems should be tailored to the needs, capacities, and sensibilities of those they serve, rather than being designed as one-size-fits-all depots. It is only through an elicitive approach that diverse experiences of conflict, values, and expectations can be addressed. An elicitive approach is one that takes its lead from the participants, rather than imposing a formula on them.[17] It allows for and invites individual and subgroup input about preferred ways of approaching conflict, optimal identities and roles of third parties, comfortable settings, communication norms, timing, identification and levels of involvement of parties and outcomes. This approach is centred on the understanding that process design is a political act as well as a functional one. Process design has a great deal to do with who participates in a process and how. If it is not carefully and collaboratively done, conflict resolution will not realize its potential as a meaningful vehicle for people to be involved in the resolution of their conflicts.

Conducting a culturally centred assessment is a fundamental challenge to the idea that dominant culture American, Canadian, or Western European models of conflict resolution are applicable to all cultural settings. Conflict process models work because they arise from social consensus about communication, conflict, and ways of making meaning. They are specific to cultural contexts. They may be stretched and applied outside the context in which they were developed, but this may be both disrespectful and dysfunctional.[18]

Implementation of an elicitive approach is complicated by the fact that there are no monocultural groups, nor monocultural conflicts. Since each of us has a multicultural identity, every conflict has some intercultural dimensions.[19] Lack of uniformity in First Nations and dominant cultural groups means that designing a conflict process mirroring cultural values of each party is challenging. Whose values are reflected when there is opposition within or between groups? How do we design processes that accommodate preferences for directness and indirectness, for unrestricted speaking time and tight limits on participation?

These questions are further complicated by dynamics of change, power, oppression, and gender within First Nations and dominant culture communities. Traditional values and modern ways combine differently in various cultural settings. For example, women in some First Nations communities have questioned the move toward wholesale adoption of circle processes. They are concerned about whether their interests are being sufficiently represented and protected. Processes have been criticized for being "soft," leaving victimized women unprotected. For these concerns to be addressed, processes must be flexible and adaptable to local conditions.

While elicitive process design may be an antidote to standardization, it is seriously challenged by these complexities. How can elicitive process design become a vehicle for bringing parties together rather than emphasizing their different ways of approaching conflict? Lederach suggests guiding multicultural process design with the metaphor of "recycling," with its associations of transforming old into new.[20] Symbolic tools such as metaphor and ritual may well assist us in devising effective ways to implement elicitive process design.

Monitoring Processes for Openness to Multiple Meanings

Once a process has been designed in a way that involves and responds to parties, it is important to inquire how the process frames the way that cultural understandings and meanings get listened to during a process – or not. This is a critical issue because the process and the norms within it shape which topics are seen as legitimate, who may address them, and how they may be addressed. When parties to a process hold different worldviews, a dominant view may operate to foreclose discussion of issues or perspectives important to others.[21] Thus, while it is common in intercultural interactions that communication norms are inadvertently violated, silencing arising from process design and facilitation from an unexamined set of cultural assumptions is more subtle and serious.

When the level of meaning is involved, the possibility that a process may yield unfair or unsatisfying results looms large. When a participant gets the message, for example, that "the meaning you attach to land" is not relevant to a discussion of the application of the legislation; when participants cannot surface an issue because it is out of order; when the bureaucratic legal culture assumes that the issues at hand all relate to money, even when some parties explicitly state that they have other interests; when histories and stories of traditional ways are not heard, there may be problems with the integrity of the processes.

An example comes from a shared decision-making process that involved a wide range of participants who came together to formulate a plan about a valley where the ecosystem was threatened by competing activities and development. This process was quite well funded, had motivated participants who received training in negotiation, and had both a good secretariat and a talented facilitator. Agreement was reached on several points, and these agreements reflected many of the interests of those involved. The process was thus seen by many, including the governments charged with implementing the agreements, as a success. It was not "win-win," since everyone did not get all of what they wanted, but this is always the case in a complex, multiparty, multi-issue negotiations. Most participants saw it as a good process that enhanced relationship and commitment among the parties to implement and follow up on agreements.

But in a conversation a few months later with a participant who had represented conservation interests at the table, an important caveat arose. The participant suggested that although the process was successful in reaching an outcome, it had been less successful in providing a forum where the views he represented were heard and factored into the outcome. During the process, he suggested, a discourse emerged that privileged values and issues that "made sense" to those funding and convening the process. Other values, issues, and perspectives were not accorded the same respect. For example, the perspective of the earth as a sacred trust, a connected web with inherent value apart from its uses, was not as deeply reflected in the interest-based result as were material concerns.

When a mediator or facilitator is aligned with a cultural perspective of one group at the table, it is more likely that concerns of those from less powerful groups may fall to the sidelines. Mediators and facilitators are constantly making microjudgments about what is relevant, productive, and appropriate in a process. As these judgments are made from a cultural frame of reference more likely to match that of funders or dominant players, it is incumbent on third parties to examine their cultural assumptions and work, where possible, in intercultural teams. Intercultural teams make it more likely that a variety of perspectives will inform interventions.

While this is the ideal, we do not always work in teams, nor do we conduct thorough cultural assessments of conflicts, involving parties in elicitive process design. There are costs to consider – efficiency is a value held by many who fund processes – and parties have understandable desires to arrive at hard outcomes rather than talk about how they will talk. After all, conflict is both uncomfortable and political. Parties rightly look to mediators and facilitators for leadership about process issues. Our task is to provide leadership that is consultative and culturally competent even as the world gives us few luxuries of time and resources to build new processes to fit specific conflicts and conflict parties.

It remains critical to try, to ask the questions, to look for hybrids and recycled ways. If instead we look for a common denominator such as the formula contained in the helpful but culture-bound *Getting to Yes*,[22] we will limit our effectiveness and ultimately the promise of conflict resolution. Why is it important to resist formulas, even those that make perfect sense from our cultural set of lenses? Some of the reasons follow:

- We have a vested interest in believing that "our way works." We may forget that "our way works for us"; we may forget to ask who is not there, whose voice is not heard, whose way of making meaning "does not make sense."

- Influence and power are attached to dominant culture ways of doing things. These come to be seen as "right" and "necessary," while other ways get labelled as "alternative." The cultural common sense of those designing, convening, and funding processes becomes influential in how things are done. This cultural common sense is the unspoken reference point for defining "normal" and "appropriate." These assignments of what is normal are often invisible and out of conscious awareness until we hear something that does not fit. Garrison Keillor in Prairie Home Companion (a weekly radio production of Minnesota Public Radio in the United States) plays on this phenomenon when he describes a Minnesota community "where all the women are strong, all the men are good looking, and all the children are above average."
- Because cultures are in constant flux, there may be loss of confidence in traditional methods, or controversy about what these methods truly are and whom these methods serve. This should not result in traditional methods being dismissed or replaced.
- Internalized oppression has operated extensively in First Nations communities, sometimes causing victims of colonization to regard their own knowledge as less when compared with that of the colonizer. This may make advocacy more difficult.
- Effective leadership may mean completely different things in dominant culture and First Nations culture. If this is true, effective leadership must take both sets of cultural values into account.

Leadership Values and Conflict Resolution

From a First Nations perspective, dominant culture leadership is characterized by these tenets: Jealously guard your reputation and status; constantly analyze resources and the opportunity structure; make others aware of their dependence on you; create a web of relationships to support your power.[23]

Contrast these descriptors with Taiaiake Alfred's identification of First Nations leadership tenets: Draw on your own personal resources as sources of power; value productivity, generosity, and non-materialistic resources; set an example; take the greatest risk needed for the good of the community; be modest and funny; minimize personality conflict and use humour to deflect anger; be aware of role models; take responsibility for educating others.

Of course, neither First Nations nor dominant cultural contexts feature only one approach to leadership. Assuming the validity of these generalizations for the purpose of discussion, which of these two styles of leadership do our conflict resolution processes most closely reflect? Conflict resolution processes are likely to assume individuals to be autonomous actors with materialistic values. Credence is given to analysis and "rational" problem solving. Dominant culture third parties bring these values, often unexamined, and thus processes tend to reflect their biases.

Conflict resolvers advocating a transformative orientation to mediation may protest that their relational focus is more likely to enhance cultural sensitivity than a problem-solving approach.[24] Yet both approaches arise from specific sets of cultural assumptions. Cultural complexity will be effectively handled only in processes where underlying cultural values have been explored and interculturally competent third parties assist.

Ongoing Self-Assessment for Third Parties

Intercultural competence is not a destination but a journey. It requires ongoing, dynamic assessment of situations and an exploration of self in context. Personal assumptions related to conflict and conflict processes will influence parties whether or not they are spoken. Skilled third parties are aware of their assumptions and make mindful decisions about how to take them into account.

Concepts of what constitutes a conflict and who is a party, what level of confrontation is appropriate, how issues should be identified and addressed, and what is seen as resolution are intricately connected to a third party's cultural experiences and perceptions. North American dominant cultural assumptions favour a direct approach of divulging all relevant information. This style may be ill-suited and even offensive to those whose norms prioritize face-saving, indirectness, and relational harmony in problem resolution. Similarly, individualist assumptions about who is involved as a party may seem atomized and reductionist to someone whose community or extended family are part of a relational web, and hence necessarily involved in any attempt at conflict resolution.

Notions of what constitutes resolution vary. Some parties may focus on relationship, apology, or reconciliation rather than on restitution. Others reject resolution unless it means overthrowing or radically changing a system. Assumptions about resolution are so central to any "common sense" of what to do in conflict, whom to deal with, and which objectives to strive for, that they should be canvassed prior to any intervention. A third party whose views about conflict or resolution differ markedly from the parties' should consider partnering with someone whose perspectives are closer to the parties' or withdrawing.

Clearly, the suitability of a third party does not depend only on communication skills, nor on awareness alone. As well as intercultural competence, third-party effectiveness depends on identity, gender, status, and role. In considering whether a given third party is appropriate, difficult choices emerge. What if a female third party discovers that the other parties find it difficult to accept her as a third party because they are from patriarchal cultures where women do not play mediative roles? In the name of cultural sensitivity, should she defer to men to do the job? Is it acceptable to push their boundaries so that they experience women in leadership or facilitative capacities? If a third party's ethnicity is likely to inspire questions about credibility for one or more of the groups in conflict, can this limitation be transcended or should the third party defer to someone else with a less controversial identity, even if he or she feels capable?

These are not simple questions. No one would seriously suggest in the name of cultural sensitivity that ethnic and cultural identities must always be matched among parties and conflict resolvers. The possible range of identities is too broad and diverse, and who would decide which aspect of a party's identity was the most salient for matching with a third party? Would gender, race, regional origin, clan, or nationality be used as the criterion for such a match? Despite the acknowledgment in the literature that some groups prefer insider partials to outsider "neutrals,"[25] aren't there also times when an insider cannot possibly bring the credibility, the fairness, and the manoeuvrability of an esteemed outsider? How are multicultural conflicts to be handled when there are many cultural groups involved with corresponding levels of complexity?

Given the impracticality and undesirability of cultural or ethnic matching between those in conflict and third parties, how do we allow for times when third-party membership in an identity group is a precondition for parties to come to the table? Those who have experienced oppression or victimization may believe they need one of "their own" to help. Anja Weiss, in her discussion of power and difference, details reasons why this may be important.[26] She points out that even when dominant parties honestly believe they are treating everyone equally, concerns of subordinated parties may go unaddressed. Cultural misunderstandings may be used strategically by those in power to retain their advantage. Also, well-meaning third parties from outside a cultural group may have difficulties appreciating the subtleties and dynamics of an issue or of a group's behaviour within a process. Even those with intercultural expertise are not immune to replicating systemic injustices; they may, in the effort to right these injustices, choose a process that is problematic for some parties to the conflict.

These concerns are illustrative of a range of issues that should be considered in an ongoing way by potential third parties in conflict. In the assessment phase, parties should be invited to identify preferred identities, desirable roles, and capacities of third parties, as well as who will represent them at the negotiation table and how the process will unfold. During the process, third parties should monitor their responses to issues, perspectives, and behaviours to be sure that those closest to their own are not privileged. Ongoing evaluation, consultation with colleagues, and requests for feedback will help ensure fairness. Effective intervention draws on all our human capacities and requires constant attention to internal and external dynamics.

Conclusion: Dancing Together

It is important to keep living these questions: For whom do our processes work? How do our processes accommodate conversations about what is important, how it is important, and for whom? Whose values do our processes mirror and whose do they exclude? Only as we do this can we build a field that addresses issues deeply and resolves them in lasting ways rather than revisiting the unfairness of the past on parties outside the dominant culture.

Notes

1 This paper was written and presented in 1999 and does not refer to research or legal authorities after that time.
2 Robin Fisher, *Contact and Conflict: Indian-European Relations in British Columbia, 1774-1890* (Vancouver: UBC Press, 1992), xi, 87-88; Paul Tennant, *Aboriginal Peoples and Politics: The Indian Land Question in British Columbia, 1849-1989* (Vancouver: UBC Press, 1990), 39-41.
3 Fisher, *Contact and Conflict,* 98, 101, 103, 111.
4 Carol Elizabeth Murray, "Transforming Environmental Dispute Resolution in Jasper National Park" (PhD diss., University of Alberta, 1999).
5 Virginia Gibson, "Conflict and Culture: The Sour Gas Plant Dispute Between Unocal Canada and the Lubicon Cree Nation" (MA thesis, University of Alberta, 1996).
6 Stella Ting Toomey, "Communicative Resourcefulness: An Identity Negotiation Perspective," in Richard L. Wiseman and Jolene Koester, eds., *Intercultural Communication Competence* (Newbury Park: Sage, 1993), 79-80.
7 Rupert Ross, *Dancing with a Ghost: Exploring Indian Reality* (Markham, ON: Octopus Books, 1992), 12 (non-interference), 25 (indirectness), 29 (not showing anger), 35-36 (choosing a time to talk).
8 Benjamin Broome, "Managing Differences in Conflict Resolution: The Role of Relational Empathy," in D.J.D. Sandole and H. van der Merwe, eds., *Conflict Resolution Theory and Practice: Integration and Application* (Manchester: Manchester University Press, 1993), 98.
9 Judith Martin, "Intercultural Communication Competence: A Review," in Richard L. Wiseman and Jolene Koester, eds., *Intercultural Communication Competence* (New York: Sage, 1993), 25.
10 Rupert Ross, *Returning to the Teachings: Exploring Aboriginal Justice* (Toronto: Penguin Books, 1996), 5 (emphasis in original).
11 P. Lane, J. Bopp, and M. Bopp, *The Sacred Tree* (Lethbridge, AB: Four Worlds Development Press, 1984), reprinted in Ross, *Returning to the Teachings,* 275-77.
12 Tennant, *Aboriginal Peoples and Politics,* 14.
13 B. Williamson, "The Pizza Syndrome," *Project North B.C. Newsletter* (fall 1989), 1-2, quoted in Tennant, *Aboriginal Peoples and Politics,* 15.
14 Broome, "Managing Differences in Conflict Resolution," 103-4.
15 Ross, *Returning to the Teachings,* 87.
16 Vamik Volkan, Demetrios A. Julius, and Joseph Montville, "An Overview of Psychological Concepts Pertinent to Interethnic and/or International Relationships" in Vamik Volkan, Demetrios A. Julius, and Joseph Montville, *The Psychodynamics of International Relations* (Lexington, MA: Lexington Books, 1990), 34, 40.

17 D. Young, "Prescriptive and Elicitive Approaches to Conflict Resolution: Examples from Papua New Guinea" (1998) 14 (3) Negotiation Journal 211 at 15, 17.

18 John Paul Lederach, *Preparing for Peace: Conflict Transformation Across Cultures* (Syracuse, NY: Syracuse University Press, 1995), 10.

19 P. Adler, "Beyond Cultural Identity: Reflections on Cultural and Multicultural Man," in L.A. Samovar and R.E. Porter, eds., *Intercultural Communication: A Reader* (Belmont, CA: Wadsworth, 1976), 362.

20 Lederach, *Preparing for Peace*, 114.

21 *Ibid.*, 89-90.

22 R. Fisher, W. Ury, and B. Patton, *Getting to Yes: Negotiating Agreement without Giving in,* 2nd ed. (New York: Penguin Books, 1991).

23 Taiaiake Alfred, *Peace, Power, Righteousness: An Indigenous Manifesto* (Don Mills, ON: Oxford University Press, 1999), 89.

24 R.A.B. Bush and J.P. Folger, *The Promise of Mediation: Responding to Conflict Through Empowerment and Recognition* (San Francisco: Jossey-Bass, 1994), 238, 242-43.

25 Lederach, *Preparing for Peace*, 94.

26 Anja Weiss, "Power and Difference: An Extended Model for the Conflict Potentials in the Negotiation of Intercultural Conflicts," Berghof Institute, Berlin, 2000, <www.b.shuttle. de/berghof>. At the time of publication, the English version of this paper was no longer available online; a German version entitled "Macht und Differenz: Ein erweitertes Modell der Konfliktpotentiale in interkulturellen Auseinandersetzungen" was available as of January 2004 at <http://www.berghof-center.org/publications/reports/complete/br7d.pdf>.

2
What Is Culture? Generalizing about Aboriginal and Newcomer Perspectives
David Kahane

In multicultural, multinational societies such as Canada, political and legal disputes often hinge not only on struggles over scarce resources but also on deep conflicts of cultural values and understandings. Ongoing confrontations over Aboriginal logging and fishing rights in eastern Canada, for example, are not merely over access to natural resources: culturally specific conceptions of the proper human relationship to the natural world are very much at stake. Legal cases often hinge on how to read treaties between Aboriginal peoples and colonizing powers as they relate to connections to land, the place of hunting and fishing in sustaining particular ways of life, and the relationship between historical and contemporary understandings of subsistence and communal flourishing.[1] Thus, defining just procedures to deal with such disputes requires a cogent account of cultural difference.

My approach lies between two fields of scholarship: on the one hand, debates within Western political philosophy over multiculturalism, justice, and democratic deliberation; and on the other, efforts to incorporate understandings of culture into theories and practices of alternative dispute resolution (ADR). These two fields have much to teach each other. Political philosophers concerned with multiculturalism tend to seek abstract conceptualizations of culture, and principled accounts of how cultural differences should be accommodated by political norms and procedures – accounts meant to provide consistent and fair guidance in particular cases. In the field of ADR, many disputes plainly involve cultural conflicts. Definitions of culture – and strategies for dealing with culture in training and process design – develop out of these local contexts, and while there are efforts to theorize intercultural dispute resolution, there is also – at least in some quarters – a suspicion of abstract, one-size-fits-all accounts. In this chapter, I bring a philosopher's eye to questions of culture, deliberation, and dispute resolution, while insisting that theoretical understanding follow practice, and be grounded in the reality of specific cases.

I begin by sketching what I take to be a dominant understanding, in both North American common-sense and liberal legal theory, of what it means to justly resolve disputes. On this understanding, justice is satisfied by appealing to a set of principles and procedures that can neutrally adjudicate between parties' rights and interests. This model of neutral adjudication has been challenged, however, as itself representing a culturally specific understanding of human identity and relationships, one held, as it happens, by powerful social groups. Principles and procedures that pretend to stand above culture may in fact operate to the advantage of some social groups and the disadvantage of others. This challenge to justice as neutral adjudication is a powerful one and has motivated attempts to develop more culturally sensitive accounts of justice and of dispute resolution.

I discuss the difficulties of incorporating cultural diversity into theories and practices of dispute resolution, given that each person has multiple cultural memberships, and correspondingly complex cultural identities. "Culture" is an essentially contested concept, and generalizations about cultural understandings and values are perennially subject to challenge. I argue that while generalizations about culture are always caught up in power dynamics within and between social groups, we need to risk such generalizations in designing processes of dispute resolution. Any attempt to avoid or transcend culture in resolving disputes subjects us to an even greater risk: that of reiterating the understandings of dominant cultural groups under the guise of neutrality.

I make the case that generalizations about cultural identities and values should play a key role in designing procedures to resolve disputes; that is, in deciding who needs to be at the table, who can legitimately represent different parties, and what structures of communication and decision making can do justice to the varying cultural perspectives involved. Claims about culture, however, always imply analyses of social power, and deciding how to incorporate culture into particular dispute resolution processes requires explicit attention to power relations between the groups involved. I describe this "politics of cultural generalization" in theoretical terms, then consider its implications for concrete elements of dispute resolution training and process design.

Liberal Neutrality and Cultural Difference

In the dominant Western political vocabulary, there is an easily available story about how to resolve disputes between groups over perceived conflicts of interests, aspirations, or access to resources: let each side make its case before a neutral third party, who will objectively decide on a just settlement. This common-sense story of just adjudication has deep roots in Western cultural, legal, and philosophical traditions and is closely tied to accounts of political legitimacy. In the venerable tradition of European liberalism, political institutions are legitimate if they can be justified as reasonable to individuals with diverse goals and values. In the Kantian vein of liberalism, principles of adjudication are reasonable if they are justifiable in abstraction from all particular ends and interests – from the point of view of reason alone. In contractarian versions of liberalism, just principles are those that reasonable parties – abstracted from the specific issues of the moment, perhaps to some hypothetical "state of nature" – would accept as fairly conducing to their interests.[2]

In its common-sense version, this story about neutrality and justice has tremendous currency in North America: it is seen as describing not only the aspirations of our legal and political systems but even their typical operation. Seen from the standpoint of Aboriginal struggles for survival, equality, and self-determination, however, this dominant Western account of justice looks deeply corrupt. Consider three bases of skepticism about the Western story of justice as neutral adjudication.

First and most dramatically, the accounts of justice that newcomers brought with them to this continent often explicitly excluded Aboriginal peoples from full membership in the political community within which justice was to prevail: from Locke to Kant to Tocqueville, liberals have defined Aboriginal peoples as beyond the scope of liberal justice – too savage, insufficiently settled, unreasonable.[3] In this context, the liberal story of justice seems like something colonizers can tell themselves about how they treat one another, while those outside of this blessed circle are exploited, displaced, or exterminated.

Contemporary liberals would respond that, in fact, this shameful history of colonization on the North American continent shows the failure of colonizers to live up to liberal aspirations – that is, to conform to the demands of justice. Yes, key figures in the history of liberalism often subscribed to the prejudices of their times, and so betrayed the aspirations of their own theories. Yet the route to justice, for Aboriginal people as for all others, is to insist that the liberal state live up to its ideal of neutral adjudication, fairly and objectively settling the conflicting claims of different individuals and groups. Liberals point to the centrality of claims to fairness and non-discrimination in the struggles of oppressed groups for equality: this agenda, they argue, needs to be extended until all remnants of irrational discrimination are overcome. Liberalism, in its truest form, is an inclusive doctrine and has space for the legitimate claims of all social groups.[4]

This attempt to rescue neutralist liberalism from an unsavoury past, however, provokes a second skeptical response: just how inclusive *is* the liberal language of neutrality and reason, even in its most fully realized forms? The past few decades have seen concerted challenges to the liberal paradigm of equality and inclusion, which is charged with requiring assimilation to standards that are not themselves neutral but in fact represent the perspective of dominant social groups. When parties to disputes are asked to step away from their parochial interests and identities to recognize the demands of reason and fairness, they are actually being forced to conform to the hegemony of some similarly parochial set of standards: feminists have argued that these norms are masculine; critical race theorists, that they are based on historically specific understandings of white identity; and neo-Marxists, that they continue to represent bourgeois interests as universal.[5] In both popular struggles and dissident theories, we find arguments that justice in fact means giving weight to the divergent and context-specific understandings of reason and justice espoused by different cultures and social groups.[6] From this critical perspective, *culture* needs to be taken seriously in debates over justice, in the sense that criteria of fairness will always have roots in particular cultural traditions, rather than in some transcultural definition of human reason, interests, or rights. And cultures exist in relation to one another, in contexts always shaped by power – the sovereign power to coerce, enslave, or exterminate tying in with epistemic privilege (the ability to dictate the terms of political debate, while denying their rootedness in particular cultural traditions). Thus it is a corollary of this perspective that *power* has insidious effects, especially insofar as established systems that claim neutrality in fact reiterate relations of group power and tend to be challenged only through mobilizations of oppositional groups.

It is also worth mentioning a third skeptical challenge to dominant understandings of justice as neutral adjudication: the idea of a neutral adjudicator presupposes some authoritative system of law and rule under which parties to a dispute are jointly situated. Yet in many political struggles involving Aboriginal peoples, the definition of parties to a dispute, and the proper site of authoritative adjudication, is precisely what is at issue. Treating Aboriginal claims as properly resolved within the supposedly neutral procedures of an existing nation state already reiterates historic injustices that ought themselves to be in question. Challenging the organization of justice within existing state institutions signals a key shift: it suggests that existing standards of justice and systems of law in colonial states cannot be taken as legitimate, in need of simple reform. These existing claims to legitimate authority need to be evaluated on an even footing with the perspectives and systems of governance of groups claiming nationhood. So again, *culture* matters: struggles between Aboriginal and non-Aboriginal groups, or between any distinct social groups, may also be struggles over the very nature of justice. And *power* matters insofar as existing governments are loath to give legitimacy, much less parity, to other units, even where historical agreements and treaties suggest such parity.

So the common-sense notion that disputes between social groups can justly be resolved through resort to some neutral system of adjudication is in many ways implausible. Seen from the critical perspectives enumerated above, the Western liberal model of fairness seems culturally biased, held in place not by its reasonableness but by the power of those whose purposes it serves. When marginalized or oppressed groups are offered a place before liberal systems of adjudication, they must first concede the power of unjust institutions, and translate their claims – at best awkwardly – into another's political, legal, and linguistic terms.[7]

How can disputes be justly resolved, though, if we set aside the liberal pretension to an adjudicative perspective that is both objective and authoritative? If conceptions of justice, reasonableness, and fairness are culturally inflected and interpreted, how can we decide disputes between culturally distinctive groups? And what deliberative processes might lead to just outcomes, given debate even over the proper sites of authority?

An interesting convergence exists, in this connection, between debates in the fields of political theory and conflict resolution. In both fields, there is an increasing recognition that intergroup disputes often involve not only divergent interests but also divergent identities, goals, understandings of conflict, and conceptions of justice. Yet there is considerable uncertainty about how to construct a just response to these dissonances. How deep do cultural differences go? If parties begin with divergent understandings of justice, might they nonetheless develop shared criteria of fairness by which to determine a mutually acceptable outcome? Or should one aim for no more than compromise between unbridgeably different perspectives? If one gives up on some standpoint from which intercultural disputes can be objectively settled, does one risk succumbing to power politics, where compromises are decided not by commonly accepted principles but by the rule of the stronger? And does the risk of power politics not also loom when one treats intergroup disputes as clashes of cultures? For in seeking descriptions of each group's culturally defined perspective (on the issues at stake and how they should be resolved), doesn't one paper over diversity within groups, letting some powerful subset of each group define identity and values on behalf of the group?

In the balance of this chapter, I suggest that justly resolving intercultural disputes requires that one treat cultural differences as deep: no single definition of justice can be fully adequate to the understandings of disputants, and communication across cultural differences will, at best, be approximate. The challenge is to design processes for resolving disputes that give weight to the range of cultural perspectives in play; this, in turn, requires that one recognize asymmetries of power that shape cultural conflicts, as well as obstacles to intercultural deliberation and dispute resolution.

Culture, Identity, and Dispute Resolution:
Conceptual Issues

This volume as a whole considers how to incorporate understandings of cultural difference into mechanisms of dispute resolution, particularly those mechanisms that fall under the heading of alternative dispute resolution. It is worth briefly reviewing the changing place of culture within ADR. Alternative dispute resolution developed as a recognizable field in the United States in the 1970s, in part in reaction to perceived limitations of conventional, court-centred methods for resolving disputes.[8] ADR described practices of problem solving, negotiation, conciliation, mediation, and arbitration that were promoted as less costly and formalistic than conventional legal responses to conflict, better equipped to address underlying interests, less likely to create winners and losers, and less corrosive of communal relationships. In the past several decades, shifts in social and legal contexts have made a greater place for these alternative forms of dispute resolution, either as components of established legal systems or as a grassroots alternative.

The most prominent versions of ADR have not tended to place great emphasis on cultural dimensions of conflict. Works such as Roger Fisher, William Ury, and Bruce Patton's *Getting to Yes* suggest that a neutral adjudicator can help parties to a dispute articulate the interests underlying initial positions, recognize the interests of other parties, and find mutually acceptable compromises. This template for conflict resolution is presented as universally applicable, though cultural differences may have to be overcome in uncovering parties' interests.[9]

Yet since the 1980s, critiques of universal, generic templates for conflict resolution have emerged from within and outside ADR, echoing the critique of liberal neutrality outlined above. Critics point out that characterizing conflicts as reducible to divergent interests may itself be culturally laden, presupposing a social ontology[10] that regards us as individual bearers of interests and maximizers of utility for ourselves or our group.[11] This underplays the extent to which disputes can arise from divergent, value-laden understandings of the issues at stake, the communities in question, and the nature of conflict itself. Critics say that because interest-based understandings of conflict and conflict resolution reflect a particular cultural background, these ADR methodologies unwittingly favour a dominant cultural perspective, especially if the third-party "neutral" is of the dominant culture. The perspectives of more marginalized parties to the dispute are systematically ignored or distorted. In these and other ways, the supposedly neutral facilitation of compromises in some dispute resolution practice systematically favours more powerful parties; indeed, the very notion of third-party neutrality may be a fiction that masks the power and ideological investments of the mediator – in F.G. Bailey's words, "the claim to be 'above the fray' is in itself, of course, an advertisement of power."[12]

Given these critiques of visions of ADR as neutrally mediating interests, some theorists and practitioners of ADR have attempted to re-craft their practice to attend to values at stake in disputes, power differentials between parties, dissonances between the cultural perspectives in play, and mediators' responsibilities to empower parties to the dispute, and to secure outcomes that do not just happen to be accepted but are just in some broader sense.[13]

The turn just described within theories and practices of dispute resolution has counterparts, as we saw above, within political philosophy: there is a burgeoning of work criticizing "universalist" accounts of justice, which suggests some perspective beyond culture from which normative political questions can be addressed. We are urged instead to develop theories that accommodate the diversity of cultural perspectives in play in particular contexts, without seeking to resolve these into some single, overarching theory.

Yet these critical currents within ADR and political philosophy run into their own problems. It is not just that universalists see dangers of cultural relativism and an abandonment of judgment in this critical response. It is that partisans of multiculturalism are faced with the difficult task of developing a working definition of culture, one that does not collapse in the face of the obvious complexity of contemporary societies and their constituent memberships. Let me now take up this task; I will make some fairly modest claims about how cultural memberships shape the perspectives of parties to disputes, then show that such claims can in fact be defended and put to use, notwithstanding the complicating effects of multiple memberships and asymmetries of social power.

I begin from what, to most readers of this volume, may be a relatively uncontroversial claim about identity and cultural membership: that we each experience the world, including the social world, through the medium of particular cultures. This is to say that individual experience is enabled (though not fully determined) by structures of understanding and belief specific to particular human communities. We thereby encounter the world from within particular cultural *horizons* – frameworks of concepts and distinctions sedimented in habits, affects, languages, and practices. The philosopher Bernard Williams expresses it as follows: "To participate in a way of life is to carry an enormous load of settled criteria of judgment, standards of appraisal, and beliefs. In sharing a language, we share, even if incompletely and imperfectly, these pre-understandings; and we bring them to bear on the specific issues and questions which arise between us."[14]

So individuals face ethical and political questions with certain interpretive predispositions and judgments already settled in the language they speak and the webs of practices within which their concepts have sense. Social practices not only give shape to a framework of concepts and distinctions but form one's sense of self, cultivating habits and patterns of affect from infancy onward. Social practices shape everything from one's sense of the meanings of hunger or love, to one's perception of time, to one's understanding of justice and of conflict. Because the practices that form understandings are shared with others in specific social contexts, different groups possess different frameworks of understandings.[15]

Where, though, are the boundaries to cultural groups? We may occasionally be tempted to view human societies as neatly parcelled into different, homogenous cultural units – oh look, there's the Azande worldview! And over there, it's the French! And of course Canadians have their own distinctive shared culture! Such fantasies of identities being dictated by monolithic and singular cultural groups disintegrate when faced with the evident complexity of our memberships, which are structured by social ascription (along lines of race, for example); cultural identification (as in the case of ethnic groups); chosen memberships (as with clubs); political affinities; and so on.[16] So, for example, if my identity is shaped by participation in social practices distinctive to particular groups, these memberships include being a Canadian of European ancestry, male, part of academic cultures, a secularized North American Jew, an Anglophone Quebecker, and much more. Each of these memberships has undoubtedly shaped my understanding of the world, but each is politicized, contested, and relevant in different ways in different contexts.[17] An account of culture and dispute resolution will have to come to grips with this complexity; moreover, it is important that such an account include an analysis of how social power shapes group identities.

In analyzing power and culture, it is important first to set aside what I call "generic multiculturalism" – the lamentable tendency in popular discourses of intercultural understanding to place all cultures on the same footing. Generic multiculturalism blandly suggests that we are all coming from different places and need to be tolerant, to understand one another, to be diversity-friendly. Generic multiculturalism treats particular cultures as autonomous and self-generating: our task as good multicultural citizens is to learn about other cultures and respect them. Generic multiculturalism ignores the hierarchies and power struggles that shape both the substance and the political interaction of social groups – dynamics that I discuss below. Without an analysis of power, though, we cannot make sense of key obstacles to intercultural communication. This sketch of generic multiculturalism is meant to capture elements of a popular discourse on diversity; no theorists I know of express such a baldly naive version of multiculturalism, but readers will hopefully recognize the tendency I am describing, and its manifestations in popular culture, workplace diversity training, school curricula, and so forth.

Cultural identities develop in the context of power-laden interactions among social groups. Many commentators have argued, for example, that it is impossible to understand the contours of contemporary African-American identity outside the context of centuries of conflict between American blacks and whites. The very meanings of blackness and whiteness in the United States – one's day-to-day experiences as a member of a racial group, one's solidarities and identifications, one's cultural practices, one's political goals – all bear traces of a history and daily reality of domination and privilege.[18] Consider four particular ways that power shapes cultures and their interaction.

First, any group identity arises out of a particular history: the foundations of racial categorization – of a schema within which people are black or white or yellow or red – lie not in biology but in ideologies born of conflict and domination.[19] This is true not only of quasi-scientific discourses of race, but of any typology of cultures and identities: the key political distinction between "Aboriginal" and "non-Aboriginal" Canadians, for example, has its place within a particular history of colonization; without these centuries of colonization, the politically salient identities on this continent would be unimaginably different.

Second, dominant ideologies of culture do not in fact tend to treat all human beings as possessing cultures – instead, marginalized groups are regarded as mired in culturally specific ways, while members of dominant groups are unmarked and individual. For example, in the popular imagination, people of colour in North America are regarded as having "races" and therefore cultures, while whites remain racially and culturally unmarked. So when college students in the United States are asked to write down descriptors of themselves, whites tend not to treat their racial classification as a key identifier, whereas blacks do. As Ruth Frankenberg writes in her empirical study of "whiteness" as racial and cultural identity, "for a significant number of young white women, being white felt like being cultureless ... Whiteness as a cultural space is represented ... as amorphous and indescribable, in contrast with a range of other identities marked by race, ethnicity, region, and class ... In fact, the extent to which identities can be named seems to show an inverse relationship to power in the U.S. social structure."[20] A further example can be found in Val Napoleon's discussion, in this volume, of ideologies of cultural difference in Australia: when the Australian Council for Aboriginal Reconciliation called for increased levels of intercultural understanding as a precondition for a just society, their presumption was that the key barrier to justice is that non-Aboriginals are ignorant about Aboriginal society. Aboriginal culture needed to be explained to culturally unmarked Australians, without reciprocity: non-Aboriginal Australians were not expected to explain their relationship to land, for example, to Aboriginals and Torres Strait Islanders.

Third, the contours of any particular cultural identity are developed through interaction and struggle between groups. I call this the "co-formation of cultures." From the moment of first contact, for example, colonizers and Aboriginal communities in North America have cooperated, fought, and otherwise influenced one another in ways that altered the understandings and identities of each; these cultural perspectives now intersect and overlap in complex ways, even as differentiations remain.[21]

Fourth, not only is each culture changed through processes of co-formation, but the lines dividing these communities and cultures are themselves complex: intense struggles are frequently involved in establishing which individuals belong to which cultures. Who in Canada, for example, counts as Aboriginal? Are those of mixed parentage Aboriginal, non-Aboriginal, both, or neither? Are those living off-reserve less Indian than those living on-reserve?

Each person belongs to a complex intersection of cultures, and we have seen from the above that typologies of cultural membership emerge from histories of domination, and that the substance of any given culture reflects a messy history of co-formation. Given these layers of complexity and these challenges to intuitions about neatly segmented, naturally occurring memberships, some may be tempted to throw up their hands and cease trying to generalize about cultural identities. Surely if we are each members of multiple groups, our identities will be pretty idiosyncratic and individual. And surely any generalization about "Aboriginal culture" or "Canadian culture" or "white culture" is going to mischaracterize and stereotype. Aren't we better off just treating people as individuals, and memberships as having too obscure a relationship to identity to be relevant to dispute resolution? Shouldn't we return to a liberal story of autonomously constituted identity, and of groups as aggregations of individual interests?

While issues of cultural identity, understandings, authenticity, and authority are complex, I argue that it would be a mistake to abandon these in our social analyses, including our analyses of disputes and dispute resolution. Identities are shaped by cultural memberships, however complicated the dynamics may be. Of course we exercise volition in sorting through our complex cultural situation to forge our goals, values, and interpretations of the world; we always work, though, with resources made available by the complex of cultures within which we move. Nor (as noted earlier) is the liberal account of individual autonomy without its own cultural baggage; to prefer the liberal account is not to escape cultural determination but to decide in favour of a particular cultural script.

While we cannot responsibly escape generalizing about cultural perspectives in understanding dispute resolution, such generalization takes place on a political terrain and is itself a political act. So we need to see ourselves as engaged not in an effort to pinpoint the truth about cultures, but rather in a *politics* of cultural generalization when we theorize dispute resolution, or seek to intervene in disputes.[22] The alternative is to ignore cultural differences and thereby to give implicit support to dominant cultures, which understand themselves as no culture, or every culture.

Generalizations about cultural values and identities will never fully capture the nuances of individual experiences and understandings. To generalize about members of a particular cultural group, however, is not to make a claim about their universally shared characteristics but rather to point to specific threads in the weave of their shared lives.[23] When viewed in this way, the activity of making general claims becomes purposive and thus political: what we choose to highlight and how we describe it are selections made with an eye to strategy and context. This makes generalization and categorization an inevitably political activity, and a value-laden one: our criteria for assessing generalizations about culture will vary with our purposes, and so defending particular assessments means coming clean about our goals and justifying these. In the context of intercultural dispute resolution, we therefore need to ask questions such as: What goals are we trying to achieve with a particular process of dispute resolution? What sorts of generalizations about cultural values will conduce to or thwart these goals? Is our goal agreement on any old compromise? Agreement with some kind of bracketing of power differentials? Empowerment in the face of histories of inequality or oppression? Different sorts of generalizations will appear justified from the standpoint of different conceptualizations of the proper goal of ADR.

Let me be explicit about the politics of the form of dispute resolution I'm espousing here: I connect justice in the resolution of disputes with resistance to entrenched power dynamics between cultures. This, in turn, requires that we identify asymmetries of power that characterize relations between parties to a dispute, and recognize the extent to which the cultural terms of dispute have previously been shaped by these power relations. In treating the dispute as *intercultural,* the focus should be on shifting authority in defining cultures and the terms of contest between them. So in generalizing about culture as part of theories and practices of dispute resolution, the challenge isn't to generalize in a way that is adequate to all nuances of individual and group identities, but to generalize in ways that resist particular sorts of domination and marginalization. This approach to dispute resolution won't resolve arguments over which cultural groupings are most relevant to a particular dispute, or how to characterize the cultural perspectives of specific groups or their histories, or what mechanisms of dispute resolution can best address these power asymmetries. Rather, the approach describes the inevitably political terrain upon which such arguments take place.

How, for example, would my approach to dispute resolution deal with issues of Aboriginality in treaty negotiations, or disputes over the proper application of treaties, such as those mentioned at the outset of this chapter? A first step would be recognizing the extent to which these negotiations and disputes have already been shaped by cultural typologies of Aboriginality and non-Aboriginality, where non-Aboriginal ways were authoritative in defining the terms of dispute, and where the power to define Aboriginal identities and perspectives was disproportionately in non-Aboriginal hands. So axes of difference between Aboriginal and non-Aboriginal cultures will be particularly important, and it will be key that Aboriginal perspectives be defined by Aboriginal disputants themselves. This prerogative of self-definition by marginalized groups obviously sets up a further set of political questions, given the internal heterogeneity and complexity of Aboriginal communities. Who belongs to a given Aboriginal culture or community? Who gets to define Aboriginal traditions, interests, perspectives in the context of a particular dispute? Giving power of naming and definition to subordinated groups doesn't erase struggle within groups, where we may find further levels of power, marginalization, and intergroup conflict. As I will suggest below, the invocation of cultural values within dispute resolution needs to be tempered by an awareness of the partiality and contingency of these claims. Such awareness in turn suggests the need for mechanisms that allow claims about cultural values to be contested from within, in a plurality of forms and contexts.

Thus a tension exists between the impetus to let claims about Aboriginal cultural ways stand in particular instances – because of histories of damaging dismissal of such claims in colonial contexts, and because without such claims the default norms are themselves culturally partial in ways inauspicious for Aboriginal goals – and the importance of acknowledging internal contest, and the contingency of any particular characterization of Aboriginal ways.

Most chapters in this volume rely on generalizations about Aboriginal and non-Aboriginal worldviews, including their distinctive conceptions of justice and community, spirituality, and conflict resolution. For example, Elmer Ghostkeeper's discussion of *Weche* ("partnership") between Aboriginal wisdom and Western scientific knowledge employs strong generalizations about each of these systems of knowledge. On the one hand, he characterizes the Aboriginal perspective as balancing emotion, body, mind, and spirit; as holistic; and as connected to nature. On the other hand, Ghostkeeper depicts a Western scientific perspective that seeks objectivity, takes things apart to understand them, and is instrumental in its approach to nature. Or, to take another example, a number of authors contrast the non-Aboriginal model of justice as punishment with Aboriginal models of justice as healing. Are these generalizations justified? This is a political question, best addressed by answering a series of further questions: Is the contingency of claims about cultural character acknowledged? Are the claims put forward as political and as subject to legitimate contestation? What authority does an author explicitly or implicitly claim in making his or her generalizations? Insofar as intracommunal heterogeneity is downplayed in these characterizations (as in Tony Mandamin's statement that "Our laws are agreement. The people make an agreement on what is to be, that agreement having been made, all follow that agreement"),[24] does this give rise to particular dangers, and how do these weigh against the importance of counteracting internalized oppression, resisting colonial institutions, and empowering Aboriginal communities?

As I will suggest below, there are procedural dimensions to these questions, involving the structures of consultation and representation that give rise to any particular claim about cultural character. There also are institutional questions, about how particular claims get sedimented into law or practice and how they might be revisited in future. Before turning to these practical questions, however, we need to address one further conceptual issue: that of prospects for intercultural translation and convergence.

I have been stressing the political importance of generalizations about cultures and identities, but questions remain about whether the cultural differences highlighted by such generalizations are simply the starting point of a process of dispute resolution, or persist right through the process. In a well-structured intercultural deliberation, ought we to hold out the hope that parties will gain a thorough understanding of the other's perspective? That parties will develop a new, shared perspective from which to decide on a just outcome?[25] Or will parties remain embedded in disjunctive worldviews, but in the best case find a resolution that is legitimate from their different perspectives? In short, what sorts of communication and agreement should well-designed dispute resolution processes aim to achieve?[26]

We can begin by ruling out two extreme positions on the possibility of intercultural understanding and agreement. On the pessimistic side, one could suggest that distinct cultures possess completely incommensurable systems of language and understanding – while accommodations could be hammered out between them, these would be deeply unstable because they are understood completely differently from the perspective of either group. Yet quite apart from the question of whether any human worldviews could be so completely divergent, it is implausible to read such divergence into the perspectives of groups that have interacted over time, struggling with and against one another to survive and flourish. Groups with such histories bear traces of one another, and there are always scraps of common understandings, vernaculars, and goals (not to mention individuals and groups whose identities and histories bridge groups, or blur the lines between groups).[27] So a full-blown pessimism about intercultural understanding and agreement appears largely unwarranted when it comes to all the cases, for example, that are discussed in this volume. Such pessimism also seems dangerous, insofar as it implies a strong epistemic and normative relativism that would allow no common basis on which to address conflicts, thereby leaving intercultural conflicts as contests of raw, coercive power.

We should also rule out an excessively optimistic view that would have intercultural dispute resolution aim to transform the divergent perspectives with which disputants enter a dialogue into substantive consensus when the dialogue is over. All complex human communication involves misunderstandings and gaps, even where interlocutors are members of the same cluster of cultures, or even the same family. Most agreements, however wholehearted, paper over certain differences of perspective and interpretation that may or may not be significant enough to become objects of dispute in the future.[28]

Thus even in well-designed intercultural deliberations, understanding is going to be possible but imperfect, and agreements – while attainable – will be incomplete (though perhaps no less just, effective, or enduring for this).[29] And so we are on a middle ground, where full commensurability is a fantasy that entrenches dominant perspectives, but where misunderstandings between cultural groups are both enabled and produced by existing structures of power and interaction.

So far, the gulf between any two cultural perspectives would seem to be of the same breadth from either side. Culture, on this symmetrical view, is a lens through which to see the world; people may generically have the tendency to privilege their own worldview, and to either assimilate other views to this conceptual scheme or denigrate them.[30] This generic view of intercultural misunderstanding echoes the "generic multiculturalism" discussed above and is equally pernicious, for when members of social groups deliberate or dispute, given a history of inequality, the cultural perspectives of the two sides are not at equal risk of being ignored, misheard, or denigrated. Many chapters in this volume bear witness to this unevenness when it comes to mistranslations and failures of dialogue in relations between Aboriginal and non-Aboriginal groups.[31] At a more general level, Larissa Behrendt, Kevin Avruch, and others address the ways that power and privilege make themselves felt in dispute resolution practice. One striking example involves the place in deliberation of emotion, as against unemotional neutrality. Drawing on Thomas Kochman's work,[32] Avruch considers the different place of emotion in African-American and European-American styles of conflict: "It is not simply two different approaches to negotiation that we see here, [but] two different sorts of social persons, for whom emotion is to be understood, and deployed, in two different sorts of ways. We can also see, here, the very real world in which power asymmetry is present and at work. There is little doubt, in negotiations over resources, who will eventually have to adapt to whose model if they are ever to get a 'fair hearing.'"[33]

So we have a gulf between cultural styles of conflict, where power forces one party to set aside its culturally specific ways, while the other party has the luxury not only of having its style of conflict prevail but of believing that its style is culturally unmarked and universally applicable. Indeed, many theorists of dispute resolution themselves treat unemotional objectivity as a transcultural goal. As Avruch writes elsewhere, "the 'politics of personhood' establishes the hegemony of one conception of it over others. As the proper and acceptable negotiator is evaluated, so too is the process of negotiation. This means that the white theory of negotiation is not simply one theory among a number of alternatives; it becomes theory for negotiation in general. The discourse of such a theory, which, conceptually speaking, is but one folk model among many, gets reified and elevated to the status of – if not science then – an expert system."[34]

The legitimate place of emotion in deliberation and negotiation is but one example of a much broader phenomenon, whereby a dominant group's very conceptualization of legitimate dispute resolution rules out reasons and understandings of justification that are compelling from another group's perspective. A further example lies in the hegemony of cost-benefit analysis, which Avruch (in his critique of Zartman) characterizes as a culturally laden form of reasoning.[35] Michelle LeBaron offers another example in practices of "active listening": while these are understood by their proponents as generically respectful forms of receptivity, LeBaron points out that they presuppose the acceptability of a symmetrical back and forth and of interjection, which are in fact disrespectful within certain cultural traditions.[36]

Culture and Dispute Resolution:
Practical Dilemmas and Responses

So how do we go on? What practical measures flow from this analysis? First, it is worth noting the many facets of deliberation and dispute resolution processes thrown into question by the analysis of culture and power outlined above. Once one sees the shortcomings of neutralist strategies as well as the necessarily political dimensions of generalizations about culture, one can be shaken out of conventional definitions of what counts as a just outcome or just process; one even may be shaken in one's sense of what counts as a dispute, and of who the parties to a dispute are. And thus one is confronted by a series of acute challenges in designing deliberative processes and dispute resolution mechanisms.

First are challenges around recognizing the presence of disputes, and deciding whether a collective or institutional response is warranted. What signals the need for a process of dispute resolution? What sorts of disputes are properly defined as public or private? What level of interpersonal or intergroup tension or conflict is sufficient to initiate a third-party intervention? There are cultural issues here, since conflict is defined and interpreted very differently within different communities and social groups. And there also are issues of power, since a corollary of social marginalization is that one's perceptions of conflict and injustice are not reliably reflected in institutional responses.

Second, once a dispute crosses the threshold of recognition, how do we establish what is at stake, and who counts as a stakeholder? Can disputes be interpreted in terms of measurable material interests, or are normative and symbolic questions also at stake? How should the issues at stake be framed? Who has a meaningful claim to be an affected party? How should the affected parties be aggregated and represented within a dispute resolution process, and how can internal divisions with particular stakeholder groups be appropriately recognized? Issues of aggregation and representation loom particularly large in disputes involving Aboriginal peoples. Richard Overstall's chapter in this volume, for example, discusses how the Canadian Crown tries to subsume smaller Aboriginal kinship groupings under established units ("Western organizational shells") for purposes of treaty and other negotiations. And a number of chapters discuss questions of the proper role of elders within processes of dispute resolution. There are pragmatic dimensions to all these questions, for the relevant stakeholders in a given instance (and the legitimate representatives of a particular stakeholding group) may be those who already have an institutional profile, or a legal stake in an issue, or the potential to derail a settlement. But there also are profound normative questions when it comes to defining the issues on the table, which groups deserve a place at the table, and who has the prerogative to speak for these groups.[37]

Third, after defining the parties to a given dispute and the stakeholders who need to be part of resolving it, how do we determine what dimensions of the dispute (and especially of misunderstandings constitutive of the dispute) are importantly intercultural? Within some dispute resolution theory and practice, the term "culture" gets thrown around pretty easily: ethnocultural groups count, but we also find discussions of the distinctive cultures of loggers and environmentalists, landowners and tenants. Yet insofar as process design is affected by the presence of deep differences in values and understandings, it seems important to figure out where a given dispute lies on the continuum between conflicts where adjudicative criteria are relatively clear and shared and conflicts where far less about the terms of the conflict and its resolution can be taken for granted.

Fourth, once a dispute has been defined, along with the legitimate stake-holders, how do we define fair terms of communication, especially in contexts of relatively deep cultural differences? Given that criteria of "reasonableness" or "neutrality" may serve to suppress certain cultural perspectives and reinforce others, how should discussion proceed? To what extent have entrenched asymmetries of power shaped the propensity and ability of members of different social groups to communicate and persuade within different dialogue structures, and how might such conversational dynamics be addressed?[38] What place should there be for emotion, storytelling, ritual, fact-finding, cross-examination, expert testimony, and so forth? It is far easier to recognize the cultural variability of such forms of disputing and dispute resolution than it is to define fair processes in light of this diversity. And power asymmetries often loom even where parties to the dispute seem to share cultural horizons.[39]

Fifth, given culturally appropriate structures of interaction between parties to a dispute, what outcome should the process aim for, and what form of decision making might establish that a just outcome has been reached? Who will the decision makers be? Is there a role for arbitration, and if so, on what basis? What place is there for voting, consensus, and guidance from elders? For apology, reconciliation, restitution? To what extent is it important that resolutions be enduring and binding, as opposed to provisional and revisable? What challenges exist in sustaining the legitimacy of outcomes with the broader communities involved? Here too, there are issues of cultural appropriateness, and power intervenes in ways that deserve both practical and normative attention.

These five dimensions of dispute resolution design all are thrown into relief by an analysis of cultural difference and power: design questions around recognizing disputes, defining stakeholders, recognizing cultural differences, crafting mechanisms for communication across these, and establishing appropriate decision procedures. Factor in the complexity of cultural memberships and the politics of cultural generalization, and these issues seem truly daunting. In addition, the very diversity of disputes and of possible cultural perspectives suggests that no universal template, developed before the fact, is going to guide practitioners through these thickets. Can any practical guidance be offered?

I will point to two ways that dispute resolution practitioners can take culture and power seriously in process design. Before doing so, however, it is worth pointing out what I take to be a signal strength of theories and practices of dispute resolution in addressing issues of culture and power and a corresponding weakness in mainstream political theory. As noted earlier in this chapter, issues of deliberation and cultural memberships loom large in much contemporary political philosophy; these philosophical debates take place, however, at a predictably abstract level, even as philosophers may aspire to guide democratic practice. By contrast, in the world of dispute resolution there is a necessary concreteness: practitioners are faced with actual disputes, and are forced to craft mechanisms that address the identities as well as the interest of parties. Part of this concreteness derives from an emphasis on effective resolution: here, practitioners of dispute resolution may manifest an indifference to principled justification of procedural norms, an indifference that philosophers would want to resist. Another part of this concreteness relates to a strong emphasis, among practitioners of dispute resolution who take culture seriously, on the fact that there are no a priori answers even about proper procedures for defining cultural identity and membership.[40] There is a greater comfort among dispute resolution theorists and practitioners with defining fair terms of conflict resolution contextually rather than before the fact; the more general pieces of guidance that follow are meant to be congruent with this sort of contextualized practice.

At the beginning of the chapter, I pointed to a dominant Kantian approach to resolving moral conflicts that seeks universally applicable rules, themselves placed outside any specific context. By contrast, my own approach resists setting up a template that will provide normative guidance in every case of intercultural conflict. This philosophical method finds sustenance in a literature on dispute resolution that works through specific cases, paying careful attention to detail and resisting the tendency to see each example as a potential archetype. More than simply using this literature to claim that one size does not fit all, however, I suggest it can be salutary for political philosophers accustomed to finding in vague generalizations the sort of evidence they need to offer liberal justifications of neutrality. Working from theory to practice to theory,[41] by contrast, provides another sort of method, where the contingent reminders I am assembling for the purpose of offering an overview can themselves be revised in light of novel experience in the context of ADR "on the ground."

Response #1: Building Cultural Sensitivity

One approach to addressing the complex issues of process design is to consider the sorts of skills, dispositions, and virtues that parties to disputes, as well as third parties, would need in order to respond adequately. This sort of an emphasis on character and communication fits well with a refusal of one-size-fits-all solutions: better to focus instead on equipping participants in disputes to deal responsibly and respectfully with one another by building cultural sensitivity, listening skills, and tools for understanding. In many accounts of intercultural dispute resolution, there is obvious faith that virtues and skills such as empathy, active listening, and reflexivity about one's own culture can conduce to the just and effective resolution of conflicts. Many commentators on dispute resolution offer useful typologies of the constituents of intercultural competence – indeed, Michelle LeBaron's chapter in this section does such work well.[42] Let me simply lay out some caveats about characterizations of intercultural competence, in light of my earlier discussion of culture and power.

First, LeBaron's chapter rightly draws attention to ways that descriptions of intercultural mediation skills can themselves reiterate cultural biases. Just as neutrality can serve as a guise for culturally specific criteria, so supposedly universal dialogical skills – LeBaron mentions active listening, eye contact, and paraphrasing – can in fact be impositional and inappropriate in some cultural contexts.

Second, intercultural training needs to be reflexive about the politics of cultural generalization, that is, about the fact that accounts of culturally specific understandings are always approximate and must be evaluated with a sensitivity to purpose and context. Otherwise, training for disputants and third parties risks reiterating stereotypes about others and so constituting new obstacles to adequate understanding. In the main, this is a point for trainers surveying how trainees use generalizations. At the same time, it is interesting to explore the implications of thematizing the contextuality of claims about culture for disputants themselves: on the one hand, an awareness of this contingency is a healthy antidote to tendencies to stereotype; on the other, the illusion that claims about cultures map some authentic truth about members will not be easily abandoned, and indeed may be a precondition of cultural claims being taken seriously, given the essentialism of dominant ideologies of culture.

Third, training in cultural sensitivity and literacy must be maintained as a route to intercultural dialogue, not a substitute for it. Natalie Oman's chapter in this volume makes the point insistently and well: no degree of imaginative competence can stand in for actual dialogue with cultural others. So cultural competencies are necessarily skills in communication, rather than legitimate routes to monological understanding.

Fourth, the gap between cultures is often asymmetrical, in that dominant groups can safely ignore other perspectives, and entrench their own worldview as the norm.[43] This not only leads to the tendency to treat marginalized cultures as the ones in need of elucidation (while the dominant culture is treated as self-evident, self-justifying, and value-neutral); it also neglects the extent to which poor skills at intercultural understanding may be both an effect and a bulwark of privilege. So certain (powerful) parties involved in disputes may be disproportionately in need of intercultural education, and disproportionately resistant to it. It is not enough for those with power to commit, with goodwill, to be reflexive about their cultural values, elicitive in process design, and so on; accounts of training for intercultural sensitivity have to incorporate an analysis of social power, and therefore to be explicitly political.

Fifth, insofar as cultural sensitivity is a character trait, it cannot be culti-vated didactically; dispositions are learned through habituation, in this case through actual practice at intercultural dialogue. So rather than being an add-on or precursor to adequate processes of dispute resolution, this form of education has to be ongoing, in the context of intercultural negotia-tion. Ultimately, a politicized understanding of intercultural sensitivity points to the importance but also the inherent limits of such training: learning intercultural skills at least arguably presupposes participation in well-structured deliberation across cultural differences. However impor-tant intercultural skills may be on the part of disputants and third parties, these must be accompanied by procedural measures that ensure the pres-ence and voice of marginalized parties to the dispute.

Response #2: Building Diversity and Representation into Process Design

It is, of course, difficult to say much in the abstract about process design, in light of the earlier injunction against pre-set formulae for culturally sen-sitive processes. But a number of reminders can be assembled.

First is the importance of an "elicitive" approach to process design, of the kind encouraged by Paul Lederach (and by LeBaron in this volume). An elicitive approach is receptive to indigenous models of conflict and conflict resolution, and recognizes the cultural presuppositions of the dis-pute resolution tools that come most readily to hand in one's own cultural contexts. With an elicitive approach, one takes the lead from participants and recognizes process design as a political as well as functional issue. Led-erach's discussion of an elicitive approach to conflict resolution primarily addresses challenges facing a third party from one culture intervening in another culture's disputes; many of the principles of an elicitive approach are also relevant, though, to designing processes for intercultural dispute resolution.[44]

Second, cultural representation is important in selecting third parties and experts for dispute resolution processes, and deliberative institutions more generally. Avruch reminds us of the cultural presuppositions in-volved in the belief (dominant in Western contexts) that the best medi-ator will be an outsider, impartial and unbiased. He suggests that "the ethnographic record in general does not support the existence of the unin-volved third party as either the norm or the ideal."[45] Rather than training outsiders as third-party mediators for distant cultural settings, Avruch sug-gests the worth of training *parties* to the conflict as mediators.[46] LeBaron, in this volume, also reminds us of the value of intercultural teams of facilita-tors (while also pointing out, however, how the diversity and complexity of cultural groupings stand in the way of a strict principle that facilitation teams should mirror the communities involved in a dispute).[47]

Third, as noted earlier, entrenched power asymmetries between groups insistently marginalize some, while establishing others as arbiters of reasonableness and neutrality. In establishing inclusive processes of dispute resolution, then, it is important to avoid reinscribing these authority relations in decisions about inclusion and representation. So elicitiveness in process design needs to be more than a sensibility on the part of members of dominant cultures, who nonetheless retain their interpretive and decision-making authority. When it comes to defining the stakeholders to a given dispute, there should be an onus in favour of including previously marginalized groups, given intrinsic limits to the possibility of representing their perspectives without their actual presence at the table.[48] And when it comes to questions of cultural representation – who can legitimately speak for a particular group – the onus should be in favour of letting groups define the terms of their own representation rather than on parties from outside the community paternalistically ruling on contests over proper representation.[49]

Fourth, the contingency of generalizations about culture, combined with the sneaky ways that power asserts and reasserts itself in intercultural encounters, should leave us especially cautious about the adequacy of any particular element of process design. There needs to be an openness to challenges from those who see exclusions and limitations in the design of a given dispute resolution process, and mechanisms to adjust procedures in an ongoing way in the light of such challenges. Natalie Oman eloquently captures this imperative in her discussion of intercultural recognition as a process: given the heterogeneous, contested, and changing character of any given culture, terms of cultural understanding can at best be a "moving consensus."

Fifth, the sorts of tentativeness and flexibility of process design urged above will (arguably) stand in tension with requirements of efficiency – of finding dispute resolution mechanisms that produce outcomes under temporal and fiscal pressures. Good intercultural processes of dispute resolution, it turns out, may be expensive, and will need to be defended against those who would treat dominant approaches to dispute resolution (including legal avenues) as more cost-effective. This simply returns us to the point that debates over culture and over dynamics of cultural inclusion are inherently political, and that an agenda of culturally sensitive dispute resolution may be intrinsically challenging to existing organizations of political, economic, and social power.

Cultural Generalization, Contingency, and Institutionalization
I have been insisting on the importance of an awareness of the contingency of cultural generalizations: it is key to remember the limitations of any particular generalization about a culture, and that the criteria of good

generalization are always established in particular contexts given particular purposes. I have also stressed the importance of preserving the openness of dispute resolution processes to challenge, and of keeping processes flexible in responding to such challenges. In this last part of the chapter, though, I would like to recognize a fairly sharp tension between this sort of an insistence upon contingency and the strong tendency for analyses of culture and for patterns of dispute resolution to become institutionally entrenched. Any new or reformed process of dispute resolution takes its place, however uneasily, within established systems of power, law, and national sovereignty. Not only do these existing systems often insist upon the clear institutional definition of new processes, but insofar as culturally sensitive dispute resolution challenges existing constellations of power, this challenge is often best sustained by struggling to make an institutional niche for such processes.

However acute one's conceptual recognition of the contingency of generalizations about culture, these generalizations take on a less contingent, often unanticipated, shape when embodied, as they must be, in institutions. Groups recognized for the purposes of some particular negotiation or deliberation develop organizational capacities and solidarities that may then be deployed elsewhere. Characterizations of culturally specific understandings or values articulated in one context become available (to members of the culture and to outsiders) in other contexts. Decisions about who may legitimately represent a group set up hierarchies within communities that may be difficult to challenge or overturn. And most generally, allocating rights or entitlements to groups requires that they have legally and politically recognized boundaries and terms of membership: this requires enduring generalizations about the group, generalizations that will stand in tension with a recognition of contingency and a continued openness to challenge from members of the group, or from other groups.[50]

A number of the authors in later chapters of this volume point to dangers inherent in institutionalizing particular claims about culture. Catherine Bell, for example, draws attention to a concern that arose persistently in the context of the Intercultural Dispute Resolution forum: to what extent might mistaken generalizations about Aboriginal peoples make processes of dispute resolution less flexible and culturally alive? As another example, Justice Yazzie's chapter discusses dangers inherent in revivalism, where indigenous communities turn to the past and tradition for comfort, success, and survival: the traditional practices thus uncovered may be incorporated into dominant systems and then used "on" indigenous peoples, reiterating existing legal and political forms of colonial imposition and control.

So there are real risks in explicitly building cultural diversity into processes of dispute resolution or political deliberation more generally.

Mistaken generalizations can take on a life of their own. Challenges by members of a community to particular characterizations of their culture can be sidelined by the power politics inherent in particular structures of representation and can be disciplined by internal restrictions. What is the appropriate response to such risks?

One response is to seek to rise above cultural particularity in designing dispute resolution processes – to rely upon putatively neutral structures of adjudication, or to seek decision criteria common to the cultures involved. The argument presented earlier shows the inadequacy of this response: structures and criteria presented as neutral are likely to be disguised versions of a dominant culture. Another version of this response – popular with liberal political philosophers – is to place substantive restrictions on the outcomes of deliberative procedures;[51] here again, though, there are acute risks of reiterating patterns of cultural domination in justifying these supposedly extracultural restrictions – whether they be formulated in terms of individual rights, prohibitions on internal restrictions, or norms of fairness.[52]

A more appropriate response to the risks of institutionalizing particular generalizations about culture is to emphasize the importance of vibrant debate within communities over the character of their culture, the nature of their traditions, and the legitimacy of existing structures of representation. Or to put it somewhat differently, the elicitiveness and openness to contingency that I have advocated in the context of designing any particular dispute resolution process needs to be recursive – practiced in multiple locations within and between communities.

An interesting example of such reflexivity about culture can be found in Ken Noskey's description of the politics of consensus within Metis communities (Noskey is president of the Metis Settlements General Council).[53] On the one hand, Noskey says, new institutions must reflect people's practices and processes in order for these new forms of governance not to be one more set of impositions; so new institutions must reflect a communal consensus. Noskey recognizes divisions of opinion even in communities that value consensus – he cites division within the Metis community over the role that should be played, in newly established dispute resolution processes, by elders and traditional knowledge. And yet he argues that such division need not – indeed must not – bring decision making to a halt: provisional agreements (in this case that elders should have *some* formal role in the process) enable the right kind of moving consensus.

So while there are tensions between contingency and institutionalization, there are also ways of negotiating these tensions – of cultivating ongoing dialogue about cultural values within communities, and of retaining openness and fluidity within new institutions. The presence of such reflexivity should stand as a criterion against which generalizations are judged. The rhetoric of cultural identities and shared cultural values is not inherently illegitimate, but needs to be made compatible with a recognition of the contingency of generalizations.

In the real world, of course, the preference just expressed for vibrant intracommunal debate – as against substantive constraints on outcomes – may seem beside the point, for particular dispute resolution processes simply do exist within broader legal and political structures, which impose all sorts of constraints on permissible outcomes, the legitimate scope of jurisdiction, and so forth. Those drafting dispute resolution mechanisms into agreements and treaties, or designing them as adjuncts to existing legal processes, or finding ways to fit such processes into the interstices of existing institutions, face very real procedural and substantive constraints.

Constraints on the authority of culturally appropriate dispute resolution processes have negative implications: while constraints may be portrayed as necessary protections for individual rights, or guarantees of fairness across systems within a nation state, they risk imposing dominant cultural values and relations of power. More specifically, limitations on the authority of Aboriginal dispute resolution mechanisms within Canada and the United States often operate to limit indigenous self-determination and to keep Aboriginal people under the sway of non-indigenous systems of law.[54] Justice Yazzie echoes this concern in his questions about who gets to be the gatekeeper for Navajo peacekeeping: is the process initiated only when a court decides it is needed? Or can the process go back to the grassroots and be relatively autonomous from the wider justice system? Bell also expresses the worry clearly: "Only in recent agreements, and under limited circumstances, are indigenous laws made paramount in their application to non-indigenous laws. For this reason, many believe that although ADR models for justice reform may help address issues of cultural stress, they are unable to effectively address the issue of colonization. Rather, the hierarchy of decision making promoted by these processes, the dominant role of non-indigenous law, and the ability of non-indigenous government to alter many of these processes if they no longer have popular support, perpetuate Aboriginal dependency."[55] So it is crucial to assert Aboriginal sovereignty and treaty rights to create genuine authority for new institutions and processes.

At the same time, any critical assessment of legal or political constraints on dispute resolution processes needs to recognize the opportunities that may lurk within these restrictions. For insofar as the contingency of generalizations about culture may tend to be lost when deliberative processes are institutionalized, countervailing institutions and laws do create opportunities for challenging particular generalizations or structures of representation. Thus there are complex valences, for example, to tensions between rights under the Canadian Charter of Rights and Freedoms and the prerogative of Aboriginal communities to establish their own structures of governance and representation.[56]

Conclusion

Those designing deliberative processes in multicultural contexts face a range of difficult judgments, made all the more challenging once we recognize the complexity of cultures and the intricate workings of power. It is tempting for members of dominant cultures to try to escape these dilemmas by appealing to neutralist models of adjudication, or by using general templates for interpreting cultures and incorporating them into deliberative processes. In this chapter, however, I have argued that this is a temptation we should strongly resist: both neutralist models and one-size-fits-all accounts of intercultural decision making tend to privilege dominant worldviews, at the expense of the perspectives and interests of marginalized groups. And so theorists and practitioners of dispute resolution and political deliberation remain on the rough ground of practice, constructing generalizations about cultures and building dispute resolution processes that are responsive to these, all in an attempt to meet the needs of parties and the demands of justice within particular disputes. Despite the stringent demands of the model I have sketched, many practitioners are successfully combining sensitivity to the complexity of culture with creative approaches to dispute resolution involving Aboriginal peoples, as the remaining chapters of this volume attest.

Acknowledgments
Thanks to David Hampton and Elizabeth Panasiuk for research assistance, and to J. William Breslin, Dale Dewhurst, Dominique Leydet, Cressida Heyes, Daniel Weinstock, Anja Weiss, Melissa Williams, and Leah Wing for helpful comments on earlier versions of this work. An earlier and abbreviated version of this argument appears in David Kahane, "Dispute Resolution and the Politics of Cultural Generalization" (2003) 19 Negotiation Journal 1, 5-27.

Notes
1 See, for example, *R. v. Simon*, [1985] 2 R.C.S. (S.C.C.); *R. v. Badger*, [1996] 2 C.N.L.R. 77 (S.C.C.); *Marshall v. Canada*, [1999] S.C.J. 55 (S.C.C.).
2 See, for example, Amy Gutmann, *Liberal Equality* (Cambridge, UK: Cambridge University Press, 1980); Stephen Mulhall and Adam Swift, *Liberals and Communitarians* (Oxford: Blackwell, 1992); Larry Siedentop, "Two Liberal Traditions," in Alan Ryan, ed., *The Idea of Freedom: Essays in Honour of Isaiah Berlin* (Oxford: Oxford University Press, 1979), 153-74; and Jeremy Waldron, "Theoretical Foundations of Liberalism" (1987) 37 Philosophical Quarterly 127-50.
3 See, for example, Carlos A. Forment, "Peripheral Peoples and Narrative Identities in Late Modernity: An Arendtian Reading," in Seyla Benhabib, ed., *Democracy and Difference: Contesting the Boundaries of the Political* (Princeton, NJ: Princeton University Press, 1996), 314-30; William E. Connolly, *The Ethos of Pluralization* (Minneapolis: University of Minnesota Press, 1995); Michael J. Shapiro, "Bowling Blind: Post Liberal Civil Society and the Worlds of Neo-Tocquevillean Social Theory" (1997) 1 Theory and Event 1, <www.press.

jhu.edu/journals/theory_&_event/v001/1.1shapiro.html>; Tzvetan Todorov, *On Human Diversity: Nationalism, Racism, and Exoticism in French Thought,* Catharine Porter, trans. (Cambridge, MA: Harvard University Press, 1993); and James Tully, *Strange Multiplicity: Constitutionalism in an Age of Diversity* (Cambridge, UK: Cambridge University Press, 1995).

4 See, for example, Will Kymlicka, *Multicultural Citizenship* (Oxford: Oxford University Press, 1996); Susan Moller Okin, *Justice, Gender, and the Family* (New York: Basic Books, 1989).

5 For feminist critiques see, for example, Alison M. Jaggar, *Feminist Politics and Human Nature* (Sussex: Rowman and Allanhead, 1983); Genevieve Lloyd, *The Man of Reason: "Male" and "Female" in Western Philosophy* (Minneapolis: University of Minnesota Press, 1984); and Iris Marion Young, *Justice and the Politics of Difference* (Princeton, NJ: Princeton University Press, 1990), 96-121. For critical race theory see, for example, Paul Gilroy, *The Black Atlantic: Modernity and Double Consciousness* (Cambridge, MA: Harvard University Press, 1993); and Todorov, *On Human Diversity.* For Marxist perspectives see, for example, Steven Lukes, *Marxism and Morality* (Oxford: Oxford University Press, 1985); and Karl Marx, "On the Jewish Question," *Selected Writings* (Oxford: Oxford University Press, 1977), 39-62, and for a consideration of class analysis in specific connection with conflict resolution, see, for example, Richard E. Rubinstein, "The Analyzing and Resolving of Class Conflict," in D. Sandole and H. van der Merwe, eds., *Conflict Resolution Theory and Practice: Integration and Application* (Manchester: Manchester University Press, 1995), 146-57.

6 A number of currents of political philosophy are implicated here as well, including communitarianism (see, for example, Charles Taylor, "Cross-Purposes: The Liberal-Communitarian Debate," in Nancy Rosenblum, ed., *Liberalism and the Moral Life* (Cambridge, MA: Harvard University Press, 1989); Charles Taylor, *Multiculturalism and "The Politics of Recognition"* (Princeton, NJ: Princeton University Press, 1992), defenders of group rights (Kymlicka, *Multicultural Citizenship*), and partisans of "identity politics" (Young, *Justice and the Politics of Difference*).

7 In his chapter, Dale Turner explores this requirement of mistranslation when it comes to Aboriginal perspectives on relationships to land which are forced into languages of Aboriginal title and sovereignty by existing systems of negotiation and adjudication.

8 See Joseph A. Scimecca, "Conflict Resolution in the United States: The Emergence of a Profession," in Kevin Avruch, Peter W. Black, and Joseph A. Scimecca, eds., *Conflict Resolution: Cross-Cultural Perspectives* (New York: Greenwood Press, 1991), 19-40. For a discussion of the development of ADR in Canadian contexts, see, for example, Alberta Law Reform Institute, *Dispute Resolution: A Directory of Methods, Projects and Resources,* Research Paper No. 19 (Edmonton: Alberta Law Reform Institute, 1990).

9 Roger Fisher, William Ury, and Bruce Patton, *Getting to Yes: Negotiating Agreement without Giving in,* 2nd ed. (New York: Penguin Books, 1991).

10 A "social ontology" is a general account of how individuals and groups fit together into social collectives.

11 Compare Avruch's critique of the realist paradigm in international relations: Kevin Avruch, *Culture and Conflict Resolution* (Washington, DC: United States Institute of Peace Press, 1998), 27-30.

12 F.G. Bailey, *"Tertius Lucans:* Idiocosm, Caricature, and Mask," in Kevin Avruch, Peter W. Black, and Joseph A. eds., *Conflict Resolution,* 63.

13 Michelle LeBaron Duryea, *Conflict and Culture: A Literature Review and Bibliography* (Victoria, BC: University of Victoria Institute for Dispute Resolution, 1992); J.P. Lederach, *Preparing for Peace: Conflict Transformation Across Cultures* (Syracuse, NY: Syracuse University Press, 1995); and Sally Merry, "Disputing without Culture" (1987) 100 Harvard Law Review 2057-73.

14 Quoted in William E. Connolly, *Appearance and Reality in Politics* (Cambridge, UK: Cambridge University Press, 1981), 110.

15 This kind of account of the social formation of identity has been a part of the Western philosophical tradition from as far back as Aristotle and finds contemporary philosophical exponents in Alasdair MacIntyre, Jeffrey Stout, Charles Taylor, and Michael Walzer. See, for example, Alasdair MacIntyre, *Whose Justice? Which Rationality?* (Notre Dame, IN: University of Notre Dame Press, 1988); Jeffrey Stout, *Ethics After Babel: The Languages of Morals and Their Discontents* (Boston: Beacon Press, 1988); and Charles Taylor, *Sources of*

the Self: The Making of the Modern Identity (Cambridge, MA: Harvard University Press, 1989). My understanding of social practices and cultural membership has been especially influenced by a neo-Wittgensteinian current in political philosophy, as best exemplified in articles collected in Cressida J. Heyes, ed., *The Grammar of Politics: Wittgenstein and Political Philosophy* (Ithaca, NY: Cornell University Press, 2003); see esp. chapters by Heyes and by Tully.

16 For a more extended critique of overly monolithic conceptualizations of culture in connection with dispute resolution, see, for example, Avruch, *Culture and Conflict Resolution,* esp. 12-16; I see more space for purposive generalizations about cultural identity than Avruch may allow.

17 Such diversity may be most evident in contemporary multicultural societies but exists in any society – one need only think of such cleavages as gender and class to recognize the fiction of claims about the homogeneous fields of social meanings typical of "traditional" societies.

18 See, for example, Ruth Frankenberg, *White Women, Race Matters: The Social Construction of Whiteness* (Minneapolis: University of Minnesota Press, 1993).

19 See, for example, David Theo Goldberg, *Racist Culture: Philosophy and the Politics of Meaning* (Oxford: Blackwell, 1993); and Michael Omi and Howard Winant, *Racial Formation in the United States: From the 1960s to the 1990s* (New York: Routledge, 1994).

20 Frankenberg, *White Women, Race Matters,* 196.

21 For an interesting example of such co-formation, see the discussions in the chapters by Dewhurst and by Bell of the Tsuu T'ina reserve, which is geographically encompassed by the city of Calgary, and where complex economic and social interdependencies unite these communities.

22 It is beyond the scope of this chapter to say much more about the social ontology implied here. I would suggest that while one can be wrong in claims about cultural values and history, the "truth" of such claims is a difficult interpretive question, and an inevitably political and contextual one. Moreover, I will suggest in what follows that because power asymmetries lead members of dominant groups to persistently mischaracterize other cultures, there is a strong case for epistemic deference, whereby members of marginalized groups are granted authority in characterizing their own cultures. For a related argument see Lawrence Thomas, "Moral Deference" (1993) 24 (1-3) The Philosophical Forum 233-50.

23 See Cressida J. Heyes, *Line Drawings: Defining Women Through Feminist Practice* (Ithaca, NY: Cornell University Press, 2000).

24 Leonard (Tony) Mandamin, "Appeal Boards Under the *Indian Act,*" 9 July 2000 (transcript on file with editors).

25 This possibility is sometimes framed in terms of the cooperative development of a "third culture." See, for example, Benjamin J. Broome, "Managing Differences in Conflict Resolution: The Role of Relational Empathy," in D. Sandole and H. van der Merwe, eds., *Conflict Resolution Theory and Practice: Integration and Application* (Manchester: Manchester University Press, 1995), 97-111, 103-4.

26 There are strong resonances between these questions and those posed within liberal and deliberative democratic theory. See, for example, Seyla Benhabib, *Situating the Self: Gender, Community and Postmodernism in Contemporary Ethics* (Cambridge, UK: Polity Press, 1992); Seyla Benhabib, *The Claims of Culture: Equality and Diversity in the Global Era* (Princeton, NJ: Princeton University Press, 2002); Jürgen Habermas, *Justification and Application: Remarks on Discourse Ethics,* Ciarin P. Cronin, trans. (Cambridge, MA: MIT Press, 1994); John Rawls, "The Idea of an Overlapping Consensus" (1987) 7 Oxford Journal of Legal Studies 11-25; and Iris Marion Young, "Asymmetrical Reciprocity: On Moral Respect, Wonder, and Enlarged Thought" (1996) 3 Constellations: An International Journal of Critical and Democratic Theory 1, 340-63.

27 Bell's discussion of the Tsuu T'ina Nation provides interesting examples here as well; she comments that its "value system is one that seeks to heal and restore relationships through promotion and teaching of values grounded in spirituality" (these spiritualities now being both traditional and Christian). And in part because of histories of co-formation, Bell suggests a convergence between Tsuu T'ina values and those entrenched in the Canadian Charter of Rights and Freedoms.

28 As I have argued elsewhere, appeals to "overlapping consensus" in political philosophy tend to fall foul of this intrinsic incompleteness of agreements; see, for example, David Kahane, "Cultivating Liberal Virtues" 29 (1996) Canadian Journal of Political Science/ Revue canadienne de science politique 699-728.

29 See Cass R. Sunstein, "Incompletely Theorized Agreements" (1995) 108 Harvard Law Review 1733-72.

30 Some of the language used by Avruch and Black tends toward this symmetrical view (though in other moments they are acute in their understanding of cultural power); see, for example, Kevin Avruch, Peter W. Black, and Joseph A. Scimecca, eds., *Conflict Resolution*, 133-34.

31 An excellent discussion of the subtle dynamics by which legal norms construct the subjectivity and speech of subordinated groups as inferior can be found in Lucie E. White, "Subordination, Rhetorical Survival Skills, and Sunday Shoes: Notes on the Hearing of Mrs. G." (1990) 38 (1) Buffalo Law Review 11-58.

32 Thomas Kochman, *Black and White Styles in Conflict* (Chicago: University of Chicago Press, 1981).

33 Avruch, *Culture and Conflict Resolution,* 79.

34 Kevin Avruch, "Introduction: Culture and Conflict Resolution," in Kevin Avruch, Peter W. Black, and Joseph A. Scimecca, eds., *Conflict Resolution,* 5.

35 Avruch, *Culture and Conflict Resolution,* 91.

36 These cultural differences in modes of conflict resolution also speak against philosophical accounts of "public reason" whereby justifications offered in political debates are legitimate only insofar as they are commensurable with the worldviews of all parties to the deliberation; once again, we find an implicit interpretation of the vernaculars of dominant groups as culturally neutral or uninflected. See, for example, Amy Gutmann and Dennis Thompson, *Democracy and Disagreement* (Cambridge, MA: Harvard University Press, 1996); and Daniel Weinstock, "Why We Don't Need Public Reason to Reason in Public" (paper presented at the World Congress of Philosophy, Boston, 13 August 1998).

37 It is worth noting that in dispute resolution theory and practice, pragmatic considerations tend to prevail in defining the parties to a dispute, whereas political philosophers pay much greater attention to the question of which parties *should* play a role; while in many cases the practical orientation of dispute resolution has lessons to teach philosophy, here I find the normative questions raised by philosophers to represent an important corrective. Though for exceptions see E. Franklin Dukes, *Resolving Public Conflict: Transforming Community and Governance* (Manchester: University of Manchester Press, 1996); and Lawrence Susskind and Jeffrey Cruikshank, *Breaking the Impasse: Consensual Approaches to Resolving Public Disputes* (New York: Basic Books, 1987).

38 For a nuanced critique of approaches to empowerment of subordinated parties within structures of mediation, see Penelope E. Bryan, "Killing Us Softly: Divorce Mediation and the Politics of Power" (1992) 40 Buffalo Law Review 441-523, esp. 498-519.

39 Given my analysis, differences in power may de facto generate differences in perspective that can broadly be labelled "cultural." For a somewhat different analysis of the separability of power and culture, see Anja Weiss, *Macht und Differenz. Ein erweitertes Modell der Konfliktpotentiale in interkulturellen Auseinandersetzungen,* Berghof Report Nr. 7 (Berlin: Berghof Research Center for Constructive Conflict Management, 2001) (also available online at <www.berghof-center.org>).

40 One finds strong resistance to one-size-fits-all solutions in Avruch, *Culture and Conflict Resolution,* as well as in the chapters in this volume by Larissa Behrendt and Michelle LeBaron.

41 Heyes, *Line Drawing.*

42 See also Milton Bennett, "A Developmental Approach to Training for Intercultural Sensitivity" (1986) 10 International Journal of Intercultural Relations 179-96; and Broome, *Conflict Resolution Theory and Practice.*

43 One way of seeing these sorts of distortions of deliberation would be to say that each party is seeing the other through a cultural lens – that the epistemic disconnect is from both sides – but that powerful parties are able to force *their* misinterpretations on the less powerful. Yet I would argue that there often are epistemic asymmetries in intercultural

dialogues, where less powerful parties may actually understand the perspective of the powerful more adequately than the powerful understand the powerless. Here the philosophical literature in feminist standpoint epistemology is relevant: see, for example, Sandra Harding, "Rethinking Standpoint Epistemology: 'What Is Strong Objectivity?'" in Linda Alcoff and Elizabeth Potter, eds., *Feminist Epistemologies* (New York: Routledge, 1993), 49-82; this literature itself has roots in the work, among others, of Frantz Fanon, *Black Skin, White Masks* (New York: Grove Press, 1967); and Jean-Paul Sartre, *Anti-Semite and Jew,* George J. Becker, trans. (New York: Schocken Books, 1948).

44 Though for doubts see LeBaron, *Conflict and Culture,* 54-55.

45 Avruch, *Culture and Conflict Resolution,* 84.

46 *Ibid.,* 107.

47 Given the complexity of memberships, it is not even always clear what should be mirrored: Ethnicities? Genders? Class backgrounds? Rather than taking this as an argument against mirror representation, it seems a reiteration of the need for politically aware generalizations about cultures (including the salience of various memberships) in the context of particular disputes.

48 Catherine Bell's chapter quotes Stein Lal on the importance of including the range of Aboriginal interlocutors in dispute resolution processes, given that one can't "borrow perspective."

49 This onus derives from weighing the risks of colonial/paternal imposition against those of oppression within groups; there is much room for debate about these risks in particular contexts, and also about the tenability of a distinction between critics without and within; see, for example, the essays collected in *For Love of Country: Debating the Limits of Patriotism,* Martha Nussbaum, ed. (Boston: Beacon Press, 1996), as well as her "Human Functioning and Social Justice: In Defense of Aristotelian Essentialism" (1992) 20 Political Theory 2, 202-46.

50 Compare Connolly, *The Ethos of Pluralization.*

51 See Gutmann and Thompson, *Democracy and Disagreement;* and Amy Gutmann, "How Not to Resolve Moral Conflicts in Politics" (1999) 15 Ohio State Journal on Dispute Resolution 1, 1-18.

52 See David Kahane, "Review Essay: Pluralism, Deliberation, and Citizen Competence: Recent Developments in Democratic Theory" (2000) 26 Social Theory and Practice 3, 509-526.

53 See Catherine Bell's chapter in this volume for a description of this politics of consensus within Metis communities.

54 Dale Dewhurst's chapter brings this out in connection with the Tsuu T'ina First Nation Court which, he argues, doesn't have too much power but too little. He suggests that Aboriginal justice systems are generally not well served by being integrated into the adversarial system as alternative, lower, or unofficial elements; among other reasons, he suggests that there is always a temptation for opponents to resort to the more "final," "official" adversarial system in controversial cases.

55 Catherine Bell, "Indigenous Dispute Resolution Systems within Non-Indigenous Frameworks: Intercultural Dispute Resolution Initiatives in Canada," Chapter 15, this volume, p. 274.

56 Consider the Native Women's Association of Canada and its use of the Canadian Charter of Rights and Freedoms to challenge patriarchal characterizations of traditional structures of decision making; see, for example, Monique Deveaux, "Conflicting Equalities? Cultural Group Rights and Sex Equality" (2000) 48 Political Studies 3, 522-39. For a perspective critical of harmony models in ADR, and that would also see opportunities in juxtaposing institutionalized rights with ADR processes, see Laura Nader, "Harmony Models and the Construction of Law," in Kevin Avruch, Peter W. Black, and Joseph A. Scimecca, eds., *Conflict Resolution;* and Laura Nader, "Controlling Processes in the Practice of Law: Hierarchy and Pacification in the Movement to Re-Form Dispute Ideology" (1993) 9 Ohio State Journal on Dispute Resolution 1, 1-25.

3
Perceiving the World Differently
Dale Turner

> The Indian and white man perceive the world in different ways. I
> take it that this is an obvious fact and a foregone conclusion. But
> at the same time I am convinced that we do not understand the
> distinction entirely or even sufficiently.
>
> – N. Scott Momaday, *Man Made of Words*

Indigenous peoples have been explaining themselves to the European newcomers since the time of first contact.[1] After five hundred years, indigenous peoples still maintain that their ways of understanding the world
are distinct. Regardless of whether we fully understand the meaning of
such a claim, indigenous ways of thinking about the world have left their
indelible imprint on the Aboriginal-newcomer relationship. However we
understand this influence, one brutal fact is deeply embedded in the
legal and political relationship: by necessity, indigenous peoples have
had to explain their beliefs – argue for their rights – in the political institutions and courts of law of the dominant culture. In the Canadian context, if Aboriginal rights are to be recognized, affirmed, and protected in
the Constitution, Aboriginal peoples must explain themselves to the dominant culture, and they must do so using Western European intellectual
traditions. Most Aboriginal peoples, and an increasing number of non-
Aboriginal people, believe that as long as this imperative characterizes
the Aboriginal-newcomer legal and political dialogues, then Aboriginal
peoples' ways of understanding the world remain of little or no importance to the relationship. The consequence of maintaining the status quo
is that just agreements, especially agreements involving Aboriginal peoples' lands, will remain elusive.

A brief note first about what I mean by the Aboriginal-newcomer legal
and political dialogues. In this chapter I am mostly concerned with the
legal dialogue on the meaning of Aboriginal rights as they have evolved
in Canadian law since 1982. The year 1982 represents an important watershed for Aboriginal rights in Canada because with the repatriation of the
Constitution, s.35(1) stated that "the existing Aboriginal and treaty rights
of the Aboriginal peoples of Canada are hereby recognized and affirmed."[2]
Aboriginal peoples have had no say in determining the content and character of their rights in Supreme Court decisions, which is telling since it
is through these decisions that the content of s.35(1) is supposed to be

determined. Legal disagreements between Aboriginal peoples and the provincial or federal governments have given rise to a field of law that has evolved into a complex set of philosophical discourses. In particular, Aboriginal rights have been subsumed within political liberalism's language of rights, rights that are foundational to a constitutional democracy. In addition, Aboriginal peoples use their rights to buttress their negotiating positions in non-adversarial contexts. Regardless, a fundamental political problem remains: the content of Aboriginal rights is articulated and understood in the discourses of the dominant culture, and therefore if Aboriginal peoples want to tell their stories in courts of law, they must engage these discourses.[3]

In this chapter I will discuss the significance of this imperative and point to a fundamental asymmetry of the Aboriginal-newcomer legal and political relationship, which the Supreme Court has implicitly endorsed in its recent *Delgamuukw* v. *British Columbia* decision.[4] Since 1982, the legal and political relationship has evolved in ways that give the illusion that Aboriginal rights are progressing along a continuum – with Aboriginal title representing the strongest expression of Aboriginal right. But the rules and conditions of the legal and political dialogue about the content of Aboriginal rights continue to be determined by the dominant culture. It is important to understand that Aboriginal peoples assert their own imperative in the legal and political dialogues over their rights: just agreements involving Aboriginal lands and resources are not possible without greater recognition of Aboriginal claims of ownership.

In this discussion, ownership is meant to be opposed to the concept of Aboriginal title. Aboriginal title is generally believed to be the most empowering legal and political option for Aboriginal peoples; that is, the strongest form of political recognition Aboriginal peoples can achieve within the Canadian state is to gain legal recognition of Aboriginal title over their homelands.[5] This approach – the rights-based approach – fails to justly engage Aboriginal intellectual traditions and, in particular, the oral traditions (traditional philosophies). Aboriginal peoples believe that their rights – what liberals characterize as cultural rights (minority ones at that) – entail legal and political powers. Yet the content of these rights, the ones that are recognized and implemented by Canadian legal and political institutions, are articulated and understood in the languages and discourses of the dominant culture. The ownership approach to Aboriginal rights does not include the voice of Aboriginal peoples in a dialogue over the meaning of their rights. The main problem with the ownership approach, then, is *how* the Aboriginal voice ought to participate in the dialogue. I believe that an indigenous intellectual culture can play a significant role in shaping the normative language that determines how Aboriginal rights are understood and used in Canadian legal and political institutions.[6]

An indigenous intellectual community, then, will play an active and vigorous role in guiding Aboriginal leaders so they can better understand the nature of Aboriginal rights discourse in Canada. Aboriginal leaders have had to be historians, anthropologists, philosophers, and lawyers whenever they entered into negotiations or courts of law. Although the relationship between community leadership and word warriors is not well-defined, it is one of the most pressing issues for contemporary Aboriginal intellectuals. Presumably, many Aboriginal communities will want to continue to assert and defend their integrity as legitimate political entities, and to do so effectively requires a knowledge of how legal and political discourses are used in Canadian institutions.

"I'll Show You Differences"

In one sense, N. Scott Momaday's "obvious fact and foregone conclusion" about the way indigenous peoples and Europeans perceive the world is unproblematic. Indigenous peoples have existed for countless generations without any influence from European cultures, and the indigenous world-views that resulted from indigenous-indigenous dialogues have evolved over long periods into distinctly indigenous ways of understanding the world. Indigenous peoples' focus on respecting life and the profound relationships between things in the world lies at the foundation of traditional philosophies. Over the past several hundred years, Western European philosophies have been greatly influenced by the rise of a capitalist, industrial, global community, which has its own ways of understanding the world. It is beyond the scope of this discussion to compare the two ways of understanding the world, and my point is a relatively uncontroversial one: there are differences between indigenous and Western European worldviews.

When we examine the early history of the legal and political relationship, we see that Aboriginal peoples used their own languages, say to negotiate the early treaties. However, by the time the treaties were written up and embedded in Canadian law, their voices fell on deaf ears. The famous case of *St. Catherine's Milling* is a telling example of this loss of voice.[7] The case involved a jurisdictional issue between the provincial and the federal governments over the legitimacy of ceded Indian lands. However, in the process of deciding jurisdictional issues, the Court unilaterally defined the rights of the Indians – "the tenure of the Indians was a personal and usufructuary right, dependent on the good will of the sovereign."[8] *St. Catherine's Milling* showed that Aboriginal rights can be characterized and legally established without the need for the Aboriginal voice. That was in 1888. The question we need to ask ourselves now is whether contemporary understandings of Aboriginal rights *require* the participation of Aboriginal voices, especially since the Supreme Court dictates in *Delgamuukw* that Canadian courts ought to find ways of accommodating Aboriginal oral traditions. That is, oral traditions ought to be considered as legitimate sources of historical evidence of knowledge.

Delgamuukw was initially viewed by many as an enormous victory for all Aboriginal peoples. However, in ordering a new trial, the Court has implicitly imposed two imperatives. First, the oral traditions must be used to justify Aboriginal title and not ownership. Secondly, Aboriginal peoples must articulate their legal arguments in the existing legal discourses of rights. While the Court explicitly recognizes the legitimacy of the oral traditions, it does so by constraining how they are to be used in Canadian courts of law. Aboriginal peoples are not willing to put their oral traditions up for negotiation, especially if they must do so in the language of the law. Will Kymlicka characterizes this imperative in *Liberalism, Community, and Culture:*[9]

> For better or worse, it is predominantly non-Aboriginal judges and politicians who have the ultimate power to protect and enforce Aboriginal rights, and so it is important to find a justification of them that such people can recognize and understand. Aboriginal people have their own understanding of self-government drawn from their own experience, and that is important. But it is also important, politically, to know how non-Aboriginal Canadians – Supreme Court Justices, for example – will understand Aboriginal rights and relate them to their own experiences and traditions ... on the standard interpretation of liberalism, Aboriginal rights are viewed as matters of discrimination and/or privilege, not of equality. They will always, therefore, be viewed with the kind of suspicion that led liberals like Trudeau to advocate their abolition. Aboriginal rights, at least in their robust form, will only be secure when they are viewed, not as competing with liberalism, but as an essential component of liberal political practice.[10]

This is a revealing statement about the nature of the Aboriginal-newcomer relationship, which I have labelled "Kymlicka's constraint." One does not have to examine too deeply the differences in political power to see that Kymlicka's constraint is a brutal reality check for Aboriginal peoples. As long as the Canadian state unilaterally enforces its power over Aboriginal peoples, I do not see how they have any other choice but to engage the discourses of the dominant culture. Whether in courts of law or sitting at roundtable negotiations, survival demands that Aboriginal peoples engage the language of the oppressor.

What this means for Aboriginal peoples is that if they want their rights, and their claims against the state, recognized and affirmed *within* the Canadian legal and political relationship, they have to articulate their arguments in the already existing legal and political discourses of the dominant culture.[11] The Aboriginal voice may participate in the dialogue, but to do so intelligibly, it must be subsumed within the existing discourses of political liberalism, nationalism, constitutionalism, and sovereignty, to name a few.[12] History has shown us that Aboriginal peoples have had very little say in determining the perspective from which their rights and sovereignty are understood and recognized. This is not to say that Aboriginal peoples don't use these discourses, because they do, but some liberal theorists argue that the virtue of rights discourse is that voice does not matter at all. Liberal understandings of equality demand that all human beings possess the same fundamental package of rights, where Aboriginal rights are a subset of a broader theory of rights.[13] Aboriginal participation is not only excluded from a theoretical articulation of rights; the Aboriginal voice is absent when their rights are applied in the real world. As Kymlicka states above, practitioners – Supreme Court justices, for example – will by necessity interpret the meaning of rights from within their own understandings and life experiences. This may be the way things are, but as long as Aboriginal peoples continue to feel left out of the processes and institutions that determine the meaning of their rights, just agreements between Aboriginal peoples and the state remain difficult, if not impossible, to achieve.

Unpacking the significance of Kymlicka's constraint involves a complex interdisciplinary intellectual investigation. The imperative has become deeply embedded in the legal and political relationship, and it is not enough for well-meaning newcomers to highlight its unjust presence in the everyday world of Aboriginal peoples. Aboriginal peoples have traditionally resisted engaging Western European intellectual traditions, because to engage them was, and still is, viewed as a sign of assimilation. Aboriginal criticisms of Western European intellectual culture have usually been voiced from the "outside"; that is, Aboriginal peoples have always maintained that they may be part of the Canadian landscape, but they remain separate from it. Former National Chief George Erasmus asserts that "all across North America today First Nations share a common perception of what was then agreed: we would allow Europeans to stay among us and use a certain amount of our land, while in our own lands we would continue to exercise our own laws and maintain our own institutions and systems of government. We all believe that that vision is still very possible today, that as First Nations we should have our own governments with jurisdiction over our own lands and people."[14]

By necessity – as a matter of survival – Aboriginal peoples have had to engage Kymlicka's constraint, especially in the context of resolving disputes over the meaning of Aboriginal rights. European newcomers moved onto Aboriginal territories, they pushed Aboriginal peoples off their homelands or onto small parcels of property whose boundaries have been defined, protected, and condoned by the force of law. It makes sense to want to be able to use the language of the oppressor to defend against such actions, because survival depends on it. Kymlicka's constraint has not simply been a way of dominating Aboriginal peoples by dictating the rules of the legal and political relationship; it has been used as a means of extinguishment.

The irony, of course, is that contemporary discourses of political liberalism, whether expressed in the courts or policy frameworks for negotiation, are viewed to be the most just way of accommodating Aboriginal rights into a constitutional democracy. That Aboriginal peoples have their own understandings of their rights is secondary for political liberalism. This is not to say that political liberalism is useless as a way of understanding the nature of Aboriginal rights. Indeed, Kymlicka points out that "Aboriginal rights, at least in their robust form, will only be secure when they are viewed, not as competing with liberalism, but as an essential component of liberal political practice."[15] The problem with his claim is that Aboriginal understandings of their rights will always "compete" with political liberalism's view of Aboriginal rights. Political liberalism has not been able to reconcile the normative content of Aboriginal rights with Aboriginal understandings of these rights. Kymlicka's liberalism, indeed most forms of contemporary liberalism, do not respect the dialogical relationship between the various understandings of Aboriginal rights in legal and political discourses and the diverse Aboriginal voices that participate in the dialogue. In other words, political liberals do not recognize that a just political relationship demands that Aboriginal peoples tell their own stories and that these stories be given some effect through resolution of rights claims.

The need to tell one's own stories is deeply rooted in the Aboriginal-newcomer relationship. While Kymlicka's constraint may continue to impose the dominant culture's rules of the legal and political relationship, Aboriginal peoples continue to resist their imposition. Aboriginal peoples may have become more adept at using the discourses of the dominant culture, but in the process they have implicitly imposed an imperative of their own on the Aboriginal-newcomer relationship. Virtually every Aboriginal community in Canada continues to assert that they have, despite the dominant culture's understandings of the Aboriginal-newcomer relationship, retained their unique relationships to their homelands. These unique relationships have profound Aboriginal explanations attached to them, and unpacking their meaning and normative legal significance in the courts and at negotiation tables will involve a difficult and complex dialogue. The political significance of these Aboriginal explanations, though, is less problematic: Aboriginal peoples assert that they still own their homelands.

The meaning of ownership is awkward at best, but as mentioned above, I use the term in opposition to what in law is called Aboriginal title.[16] Title is arguably the strongest form of Aboriginal right in Canadian law, and it no doubt empowers Aboriginal communities. But recognition of title, by necessity, facilitates a legal reconciliation between two competing claims: recognition of Aboriginal ownership before contact with the unequivocal assertion of Crown sovereignty. The legal content of Aboriginal title is premised on the assumption that the unilateral assertion of Crown sovereignty trumps Aboriginal claims of ownership.[17] The problem with this claim is that the Canadian legal system has a definitive beginning, which Aboriginal ownership by necessity predates. How this reconciliation is supposed to occur and which processes are best suited to facilitate this reconciliation is the topic of great controversy. Ownership arguments, on the other hand, do not work with this "reconciliation" assumption. Making sense of the transition period between the time of Aboriginal ownership – from time immemorial – and the assertion of Crown sovereignty – somewhere in the early seventeenth century, at its earliest – is one of the most challenging problems in Canadian law, which in turn affects the negotiation of new political relationships.

One reason why treaties are so important for Aboriginal peoples is that they represent binding political agreements between mutually recognized political entities. Without them, the doctrine of extinguishment, applicable from the moment of the unilateral assertion of Crown sovereignty, would have succeeded in Canadian courts of law to completely extinguish Aboriginal rights in Canada.[18] The idea behind the doctrine of extinguishment is that, for better or worse, Aboriginal peoples have become subsumed – incorporated – into the legal and political institutions of the Canadian state. Aboriginal peoples may initiate claims against the state, but they are claims undertaken by entities that are intrinsically situated within the state. In fact, in the rights-based approach it literally does not make sense to claim that Aboriginal peoples possess some form of sovereignty outside the existing legal and political institutions of the Canadian state.

Yet, this is precisely what Aboriginal peoples have been claiming since the earliest times of the relationship. The confusion, which Aboriginal peoples have played some role in perpetuating, is that their arguments to support ownership have been mostly couched in the language of sovereignty. But political sovereignty has not been viewed as a dynamic, evolving concept, the meaning of which is determined by its use in different contexts; rather, sovereignty has been understood in the narrow context of the European nation-state.[19] The argument is that Aboriginal peoples constitute nations in the strongest sense of nationhood, the "nation-state," and therefore they ought to be accorded equal recognition in the international forum. My response to this oft-cited objection to indigenous ownership arguments has been to counter that the term "Aboriginal" in front of "sovereignty" – Aboriginal sovereignty – profoundly changes the meaning of sovereignty as it is understood in the context of the European nation-state. Aboriginal sovereignty is an attempt to explain Aboriginal ownership while being acutely aware of Kymlicka's constraint. Sovereignty-type arguments may not prove to be the best intellectual strategies available to indigenous peoples, but the approach ought to be viewed as a way of engaging the existing discourses of law and politics, guided by the imperative that Aboriginal peoples still own their homelands. As long as Aboriginal sovereignty is viewed solely as a legal-political term, its meaning remains safely embedded in Western European legal and political traditions.

The recent work of Taiaiake Alfred is instructive here. He argues that the discourse of sovereignty is not the best intellectual strategy for indigenous peoples. He states: "Sovereignty is an exclusionary concept rooted in an adversarial and a coercive notion of power. Indigenous peoples can never match the awesome coercive power of the state; so long as sovereignty remains the goal of indigenous politics ... Native communities will occupy a dependent and reactionary position relative to the state. Acceptance of 'Aboriginal rights' in the context of state sovereignty represents the culmination of white society's efforts to assimilate indigenous peoples."[20] Instead, Alfred prefers to engage the discourse of nationalism, or, more precisely, the language of indigenous nationhood. But in the context of Western European political philosophy this merely shifts the normative discussion from one discourse to another – from sovereignty to nationalism or nationhood.[21] Aboriginal peoples use concepts such as Aboriginal sovereignty and indigenous nationhood to support the claim that they ought to be recognized as legitimate political communities that have survived the unilateral assertions of state sovereignty. Our intellectual strategies are guided by the same imperative: if Aboriginal peoples are to gain recognition of their rights in their most robust form, we must generate explanations that make sense to people who possess the power to enforce them, *but* we must do so guided by our own intellectual traditions. This is because indigenous arguments for ownership are rooted, deeply embedded, in indigenous philosophies (oral traditions).

What indigenous peoples mean by ownership is difficult to articulate, and the indigenous-indigenous dialogues required to explain its meaning, especially to the dominant culture, are desperately needed in indigenous intellectual culture. Regardless, Aboriginal peoples will never give up their ownership-based arguments; it literally does not make sense in Aboriginal worldviews to do so. The dominant culture may impose the normative terms of the legal and political discourses, but they do so in a context where Aboriginal peoples assert that they still own their homelands. Alfred's manifesto argues that indigenous peoples, especially their leaders, must turn and embrace their traditional values in order to find solutions to their legal and political problems. While some indigenous communities may not be able, or willing for that matter, to make such a radical shift in worldview, one imperative remains. If an indigenous group wants to make ownership arguments against the state, it will have to explain its traditional philosophies in the discourses of the dominant culture.

One problem with taking this approach is that many Aboriginal communities do not, as communities, understand their traditional philosophies in their own languages. English or French has become so deeply embedded in Aboriginal daily life that concepts such as rights or ownership cannot be unwoven from the ways they are used in the dominant culture. No doubt this is a serious issue, as it goes to the very core of what it means to assert one's indigeneity, not just to oneself and one's community but to the world. Alfred is fortunate because, as a Mohawk political thinker, he can draw from a venerable Iroquoian philosophical tradition.[22] The reality, however, is that many communities have lost their language to the point where it is no longer spoken in the everyday. The problem of language is a difficult one but not an impossible one to come to terms with, especially in the context of the legal and political dimensions of the Aboriginal-newcomer relationship.[23] I believe that this is one area where an Aboriginal intellectual culture ought to focus its energy. Aboriginal intellectuals need to make more explicit connections between their traditional philosophies, the legal and political discourses that are used to determine indigenous rights, and the imperative of cultural and political survival. The recent *Delgamuukw* decision is a good example of how traditional philosophy, dialogue, and survival relate to each other. More importantly, however, the case shows how crucial it is for Aboriginal intellectuals to become more active in mainstream Canadian intellectual culture.

If the oral traditions are to be accommodated in Canadian courts of law, the immediate question arises of how they ought to be listened to. Second, who should do the speaking? I mention above that the reconciliation between Aboriginal title and Aboriginal ownership before the assertion of Crown sovereignty is a controversial legal and political problem. Aboriginal peoples have answers about how to resolve this complex legal issue. The need to survive demands that we, and in particular indigenous intellectuals, engage these issues. How we do so remains to be determined, but indigenous thinkers such as Taiaiake Alfred (Mohawk), Susan Tuhiwai Smith (Maori), Robert Warrior (Osage), Jace Weaver (Cherokee), and Audra Simpson (Mohawk) are engaging Western European intellectual discourses with their feet firmly rooted in their indigenous intellectual traditions.[24]

One goal of an indigenous intellectual community is to have a greater influence on the way the courts interpret and implement Aboriginal rights – ideally, there should be more indigenous judges deciding indigenous cases. Rights-based litigation, though, will always be rule driven, and articulated in a non-indigenous language, which makes the task of an indigenous intellectual community simple: find ways of influencing the way the rules are understood and put to use. This is not an earth-shattering revelation about the Aboriginal-newcomer relationship. There are many reasons why Aboriginal peoples have not developed a rich intellectual culture within the mainstream legal and political communities. Most Aboriginal communities are struggling to survive, to fulfill basic life needs, rather than devoting their time to studying the white man's ways of thinking. So while I advocate the need for an intellectual community of word warriors, I am fully aware that this is a vision and will require enormous changes in Indian Country.

Nonetheless, I believe it is something the indigenous community should strive for. Understanding how to navigate one's way around the dominant culture's ways of thinking is necessary for survival, just as food and shelter are necessary for survival. More importantly, understanding who we are as indigenous peoples, and the ways of thinking that make us indigenous, ought to provide the foundation for how we learn to navigate our way in the dominant culture. I believe this would situate our leaders in a richer indigenous context, one with a better understanding and appreciation of the complex nature of the problems at hand. Only a community can answer questions such as: What should Aboriginal children be learning in school? What do we mean by traditional knowledge and what role ought it play in the day-to-day lives of Aboriginal peoples? What is the proper relationship between indigenous forms of knowledge and the legal and political discourses of rights, sovereignty, and nationalism? There are no shortages of tough questions to ask Aboriginal peoples; the point is that Aboriginal peoples must ask these questions themselves and then answer them.

What I have implied in this discussion is that indigenous peoples should not expect the dominant culture to change its ways of thinking, especially about indigenous peoples. A cursory understanding of the Aboriginal-newcomer relationship shows clearly that the dominant culture, in particular governments, have either not understood Aboriginal peoples, ignored them, or distorted Aboriginal ways of understanding the world. The dominant culture has dialogued with Aboriginal peoples on the assumption that Aboriginal peoples' ways of understanding the world can be explained away: it is simply a matter of finding the right words – English words. It is this explaining away that must change. By being more aware of the translation process, especially when normative language is translated from an indigenous language into English, non-indigenous negotiators can begin to appreciate the differences in the ways of understanding the world.

Indigenous leaders and intellectuals need to make the relationship between indigenous ways of understanding the world and the legal and political discourses that define their rights an explicitly political one. This means that the indigenous ways of understanding the world are not up for negotiation; more importantly, they cannot be explained away. Instead, indigenous intellectuals engage the legal and political discourses in ways that assert and protect the dignity and integrity of indigenous worldviews. Hopefully, by forcing the indigenous voice into the hostile intellectual culture of the dominant society, the way indigenous rights, sovereignty, and nationalism are understood and put to use will finally be of benefit for indigenous communities.

Epilogue

What have I attempted to do in this brief discussion? My point is a simple one: Aboriginal peoples assert that they possess unique ways of understanding the world, that they have never relinquished their profound relationships to their homelands, and that these sui generis relationships give rise to legal and political rights that ought to be recognized by the dominant society. Of course, what indigenous peoples believe and what the dominant culture dictates are two very different things. The dominant culture has imposed its will on indigenous peoples for so long that many indigenous peoples do not believe that Kymlicka's constraint is in fact a constraint. The brutal reality is that many Aboriginal people in positions of power could care less about traditionalism, especially if it means that they will no longer control the purse strings of the community. There is a deeper issue here, though, and it is that traditional knowledge does not function like an off-on switch, but permeates indigenous everydayness. In a way, traditionalism has never left the communities; the difficulty for communities is to reconcile what makes us unique as indigenous people with the forms of life that have been imposed upon us. This is yet another serious issue for Aboriginal leadership and now for an Aboriginal intellectual community.

It matters how indigenous peoples participate in the legal and political life of society: we can speak with many tongues (even forked ones), but we will always insist – no, demand – that we tell our own stories in our own ways. How we tell our stories matters, and how our stories are listened to matters – to us, and for society as a whole.

Notes

1 I use the term "indigenous" to refer to the original peoples who inhabited the territories of contemporary nation-states before the arrival of colonizing Europeans. In other words, the use of "indigenous" implies an international context. I shall use the term "Aboriginal peoples" when I specifically refer to the indigenous peoples of Canada, but the terms are interchangeable.
2 Constitution Act, 1982, s.35(1).
3 Discourses such as those on rights, sovereignty, and nationalism have evolved over the

past few centuries into complex sets of overlapping dialogues. For example, the language of rights is central to the theory of political liberalism. Aboriginal rights, as a class of minority rights, are subsumed within a more general theory of individual rights, so Aboriginal rights are not anomalous to political liberalism but consistent with it. Liberals may disagree over how to characterize Aboriginal rights – that is, whether they are expressions of individual or collective rights – but they agree on the primacy of the individual as the fundamental moral and political unit of a just political society. The point I want to make here is that the discourse of rights has evolved with little or no input from indigenous peoples, who have their own intellectual traditions from which to understand the relationships between individuals, communities, and a just society.

4 *Delgamuukw* v. *British Columbia* (1991), 79 D.L.R. (4th) 185 (B.C.S.C.); see also Stan Persky, *The Supreme Court of Canada Decision on Aboriginal Title* (Vancouver: Greystone Books, 1998).

5 Chief Justice Lamer states at s.117 of *Delgamuukw* v. *British Columbia*, [1997] 3 S.C.R. 1010: "I have arrived at the conclusion that the content of Aboriginal title can be summarized by two propositions: first, that Aboriginal title encompasses the right to exclusive use and occupation of the land held pursuant to that title for a variety of purposes, which need not be aspects of those Aboriginal practices, customs and traditions which are integral to distinctive Aboriginal cultures; and second, that those protected uses must not be irreconcilable with the nature of the group's attachment to the land."

6 I have characterized indigenous intellectuals as "word warriors" because they engage the legal and political discourses of the dominant culture guided by their indigenous traditions. See Dale Turner, "Vision: Towards an Understanding of Aboriginal Sovereignty," in Ronald Beiner and Wayne Norman, eds., *Canadian Political Philosophy: Contemporary Reflections* (Oxford: Oxford University Press, 2000).

7 *St. Catherine's Milling and Lumber Company* v. *The Queen* (1888), 14 App. Cas. 46 (P.C.).

8 *Ibid.*, 27. See also Peter Kulchyski, *Unjust Relations: Aboriginal Rights in Canadian Courts* (Oxford: Oxford University Press, 1994).

9 Will Kymlicka, *Liberalism, Community, and Culture* (Oxford: Oxford University Press, 1989).

10 *Ibid.*, 154.

11 I would argue that whether one addresses the rights of Aboriginal peoples inside or outside the Canadian state, Kymlicka's constraint remains. All that changes are the intellectual strategies indigenous peoples adopt. The discourses that support one's claims for, say, stronger forms of nationhood still have to convince nation-states of their legitimacy. In other words, recognition of political legitimacy is never a given as long as indigenous peoples are in the disadvantaged position of having to justify the ownership of their territories to the dominant culture.

12 Cf. note 4. For a generous view of Aboriginal rights in political liberalism see Will Kymlicka, *Multicultural Citizenship* (Oxford: Oxford University Press, 1995). For a more hostile view of Aboriginal rights in a liberal society see Melvin Smith, *Our Home or Native Land* (Victoria, BC: Crown Western, 1995).

13 There are a number of competing accounts of political liberalism, but contemporary liberalism is built upon the moral primacy of individuals per se, not individuals as they are richly identified in society. Indigenous rights are special in virtue of indigenous peoples' membership in minority cultures, which are understood to be threatened by the dominant culture. Minority rights are cultural rights, bestowed upon a minority culture by the dominant society. Ownership arguments, on the other hand, begin with rights of self-determination – political rights – and have no need to refer to culture, never mind characterizing indigenous cultures as minority cultures. See Kymlicka, *Multicultural Citizenship*. For an indigenous response to Kymlicka's theory of minority rights see Dale Turner, "Liberalism's Last Stand," in *Aboriginal Rights and Self-Government: The Canadian and Mexican Experience in North American Perspective* (Montreal: McGill-Queen's University Press, 2000).

14 George Erasmus, "Introduction: Twenty Years of Disappointed Hopes," in Boyce Richardson, ed., *Drumbeat: Anger and Renewal in Indian Country* (Toronto: University of Toronto Press, 1989), 1-2.

15 Kymlicka, *Liberalism, Community, and Culture*, 154.

16 Cf. note 6. For an excellent article discussing the problem of reconciling ownership and title arguments see Kent McNeil, "Aboriginal Title," in Michael Asch, ed., *Aboriginal and Treaty Rights in Canada: Essays on Law, Equality, and Respect for Difference* (Vancouver: UBC Press, 1997).

17 This is why Aboriginal title is a "burden" on the Crown. Justice Lamer states at s.145 of *Delgamuukw,* "Aboriginal title is a burden on the Crown's underlying title. However, the Crown did not gain this title until it asserted sovereignty over the land in question."

18 The doctrine of extinguishment is the colonial practice that exterminates Aboriginal ownership claims. The doctrine of extinguishment ignores the claim that Aboriginal ownership is preserved throughout the Aboriginal-newcomer relationship. Instead, ownership claims are nullified by the unilateral imposition of Crown sovereignty, and any agreements (e.g., treaties) made between the Crown and Aboriginal peoples are understood to concomitantly extinguish Aboriginal interests in their homelands.

19 The field of international relations has a growing literature on the evolution of the nation-state in the international order. See, for example, Andrew Linklater, *The Transformation of Political Community: Ethical Foundations of the Post-Westphalian Era* (Columbia, SC: University of South Carolina Press, 1998); and Alex Wendt, *Social Theory in International Relations* (Oxford: Oxford University Press, 1999).

20 Taiaiake Alfred, *Peace, Power, Righteousness: An Indigenous Manifesto* (Oxford: Oxford University Press, 1999), 59.

21 Alfred prefers nationhood approaches because the Iroquois argue that they constitute a nation in a European sense and ought to be respected as such in the same way the Canadian state is recognized as a nation in the international context. Iroquoian political thought has a long and venerable tradition, and its influence on nascent forms of American political thought has been the subject of much scholarship and controversy. The framers of the American constitution may have been "influenced" by the Great Law of Peace, but they put their understandings to use in Eurocentric ways. The lesson from this kind of investigation is not to see Iroquoian political thought as "similar" to American political thought, or vice versa, but that even when European intellectuals make use of indigenous ideas, they still get them wrong and then use them to their own benefit. See Donald Grinde, Bruce Johansen, and John Kahiohhes Fadden, *Exemplar of Liberty: Native America and the Evolution of Democracy* (Berkeley: University of California Press, 1991); and Oren Lyons et al., eds., *Exiled in the Land of the Free* (Santa Fe: Clearlight Publishing, 1991).

22 Although even the Mohawk have been known to listen to the occasional Anishnabe.

23 One point worth mentioning is that the issue of language, and the philosophical and political problems associated with using it more explicitly in the Aboriginal-newcomer relationship, is an Aboriginal problem and therefore ought to be resolved by Aboriginal peoples. Non-Aboriginal peoples may play an important role in facilitating understanding and implementing solutions, but they do so more as consultants than as participants.

24 See, for example, Taiaiake Alfred, *Heeding Our Ancestors: Kahnawake Mohawk Politics and the Rise of Native Nationalism* (Oxford: Oxford University Press, 1995); Susan Tuhiwai Smith, *Decolonizing Methodologies: Research and Indigenous Peoples* (New York: Zed Books, 1999); Robert Warrior, *Tribal Secrets: Recovering American Indian Intellectual Traditions* (Minneapolis: University of Minnesota Press, 1994); Jace Weaver, *That the People Might Live: Native American Literatures and the Native American Community* (Oxford: Oxford University Press, 1997); and Audra Simpson, "Paths Toward a Mohawk Nation: Narratives of Citizenship and Nationhood in Kahnawake," in Duncan Ivison, Paul Patton, and Will Sanders, eds., *Political Theory and the Rights of Indigenous Peoples* (Cambridge, UK: Cambridge University Press, 2000).

4
Paths to Intercultural Understanding: Feasting, Shared Horizons, and Unforced Consensus
Natalie Oman

Theories of intercultural understanding are generally required and formulated in response to conflict between members of different cultures, when differing belief systems or worldviews grate against one another more sharply in the presence of a specific contested resource, value, or belief. In such a situation, a theory of intercultural understanding serves as the underpinning for a practical approach to intercultural negotiation aimed at resolving the conflict. In the wake of a general apprehension by Europeans of the existence of the profoundly different civilizations of the inhabitants of other continents in the sixteenth and seventeenth centuries, and the colonial era that followed,[1] such situations of conflict have arisen with destructive frequency between members of the dominant societies of "post"-colonial powers and members of formerly colonized peoples within those states or their former satellites.

The following story drawn from the long history of these clashes helps to illustrate why approaches to intercultural negotiation that do not place a premium upon the pursuit of intercultural understanding are unhelpful in achieving lasting resolutions of such disputes.

The Significance of Intercultural Understanding
The "Kitsegukla incident" refers to the period of several months in 1872 when Gitxsan chiefs blockaded the passage of trade goods along the Skeena River in the British Columbia interior in reaction to the accidental burning of the Gitxsan village of Kitsegukla by a party of mainly white miners. The blockade was eventually lifted as a consequence of negotiations between the Gitxsan chiefs and the lieutenant-governor of the then colony of British Columbia, conducted aboard a British navy gunboat moored at Metlakatla on the northern Pacific coast.[2]

It is evident from the oral history of the Gitxsan and the newspaper and journal accounts of the colonial participants that two quite contradictory versions of the purpose and meaning of the negotiations that occurred on the gunboat at Metlakatla were generated, even as those events were occurring. These two accounts are remarkable insofar as they agree in all important matters of narrative detail, while differing in every particular concerning the significance of the events they describe.

The Gitxsan chiefs who attended the Metlakatla meeting believed they had taken part in a form of feast lasting three days that included the following elements: an explanation of the offence that led up to the blockade of the Skeena River; the indispensable storytelling that contextualized that account; the sharing of oral histories; the acceptance of gifts of money and goods that signified the newcomers' acknowledgment of responsibility for wrongdoing and recognition of Gitxsan jurisdiction; the witnessing of an agreement, attested by the signing of a paper, that confirmed both parties' obligation to respect the authority of the other within their appropriate spheres; and a celebration marking the occasion of that agreement.[3]

From the viewpoint of the colony's lieutenant-governor and his men, they had spent three days in meetings with representatives of the offending Indians that included: a recitation of the grievance that provoked the Native group to blockade the river; the recounting of various songs and stories (to which the colonial delegation acquiesced in order to speed a resolution); the payment of a token sum to the Native leaders in exchange for their agreement to permanently discontinue the blockade; the signing of a statement confirming the amicable intentions of both parties;[4] and a symbolic show of force consisting in the firing of the gunboat's cannon, to mark the conclusion of the discussions and help ensure the future quietude of the Natives.

Unsurprisingly, the "agreement" that resulted from these two distinct sequences of events was not an effective means of bringing about the goals of either party. The Gitxsan believed that they had received honourable compensation for damages suffered and had reached an accord in which their sovereignty was acknowledged and a foundation for future intercultural cooperation had been forged;[5] the representatives of the settlers perhaps thought that they had eliminated the immediate obstacle that the blockade posed by paying off a few troublemakers who were attempting to extort from the rightful government of the land, and had ensured that similar problems would not occur again by intimidating the ringleaders with their ship and their display of arms. In fact, while each party seemed to have achieved its short-term goal at the time, Gitxsan sovereignty remains essentially unrecognized over a century later, and the provincial government of what is now British Columbia continues to struggle with constant challenges to its authority.

Neither side procured the outcome it believed it had secured at Metlakatla, precisely because each group brought unique expectations and assumptions about the process of resolving intercultural conflicts to the negotiation process. The agreement that arose from the Metlakatla discussions was interpreted by the Gitxsan and the colonists in light of these divergent background understandings and, accordingly, had a distinctive meaning for each. As a consequence, the resolution to this intercultural dispute proved to be both ineffective and short-lived.

One of the lessons of this incident is that the motives and background understandings of other-cultural parties to a dispute matter greatly for the outcome of that dispute, and thus, efforts to build intercultural understanding (as a means to comprehending the motives and background understandings of others) ought to be a fundamental feature of attempts to settle intercultural conflicts.

In cases in which one party to an intercultural conflict holds the preponderance of power, as at Metlakatla and its modern-day variants played out at Oka, Ipperwash, Gustafsen Lake, and Burnt Church, the possibility of achieving a mutually satisfactory resolution in the absence of intercultural understanding is not only reduced but gravely endangered.[6] The almost overwhelming tendency – which may not even reach the level of conscious temptation for the particular individuals involved – is for members of the dominant group to impose their standards of value and worldview upon the less powerful party. Even when agreements *are* concluded under such circumstances, their reliability remains doubtful, because the conditions of negotiation and the range of conceivable solutions that were open to discussion have often been dictated, sometimes through very subtle means, by the more powerful cultural group.[7]

Thus, reciprocal understanding of the motives of the other party to an intercultural negotiation and of the meaning the process of negotiation holds for members of that group is an indispensable element of intercultural agreements that are intended to be both effective and lasting, particularly in cases in which the resources of the parties to the dispute differ significantly. The tactics that will be most appropriate for fostering intercultural understanding (and thus creating the conditions to build intercultural agreements) between parties to any specific conflict will depend directly upon those parties' motives and the constructions they place upon the negotiating process.

Theories and Techniques of Intercultural Understanding
What follows is a rough assemblage of key elements of theories and methodologies for the resolution of intercultural disputes that all aim in some part at fostering intercultural understanding. This brief survey is restricted to approaches in which the techniques of bestowing recognition and cultivating dialogical relationships are assigned central roles. What distinguishes their authors and adherents from those who do not assign as great a value to the pursuit of understanding in their efforts to theorize

intercultural negotiation is their acceptance of the ethical challenge posed by cultural diversity. This exercise generates what Ludwig Wittgenstein described as a "perspicuous representation" of the process of crafting intercultural understanding itself, and reveals the unique strengths of two convergent approaches in particular.

One of the purposes of this eclectic account is to illustrate how human beings make use of a gamut of techniques entailing a variety of forms of recognition that aid us in building intercultural understanding in order to deal with intercultural difference. These techniques can be assembled to form a continuum of possible approaches to intercultural relations that reveals interesting relationships among its constituent elements (Wittgenstein refers to such relationships as "connecting" or "intermediate" links[8]). These approaches to intercultural relations range from tactics involving the egregious misrecognition of others, through techniques designed to bestow solely instrumental recognition of others, to approaches justified both in terms of the instrumental purposes they serve and as ends in themselves, which entail more comprehensive forms of recognition that take account of the self-understandings of the others being recognized. (Due to considerations of length, the overview that follows will be limited to approaches of the latter sort.)

Techniques involving profound misrecognition are based on the conviction that "others" are lesser moral beings, or perhaps lack moral status altogether, while approaches situated somewhat closer to the middle of the continuum tend to endorse a broadening of membership in the "we" of equal moral agents to include members of other cultures. This move entails recognizing those others as possessing the same morally relevant qualities that "we" have; in other words, recognizing others as analogues of ourselves in a fashion that may take little account of the qualities that the others *themselves* regard as morally valuable. Toward the other end of the continuum, tactics for building intercultural understanding involve an acknowledgment that my interlocutor has an irreducible perspective born of particular experiences, that must, in some part, remain unknowable to me.[9] My conception of the qualities that define moral agency begins to be transformed under the influence of alternative conceptions of personhood as I question the hegemony of my culture-specific standards of value, and the form of recognition that is bestowed through our interaction comes to be informed by the self-understandings of my interlocutor.

Taken together, the elements of this continuum illustrate the process of building intercultural understanding, but the fact that techniques situated near the comprehensive recognition pole of the continuum seem to offer superior means of encouraging intercultural understanding to those located close to the misrecognition end of the continuum may be somewhat misleading. This picture of the relationships among different approaches to intercultural understanding is not meant to imply that a linear, uni-directional progression from one technique to another ever occurs in real-world attempts to forge intercultural understanding. Most intercultural relationships encompass a wide range of these different tactics and, correspondingly, involve a variety of different modes of recognition. And even when these diverse approaches result in the creation of a significant degree of intercultural understanding, this success can never signal a cessation of effort on the part of the interlocutors or the cultural groups they belong to, because any understanding that is reached is necessarily transitory, since it is an understanding of finite aspects of a living culture that is heterogeneous, contested, and changing. It follows that any agreement based on such an understanding must be in the nature of a "moving consensus" – an accord that must be open to renegotiation and fine-tuning over time.

Approaches to intercultural relations that are not principally concerned with the valorization of understanding (such as, for example, philosopher John Rawls's theory of overlapping consensus)[10], are much less likely to facilitate this ongoing process of readjustment. Because the achievement of intercultural understanding is not necessarily a primary goal for their advocates (although it certainly plays a role in Rawls's view), these approaches seem apt to produce more obstructive forms of (mis)recognition than those associated with models that assign greater significance to the process of creating intercultural understanding as such.

I will argue below that two complementary approaches to intercultural understanding that entail a highly comprehensive form of recognition – that associated with the Gitxsan-Wet'suwet'en model of intercultural relations and the theory developed in Charles Taylor's most recent work on intercultural negotiation of human rights standards – can play a particularly useful role in helping to build flexible intercultural relationships capable of evolving and adapting over time. To develop this argument, key positions along the continuum of intercultural understanding will be mapped by surveying representative features of arguments drawn from a variety of influential "Western" disciplines, including legal theory, philosophy, and political science, and from a First Nations perspective shared by many members of the Gitxsan and Wet'suwet'en peoples.[11] This methodology has important limitations, since it involves reducing complex theoretical positions to a few elements selected not only because I regard them as representative of the authors' broader arguments but also because those particular features serve to flesh out the continuum of approaches to intercultural understanding. In reality, all of these authors and individuals combine elements from different parts of the continuum, just as people engaged in practical efforts to craft intercultural understanding employ a shifting patchwork of diverse methods and achieve degrees of understanding that vary over time. However, with these limitations in mind, I believe that the reductionism inherent in this method is justified by the insights that the activity of assembling a "perspicuous representation" reveals about the nature of intercultural understanding.

Legal Contextualism

Former Supreme Court of Canada (SCC) Justice Bertha Wilson's contributions to the tactics of intercultural understanding arise in connection with her development of an innovative judicial methodology dubbed "contextualism," which some believe is coming to play a dominant role in shaping the decisions of the current SCC.[12] As the first woman to serve on the SCC, appointed to the Court seventeen days before the Charter came into force, Justice Wilson self-consciously sought to construct an alternative to the ethnocentric, class, social, and gender biases inherent in existing mainstream approaches to judging. The established ideals of judicial decision making – impartiality, neutrality, dispassionate disengagement – became targets for Justice Wilson's critical reexamination.

Justice Wilson accomplished this reexamination through the application of a method of judicial decision making that evolved through both her decisions and her public speeches. The precise description of this contextualist approach to judicial decision making is contested, as the methodology was developed by Justice Wilson and her colleagues on a decision-by-decision basis, and continues to be modified by the SCC today.[13] But the essential Wittgensteinian insight on which it rests is that linguistic (and every other form of) meaning is based on use.[14] For contextualist legal scholars, the meaning of law depends upon the way that the language with which it is concerned is conventionally employed by communities of speakers at any given moment. It follows that understanding the context that lends meaning to the language at issue in any particular case, whether it be the language of the Charter, of ordinary legislation, or words employed by parties to a proceeding that form part of the evidence under consideration, is the key step in the contextualist method.[15]

In practice, this requirement for an appreciation of context entails a need for intersubjective understanding, whether of individuals seeking interpretation of their Charter rights or freedoms, of the members of a broad community whose standards are at issue, or of litigants in other more commonplace forms of dispute. In the multicultural Canada of today, the nature of the intersubjective understanding that is sought is frequently intercultural.

How is this intersubjective and often intercultural understanding to be attained? Justice Wilson prescribes a methodology involving the bestowal of recognition and the fostering of a form of dialogue. As she explains in her most famous public comments on the subject, the crucial step in the contextual approach to judicial decision making is "to enter into the skin of the litigant and make his or her experience part of your experience and only when you have done that, to judge."[16] The resources that can assist a judge in making this step are varied. Social, political, and psychological theory; historical and statistical academic studies (both those properly before the court and those that might be expected to contribute to the common knowledge of the average citizen); personal experience; imagination; and empathy are all important tools that can enable judges to develop intersubjective/intercultural understanding.

R. v. Hill[17] provides a typical example of the application of the contextual approach to judicial decision making. This appeal of a second-degree murder conviction involving a sixteen-year-old defendant turned on the issue of the provocation defence and the "ordinary person's" standard of self-control. In her dissenting judgment allowing the appeal, Justice Wilson introduces the argument that in order to assess the ordinary person's self-control, the seriousness of the particular provocation at issue must be considered, necessarily with reference "to the context in which the insult occurs, including the relationship between the parties, their age, culture, physical and mental attributes."[18] In this way, Justice Wilson makes the employment of the curial concept of the reasonable person dependent upon the judicial act of "enter[ing] into the skin of the litigant and mak[ing] his ... experience part of [the judge's] experience."

Hill demonstrates the revolutionary implications of the contextualist method for a judge's construal of the "identity" imputed to the ubiquitous reasonable person of curial discourse. By considering contextual factors to determine ordinary standards of conduct for a reasonable person possessing specific characteristics, this approach challenges the hegemony of the "invisible norm" that has historically functioned as a means of assigning the features of a dominant group to what purports to be a universally representative legal construct. As Hester Lessard suggests, this contextual method "creat[es] a space for telling different sorts of stories about what ordinariness means."[19]

While relying on a method of intersubjective/intercultural understanding for its accomplishment, Justice Wilson's ultimate purpose is to render just judgments. In assessing the limitations of the contextualist approach, it is important to keep this fact in mind, particularly when appraising the effectiveness of contextualism's contribution to the creation of the dialogical relationships upon which intercultural understanding depends.

The rather monological means of seeking dialogical relationships prescribed by the contextualist method is a weakness common to many academic approaches to intercultural understanding. It is, of course, a structural constraint of the existing Canadian legal system that the process of appellate review does not allow for direct exchanges between litigants and appeal judges, but instead relies (traditionally) upon factums provided by the litigants' legal counsel and transcripts of the trial court proceedings, in addition to relevant legislation. By drawing upon additional resources such as expert reports and judges' personal knowledge about social conditions, Justice Wilson's approach does, however, go some way toward ameliorating the effects of this absent opportunity, and perhaps as the use of contextualism spreads to lower courts, a less interrogative and more dialogical process of interaction between litigants and judges will become characteristic. (Research in the field of comparative legal theory indicates that a much greater degree of dialogicality can be accommodated by other formal legal systems. For example, both Lawrence Rosen and Sally Engle Merry provide interesting discussions of how the *qadi* courts of Morocco depend upon many of the conventions of conversational exchange.[20])

Despite the structural impediments to the establishment of dialogical relationships, Shalin M. Sugunasiri writes approvingly of the "dialogic" nature of the contextualist method of judicial decision making. "By 'dialogic,'" he says, "I mean no more than the fact that such decision making is discursive in nature. To put the matter more plainly, contextualist decision making is about conversations – it is about the conversations judges have with themselves, the conversations they have with each other, and the conversations they have with the parties, the legislators, and always, in one way or another, with the general public."[21]

Notwithstanding Sugunasiri's contention that the contextualist approach does involve an important element of dialogue, according to Justice Wilson the primary aspect of contextualist methodology remains the empathetic act of imagining what it is like to be the other. When the key to your method is getting inside the skin of the litigant, but your method for doing so involves only a highly limited degree of dialogue with the specific interlocutor(s) concerned and does not emphasize the development of actual dialogical relationships with concrete individuals, you have to worry about how genuine the form of recognition you are bestowing actually is: because you are not really in conversation in the conventional sense, you don't have an independent authoritative check on whether your insights – and the form(s) of recognition you are bestowing based on those insights – are accurate or not.

This lack of authentically dialogical guidance has an additional implication: without a "native" interlocutor to provide a constant reminder of the irreducibility of difference, the tendency when using an empathetic method could easily be to put *oneself* in the place of the other without realizing that that is what you are doing; in other words, thinking that you have achieved a sufficient understanding of how the other feels and thinks and reacts as a result of making the imaginative and empathetic efforts prescribed by the contextual approach.

Another concern about the contextualist approach arises in connection with the central role it assigns to the imaginative and emotional exercise of empathy. While empathy clearly has an important place as a fairly universally available technique for seeking intersubjective understanding, this further problem may arise when it is unreflectively or exclusively depended upon. In a classificatory discussion of various legal conceptions of impartiality, Richard Devlin suggests that any theory like Justice Wilson's that relies upon entering the skin of the litigant – in essence, becoming another and "mak[ing] his or her experience part of your experience" – in an effort to forge understanding raises the spectre of appropriation. "In the effort to empathize with the marginalized, those who have privilege may begin to speak on behalf of the excluded," he asserts, "usually mistranslating their experience and thereby reinforcing their silence."[22] When significant power differentials between parties to an intercultural conflict exist and the very framework for negotiation is at issue, the ramifications of such an unintentional imperialism can be disastrous.

Symmetrical Reciprocity
During the last fifteen years, debates over the goals and epistemology of feminism have given rise to a rich literature concerning the problem of seeking understanding across difference. Feminists' struggles with the practical challenges posed by racism, classism, and heterosexism within the movement have generated theoretical insights that have been applied, notably by authors Seyla Benhabib and Iris Marion Young, to the subject of deliberative democratic theories of politics.[23]

The account of "symmetrical reciprocity" Benhabib provides in *Situating the Self* is a description of a form of moral conversation, intended to remedy what she argues are weaknesses within Jürgen Habermas's theory of communicative ethics. Benhabib quite consciously means her approach to apply in situations of intercultural conflict, at least within the bounds of multicultural societies, as well as in contexts where other forms of difference are at issue. Benhabib's model builds upon Hannah Arendt's uncompleted work developing Immanuel Kant's notion of "enlarged thought." The central premise of Benhabib's argument is that attempts to reach agreement across difference (of whatever sort – gender, life experience, socioeconomic status, age, skin colour, sexual orientation, culture, and so on) require the cultivation of a "capacity for reversing perspectives." This capacity is exercised through acts of imagination where, in Arendt's words, I "anticipate ... communication with others with whom I know I must finally come to some agreement."[24]

Benhabib suggests that this approach to the problem of achieving understanding across difference is a natural one since it relies upon the same skills that we employ in everyday conversation: "In conversation, I must know how to listen, I must know how to understand your point of view, I must learn to represent to myself the world and the other as you see them. If I cannot listen, if I cannot understand, and if I cannot represent, the conversation stops, develops into an argument, or maybe never gets started."[25] In order to employ the method of enlarged thinking in a situation of potential conflict arising from difference, I must strive to imaginatively create "a condition of actual or simulated dialogue" with an other-cultural conversation partner. This imagined conversation is designed to allow me to think from the standpoints of others, but Benhabib is careful to follow Arendt in maintaining that this reversal of perspectives is *not* a form of empathy. Success in reversing perspectives does not involve "emotionally assuming or accepting the point of view of the other"; rather, "it means merely making present to oneself what the perspectives of others involved are or could be, and whether I could 'woo their consent' in acting the way I do."[26]

It seems that Benhabib's strategic goals here are to foster recognition and a form of dialogue, but how effectively can recognition be cultivated if the deliberation that gives it rise is monological? For the dialogical relationships that provide the foundation for intercultural understanding on Benhabib's Arendtian theory are solely hypothetical, consisting in "*making present to oneself* what the perspectives of others involved are or could be" with no enjoinder to engage in actual moral conversation with living partners. Surely intercultural understanding is something that is created *with* specific other people, at its most fundamental level. If the understanding that I attain is to be contextualized and sensitive to the implications of power inequalities between myself and those I seek to build understanding with, it must be dialogical. Such an approach cannot be about speaking for, but must aggressively emphasize the importance of speaking with.

While Benhabib, like Justice Wilson, advocates the method of "putting myself in your place" in order to achieve intercultural understanding, her argument introduces an important shift in accent. Benhabib emphasizes that while I am imagining myself in your place, I ought to think about what *your place* is like; whereas for Justice Wilson, the act of putting myself in your place can all too easily be primarily about *myself*.[27] That is to say, Benhabib is concerned with the activity of my thinking about your difference, while Justice Wilson's empathetic method may endorse my thinking about our *sameness*. As we trace the continuum from Wilson through Benhabib and beyond, the recognition that is accorded to the other shifts from "solidarity" that acknowledges the other's moral equality-in-sameness into a more complex and challenging recognition of the other's moral-equality-in-difference. In this way, the form of recognition imparted to the other begins to be less a recognition of how she is like me and more a recognition of her in terms she might employ to describe herself. So while both authors argue in favour of broadening the constituency of the "we" of equal moral agents, the manner in which those agents are defined changes subtly from one approach to the next.

Taylor and Young on the Limits of Description

During the last decade, Charles Taylor has devoted his occasional writings on intercultural understanding to exploring means of fostering recognition of the other's moral equality-in-difference.[28] He explores the general issue of intercultural understanding as it relates to the particular case of disagreement over human rights standards, and privileges the process of dialogical interaction above all. For Taylor, the dialogical method must extend beyond dialogue itself to *participation* in other-cultural practices. Dialogue alone cannot be the sole means of communicating the standards of value of one culture to members of another, because the language of each cultural group initially limits the concepts that can be conveyed. Because the broader "cultural codes" of which languages are a part open up the possibility of experiences that may not be easily communicable to others whose languages lack concepts to express those experiences, a serious effort to achieve intercultural understanding requires a greater commitment, at least by some members of the groups involved, than is involved in simple dialogue.[29]

Iris Young also proposes a dialogical approach that, like Benhabib's, is intended to apply to situations in which intercultural understanding (among other types of understanding across difference) is being sought within a single society. In a similar vein to Taylor, she argues that most deliberative democratic theories restrict their conception of the democratic process to critical argument and thereby "assume a culturally biased conception of discussion that tends to silence or devalue some people or groups."[30] Young holds that other modes of interaction beyond argumentation, such as greeting, rhetoric, and storytelling, are necessary if a more comprehensive intercultural understanding, and a just process for crafting it, are to be sought.

Young concurs with Benhabib in endorsing the idea of reformulating discourse ethics by attempting to preserve "the standpoint of the concrete other" in order to ensure respect for the specificity of those engaged in the attempt to achieve intercultural understanding. However, the means she proposes for bringing about this end are designed to redress what she regards as a serious flaw in Benhabib's method. In opposition to her reading of Benhabib's position, Young argues that moral respect (expressed in the form of recognition) rests upon a relation of *asymmetrical* reciprocity in which the *impossibility* of taking another's place imaginatively – as Benhabib's methodology of symmetrical reciprocity requires – is acknowledged, and the activity of listening is preeminent. As Young explains,

This reciprocity of equal respect and acknowledgement of one another ... entails an acknowledgement of an *asymmetry* between subjects. While there may be many similarities and points of contact between them, each position and perspective transcends the others, goes beyond their possibility to share or imagine. Participants in communicative interaction are in a relation of approach. They meet across distances of time and space and can touch, share, and overlap their interests. But each brings to the relationships a history and structured positioning that makes them different from one another, with their own shape, trajectory, and configuration of forces.[31]

I believe that Benhabib shares this realization concerning the non-identity of interlocutors but fails to thematize it explicitly or consistently. She captures the essence of this idea in her citation of a comment by Arendt, in which Arendt describes mutual respect – akin to what I am calling recognition – as "a kind of 'friendship' without intimacy and without closeness; it is a regard for the person *from the distance which the space of the world puts between us.*"[32]

"Sharing" Horizons

Taylor develops the insight about the irreducibility of difference in another way. Revealing the roots of his position in the Gadamerian conception of "prejudice,"[33] Taylor believes that a qualitative difference exists between intracultural understanding and intercultural understanding. Precisely because I draw primarily upon familiar language and concepts when I attempt to forge an understanding with another person who is shaped by many of the same cultural influences, what Taylor describes as a "fusion of horizons" occurs when we succeed. On his account, understanding is achieved by means of the creation of a "language of perspicuous contrast" that develops out of the discourse of members of the participant cultural groups. For Taylor, this would be "a language in which we could formulate both their way of life and ours as alternative possibilities in relation to some human constants at work in both,"[34] a language of negotiation. Because in this situation the participants share many sources of background understandings, our standpoints are generally (although not always, of course) relatively close to begin with, and although I don't "become" you, or imagine myself in your place, when we grasp one another's standards of value and life situations through dialogical exchange over time, our horizons of background understandings might, without great inaccuracy, be said in many cases to be "fused," just because of this initial proximity.

However, in the more complex cases of *inter*cultural understanding, where the source cultures diverge significantly and have had little mutual influence, the extent to which our horizons are common to begin with is correspondingly smaller. In such cases, recognition would minimally consist of abandoning the unreflective favouring of our own culture-specific conceptual categories and cultivating an awareness of the importance of acknowledging our interlocutors in their own terms and traditions (an activity distinct from an arbitrary acceptance of the terms of the others' self-description). The dialogical process that gives rise to a meta-language of negotiation in this situation provides the participants with the opportunity to discover a broader horizon against which their home conceptual systems can be more revealingly located in relation to the conceptual systems of others.[35]

In relationships of this sort that tend toward the genuinely "cross"-cultural end of the spectrum where the difference in standpoint to be bridged dialogically is much greater, it seems more accurate to speak of the understanding that may be achieved through this process as a sharing of horizons, rather than a seamless fusion.

I invoke this particular alternative metaphor not only to draw an analytical distinction but also to signal my disaccord with Young's ambivalence concerning the concept of sharing (see the quoted passage above), which she regards as necessarily implying a relationship of perfect symmetry. Rather, I suggest that a full and equal appreciation of all aspects of horizons jointly surveyed by interlocutors seeking intercultural understanding is one potential expression of a relationship of sharing, but that this expression represents only one extreme of the range of possibilities that sharing can encompass. Sharing is not distinguished by the interchangeability of the experiences of partners – in other words, by their having had identical experiences of the horizons they share – but by the quality of invitation, and of possibility, that each brings to the relationship.

The Feast as an Invitation to Share Horizons

This notion of sharing horizons seems to express the animating principle of traditional Gitxsan and Wet'suwet'en strategies of international relations as well.[36] The Gitxsan and the Wet'suwet'en First Nations of northwestern British Columbia are culturally and linguistically distinct peoples who share a border and a historical relationship marked by close cooperation and frequent intermarriages. Their common history has given rise to similar social and political institutions: both peoples employ a form of governance in which house chiefs and sub- or wing-chiefs play a leading role among the wider body of name-holders who conserve the history and the territories in the keeping of each of the houses, and both the Gitxsan and the Wet'suwet'en engage in the practice of feasting as their primary means of securing political, legal, social, and cultural continuity.[37]

Traditionally, the Gitxsan and the Wet'suwet'en also shared the belief that the world consists fundamentally in a web of relationships. Thus, intercultural relationships, and the intercultural understanding that allows such relationships to flourish, play a key role in the Gitxsan and Wet'-suwet'en worldview.[38] It follows that in their capacity as stewards of their traditional territory and culture, Gitxsan and Wet'suwet'en people work to sustain a balance among the diverse, and equally legitimate, human and animal societies that are inextricably linked to one another. As Susan Marsden (a scholar who was employed by the Gitxsan as an expert witness in the *Delgamuukw* land claim case)[39] summarizes, "this balance is based on the understanding that all forms of life and all peoples are intrinsically complementary, and will flourish if the domain of each is perceived and respected."[40] The art of accomplishing these dual tasks of observation rests in turn upon the successful forging of intercultural understanding. And the path to intercultural understanding for the Gitxsan and the Wet'-suwet'en is through the formal recognition of other-cultural interlocutors and the activity of engaging in ritualized but highly meaningful dialogue with them in the medium of the feast.

The telling of *adaawk* and *kungax* (Gitxsan and Wet'suwet'en oral histories, respectively) is the vehicle for dialogue during a feast. As each chief tells the story of the part of their society's history for which he or she is responsible "in the living context of the knowledge in others' minds," that shared history and the physical boundaries of the territory it imbues with meaning acquire an "accumulated validation."[41] On important occasions, all of the custodians of the histories pertaining to the subject(s) at issue assemble the complementary and contradictory viewpoints that capture the refracted quality of the lived experience of complex social events. By exposing the witnesses to diverse perspectives on the same incidents, this telling is designed to inspire reflection on the varieties of distance that separate each participant and the multiplicity of their truths.

The immanent ideal of intercultural understanding embodied in this practice of feasting was put into practice during the *Delgamuukw* land claim trial concerning Gitxsan and Wet'suwet'en ownership and jurisdiction over their traditional lands. In essence, the Court was invited to participate in a form of feast as, through stories and explanations in their own languages and the language of the Court, through songs and demonstrations and showings of many kinds, the Gitxsan and the Wet'suwet'en sought to reveal what it means to "know how to go on" for members of their societies. The purpose of this attempt was simply to offer the Court guidance in learning a technique of intercultural understanding analogous in spirit to the Taylorean approach described above.[42] Taylor offers an account of principles that can and must be actualized uniquely in every specific effort to build intercultural understanding, according to the context of disagreement or harmony, and the parity or inequality of power

among participant cultures. The Gitxsan-Wet'suwet'en model provides an
example of a similar sensibility, rooted in a different cultural tradition.

Relativism and the Possibility of Moral Judgment

A further parallel between Taylor's view and the Gitxsan-Wet'suwet'en
model is the role assigned by both to moral judgment. Each approach
valorizes the process of seeking intercultural understanding, yet in its own
way retains a commitment to moral judgment as well. Benhabib provides
a particularly lucid account of the conviction that underlies this common
position and also serves as the basis for her phenomenology of moral
judgment:

> Moral judgement differs from [political and other forms of judgment] in
> one crucial respect: the exercise of moral judgement is pervasive and
> unavoidable; in fact, this exercise is coextensive with relations of social
> interaction in the lifeworld in general. *Moral judgement is what we "always
> already" exercise in virtue of being immersed in a network of human relation-
> ships that constitute our life together.* Whereas there can be reasonable
> debate about whether or not to exercise juridical, military, therapeutic,
> aesthetic, or even political judgement, in the case of moral judgement this
> option is not there. The domain of the moral is so deeply enmeshed with
> those interactions that constitute our lifeworld that to withdraw from
> moral judgement is tantamount to ceasing to interact, to talk and act in
> the human community.[43]

On this view, moral judgment is inevitable, and the only issue it raises
for the theorist of intercultural understanding is whether she chooses to
acknowledge that inevitability or not. In this regard, Young chooses differently from Taylor, adherents to the Gitxsan and Wet'suwet'en approach,
Benhabib, and Wilson.

Young's concern for the implications of the asymmetrical relationship
between intercultural participants leads her to remain largely silent about
the issue of intercultural moral judgments. She seems to tend toward with-
holding or attempting to forestall such judgments on the grounds that
"each party must recognize that others have irreducible points of view,
and active interests that respectful interaction must consider."[44]

There are certain kinds of judgments – at a minimum, moral judgments
in hard cases – that by their very nature must be universal. In such cases,
our judgments are expressed as universal assertions: "unprovoked murder
is wrong"; "landmines should not be disguised as children's toys." If we
appreciate the extent to which human beings are immersed in particular cultural contexts and the background understandings that constitute
them, we know that any such moral judgment can only be justified by

relativistic or culture-specific reasons, and so we typically infer the existence of the implicit "I believe that" clause preceding the assertion, yet the universal force of the moral judgment cannot be lessened by the explicit inclusion of that clause. Thomas Morawetz explains Wittgenstein's appreciation of this point in *On Certainty:*[45]

> It is a fallacy to say that because my claims, as seen by *others,* are "merely" personal and because "my certainty is my own" [s.174] I ought to (or can) subject my own ways of proceeding to the same kind of scrutiny and evaluation as I do the claims of others. This is nonsense: what could I use to check my picture of the world and my practices as a whole but my picture of the world and my practices? The recommendation that I treat my own claims as merely personal is incoherent. It involves the misconception that I can stand impartial between my own ways of proceeding and those of others.
>
> ... I can admit the possibility that I will come to think differently (that "my eyes" will be "opened" [s.578]) but I cannot accommodate this standing possibility ("so far as one can know such a thing" [s.623]) by disclaiming my own certainty.[46]

By taking the argument concerning the inevitability of moral judgment seriously, I acknowledge that my embeddedness in a particular (inter)cultural context must be assigned as much significance as the embeddedness of an other with whom I am trying to build understanding; in hard cases, I cannot abandon my allegiance to the standards of value that constitute me by defining my notion of personhood. Therefore, in such cases, when I am unable to grasp or recognize the legitimacy of a set of other-cultural standards of value, I have no choice but to employ my own in exercising moral judgment.[47] At the same time, I always hold open the possibility of self-transformation through the discovery of "experiences recalcitrant to my way of understanding" that may be encountered in the process of seeking intercultural understanding.[48] (In the Gitxsan and Wet'suwet'en practice of feasting, the performance of *adaawk̲* and *kungax* crystallizes different perspectives on historical events and thus creates opportunities for such moments of realization.) This perpetual openness to the potentialities of dialogical interaction precludes zealotry or dogmatism in intercultural relationships.

It follows that no conflict is necessary between the goals of pursuing intercultural understanding and of acknowledging the inescapability of moral judgment; both can be accomplished by attending equally to the facts of my embeddedness and of my other-cultural interlocutor's. Adoption of this middle-ground position serves to defuse the dangers of relativism. And refusal to relinquish the possibility of moral judgment, and simultaneous attention to the constitutive role played by our immersion in specific cultures, provides the groundwork for a "domesticated relativism" that reconciles the need for action and choice in the real world with the ethical challenge posed by difference.

One of the greatest strengths of an approach to negotiation that relies upon intercultural understanding in this way is that it does not require a shared set of standards of value to be effective. In situations in which one party to a conflict is substantially less powerful than the other, as is generally the case when formerly colonized peoples are negotiating with their former (and present) colonizers, the rules of the negotiating game are largely determined by the colonizers. So although the terms of debate can be altered by the less powerful party (the Gitxsan and the Wet'suwet'en's continuing impact on Canadian and British Columbia government Aboriginal policies through their actions in the *Delgamuukw* case and their ongoing dealings with both governments are a case in point), the limits of debate and the conceivable possibilities for negotiated outcomes are for the most part determined in advance by the more powerful party. What this means is that the standards of value of the more powerful party generally define the reality that is admitted as imaginable within the walls of the negotiating room. If intercultural understanding is assigned a central place in the negotiating process, the fact that alternative *legitimate* (whether comprehensible or not) standards of value – and the worldviews they underpin – exist becomes inescapable, and the possibility of outcomes that challenge the assumptions and expectations of both parties becomes real.

Taylor describes the goal of seeking solutions to intercultural conflicts based on such a sensibility as "unforced consensus." He uses this term to indicate that in a negotiating process based upon the insights of shared horizons, no single party's frame of reference would be imposed to define the purposes and possibilities of negotiation. A consensus of the sort he advocates would eventually come to include "agreement on norms, yes; but a profound sense of difference, of unfamiliarity, in the ideals, the notions of human excellence, the rhetorical tropes and reference points by which these norms become objects of deep commitment for us."[49] It is this sense of difference that inspires the moments of self- and cultural-transformation that must serve as the foundation for lasting and adaptable solutions to intercultural conflicts.

Conclusion

The resolution of specific intercultural conflicts at both the intranational and international levels is facilitated by the pursuit of intercultural understanding, since an appreciation of the influence of the mode of negotiation upon the agreement, and of the meaning of the agreement itself for each party, can be achieved only on the basis of some insight into the background understandings that are specific to the cultural groups involved. (A brief survey of the history of Aboriginal-settler relations in the Americas indicates at the very least that the absence of such an understanding is often a factor associated with the failure of such agreements.[50]) At the same time, this is not to say that the attainment of meaningful intercultural understanding is any guarantee of success in the negotiation of resolutions to specific disagreements. Interests, however well understood by both parties, can genuinely be in conflict, and differences of opinion about standards of value – however comprehensively appreciated by other parties – can still legitimately occur. But while a commitment to a process of seeking intercultural understanding does not offer a simple panacea to intercultural conflict, it does seem to provide a logical starting point.

The particular usefulness of the approach to intercultural understanding sketched in Taylor's recent work and instantiated in the practices of the Gitxsan and Wet'suwet'en feasts lies primarily in the fact that it is recommended not only by pragmatic reasons of the commonsense sort outlined above, but also by an open-ended and potentially culture-specific set of normative reasons. As Taylor has argued, because such agreements would be locally justified in the terms and traditions familiar to members of the particular cultural groups involved, intercultural agreements achieved through this type of process would be unlikely to be regarded as imposed from outside, or as the mere product of realpolitik. Instead, intercultural agreements such as multilateral international agreements would develop a genuine normative force; (most) members of cultures in which the aggregation of thoughtful adherents to an idea is considered a sign of the idea's worth would tend to be favourably impressed by agreements or standards endorsed under such circumstances.[51] This kind of convergence would not come, Taylor writes, "through a loss or denial of traditions all around, but rather by creative re-immersions of different groups, each in their own spiritual heritage, travelling different routes to the same goal."[52] Because this approach to intercultural understanding relies upon local justifications, it also possesses the virtue of moderation: it does not comprise a totalizing metaphysical doctrine, and it does not purport to provide a solution to every conflict; it simply offers a sensible, adaptable set of guidelines for working toward the resolution of intercultural disagreements.

This "sharing of horizons" approach assigns a central role to the bestowal of a form of recognition that takes account of the self-perception of the one being recognized. It endorses a generous and faith-full, trusting attitude toward other-cultural interlocutors, and while it begins with a commitment to the idea that the moral agency of others is, at a minimum, the same in character and worth as our own, it encourages us to be open to new conceptions of what moral agency might consist in.[53] This prescription can accommodate a history of misrecognition, and assumes the incremental development of intercultural understanding by means of a fluid combination of different techniques drawn from the continuum outlined above.

While approaches that entail more "genuine" forms of recognition of "others" foster more comprehensive degrees of intercultural understanding, each of the techniques can contribute to the complex endeavour of creating intercultural understanding. Although approaches based on solely instrumental justifications for seeking intercultural accommodation tend to prepare the ground for the exercise of approaches that are *also* justified as ends in themselves (for example, asymmetrical reciprocity), in real-life intercultural relationships, no rigid hierarchy prevails: most people involved in the process of seeking intercultural understanding employ a gamut of different approaches, sliding from one technique to another, treating their partners with greater and lesser degrees of recognition from one conversation to the next.[54]

This approach constitutes a sensibility, rather than a blueprint. The condition of shared horizons is not something that can be brought about in the same way twice; in every particular case, the approach will be implemented differently, and even within a single case, the techniques employed to build intercultural understanding will change over time. In his more recent work, Taylor makes this feature of his approach explicit, and in so doing, acknowledges the struggle over cultural values that is a feature of every cultural group. Because of this inescapably contested character of culture, intercultural agreements, and the intercultural understanding that may have contributed to their achievement, can never be regarded as fixed. Since the cultures of all parties to such agreements are always undergoing change and reformulation, a moving consensus that can adapt to these transformations – that are themselves partly a consequence of the phenomenon of "interculturality" itself – provides the best long-term hope of those who seek intercultural stability. The approach to intercultural understanding expressed by Taylor in his recent writings, by the Gitxsan and Wet'suwet'en through their historical practices of intercultural feasting, and, most notably, by the manner of their conduct in the *Delgamuukw* case, is based upon a rejection of the illusion that intercultural understanding can be a static accomplishment; their "shared horizons" approach instead affirms the process of self- and cultural-transformation that the quest for a moving consensus implies.

Notes

1 This chronology is complicated by the fact that "Europeans" had varying exposure to information about the inhabitants of distant lands, depending not only on their own socioeconomic class but also on the particular country in which they lived. For example,

Spain and Portugal had had close contacts with the Arab world through the Arab occupation of much of Spain in the medieval era, and the Portuguese were early and avid explorers of Africa. During the sixteenth century, the printing press facilitated the popularization of travel literature about African and Asian peoples in those countries and throughout Europe, but although both Spain and Portugal committed great resources to the exploitation of the Americas during that century, the indigenous inhabitants of the "new" continents did not apparently stir much interest in Europe until toward the end of that century and the beginning of the next, when France and England, among others, began to establish North American colonies. On the history of Spanish conceptions of American indigenous peoples, see, for example, Lewis Hanke, *Aristotle and the American Indians* (Bloomington: Indiana University Press, 1959), chap. 1; and on other European ideas about the "others" inhabiting the Americas, Anthony Pagden, *European Encounters with the New World* (New Haven, CT, and London: Yale University Press, 1993), and Robert A. Williams Jr., *The American Indian in Western Legal Thought* (New York: Oxford University Press, 1990).

2 These events are explored insightfully in R.M. Galois's "The Burning of Kitsegukla, 1872" (1992) 94 BC Studies 59, a paper that resulted from research commissioned by the Office of the Hereditary Chiefs pursuant to the *Delgamuukw* land claim case. I have drawn upon Galois and the relevant material included in Gisday Wa and Delgam Uukw, *Spirit in the Land* (Gabriola, BC: Reflections, 1989, 1992), 51-54, in this brief discussion.

3 See below for a more detailed discussion of the practice of feasting among the Gitxsan and the Wet'suwet'en First Nations.

4 Newspaper accounts of the day produced by the settler population provide little information concerning the details of this agreement, and seem to have regarded it as of minor importance. See Galois, "The Burning of Kitsegukla."

5 It seems possible that the Gitxsan did not fully appreciate the profundity of the difference between the newcomers' worldview and their own, and that this oversight prevented them from fully applying their own model of intercultural relations in this case. They may have underestimated the importance of the task of building intercultural understanding before reaching an agreement with the colonial government, or perhaps felt compelled to break with their traditional model because of rumours of the superior force that the newcomers had brought to bear against other Native peoples in other parts of North America. See Natalie Oman, "Sharing Horizons: A Paradigm for Political Accommodation in Intercultural Settings" (PhD diss., McGill University, 1997) for more detail.

6 I employ the notoriously nebulous term "power" in this chapter for want of a reasonable alternative. In what follows, power refers simply to the potential for influencing both the outcomes of particular interactions and the terms in which those outcomes are judged, that flows from the concatenation of material, human, and technological resources.

7 One example of this kind of exercise of power is occurring in British Columbia's treaty negotiations. The "land selection model" promoted by the provincial government and adopted as the standard that would determine the structure of all future negotiations was agreed to by the members of the First Nations Summit of BC in the discussions with the provincial government that led up to the inauguration of the contemporary treaty process in British Columbia (in which the Gitxsan and Wet'suwet'en did not participate). A refusal to accept the general type of outcome dictated by this model (which eliminates the possibility of gaining recognition of territorially based forms of sovereignty) essentially precludes a negotiated settlement.

8 Ludwig Wittgenstein, "Remarks on Frazer's Golden Bough," in C.G. Luckhardt, ed., *Wittgenstein: Sources and Perspectives* (Ithaca, NY: Cornell University Press, 1979), 69.

9 Iris Marion Young suggests that "moral humility" is a necessary basis for this kind of insight; Iris Marion Young, "Asymmetrical Reciprocity: On Moral Respect, Wonder, and Enlarged Thought" (1997) 3 Constellations 4, 354.

10 For a discussion of the instrumental character of Rawls's early use of the concept of overlapping consensus, see Natalie Oman, "On the Universalizability of Human Rights" (April 1996) 1 The European Legacy 530.

11 There are a variety of accepted spellings of the names of these northwestern BC First

Nations. "Gitx̲san" is a form of the older "Gitksan" and is now employed by the hereditary leaders and treaty negotiators of the Gitx̲san Nation, while "Wet'suwet'en" is the version of the name "Witsuwit'en" presently used by their neighbours.

12 See, especially, Shalin M. Sugunasiri, "Contextualism: The Supreme Court's New Standard of Judicial Analysis and Accountability" (spring 1999) 22 Dalhousie Law Journal, 126-84 on this point.

13 Alternative versions of the main features of contextualism in law are available in R.E. Hawkins and R. Martin's critical discussion of what they regard as the dangers of the contextual approach in their "Democracy, Judging and Bertha Wilson" (1995) 41 McGill Law Journal 1; in Shalin M. Sugunasiri's laudatory discussion of legal contextualism in the form of a detailed analysis of the nuances of the application of the contextual method to Charter interpretation, to the interpretation of ordinary legislation, and to the development of the common law in the provocative "Contextualism: The Supreme Court's New Standard of Judicial Analysis and Accountability"; and in Danielle Pinard's "The Constituents of Democracy: The Individual in the Work of Madame Justice Wilson" (1992) 15 Dalhousie Law Journal, 81-114.

14 An extraordinarily illuminating discussion of the relationship between meaning and use in general and, in particular, of the manner in which non-linguistic forms of meaning are informed by convention is contained in Charles Taylor's "Heidegger versus Davidson" (unpublished paper, McGill University, 1990).

15 Wilson states the implications of the contextualist approach most clearly in connection with Charter interpretation, for example in her concurring majority opinion in *Edmonton Journal* v. *Alberta (Attorney General)*, [1989] 2 S.C.R. 1236; 64 D.L.R. (4th) 584: "It is my view that a right or freedom may have different meanings in different contexts. Security of the person, for example, might mean one thing when addressed to the issue of over-crowding in prisons and something quite different when addressed to the issue of noxious fumes from industrial smokestacks."

16 Bertha Wilson, "Will Women Judges Really Make a Difference?" (1990) 28 Osgoode Hall Law Journal 521.

17 *R.* v. *Hill*, [1986] 1 S.C.R. 313.

18 I owe this useful summary to Hester Lessard, "Equality and Access to Justice in the Work of Bertha Wilson" (1992) 15 Dalhousie Law Journal 40.

19 *Ibid.*

20 Lawrence Rosen, *The Anthropology of Justice: Law as Culture in Islamic Society* (Cambridge, UK: Cambridge University Press, 1989); and Sally Engle Merry's review of Rosen, "The Culture of Judging" (1990) 90 Columbia Law Review 2311.

21 Sugunasiri, "Contextualism," 175, note 225.

22 Richard Devlin, "Judging and Diversity" (fall 1996) 20 Provincial Judges' Journal 13.

23 Deliberative democracy is defined by Young as a "discussion-based ideal of democracy" devised as an alternative to interest-based theories. Prominent deliberative democracy theorists include Jürgen Habermas – whose theory of communicative action also serves as the basis for most accounts of deliberative democracy – Joshua Cohen, Jane Mansbridge, Benjamin Barber, Jean Cohen, and Amy Gutmann. For examples of relevant texts, refer to Iris Marion Young, "Communication and the Other," in Seyla Benhabib, ed., *Democracy and Difference* (Princeton, NJ: Princeton University Press, 1996), 133, note 2.

24 Seyla Benhabib, *Situating the Self* (New York: Routledge, 1992), 137.

25 *Ibid.*, 52.

26 *Ibid.*, 137.

27 Young also analyzes Benhabib's argument in connection with the analogy of "putting myself in your place," although she draws a different conclusion. She argues, roughly, that Benhabib fits into the same stratum of the continuum as Wilson. I believe that in making this assessment, Young is assigning too much weight to the particular phrase – "reversing perspectives" – Benhabib has chosen as a form of shorthand for her approach and too little to the explanation that constitutes it. See Iris Marion Young, "Asymmetrical Reciprocity: On Moral Respect, Wonder, and Enlarged Thought" (1997) 3 Constellations, 349-50.

28 A few of Taylor's most controversial works of the last decade have dealt with the subject of intercultural understanding and the issue of human rights, including "The Politics of Recognition," in Amy Gutmann, ed., *Multiculturalism* (Princeton, NJ: Princeton University Press, 1994); "Conditions of an Unforced Consensus on Human Rights" (paper presented at the Cultural Sources of Human Rights in East Asia Conference, Chulalongkorn University, Bangkok, March 1996); and the report cowritten with Vitit Muntarbhorn, *Roads to Democracy: Human Rights and Democratic Development in Thailand* (Bangkok and Montreal: International Centre for Human Rights and Democratic Development, 1994).

29 Gitxsan and Wet'suwet'en strategists in the *Delgamuukw* land claim case demonstrated their appreciation of this point through their trial court tactics – they did not restrict themselves to an exegesis of their beliefs and values, but insisted upon the importance of inducting members of the court into their practices by treating them, as far as was possible, as *participants* in a feast.

30 Young, "Communication and the Other," 120.

31 Young, *Asymmetrical Reciprocity.*

32 Hannah Arendt, *The Human Condition*, 8th ed. (Chicago: University of Chicago Press, 1973), 243, quoted in Benhabib, *Situating the Self*, 196; emphasis is mine.

33 For Hans-Georg Gadamer, the condition of being "prejudiced" in the sense of participating in a shared tradition is a prerequisite of the possibility of understanding. Taylor develops a different basis for commonality that is better suited to the task of building intercultural understanding in his own version of the fusion of horizons model. See Oman, *Sharing Horizons*, chap. 3 for further detail.

34 Charles Taylor, "Understanding and Ethnocentricity," in *Philosophy and the Human Sciences*, vol. 2 of *Philosophical Papers* (Cambridge, UK: Cambridge University Press, 1985), 125.

35 Such a meta-language would be a language "about" or encompassing the original two languages.

36 The following discussion of the feasting practices of the Gitxsan and Wet'suwet'en is heavily dependent on research I conducted in the summer of 1996 in the Hazeltons and Smithers region of the Gitxsan and the Wet'suwet'en traditional territories. My views are informed by conclusions I drew from conversations in which members of these two First Nations and their broader communities generously shared their thoughts concerning the *Delgamuukw* trial court case and their histories of intercultural negotiation. I am particularly indebted in this area to Don Ryan (Mas Gak), Herb George (Satsan), Richard Overstall, Neil J. Sterrit, and Dora Wilson, and also to Susan Marsden's *An Historical and Cultural Overview of the Gitksan*, vol. 1 (Hazelton, BC: Gitxsan Treaty Office archives photocopy, 1987). See Natalie Oman, *Sharing Horizons*, for a more detailed discussion of this subject.

37 There are a variety of sorts of feasts devoted to accomplishing different functions, including most commonly funeral feasts, shame feasts, and pole-raising feasts. A series of the rarer feasts dedicated to intercultural dispute resolution have occurred in recent decades in connection with Gitxsan and Wet'suwet'en efforts to settle outstanding disagreements about territorial boundaries with various neighbouring First Nations. In all these variations of feasting, the bestowal of recognition and the nurturing of dialogical relationships are central activities.

38 I do not mean to suggest that all Gitxsan and Wet'suwet'en people agree upon the elements of a single, uncontested worldview, or that they all share a single worldview. However, Gitxsan and Wet'suwet'en people themselves use this terminology of a shared worldview to indicate the closeness of their historical relationship and their distinctiveness from non-Native Canadians in this regard. I believe that highlighting the gulf between mainstream Canadian understandings of the political, social, legal, and spiritual aspects of human experience and those of First Nations people by a conscious simplification of this sort is defensible as a means of underlining the oppressive consequences of the continuing hegemony of the conceptual categories and standards of value associated with the belief systems of Western European peoples.

39 *Delgamuukw* v. *British Columbia* (1991), 79 D.L.R. (4th) 185 (B.C.S.C.); (1993) 104 D.L.R. (4th) 470 (B.C.C.A.); [1997] 3 S.C.R. 1010.

40 Susan Marsden, *An Historical and Cultural Overview,* 1.
41 Gisday Wa and Delgam Uukw, *The Spirit in the Land* (Gabriola, BC: Reflections, 1989, 1992), 39.
42 It is well known that the trial court failed to accept the guidance proffered by the plaintiffs in *Delgamuukw.* But the case was only one example of the multiple tactics of accommodation/resistance devised in concert by the contemporary Gitxsan and Wet'suwet'en leadership to bring the Canadian provincial and federal governments to the negotiating table.
    Members of these First Nations have faced an unprecedented problem in their efforts to employ their traditional approach to intercultural negotiation with the newcomer population: the various governments of Canada who have asserted jurisdiction over them have demonstrated a profound lack of interest in engaging in any recognizable form of negotiation with them. The historically justified assumption underlying the Gitxsan and Wet'suwet'en approach had been that both parties to any intercultural dispute would be similarly, if not equally, motivated to seek a resolution via the fostering of intercultural understanding. That assumption has been revised in light of Gitxsan and Wet'suwet'en experiences with an interlocutor that lacks any corresponding normative commitment to the recognition of others and possesses vastly greater resources for imposing its worldview.
    The accommodation/resistance tactics of the contemporary leaders are designed to motivate the various newcomer governments of Canada to seek intercultural understanding with them for a variety of reasons, while also in most cases performing a pedagogical function concerning the Gitxsan and Wet'suwet'en worldview as well. See Oman, *Sharing Horizons,* chap. 4 for a detailed analysis of these tactics.
43 Benhabib, *Situating the Self,* 125-26.
44 Young, *Asymmetrical Reciprocity,* 351.
45 Ludwig Wittgenstein, *On Certainty,* G.E.M. Anscombe and G.H. von Wright, eds. and trans. (Oxford: Blackwell, 1969).
46 Thomas Morawetz, *Wittgenstein and Knowledge* (Amherst, MA: University of Massachusetts Press, 1978), 134.
47 Orson Scott Card provides an instructive examination of this issue in his novel *Speaker for the Dead* (New York: Tom Doherty Associates, 1986).
48 Morawetz expands upon this point: "Men do not 'know the truth with perfect certainty' [*On Certainty,* s.404] because there remains a series of impotent possibilities – possibilities because they cannot be discounted, because life is unpredictable, impotent because the awareness of their possibility is not the sort of thing I can weigh as evidence for or against any grounded beliefs"; Morawetz, *Wittgenstein and Knowledge,* 135.
49 Taylor, "Unforced Consensus," 12.
50 Statistical evidence for this hypothesis falls outside the purview of this study; however, much historical evidence suggests that in many past incidents involving intercultural negotiation between Aboriginal peoples and settler populations in North America, a pattern of misunderstanding and divergent interpretations (as well, of course, as deliberate misrepresentation) occurred that serves as a source of serious conflict today as in the case of the Kitsegula incident and the resulting agreement reached at Metlakatla. See, for example, J.R. Miller, ed., *Sweet Promises* (Toronto: University of Toronto Press, 1991); Norman Z. Zlotkin, "Post-Confederation Treaties," in Bradford W. Morse, ed., *Aboriginal Peoples and the Law* (Ottawa: Carleton University Press, 1991); J.R. Miller, *Skyscrapers Hide the Heavens,* rev. ed. (Toronto: University of Toronto Press, 1989); John Goddard, *Last Stand of the Lubicon Cree* (Vancouver: Douglas and McIntyre, 1991); and Michael Pomdeli, "Treaty Number Three: Letting Ojibwa Voices and Ceremonies Speak" (paper presented at the Sacred Lands Conference, University of Manitoba, October 1996).
51 One demonstration of the effect of the persuasive force that such an approach can exercise seems to have occurred with the signing of the draft treaty banning the use of anti-personnel mines by the majority of the world's states in Oslo in September of 1997. Despite the fact that a number of major powers including the United States, Russia, China, and India had not endorsed the treaty at the time of the draft signing, enormous

pressure has since been brought to bear on these countries as a consequence of the stigma now attached to the use of such land mines through the publicly recognized international mechanism of the draft treaty, and several of them seem on the verge of dropping their objections in order to participate in the formal signing ceremony for the final version of the treaty in December of 1997.

52 Taylor, *Unforced Consensus*, 19.

53 Young comments perceptively on the sense in which this manner of initiating a dialogue "is always a *gift* ... [since] the trust to communicate cannot await the other person's promise to reciprocate, or the conversation will never begin"; *Asymmetrical Reciprocity*, 351.

54 To appreciate the unstudied character of such transitions, think of a conversation between adult siblings. The tone of the dialogue can seamlessly slip from respectful deliberation over a common problem to gentle, yet patronizing, scolding, marking a shift from a more comprehensive form of recognition to an impoverished mode of recognition that diminishes the sibling to whom it is directed. Such shifts in tone can characterize our relationships with those we most love and respect, and correspond to the variations in approach that similarly typify our dealings with other interlocutors, including other-cultural ones.

5
Commentary:
When Cultures Collide
Julie Macfarlane

One of the central issues for this collection is what should we expect when very different cultures of conflict resolution meet – or, perhaps more descriptively, collide? The awkward and halting steps taken in efforts at dialogue and formal negotiations between Aboriginal and non-Aboriginal peoples are an obvious, but just one, example of this phenomenon. Michelle LeBaron in her chapter in this section poignantly describes the "parallel activities" or "dances" that take place between First Nations and government negotiators without any real connection or understanding. Other processes appear, at least at first glance, to have been more successful at blending different cultural approaches, an obvious example being the development of sentencing circles in some First Nations communities that have adopted the traditions of the talking circle within the context of Western criminal justice norms and procedures. Another cultural "blend" or "merger" that comes to mind is the introduction of compulsory early mediation in many provincial superior courts, in many ways an odd juxtaposition of restorative and adversarial principles of conflict resolution.

Each of the chapters in this first section struggles with the dilemma of how to facilitate dialogue between different understandings of the world, and what the implications might be for those who participate. Much of what is happening in conflict resolution initiatives involves cross-cultural dialogue. These efforts can be held up as models of increased sensitivity and power-sharing, or as simply another means of the dominant cultural group imposing its agenda on others with an aura of respectability. To be able to evaluate these initiatives and to have any chance of developing authentic efforts to build cross-cultural understanding, we need to know more about what might happen when different cultures – traditions, systems, and norms – of conflict resolution are thrown together or collide. This short response will articulate and tentatively evaluate some of the possible scenarios that we see emerging.

As each chapter in this section recognizes, there is first a need for an acknowledgment of the entrenched dynamics of the dominant culture of discourse. Historically, one culture (Western legal-adjudicative culture) has swallowed all others (including Aboriginal conflict resolution traditions) by imposing its own criteria of substance and process. Dale Turner writes of the "translation" of Aboriginal concepts into the language of Western adjudication. "Aboriginal people must explain themselves to the dominant culture, and they must do so using Western European intellectual traditions," and, he continues, "the content of Aboriginal rights is articulated and understood in the discourses of the dominant culture, and therefore if Aboriginal peoples want to tell their stories in courts of law, they must engage these discourses." In his chapter, David Kahane is at pains to remind us that the terms of this engagement always reflect existing relationships of power. "Cultures exist in relation to one another, in contexts always shaped by power ... tying in with epistemic privilege (the ability to dictate the terms of political debate, while denying their rootedness in particular cultural traditions)." Blindness to or ignorance of this dynamic means that efforts at cross-cultural dialogue become simply a matter of accommodating (fitting within, adjusting) all other cultures to the dominant discourse; for example, how can we (non-Aboriginals) take and use the talking circle so that it works for us? Or, how can we bring forward our (non-Aboriginal) agenda in a way that is acceptable to First Nations people? Authentic dialogue between different cultures of conflict resolution demands that we recognize this innate privileging and strive to avoid its assumptions.

In order to explore what may happen when different cultures meet, it is helpful to first look at what happens when we communicate about difficult or conflictual issues with those who come from the same or similar culture to our own. First, the dialogue between us is framed implicitly by our many shared norms and expectations over the moral basis of the argument we are having. This is the case even where persons from a similar culture are challenging one another – for example where a white woman academic tells a white male academic that she finds his attitude toward feminist scholarship chauvinistic – because both sides recognize and understand the existence of a dominant discourse (in this case, the historically privileged place of males and masculine epistemologies in academia), even where one rejects it. These types of differences between those who share cultural similarities – both white, both academics – reflect the lack of homogeneity within individual cultures that David Kahane writes about in his chapter, as well as the intrinsic power differences which exist within every relationship. Michelle LeBaron provides an important example of this when she refers to the concerns raised by some Aboriginal women about the use of circles, especially for issues involving violence toward women. Within similar cultures there is plenty of scope for misunderstanding, miscommunication, and outright conflict. Despite all this, however, the man and the woman in my example are essentially speaking the same language to one another, and they can communicate using shared concepts (however they might individually orient themselves to those concepts). Natalie Oman makes this point in her chapter using Charles Taylor's concept of "fusion" of horizons to demonstrate what is possible between those who share many of the same cultural influences. Furthermore and significantly, our two academics will probably also have a shared anticipation of the process they shall use to conduct their debate or dispute. This likely includes expectations over what will be discussed and what might be considered inappropriate or off limits; how the discussion will affect their future professional relationship; and what might be realistic in terms of resolution (a truce? changed behaviour? inevitable continuing hostilities?).

The ritual of lawyer-to-lawyer interaction in litigation is a rich source of examples of shared cultural meaning within the Western adjudicative model of dispute resolution. Multiple shared meanings exist and are assumed, and these grease the wheels of communication. Anyone standing outside this particular culture (an individual who is not legally trained, or even a legally trained person who finds themselves a litigant) would find quite different and perhaps unintended meanings in many of these communications. Examples include the traditional "letter before action" (which in a non-legal context would probably be seen as aggressive, formalistic, and hectoring); the accusatory language of pleadings (which often takes on a quite different level of personal meaning for the parties than for their lawyers); and the ritual dance of outrageous opening offer followed by derisory counter-offer in settlements negotiations. Similar examples of assumptive behaviours and rituals of meaning can be found elsewhere, of course; for instance in the patterns of management-labour negotiations; in the ways a parent scolds her child; and perhaps most graphically in the comfortable bickering of life partners.

The complexities of conflict resolution within cultures are magnified many times over when different cultures meet or collide. The limitations of our understanding of these complexities are exacerbated by the historical dominance in Western intellectual thought of a rational, predictive model of conflict, epitomized in game theory. This model posits that the key to success in conflict resolution is the development of a rational, predictive, risk management strategy that will always seek to maximize personal gain (perfectly illustrated in Machiavelli's *The Prince*). This approach to understanding conflict is sometimes described as the "monologue" model, where the focus is on what one person does. This approach tends to either assume or disregard the impact of the behaviour on others, or the ways in which relationships affect conflict resolution strategy and choices. Not only is this model culturally determined by its roots within Western individualism but it is also an inadequate explanation of what really occurs in conflict and resolution where the behaviour and reactions of others are crucial influences on both our chosen course and the end result. What is more, our ability to predict with any degree of accuracy how others might respond to our strategy is considerably reduced where we are talking with others from cultures different to our own. The monologue approach is sometimes contrasted with the "dialogue" model in which the relationship formed between the disputing parties is regarded as having a critical impact on the outcome of the conflict. Generally, our overestimation of the practical potential of a "solo" approach to conflict resolution may have blinded us to the importance of learning about and from other cultural approaches to conflict.

The complexity of cross-cultural dispute resolution is multiplied by individual differences between the players themselves – the parties to the conflict – and differences between the conflict resolution process or processes they assume to be appropriate and fair. First, the parties come to the moral arguments quite differently. Such differences are sometimes described as "irreducible" or "incommensurate," where they flow from fundamentally different paradigms of values such that they cannot be "'mapped onto,' expressed as, or reduced to"[1] the moral order of the other. Moral order is a critical element in social reality. Different social realities include the meanings given to experience, assumptions, and beliefs. When intertwined with a "grammar of action" (those practices and behaviours that are expected and acceptable), this produces a related culture of communication – including language, forms of expression, accepted meanings, and styles of rhetoric. In addition – and perhaps critically for conflict resolution – these different moral orders and cultures of communication also produce different culturally based ideas about power and empowerment. For example, perspectives on the relative power of men and women within a particular culture, on the expression of emotion as weakness or as strength, the importance of honour and saving face as empowerment, and the significance of self-expression as an expression of power will all depend on the moral ordering of that culture or subculture. None of these particular approaches or interpretations is morally privileged, but they are (as Natalie Oman argues) inescapable and inevitable for the members of that cultural group. Equally, none of the moral positions we adopt is "neutral"; this claim is generally a cover for "dominant" (see David Kahane's eloquent critique of the liberal paradigm). Within our different moral orders, our criteria of fairness will also be different. However, it seems equally important to avoid the assumption that the adoption of a particular model of fairness – or communication, or power – within a particular culture means that the conceptual and analytical frameworks it uses are forever exclusive to that culture, and incapable of being adjusted and applied across different cultural traditions. For example, it has recently become fashionable to argue that an "interests-based" approach to understanding and resolving conflict is a Western cultural construct that assumes the primary motivation for conflict resolution is individual resource maximization. While the maximization of individual self-interest is a widely accepted value in Western political culture, and this motivation would clearly be out of place in many other cultures, there seems to be no good reason why an interests-based approach – variously interpreted as resource allocation, wealth maximization, relationship building, and a means to strengthen pragmatic collaborative partnerships – should be restricted exclusively to an individual resource-maximization model. There is a complex relationship between values and interests in conflict, and each culture – and each subculture – resolves such conflict differently and in accordance with its internal moral order and external grammar of action.

Second, where we do not share cultural similarities with those with whom we are in conflict, we are unlikely to share common values or expectations over the process we shall use to have our discussion or resolve our impasse. Our understandings of the role and place of authority within that process, and who those authority figures are or should be, will be very different, for example, in collectivistic Aboriginal cultures than in more individualistic Western political cultures. Our moral orders also affect our ideas about how conflict should be handled. This includes expectations over how we shall talk and how we show we are listening (LeBaron points out that, "while listening well is certainly an important feature of all communication, the [ubiquitous] skill of active listening has cultural assumptions built into it"); what will be revealed or concealed; what we consider to be appropriate (sometimes seen as inevitable) emotional responses to particular situations; which topics and modes of expression are off limits; how a resolution will feel and look; and what might be forthcoming in terms of resolution. Some of the more powerful differences between different cultural expectations of appropriate conflict processing and outcome are evident when we look at instances where individuals from different cultural traditions have tried to resolve conflict, or where processes and cultures are apparently mismatched, as in the story related below.

One might hypothesize a number of possible scenarios resulting from a collision of different cultures of conflict resolution. First, it seems most likely that where a dominant (economically, politically, historically) culture meets a less powerful one, the consequence will be simply the assimilation and absorption of the latter by the dominant tradition. Examples of this include what seems to be the hijacking of court-connected mediation by a small group of highly evaluative retired judges (memorably described by James Alfini as the "hashers, bashers and trashers"),[2] or the instrumental use of mandatory mediation as an early, cheap discovery process. In his chapter, Dale Turner describes the assimilation of Aboriginal understandings of land ownership within Western concepts of title to property (despite the assertion of legal reconciliation). If there were no alternative to assimilation, or the swallowing up of one culture by the other, there would be no purpose to the intellectual and practical energies that have prompted this book. Instead we have to try to imagine other possible consequences of the collision of different cultures of conflict resolution that could have profound and lasting benefits both for those directly affected and for those looking on and hoping for inspiration.

One possibility when different cultures of conflict resolution collide is that some convergence might occur. By convergence I mean mutual influence and cross-fertilization, but short of transformation, integration, or the creation of a new, substitute paradigm. As a consequence of convergence, each culture of conflict resolution takes on some of the ideas and values and practices of the other, and there is an intertwining of cultural norms and traditions. The convergence of different cultures, despite falling short of the creation of a "new" something, may still be important and exciting; the result might be compared to a chemical combination, where the essential properties of each process or culture are significantly changed as a result. It might be argued, for example, that a consequence of imposing a mandatory mediation step in civil matters is that mediation practices have adapted to the court-connected context (for example, by formalizing rules on exchange of documents and the increasing use of evaluative mediators) and that litigation practice has also been altered (for example, by challenging the assumption that settlement negotiations should not be contemplated until after discoveries, or that clients should not participate in negotiations).

Of course, both the authenticity, and the desirability, of what I am describing as "convergence" is often questionable. One might view the development of the modern welfare state as the consequence of the influence of principles of Marxism and collectivism on industrial capitalism, or a minimally costly means of defusing opposition and stabilizing the system under the control of the corporate classes. Natalie Oman's description of the Metlakatla negotiations between the Gitxsan and the British, in which the British tolerated but utterly failed to comprehend the significance of the inclusion of traditional Gitxsan rituals of storytelling and feasting, could be understood as an example of convergence or simply as a polite form of assimilation. In the same way, the establishment of commercial dispute resolution facilities promoting evaluative mediation and fact-finding services might be seen as evidence of the impact mediation and consensus-building principles have had on the development of dispute resolution services, or simply a fashionable "front" for what is essentially the same lawyer-driven, rights-based model. From those taking this latter position comes the criticism that the real values of mediation are being compromised by such a metamorphosis, and that mediation is tainted and co-opted by the adversarial system as a result. Certainly, some manifestations of convergence create strange affinities. An obvious example is the embracing of mediation by many in the business and insurance community. This suggests a coincidence of interests between private market capitalism and informal, confidential mediation processes for commercial disputes – a coincidence that might be unexpected – and resisted – by those who promote mediation as a therapeutic, restorative, empowering process for individual disputants. What many would see as a vehicle for social and personal transformation (mediation and consensus building) may in fact double handily as a means to produce private, unregulated, efficient, and highly pragmatic business solutions for corporations.

Another possibility is that rather than convergence, what more often occurs when different cultures meet is divergence. When divergence occurs, different approaches and understandings of conflict are reinforced and further entrenched with little or no enhanced mutual understanding. When two different cultures are speaking different "languages" of redress and resolution – as occurred recently in the standoff between the Chinese and the Americans over the downing of a Chinese plane and the subsequent holding of American pilots – divergence may lead to escalation. This incident appears to have led to a heightened sense of difference and distance between China and the United States. The introduction of a new approach to conflict resolution – for example, a new grievance process introduced into a workplace – may also result in the fragmentation and divergence of interests. In this way, divergence might occur within an existing culture of conflict resolution; for example, in the recent development of separate camps of believers and oppositionists within the legal profession in reaction to the growth of mediation. The reinforcement of difference and divergence may also occur as a result of unsatisfactory interaction between different cultures of conflict, which ultimately serves only to highlight different understandings and values.

During the past year I worked with a First Nations community where two lawsuits had been brought by band members against the band council, one involving an employment matter and the other a construction dispute. Each plaintiff had hired a white lawyer from outside the community and the band council had gone to their lawyers (also non-Aboriginal) for advice. Each case followed the same pattern. In each, a settlement had been proposed by the plaintiffs' lawyers, and then considered by the lawyer for the band council. In each, the defence lawyer recommended that the chief and council reject the settlement offer, advising them that the plaintiffs were unlikely to do as well in court. Finally, in each case, the plaintiff insisted that he or she had not in any event acquiesced in the settlement offer proposed by his or her lawyer.

I was asked to co-mediate both disputes along with a band member. The parties in each lawsuit decided in advance of mediation that they did not want their legal representatives present, nor did they wish to review any settlement proposals that emerged from mediation with their counsel before making a decision. Since my own cultural norms suggest that for a party to a lawsuit to entirely dispense with legal advice might be prejudicial to their interests, I spent some time checking with each side that this was indeed their wish and going over with them the implications of making a binding agreement in mediation. My co-mediator, a respected band member and a lawyer herself, assured me that the parties were comfortable with this arrangement – in fact, they would not agree to mediation on any other basis. Everyone was clear that an agreement reached in mediation would be a matter of honour, agreed fairness, and a decision for the community, and this was not something that they would seek legal advice on.

Both disputes settled in mediation. In each case, the amount agreed in settlement – plus a series of non-monetary undertakings – was considerably higher than the sum the council's lawyers had advised them to reject in the earlier settlement offer. Each settlement was taken to the full band council for review. No one there suggested that the fact that the settlement sums were higher than the earlier offers which the council had been advised by their lawyers to reject was a relevant consideration; instead, discussions were limited to the perceived fairness, appropriateness, and practicality of the settlement in each case. Once satisfied, the council members ratified the settlements and the suits were discontinued. The only conflict that remained then was between the litigants and their lawyers (whose reactions to the settlements ranged from incredulity to bemusement) over the size of the legal bills.

The disjuncture between the two cultures of conflict represented here was a stark one. There was no convergence between the two worlds – the one of Aboriginal collectivist traditions and the other of Western legal rights and procedures – just a highly unproductive and dysfunctional series of interactions that left everyone feeling dissatisfied. It would appear that as a result, the band members involved have even less faith in, and still less respect for, this model of lawyer-driven civil litigation – and that the lawyers who represented them failed to comprehend either the basis of their dissatisfaction or the eventual outcome (indeed, at the time of writing, one of the lawyers is still resisting the discontinuation of that action). So just how realistic or desirable is it to imagine the integration or fusion of different cultural traditions, in this or any other context of "collision"? A fourth possibility is that we at least aspire to a conscientious and respectful dialogue between different realities in order to achieve some understanding via participation. One useful conceptual framework here is the notion of transcendent dialogue developed by Barnett Pearce and Stephen

Littlejohn.[3] In transcendent dialogue there is an explicit acknowledgment of differences and a commitment to dialogue as a means of understanding and coordinating those differences, not transformation. The key question for cross-cultural dialogue becomes not how can I accommodate your norms to fit within mine? (assimilation), how can I ensure that my culture is not tainted or changed in any way by yours? (divergence), or how might we mutually influence each other's traditions (convergence)? Instead it is, how can I understand the moral order and social reality that leads you to think that way? In other ways, transcendent dialogue seeks to facilitate the coexistence and acceptance of two parallel realities, via the development of what Natalie Oman describes as a "meta-language of negotiation." This holds out promise for the building of mutual respect, the avoidance of violence and confrontation, and the enhancement of participation, both between and within cultural groups.

But when different dispute resolution traditions are forced together, will this not eventually mean changes in practices and norms? Natalie Oman suggests that one's values are inevitably transformed in the process of observing another's culture. Can we go further than transcendent dialogue and imagine the creation of new and better paradigms for conflict resolution – in short, transformation? It is difficult to believe that those who advocate dialogue and participation are not also committed to actual change via the evolution, adjustment, and eventual resolution of conflicting moral and cultural norms. But when different cultures of conflict resolution are thrown together, ambiguity and uncertainty – and sometimes mistrust and defensiveness – replace the stability of established norms and authority structures. Every effort at dialogue across different cultures of conflict resolution, and each genuine attempt at interaction and cross-fertilization between different disputing models or traditions, potentially challenges the traditional constructs of authority, legitimacy, and status within each culture. Different values and ideologies of dispute resolution are reflected in the powerful self-interests of those who sustain their position – chief, lawyer, government representative – on the basis of that current ideology. Moving away from an established tradition of conflict resolution will sometimes imply the giving up of powerful positions by an expert elite. Furthermore, experiencing and responding to different models of conflict resolution often impacts the core identity of the players themselves, both personal and professional. Significantly perhaps, anthropologist Clifford Geertz has argued that it is at this point that significant change in cultural paradigms is most likely to occur – when the practices of the various actors change to the extent that they begin to impact on their core notions of role and identity.[4]

Which if any of the five scenarios described in this chapter should be our goal? And can we anticipate and create the conditions under which that particular consequence – for example, convergence rather than divergence, or transformation rather than mere convergence – is most likely to occur? First, we can reject assimilation, and with it the cultural blindness that has perpetuated the reproduction of the conditions of oppression under which assimilation occurs. The four other scenarios suggested here – convergence, divergence, transcendent dialogue, and transformation via paradigm change – can and do occur in many different manifestations, and with differing impacts, at different historical and political moments. It is next to impossible to draw moral judgments about which scenario is the most desirable, since historical context, individual and community needs, and political circumstances present so many potential variables. Is it better or worse for the future of mutual understanding between First Nations communities and lawyers trained in the Western adjudicative model that on the occasion described above everyone concerned experienced such a stark disjuncture of aims and objectives? Is it better or worse for the development of an accessible and fair civil justice system that particular lawyers specialize in alternative dispute resolution and others continue to act as traditional gunslingers? Are there indeed new paradigms out there that are somehow better than the old?

Perhaps the best that we can do is to aspire to the development of a transcendent dialogue of understanding, and with it the acknowledgment of parallel realities, as a critical prerequisite to whatever might emerge over time as a result of the interaction of different conflict cultures. Making specific predictions of the consequences of blending different cultural traditions may be to forget that even well-established conflict resolution practices vary widely according to content and conditions. Instead, it is our responsibility to think carefully and clearly about the range of consequences that might be both likely and desirable. Only then can we properly appreciate the complexity of the relationships between our different moral orders and their conflict resolution norms and systems, anticipate some of the problems that we might face in blending different cultural approaches, and be alert to the potential for both enhanced insight and the reinforcement of mutual mistrust.

Notes
1 W. Barnett Pearce and Stephen Littlejohn, *Moral Conflict: When Social Worlds Collide* (Thousand Oaks, CA: Sage, 1997), 15.
2 James Alfini, "Trashing, Bashing and Hashing: Is This the End of Good Mediation?" (1991) 19 Florida State University Law Review 47.
3 Pearce and Littlejohn, *Moral Conflict*.
4 Clifford Geertz, *The Interpretation of Cultures: Selected Essays* (New York: Basic Books, 1973).

Part 2:
International Contexts

Dispute resolution in Aboriginal contexts is shaped and constrained by colonial histories: this applies both to disputes between Aboriginal and non-Aboriginal communities, and to disputes within and between Aboriginal communities. The chapters in Part 2 show, at a broad level, the different negotiations of culture and power involved in setting up dispute resolution mechanisms in varied national contexts: in the Navajo Nation in the southwest United States, in Aboriginal Australia, and in Aotearoa/ New Zealand. Each of these colonial contexts raises important questions about how indigenous dispute resolution processes can and should fit with non-indigenous systems of law; dangers of appropriation and co-optation by mainstream legal and political institutions; and the embeddedness of dispute resolution within the rich ways of life of particular communities.

6

Navajo Peacemaking and Intercultural Dispute Resolution[1]

Chief Justice Robert Yazzie

The first formal European recognition of indigenous law was made by Holy Roman Emperor Charles V on 9 August 1555.[2] After that, indigenous dispute resolution seems to have disappeared. At least, it disappeared from our European visitors' point of view. In the early days, the Spanish established the General Court of Indians to handle disputes between Indians and Spaniards.[3] One study says that there was a heavy Aztec flavour to the court in the beginning, but that gradually disappeared when Spanish, rather than the Aztec language, became the court's primary tongue.[4] As British colonialists fanned out across the world, they established village courts as a means of control. That was probably the model for the Indian courts created in the United States in 1883 and the foundation for Indian courts there today. What happened to indigenous methods? They went underground, along with Indian religion.

The non-Indian world had little interest in genuine Indian law. A few Spanish writers dabbled in it, including a Spanish judge in the late sixteenth century.[5] The first book on Indian law in North America wasn't written until 1940.[6] In recent years, Indian nation leaders have been seeking to revive their traditional law and bring it back to the surface again. Why? Because English common law as it was imported to this continent has not worked for us. It has been used to put us down and keep us down. Indian law in the United States is so bad that I shudder every time an appeal comes before my court. We are reviving our traditional law to survive.

The non-indigenous world has also become very interested in traditional indigenous law and our dispute resolution processes, particularly in the areas of criminal and domestic law. Again I ask, why? The reasons are obvious. The prisons are full of people of colour. We are telling national governments that there is something a little strange about having Anglos dominate the police, bench, and bar while it is the people of colour who are treated as the most likely suspects. Wider society is also beginning to understand that punishment does not work. It is time to try something else. Why not indigenous justice methods?

Navajo Peacemaking

The judges of the Navajo Nation revived their traditional justice method within the Courts of the Navajo Nation in 1982. It is called Hozhooji Naat'aanii or "Navajo Peacemaking" in English. It is successful. We say that Navajo peacemaking is successful for several reasons. First, since its reintroduction in 1982, Navajos have voiced their acceptance of the revival. Second, people are using it. A few years ago, the court staff attorneys who serve the trial courts were asked to report on the implementation of the Navajo Nation's domestic violence code and the use of peacemaking in domestic violence cases. Staff attorney Sarah J. Foster (who served the Window Rock and Chinle judicial districts) reported back that, for reasons unknown to her, Navajo women in the Window Rock district preferred peacemaking over the modern domestic violence code. Third, people express their satisfaction with decisions achieved in peacemaking, and in some instances say they prefer it to the Western method of adjudication. Fourth, we have been concerned about the success of peacemaking, and have cooperated with scientific studies and interview-surveys on the process, which report that it is successful in terms of outcomes and "customer satisfaction."

At the start of this process, we did something fairly simple. We identified our traditional norms or ways of doing things. I call these "Navajo thinking." We then identified our traditional institution for dispute resolution and leadership. It is a form of leadership based on respect for traditional leaders. These leaders are chosen by consensus in the community, and disputes are resolved by "talking things over in groups." Traditional Navajo civil leadership is based upon the (often informal) selection of individuals as leaders who have proven themselves to be successful in speaking, planning, and spirituality. They are leaders whom the people listen to when discussing a community dispute. The civil leader or *naat'aanii* will call people together when there is a dispute so they can "talk it out." This process involves prayer, to commit people to serious and respectful discussion of the dispute; recounting the facts of the dispute (actual and perceived, including opinions about the facts and the emotional impact of what happened); teachings of traditional approaches to the problem by the *naat'aanii*; plans for future action; and finally, a consensus decision by the group. The success of peacemaking is often the product of traditional Navajo concepts of solidarity, mutuality, and reciprocal obligations, which badly translate from English back to Navajo in the simple word *k'e*. Traditional Navajo leadership is not authoritarian or bossy. It can be described as persuasive, but it is stronger than that. A *naat'aanii* is more of a teacher and planner in his or her leadership role, and the strength of a *naat'aanii's* advice comes from a reputation for wisdom and knowledge of traditional lore.

In recent years, Navajo peacemaking seems to have captured the attention of the world. Visitors from Canada, Fiji, Austria, New Zealand, Australia, and South Africa have come to learn about peacemaking. The Royal Commission on Aboriginal Peoples visited us for a week, and a few years later, some of its members returned with the Canadian Minister of Justice and the Minister of Indian and Northern Affairs.[7] We can expect that every January, Canadian delegations will arrive on our doorsteps; they are welcome. During the conference that gave rise to this volume, an academic from Rutgers University in New Jersey was in my offices, trying to figure out how peacemaking works. The municipal court of Norfolk, Virginia, obtained a copy of our peacemaking manual and set up a peacemaking program. The City of Philadelphia is currently studying Navajo peacemaking for juvenile cases. Some US Justice Department papers also point to Navajo peacemaking as a "promising practice" and as a model for community courts.[8]

However, the issue of whether indigenous justice methods can be used in non-indigenous communities by non-indigenous institutions is controversial. For example, Carole Goldberg, known for her fine work in Indian law, wrote a thoughtful article in the *University of Washington Law Review* which says that indigenous justice, and Navajo peacemaking in particular, cannot be replicated.[9] She points to peacemaking's foundations in Navajo spirituality and language and says that those aspects are so culturally specific that the process cannot be used as effectively elsewhere. A lawyer on my staff, James W. Zion, also wrote an article on the social psychology of peacemaking.[10] He thinks that certain human universals make it possible for peacemaking to be used anywhere people understand and apply its dynamics.[11] One of these universals is the utilization of three methods of persuasion: compliance, identification, and internalization. Compliance is the threat of punishment or the fear of being caught. It is the concept that is so familiar to Western criminal law of sanctions. Peacemaking does not use punishment as such. However, there is a fear of being talked about and of humiliation, so the existence of a forum where one may be talked about does have some deterrent effect. Identification is the process of someone changing his or her mind about behaviour out of respect for a teacher. In the Anglo world, that can be a parent, respected aunt or uncle, or a brother or sister. In peacemaking, there is respect for the peacemaker because of his or her position as a civil leader, and the process of prayer to open the session; a peacemaker's guidance for respectful "talking things out" reinforces the power of identification. Internalization is a process that seeks to tap values held within. In the Western world, those values can include common-sense morality, Christian principles or other commonly-held values. In the Navajo way, the internalization process uses deeply held traditional Navajo values (which the listener may know consciously or hold within as emotional prompts). There may be differences in the way these three human universals work from a cultural or linguistic perspective, but compliance, identification, and internalization are three methods of changing a person's mind that are recognizable dynamics in any method of dispute resolution.

While it is possible that indigenous justice methods can be used elsewhere, it is important to understand their context and why they work. For example, Navajo justices have been attending restorative justice conferences and considering the relationship of our indigenous justice methods with that movement. At one conference held at the Eastern Mennonite University in Virginia, we discussed *sulha,* the traditional Palestinian method of dispute resolution. We spent a day and a half trying to figure out how to replicate a traditional justice method such as *sulha,* but did not get very far. *Sulha* is something like shuttle diplomacy, where the family members of an offender will approach the family members of an injured person to open negotiations. If and when a resolution is achieved, public ceremonies are held to celebrate the reconciliation. A room full of restorative justice professionals tried to identify the essentials of *sulha* for replication, through an articulation of its principles. However, the attempt at translation simply was not successful, perhaps because of the problem of intercultural communication. We are at only the beginning of a process to attempt to identify and explain how traditional justice works, whether it is traditional Navajo justice or Palestinian *sulha.*

This is the first challenge. When designing effective dispute resolution mechanisms, one cannot simply look at a method or procedure for doing things, write down a checklist of what to do, and implement it anywhere. We did two very important things when we revived peacemaking. First, we looked at Navajo values and thinking. Second, we identified the traditional Navajo procedure and the leaders who use it. Those are Navajo-specific cultural values. If your community wants to revive effective indigenous dispute resolution practices, it must engage in a similar process. Each of you must ask yourself: What is the basis for my culture's ideas of right and wrong and how to do things? Which institutions in my community could learn and use indigenous methods? Navajos are lucky. We are very close to our traditions because our culture was relatively untouched until the start of the Second World War. Other cultures may be distant from their traditions. We know, for example, that the British first experimented with their Indian policies when they invaded Ireland and Scotland.[12] The Irish and Scots were still tribal people then. While there is an Irish revival going on now, will the revivalists be able to capture their Irish roots?

The dominant culture and the Navajo culture are going through what anthropologists call "revivalism."[13] It is a movement in which you look around you and see that things quite obviously are not right. Although detailing "what is not right" from the Indian perspective would fill a book in itself, when we consider widespread discrimination against Indians, highly disproportionate Indian incarceration rates, and pressures on Indian national sovereignty and government, it is clear there is a great deal of incentive for revivalism. The revivalism movement maintains that we must return to our past and our traditions for comfort, success, and survival. Consequently, we look to the past in hopes that a return to the thinking and ways of the past will change things for the better. I agree with former Justice Raymond D. Austin of our Supreme Court when he explains it as looking "back to the future."[14] I think this process will work for Navajos; you must all ask yourselves if it will work for you. For us, Navajo peacemaking and indigenous justice are the original method of justice. The methods predate the modern state. The question we face is, can these be revived?

In this revival process we face some dangers. For example, Maori traditional law had a lot of influence on family group conferencing in New Zealand. What did the government of New Zealand do with it? Rather than say to Maoris, "Go ahead and use your traditional methods of solving problems and we'll support you and recognize your decision," it said, "We're going to take your procedure, incorporate it even though it is not our law, and use it on you." Family group conferencing was then tried in Australia, where the police said, "Hey, Aboriginal folks, we've got a nifty traditional Maori procedure for you! Bring your kids down to the police station and we'll use it on them." Do you see my problem with this process? One writer calls this process "orientalism."[15] Another calls it "indigenization."[16] The idea is the same: while it may be all right to study another indigenous justice method and incorporate it into your justice systems, the issue of who the method will be used on remains. One of the problems indigenous people are trying to escape is having things done "to" them, rather than doing things for themselves. The core problem is who has control.

Respect as the Key to Intercultural Dispute Resolution

Respect is a major value of Navajos. Talking things out in a good way is another. We have heard our elders say, "Do things in a good way." While a non-Indian may not understand what that means, we know very well that it means a way of dealing with each other that is respectful, gentle, peaceful, and promotes good relationships. Planning is also a major part of our concept of justice. It is important because a great deal of care needs to be taken when incorporating indigenous methods into a non-indigenous justice framework so that indigenous values will not be lost.

One of the questions we addressed early in the process was, who can do peacemaking? Anyone can do it, but not everyone can do it. What does that mean? Our peacemakers are chosen by each of the Navajo Nation's 110 local governments, called chapters. They are not really elected, and they are not exactly appointed. That is, chapters have meetings to discuss things, and they will choose peacemakers they respect. Certain people in our communities show their spirituality through what they do, demonstrating their ability to plan. And so they take on a leadership position not by seeking it but by being selected. These people understand the importance of natural leadership. For example, a person who always helps others and can be looked to for help is a natural leader. There are also people who know our Navajo traditions well and apply them to everyday situations. These are our natural leaders. We do not pick them because of their formal education. We look to them because their life is a model of success.

I sometimes worry about what happens when a new justice fad comes along – how will this impact on revival of our justice systems? Take alternative dispute resolution, for example. What happened when it first became popular? First, the lawyers and social workers got into a battle over who would control mediation and who the mediators would be. In the United States, the lawyers mostly won. Now, if you burn out practising law, you can always become a mediator. Laura Nader, known for her studies on how justice methods work, was once asked where alternative dispute resolution (ADR) would be in the year 2000.[17] Although she essentially said she didn't know, Nader did state the problem that existed in the mid-1980s: she said that the moral objective was "justice for the masses; the many," but went on to say that people were so busy trying to make money in ADR and scramble to control it that they often ignored the moral issue.

While we are willing to share what we have with others, let me give a warning: if we hear of people making money off Navajo peacemaking or if we see self-inflated "professionals" trying to dominate it, we will report them immediately. We will expose such people as frauds. That is not what peacemaking is about. While it may be a lot to hope for in the modern context of money and materialism, we hope that Navajo peacemaking will remain a grassroots movement. We want people to return to the tradition of dispute resolution by respected and accepted community leaders and we hope that they will be involved because of their commitment to their community, not because they want to make money. Peacemaking is not a dispute resolution technique. It is not a justice method as such. It is a way of thinking and living in respectful relations with others that can be described as a method but which in reality is grounded in the fundamentals of Navajo moral values.

Right now, we are discussing something interesting in the Navajo Nation: privatizing peacemaking. We incorporated it in an institution, the

Navajo Nation Courts, in 1982, and now we are asking ourselves if it belongs there. That is, Navajo peacemaking used to operate on its own in communities; it was an institution unto itself. When peacemaking died out because of the Western system of police and adjudication, the Navajo Nation judges revived it in the court as a governmental institution. The original model was for the judge to decide what cases went into peacemaking, but when we began using peacemaking on a wider scale in 1991, we discovered that the judges acted as gatekeepers and referred few cases to peacemaking. As the court program grew, we found that people were self-selecting the remedy and that 60 percent or more of peacemaking cases were "walk-ins," where members of the public asked for peacemaking. More recently, the Navajo Nation judges have been saying that peacemaking should continue to operate in its original, grassroots community context, and peacemakers are beginning to form their own organizations to exercise greater control over the process and to regulate their own conduct. This suggests that it might be possible and desirable to give peacemaking greater independence from the judicial system and to allow greater flexibility for community control over the process. There will still be relationship issues, as with situations where an agreement in peacemaking should be reduced to a court judgment, but now that peacemaking has become popular again, those kinds of issues can be addressed.

Another problem that arises when an indigenous justice method is institutionalized is reflected in the simple question, who are the gatekeepers? For example, in circle sentencing in Canada, a non-Indian judge, a non-Indian prosecutor, and a non-Indian defence lawyer decide when a case will be determined through the circle sentencing process. Circle sentencing is community justice: it belongs in the community, under the control of the community. Studies of restorative justice in juvenile cases in the United States shows that judges act as gatekeepers.[18] This might be all right if the judges are committed to the process and believe in it. But that is not always the case. Earlier this year, my solicitor and I went to Long Beach, California, to make presentations on peacemaking in sessions held for judges and court personnel. A few judges said they were already using something like peacemaking in their courts and that it worked well. However, it was a hard sell to the skeptics in the audience who simply could not understand how a process that doesn't use punishment as a dispute resolution device can work.

Conclusion

In discussing appropriate methods of dispute resolution, it is important to understand the difference between law and justice. Law is a rational process. It uses the mind. One study of Navajo peacemaking says that it works to the satisfaction of the disputants and the community because the "talking out" procedure moves people from "head-thinking" to "heart-thinking."[19] Justice comes from the heart. It is a feeling. It is also knowing that those around you are concerned about you. Although they may be angry with you for what you have done, they do not put you down. Instead, they focus on what you did, ask why it happened, and then go on to talk about what to do about it. The Navajo peacemaking process is based on respect.

Can respect be institutionalized? Can it be packaged? Can manuals be written about it? As I've travelled around the world to talk with indigenous leaders, the idea that respect is the basic foundation of indigenous justice has hit home more than once. When you start to look at "law," "justice," and parallel words in indigenous languages, you will see that indigenous law and justice are built on concepts of respect, solidarity, relationships, and good feelings. A good feeling can be an attitude – the fancy word is "internalization," which means accepting something to such an extent that you move it into your gut; it becomes a habit. If we have problems in contemporary society, it is because we have lost the habits of respect and tolerance. We rely on power and authority, and that is not the way.

I am optimist, however. I think that indigenous justice has a lot to teach Anglo law. I think that people of goodwill can do a lot, if goodwill can prevail over bureaucracy. I will offer one last intercultural suggestion: If you can strike up a conversation with an Indian, Inuk, or Metis person, ask that person why he or she is uncomfortable with people from the dominant society. You may get an answer or you may not. The answer (or non-answer) is a mirror of non-indigenous society. What *is* the answer?

Consider the Navajo word for lawyer: *agha'diit'aahii*. It means "someone who pushes out with words" – someone who is aggressive, demanding, and insists on having his or her way; someone who is controlling. Before my lawyer friends get angry with me, I should say that many lawyers recognize this shortcoming and are trying to do something about it. The problem is that the system of law we have encourages such behaviour. It is just the opposite with indigenous justice.

We all need mirrors with which to look at ourselves. Where can we find them? If you make friends with the person next to you and build trust, that is your mirror – respect and relationship. Respect and relationship are not qualities you can measure, and it is difficult to institutionalize them. However, they are the keys to indigenous justice and essential if you wish to incorporate indigenous methods into non-indigenous frameworks.

Notes
1 This chapter is an edited version of the paper delivered by the Honourable Irene M. Toledo, Associate Justice Designate, Family Court judge of the Navajo Nation at the forum on Intercultural Dispute Resolution: Opportunities and Issues, Faculty of Law, University of Alberta, 9 July 1999.

2 S. Lyman Tyler, ed., *Spanish Laws Concerning Discoveries, Pacifications, and Settlements Among Indians* (Salt Lake City: American West Center University of Utah, 1980), 50.

3 Woodrow Borah, *Justice by Insurance: The General Indian Court of Colonial Mexico and the Legal Aides of the Half-Real* (Berkeley: University of California Press, 1983).

4 Susan Kellogg, *Law and the Transformation of Aztec Culture, 1500-1700* (Norman: University of Oklahoma Press, 1995).

5 Alonso de Zurita, *Life and Labor in Ancient Mexico: The Brief and Summary Relation of the Lords of New Spain,* Benjamin Keen, ed. (New Brunswick, NJ: Rutgers University Press, 1963).

6 Karl N. Llewellyn and E. Adamson Hoebel, *The Cheyenne Way: Conflict and Case Law in Primitive Jurisprudence* (Norman, OK: University of Oklahoma Press, 1941).

7 The author participated in the visit.

8 David Rottman, "Community Courts: Prospects and Limits" (1996) 231 National Institute of Justice Journal 46.

9 Carole Goldberg, "Overextended Borrowing: Tribal Peacemaking Applies in Non-Indian Disputes" (1997) 72 Washington Law Review 1003.

10 James Zion, "The Dynamics of Navajo Peacemaking" (1998) 14 (1) Journal of Contemporary Criminal Justice 58.

11 *Ibid.*

12 William C. MacLeod, "Celt and Indian: Britain's Old World Frontier in Relation to the New," in P. Bohannan and F. Plog, eds., *Beyond the Frontier: Social Process and Cultural Change* (Garden City, NY: Natural History Press, 1967), 25.

13 Anthony F.C. Wallace, "Nativism and Revivalism," in D.L. Sills, ed., *International Encyclopedia of the Social Sciences* (New York: Macmillan, 1968), 11, 75.

14 Raymond D. Austin, "Freedom, Responsibility and Duty: ADR and the Navajo Peacemaker Court" (1993) 32 (2) The Judges' Journal 8.

15 Harry Blagg, "A Just Measure of Shame? Aboriginal Youth and Conferencing in Australia" (1997) 37 (4) British Journal of Criminology 481.

16 Gloria Lee, "The Newest Old Gem: Family Group Conferencing" (1997) 2 (2) Justice as Healing 1; see also the alternative citation <www.usask.ca/nativelaw/jah_lee2.html>.

17 Laura Nader, "Where Is Dispute Resolution Today? Where Will Dispute Resolution Be in the Year 2000?" (April 1985) Dispute Resolution Forum 5.

18 For example, see Gordon Bazemore, "Crime Victims and Restorative Justice in Juvenile Courts: Judges as Obstacle or Leader?" (1998) 1 (1) Western Criminology Review 1; see also the alternative citation <www.wcr.sonoma.edu/v1n1/bazemore.html>.

19 Laurie Grohowski, *Cognitive-Affective Model of Reconciliation (CAMR)* (MA thesis, Antioch University, 1995).

7
Cultural Conflict in Colonial Legal Systems: An Australian Perspective
Larissa Behrendt

When a legal system looks neutral on the surface, many will assume that it produces fair results. This assumption is incorrect, as the experience of Aboriginal Australians bears out: seemingly neutral institutions can often contain inherent biases, and can generate biased results.

I want to explore and explain how Australia's seemingly neutral laws contain and create bias, and how this cultural conflict extends to popular methods of alternative dispute resolution, particularly mediation models.

I will begin by looking at the Eurocentric nationalistic imagery and ideals that feature prominently in Aboriginal policy and in the way that the legal system treats Aboriginal rights, particularly in relation to land. This will assist in highlighting the ways in which laws contain bias and so work, in often unnoticed ways, to create an unequal power balance that disadvantages Aboriginal people. This highlights the need for "alternatives" to the legal system as a way of providing fair, equitable, and just outcomes to disputes. From here I will explore dispute resolution mechanisms used in indigenous cultures and suggest ways that those assist in the identification of cultural conflict with dominant Australian culture's legal system. I then seek to draw out these cultural conflicts in relation to commonly used mediation models to show that mediation, as structured in many models, is not an "alternative" to the dominant legal system but an extension of it.

A Historical Legacy
May 26 is now Sorry Day in Australia. It was so named to mark the handing down on that day in 1997 of *Bringing Them Home: A Guide to the Findings and Recommendations of the National Inquiry into the Separation of Aboriginal and Torres Strait Islander Children from their Families,* commissioned by the Australian Human Rights and Equal Opportunity Commission.[1] The report investigated the government policy of removing Aboriginal children from their families and mapped out the impact that policy of family destruction and cultural genocide had had on our communities.

Despite the clear links the report made between past government practices and contemporary legacies of cyclical family breakdown, substance
abuse, mental health problems, and suicide, the federal government has
denied these links. In a submission from Senator John Herron, the Minister
for Aboriginal and Torres Strait Islander Affairs, signed off on a submission
to the Senate Legal and Constitutional References Committee on the "Inquiry into the Stolen Generation." In that submission, the government stated:

- "There was never a 'generation' of stolen children."
- "Emotional reaction to heart-wrenching stories is understandable, but it
  is impossible to evaluate by contemporary standards decision that were
  taken in the past."

Australian history says little of the practices of the Aborigines Protection
Board. Before the Royal Commission into the "stolen generations" brought
the matter to the attention of the nation, very few Australians even knew
of its existence. Many Australians felt moved by the revelations of the
report, including Governor General Deane, who stated: "It is vital that
we acknowledge past injustices and recognize wounds inflicted in our earlier policy of denial."[2] A different response came from Australians who
envisaged the Australian identity in a colonial manifestation. This can
be summarized in Prime Minister John Howard's response to the report:
"Australians of this generation should not be required to accept guilt and
blame for past actions and policies over which they have no control."[3]

These attitudes are perhaps the biggest impediment to the protection of
indigenous rights in Australia today; this attitude – shared by a sector of
the community – continues to refuse to acknowledge Aboriginal experience and perspective.

Australia is an ideologically divided country. There is an Australia that
welcomes our transformation into a nation with a multicultural, diverse,
and tolerant ideology. Then there is the other Australia, one that clings to
its English roots, its European values, and its monocultural identity. Reactions to Sorry Day are just one point in which those conflicting visions of
Australia, this tug-of-war over what Australia's national identity should
look like, play out.

Australia splits between those who embrace the idea of becoming a
republic that breaks with its constructed colonial, monocultural, and Eurocentric past and those who wish to continue to define our country by its
British, colonial values and heritage. And again, it is the Aboriginal people
within Australia who have become the litmus test for this split. Those who
want to become a republic generally favour a constitutional preamble that
will recognize the prior ownership of Australia by indigenous people;
those against the republic do not favour such acknowledgment.

There are Australians who seek reconciliation with Aboriginal people and greater protection of their cultural and legal rights as part of the move to become a new nation, and those who believe that Aboriginal people should simply be treated the "same as everybody else." This notion of formal equality is pervasive throughout the rhetoric of the conservatives. The prime minister, John Howard, is a great advocate of this approach to Aboriginal rights, but it is a model that is ineffective because it is devoid of the historical context and an awareness of the legacies of past government policies of dispossession and genocide.

It is this Australia that enabled the rise of the One Nation Party led by Pauline Hanson. Although Ms. Hanson lost her seat in Parliament at the last election, her party polled 10 percent of the vote; it was Australia's preferential voting system that kept her from reelection, not a fundamental shift in the ideologies of the party or a rejection of her policies by the electorate. Pauline Hanson's right-wing, conservative rhetoric diverted attention from the fact that her vision of a white Australia that does not give special recognition to the rights of indigenous Australians was shared by the Howard government, which put its agenda into a slicker political package. Nowhere has the impact of this been more evident than in the area of Native title rights. (Ms. Hanson's election platform was to extinguish them; Howard's election platform was effectively the same – which of the two leaders was elected made little difference to the protection of indigenous property rights).

The prime minister has stated: "Australia's farmers, of course, have always occupied a very special place in our heart ... They often endure the heart break of drought, the disappointment of bad international prices after a hard-worked season and quite frankly I find it impossible to imagine the Australia I love, without a strong and vibrant farming sector."[4] There is, of course, no such romanticized or idealized place for Aborigines in Mr. Howard's view of Australia.

Although many define this difference as a debate of mere symbolism and imagery, these ideologies and nationalistic visions impact on indigenous people by denying them basic rights and freedoms. As Howard has shown, treatment of indigenous people's perspectives and experiences as "other" denies protection in a substantive way when Aboriginal property rights are treated as being lesser than the property rights held by all other Australians.

But first we need to go back to 1770, despite warnings from our conservative politicians that we should not be chained to our past. When Captain James Cook claimed Australia on behalf of the British Empire in 1770, he claimed it on the basis that it was *terra nullius* – vacant, without people or sovereign. No treaties were signed and, as a result of this, no interests in land were recognized until 1992, when the High Court in the *Mabo* case[5] found that Native title did occur in very specific circumstances. The majority of the High Court rejected the doctrine of *terra nullius,* considering it bad law.

According to the decision in the *Mabo* case, Native title is recognized only where:

- An Aboriginal community can show that there is a continuing association with the land.
- There has been no clear and plain intention of the government, federal or state, to extinguish that title.

According to *Mabo,* Native title is:

- held communally
- exists in the manner in which it is defined by the Aboriginal community, i.e., the laws and customs of the Aboriginal community will determine the parameters of the Native title interest
- only extinguished by legislation with a clear and plain intent.

If the government wishes to show that the Native title interest has ended, it must show that there was an act, such as the passing of legislation or the granting of a lease, that showed a clear intention to extinguish Native title. This definition of Native title means that for most indigenous Australians, their interest in land has long since been extinguished under the Australian legal system, since the practices of dispossession and removing Aboriginal children from their families was so widespread across the Australian continent.

The High Court also held that where a Native title did exist, there was no common-law right to compensation when the property interest was extinguished. However, because the Racial Discrimination Act, 1975 (Cth), prohibits discrimination on the basis of race, any Native title that is extinguished after 1975 is in breach of that act. This means that any Native title extinguished after the passing of the Racial Discrimination Act would give rise to a claim for compensation.

It is important to note that the issue of the sovereignty of Aboriginal people was avoided by Australian courts in the *Mabo* case, subsequent Native title cases, and in other contexts where the issue was raised. To date, there has been no recognition of sovereignty or an inherent right to self-government. Indeed, legislation was introduced to limit and institutionalize the recognition of Native title. The Native Title Act, 1993 (Cth), made provision, *inter alia:*

- for the validation of all existing land grants with Native title to be extinguished except in relation to mining leases

- that lessees' rights will have primacy over those of Native titleholders. Aborigines will be able to negotiate over land use but cannot veto it
- that the federal government will allow validation of titles granted and will pay more of the compensation for the post-1975 extinguishment of Native title.

A statutory body, the National Native Title Tribunal, was established to review Native title claims. Administered by non-Aboriginal people, it was designed to streamline the claims process and avoid costly litigation through the federal courts.

The *Wik* case[6] further clarified the common law in this area. The Wik and Thayorre peoples sought to have recognized a Native title interest in a piece of land that had been the subject of a pastoral lease. The lease had expired. The majority of the court answered that the existence of a lease will not necessarily mean that Native title interests are extinguished. If the interests can coexist, they will both survive. However, the court noted that where there was a conflict between a Native title interest and an interest under a pastoral lease, the interests of the pastoralist would prevail. Whenever there is a conflict between the use under the lease by the pastoralist and the indigenous people's Native title interest, the interest of the farmer will always trump.

Wishing to end what they had termed "uncertainty," state governments, pastoralists, and mining companies pressured the federal government to extinguish Native title interests on pastoral leases. The Howard government responded to these industry demands by passing the Native Title Amendment Act, 1998 (Cth). This legislation embodied what the prime minister referred to as his "10 Point Plan." Main effects of that legislation included:

- reducing the say Native titleholders have about exploration in their traditional country: there will be some schemes of consultation
- allowing states and territories to replace the right to negotiate on pastoral leases
- permitting a full range of primary production activities on pastoral leases without negotiating with the Native titleholders
- making it harder for Native titleholders to present their case in a claims hearing.

On 24 March 2000, the Committee to Eliminate Racial Discrimination noted, *inter alia*, its concern over "the absence from Australian law of any entrenched guarantee against racial discrimination. It also condemned aspects of the Native Title Amendment Act, 1998 (Cth) that were seen as breaching the Convention on the Elimination of Racial Discrimination (CERD).

Yet Australian law has an expansive interpretation of a property right.[7] Property rights enjoy constitutional protection (under s.51 [xxxi]), and Australian courts have held that property rights "extend to every species of valuable right and interest,"[8] including "any tangible or intangible thing which the law protects under the name of property."[9] While the law provides this tenacious protection to property rights, the extinguishment of Native title interests and the repeal of the protections of the Racial Discrimination Act, 1975 (Cth), from applying to Native title show that these legal protections enjoyed by all other Australians do not extend to Aboriginal titleholders.

What I have attempted to show with this brief synopsis of some of the developments in relation to Native title is that the legal system is not operating fairly to Aboriginal people. It fails to protect where it tenaciously protects the interests of non-Aboriginal Australians. This failure to protect equally is a historic colonial legacy. The failure to protect Native title rights is merely an extension of the doctrine of *terra nullius* that the *Mabo* case overturned but that seems firmly entrenched in the Australian psyche.

The most contact that Aboriginal people have with the law is with the police. This contact also has a historical context since law enforcement officers led massacres of Aboriginal people and came to take children away. Police officers are rarely from the Aboriginal community and often believe the stereotypes perpetuated about Aboriginal people; this has played no small part in the high levels of incarceration of Aboriginal people.[10] Aboriginal people make up around 2 percent of the population but are around 20 percent of the prison population; for Aboriginal women and children, the overrepresentation is even higher. One in four of our men are in jail. An Aboriginal person is twenty times more likely to die in prison than a non-Aboriginal person. Aboriginal people are more likely to be arrested for a summary offence than are non-Aboriginals. Aboriginal people are held in police custody for longer periods than are non-Aboriginal people.[11]

If most Australians do not question the fairness and neutrality of Australia's legal system, this is not true of Aboriginal Australians. The first encounter that Aboriginal people had with the law of the British was when Captain Cook claimed the continent of Australia for the British sovereign. The legal doctrine of *terra nullius* kept Aboriginal people dispossessed until 1992. The law is an instrument of colonization that allowed the state to legitimate its control over the lives of Aboriginal people while failing to protect their rights.

Cultural Traditions and Dispute Resolution

Land has always meant different things to Aboriginal and non-Aboriginal Australians. We bond with the universe and the land and everything that exists in the land. As my father says, "You can no more sell our land than sell the sky." He would describe our relationship to the land in the following way: "Our affinity with the land is like the bonding between a parent and a child. You have responsibilities and obligations to look after and care for a child. You can speak for a child. But you don't own a child."

Even though Aboriginal people have been moved off their traditional lands, land remains an important need of Aboriginal communities. Even urbanized communities maintain links with their traditional lands. Traditional land is needed so sacred sites that remain can be protected. Non-Aboriginal Australians have destroyed and defaced Aboriginal sacred sites. Non-indigenous concern for land is mostly economic.

The values and priorities of the Aboriginal community conflict at many points with those of the dominant legal system. While acknowledging that there is vast diversity between the lifestyles and cultural practices and values of indigenous Australians, it is also fair to say that several similarities exist. The notion of a creation period in which laws were created, a "Dreamtime," is one such commonality. The interconnection with the land – whether you call it custodianship or ownership or guardianship – exists throughout all Aboriginal groups. Interconnection occurs with all living entities and people through a totemic or clan system. Our culture is oral; this is how law and responsibility were handed down. Learning is gained through the example set by others, leading to more respect for those with life experience and wisdom. This worldview is much more focused on the community than on the individual. The smallness of groups and their reliance on each other to ensure survival facilitated a strong sense of interdependence, loyalty, and responsibility to the group that today still facilitates notions of cooperation and consensus. There was also no hierarchical structure analogous to European class structures in our communities; in this sense, it can be asserted that Aboriginal culture was more egalitarian than European or Western culture.

These cultural values are reflected in the process by which conflict was resolved in pre-invasion Aboriginal communities. Grievances were dealt with in several ways. The following examples were taken from a specific area, so there will be some elements that are shared with other groups and some that are unique to the area. They will help to map out the values and processes in an indigenous dispute resolution model.

A group of elders would make decisions for groups and would also intervene in disputes if they had not been resolved between family members. Meetings between elders were usually convened when groups met for ceremonies. These groups were not judicially formed bodies; no one had a vested authority to decide the outcome. Decision making was less formal and less systematic. Women had a prominent part in the process, having the power to make decisions if the person who had broken the law was a woman.[12]

In an example from the lower Murray,[13] two clans sought to settle a dispute in the following manner: members of each clan sat facing each other, arranged around their spokespeople; a general discussion was undertaken; and aggrieved parties then spoke, along with their family members and any other person with an interest in the proceedings. In grievances between individuals, aggrieved parties were given the chance to express the way they felt – even through shouting, yelling, and screaming. Open displays of anger were seen as part of the resolution process. Disputants were encouraged to spend time getting their emotions under control before they faced the person with whom they were in dispute. Women were especially important in this process, playing an active role. Facilitation of a resolution was aided by the use of the interconnection of the community, for social pressure can be very powerful in a small, close-knit, and interconnected community.

From this example, several points of conflict with Australia's dominant legal culture and legal system become apparent.

Cultural Conflict and Mediation

With these cultural conflicts endemic when indigenous people have contact with the legal system, it is easy to see the attraction of mediation in these circumstances. Mediation was hailed as a way of alleviating these cultural conflicts and countering systemic racism and historical legacies. It has become a process employed by the National Native Title Tribunal and is required in most disputes brought before the Family Court of Australia.

Mediation does recognize the inadequacy of litigation, which in certain circumstances is costly and intimidating. Mediation streamlines the court system and allows parties a better opportunity to express their opinions.

Table 7.1

Aboriginal dispute resolution and the British legal system

Aboriginal disputes	British legal system
Emotional response	Controlled response
Oral	Written
Disputants often live together	Disputants often strangers
Experience as training	Formal legal training
No rules of evidence	Strict rules of evidence
Process in front of the community/family	Process in front of strangers
Disputants speak	Use of advocates
Time not an issue	Deadline intensive
Informal	Formal
Communal	Hierarchical

Despite these benefits, there are still fundamental conflicts that arise in mediation models.

It is claimed that mediators are especially useful in dealing with disputes where there are cultural differences between the parties and that a mediator can reduce obstacles to communication through identifying cultural issues. It is asserted also that mediation allows discussion of cultural beliefs and attitudes, thus giving them importance and encouraging respect for those values without making people change their own values.[14] Mediation assumes that people can resolve their issues. It allows disputants the control and the responsibility to decide the content of the conflict and the power to make a decision. In this way, mediation encourages people to choose their own options for resolving disputes, thereby empowering disputants. This allows consensus in the outcome of the dispute, meaning that it is more likely to be implemented by the parties involved. The obvious advantages of mediation have made it the model employed in pilot programs to implement alternative dispute resolution into the Aboriginal community, especially in areas related to families and land.

Mediations between parties from different cultural backgrounds can lead to specific types of problems; proponents of mediation are quick to point to the following "cultural issues":

- *Language issues* that lead to miscommunication and misinterpretation
- *Incorrect assumptions* about diverse cultures
- *Expectations* that others will conform
- *Biases* against the unfamiliar
- *Values in conflict* when the values of the dominant culture conflict with those of another culture.[15]

One goal of mediators is to counter the cross-cultural bias through cross-cultural training. Another is to train Aboriginal people as mediators. Although cross-cultural training sometimes includes components on Aboriginal history and culture, many such sessions last a day or less. (Indeed, it is hard to believe that even a week of study could really allow someone to immerse himself or herself in an indigenous worldview.) This is inadequate to provide a thorough understanding of the weight of Aboriginal experiences and perspectives. These methods of trying to compensate for bias do not address the fundamental cultural conflicts in the mediation model and fail to alter the inherent bias in alternative dispute resolution.

Fundamental conflicts occur in the mediation model in the following ways:

- *The use of a neutral third party:* the mediation model relies on a neutral, impartial third party to facilitate. This poses a special problem for use in indigenous communities in that it is counter to conceptions of who has the right to speak within the community. Getting over the hurdle of giving a stranger, an outsider, the power to facilitate the dispute resolution is not something addressed within the mediation model.

- *The training of mediators:* the use of trained mediators gives rise to an inherent cultural conflict by placing the emphasis on formal training rather than on life experience. This is in conflict with the value of life experience in indigenous communities. It also inadequately "trains" the mediator to have an understanding of indigenous cultural and historical perspectives.
- *The power imbalance between the parties:* the mediation model does not level the economic or legal playing field. Large corporations with lots of money and large legal teams will still have an advantage, especially if governments support their economic goals. It is also true that the power imbalance will not be eradicated while the option to return to the litigation process is available to companies that have no bona fide interest in dealing with Aboriginal communities.
- *Focus on the individual:* the mediation model is concerned with settling disputes between parties but deals primarily with disputes between individuals. When the dispute involves a community, mediation usually operates by resolving the dispute through representatives rather than providing for a broad range of input.
- *Cultural bias:* the mediation process is not derived from Aboriginal and Torres Strait Islander methods of dispute resolution. Any cultural compatibility is purely coincidental. In fact, the logic of using mediation models in Aboriginal communities derives from the belief by proponents of the mediation process that because their methods work well in other contexts, they will do so in Aboriginal and Torres Strait Islander communities.

Mediation is really just an extension of the legal system and all of that system's problems, not an alternative to these. This fact is lost on those proponents of mediation who are not conscious of or interested in challenging the fundamental aspects of that system. Their focus is usually on diverting indigenous people from the litigation process, and alleviating the impact of litigation. While this is a worthwhile pursuit that can have benefits for indigenous people who would otherwise be facing a court case, it has its limitations.

Training Aboriginal people as mediators is a better option and overcomes the problems of trying to give a different cultural perspective and experience to someone else, yet even this approach is flawed. Two points are worth noting:

- Indigenous mediators will not necessarily counter a cultural bias. An indigenous person will be able to have a much better understanding of the indigenous experience, such as the way that things like the Aborigines Protection Board has permeated the lives of our people, and to know what kind of racism is experienced by indigenous people. But this may not be enough. Indigenous communities are not culturally homogenous. These cultural differences may not all be countered if the person is not from the community in which the mediation is taking place.
- Indigenous mediators may not solve the problem of a "neutral" third party acting as facilitator unless the person is in some way connected with the group in conflict; otherwise, distrust may be generated when a stranger seeks to resolve the dispute.

Empowerment through Dispute Resolution

Aboriginal people in Australia have not been given space within which to exert their own jurisdiction because there is no recognition of Aboriginal sovereignty or the inherent right to self-government. Control over decision making is delegated to indigenous communities in circumstances in which ultimate control is still exercised by the dominant culture and its institutions, though Aboriginal communities do assert control over such processes in subversive pockets. This situation will change only if Aboriginal sovereignty and inherent rights to self-government are recognized – and recognized in such a way as to acknowledge Aboriginal jurisdiction and decision-making powers. In addition, space needs to be made available for Aboriginal communities to develop and exercise control over their own decision-making and civil and criminal processes. Mediation models need to be developed that embrace Aboriginal values and processes, to ensure that culturally appropriate mechanisms are available to assist in fair resolution of disputes.

Until real alternatives to the dominant legal system are provided for Aboriginal disputants, Australia's Aboriginal communities will continue to be disadvantaged by institutional racism and biases within the legal system. Empowerment through dispute resolution processes that are faithful to Aboriginal cultural values and processes is a small step forward in asserting the Aboriginal self-determination that colonization has sought to curtail.[16]

Notes

1 Human Rights Commission, *Bringing Them Home: A Guide to the Findings and Recommendations of the National Inquiry into the Separation of Aboriginal and Torres Strait Islander Children from their Families* (Canberra: Australian Government Publishing Service, 1997).
2 "Governor Joins Call for Apology," *Sydney Morning Herald,* 3 June 1997.
3 "PM's Apology Draws Protest," *Sydney Morning Herald,* 27 May 1997.
4 "The Sooner We Get this Debate Over the Better for All of Us," *The Age,* 1 December 1997.

5 *Mabo et al.* v. *Queensland* (No. 2) 175 C.L.R. 1.
6 *Wik Peoples* v. *The State of Queensland; The Thayorre People* v. *The State of Queensland* (1996), 187 C.L.R. 1.
7 *Minister of State for the Army* v. *Dalziel* (1944), 68 C.L.R. 261, per Starke J., 290.
8 *Ibid.*
9 *Ibid.*, per J. McTiernan, 295.
10 See Human Rights and Equal Opportunity Commission, *Racist Violence: Report of the National Inquiry into Racist Violence in Australia* (Canberra: Australian Government Publishing Service, 1991).
11 Sources: Aboriginal and Torres Strait Islander Commission; Human Rights and Equal Opportunity Commission; and Australian Bureau of Statistics.
12 Fay Gale, ed., *Women's Role in Aboriginal Society* (Canberra: Australian Institute of Aboriginal Studies, 1986).
13 Ronald and Catherine Berndt, *The World of the First Australians* (Sydney: Lansdowne Press, 1977, 1981).
14 Kayleen Hazlehurst, *A Healing Place: Indigenous Visions for Personal Empowerment and Community Recovery* (Rockhampton: Central Queensland University Press, 1994).
15 See Selma Myers and Barbara Filner, *Mediation Across Cultures: A Handbook about Conflict and Culture* (San Diego: Intercultural Development, 1993).
16 For further reading, see Richard Bartlett, *The Mabo Decision* (Sydney: Butterworths, 1993); Richard Bartlett, *Native Title in Australia* (Butterworths, 2000); Larissa Behrendt, *Aboriginal Dispute Resolution* (Sydney: Federation Press, 1995); Ronald Berndt, *The World of the First Australians* (Canberra: Aboriginal Studies Press, 1988); Human Rights Commission, *Bringing Them Home: A Guide to the Findings and Recommendations of the National Inquiry into the Separation of Aboriginal and Torres Strait Islander Children from Their Families* (Canberra: Australian Government Publishing Service, 1997); Henry Reynolds, *Frontier: Aborigines, Settlers and land* (Ringwood: Penguin Books, 1992); Henry Reynolds, *The Law of the Land* (Sydney and Boston: Allen and Unwin, 1987); and Royal Commission into Aboriginal Deaths in Custody, *National Report: Overview and Recommendations*, 2 vols. (Canberra: Australian Government Publishing Service, 1991).

8
The Waitangi Tribunal's Roles in the Dispute Resolution of Indigenous (Maori) Treaty Claims
Morris Te Whiti Love

This chapter looks at the main dispute resolution process for the resolution of indigenous (Maori) claims dating back to 1840 and the original signing of the Treaty of Waitangi, a treaty between the British Crown and Maori tribes from throughout *Aotearoa* (New Zealand).[1] These disputes are dominated by claims concerning the appropriation and alienation of Maori land to the Crown and private individuals over a period of 160 years. The chapter begins with an overview of the nature of the disputes and the history leading to the establishment of the Waitangi Tribunal in 1975. This is followed by a discussion of mechanisms established by the tribunal for negotiation and settlement of claims between Maori tribes and the New Zealand government (the Crown). As the process for solving these macrodisputes gives rise to microdisputes between tribes and among subgroups within tribes, less formal processes of dispute resolution designed to address conflict between and within tribal groups will also be examined.

Historical Origins of the Main Dispute
The formal and acknowledged start of the colonization of *Aotearoa* (New Zealand) by the British Crown was 6 February 1840.[2] On that day, as a result of some hasty drafting, a single-page treaty was presented for signature to a large group of Maori gathered in the north of New Zealand at a place called Waitangi. Following exploration by Captain James Cook in the eighteenth century, New Zealand became the subject of French interest. Sealers and whalers, especially Americans, also plied the waters to great profit. Although they sent James Busby to be the official British resident in 1833, the British in New South Wales, Australia, had no great desire to extend their formal relationship with New Zealand at this time. Busby's appointment was, in part, a response to incidents involving British merchantmen and Maori that resulted in considerable bloodshed. He was also sent to regulate the burgeoning shipping industry out of New Zealand. In England, the New Zealand Company, a private colonization

venture in the 1830s, was also preparing to bring its first batch of British colonists to New Zealand. The colonists arrived in Wellington in early 1840. This action forced the hands of the British administration in New South Wales. They sent a young naval officer, Captain William Hobson, to be lieutenant-governor of New Zealand and to discuss a treaty with the Maori people.

The chiefs of many of the northern *hapu* (subtribe) gathered at Waitangi in early February 1840 to discuss the treaty to be proffered by the British. Waitangi was just across the water from a town called Kororareka (now called Russell). This town was known as the "hell hole of the Pacific," where traders, whalers, sealers, and others, including some Maori, plied drink. Maori provided women in exchange for goods and liquor. However, many of the chiefs had converted to their own form of Christianity. For them and other Maori, law and order was a major issue. The treaty promised to bring European law and order to this unruly town. The treaty also held the promise of trade for Maori and the possibility of prosperity in markets such as Australia and those further afield. Nevertheless, on 5 February 1840, most of the chiefs rejected the notion of a treaty and were preparing to go home. However, that night, the drafting of the Waitangi Treaty was completed and in the morning, the chiefs, led by one of the most vigorous opponents, came to sign the Treaty of Waitangi.[3]

The treaty is a simple and pithy document, consisting of a single page of text. It begins with a preamble stating the desire of the Queen of the United Kingdom to "protect [the Maori's] just rights and property and to secure to them the enjoyment of Peace and Good Order." Having set out the intention of the treaty in the preamble, the three articles that follow are the operative parts of the treaty. The articles are remarkable for their simplicity and for their lack of precision in drafting.

1   The first article of the treaty cedes sovereignty (or "governorship" in the Maori version) to the British Crown.
2   The second article guarantees to the chiefs full, exclusive, and undisturbed possession of their lands, estates, forests, fisheries, and other properties they wish to retain. Also, Maori land can be sold only to the Crown.
3   The third article extends to Maori all the rights and privileges of British subjects.

The treaty was taken around the country for signature by those tribes not present at the initial signing. Although some tribes did not sign the treaty, it was gradually seen to have general application throughout the whole country. It signalled the introduction of British law and of a British form of government. The formalization of this process through legislation came later.

The treaty was soon regarded by the British as a treaty of cession, and not a means to protect the rights of Maori. Agents of the British Crown actively set about purchasing much of the South Island (152,232 square kilometres) with the intent of providing extensive reserves for Maori. However, promised reserves were reduced in some cases to no reserve at all.[4] Just after the turn of the century, the situation for a number of Maori was so bad that an Act of Parliament, called the South Island Landless Natives Act, 1906, was passed.[5] The need for this legislation is indicative of the fact that the Maori did not get a good deal and that the main beneficiary of the land provisions under the treaty was the Crown.

The period from 1840 to 1865 saw significant Crown purchasing of Maori land, but for various reasons, especially as a result of stolid resistance from Maori, the land sales slowed significantly after this time. As the settlers' demand for land increased, the government was pressured to find new mechanisms to acquire land. As land throughout the country was derived through a Crown grant and the Maori no longer retained Aboriginal title to the lands they held, Maori lands were brought into a system of land transfer managed by a Native land court. The purpose of the court was ostensibly to ensure that Maori maintained sufficient land for their subsistence, but the unstated purpose was to find new and innovative ways to separate Maori from their land. One of the principal tools was the process of "individualization of title."[6] That process saw the allocation of blocks of land divided from *hapu*, or collective ownership, to a group of owners, each with individual rights to alienate. Initially, no matter how many individuals had rights to the land, only ten owners were featured on the title. Any owner could enter into a process for the alienation of land. This mechanism proved to be very effective in facilitating the alienation of Maori land and the settlement of European farmers and landlords.

As resistance to alienation became stronger, the government adopted other tactics. In Taranaki, Waikato, and the Bay of Plenty, armed troops were brought in, purportedly to protect the European population. However, this led to a war in which British troops attacked Maori. The British were surprised to find the Maori more than a match for the well-trained British regiments fresh from campaigns in India, South Africa, and Europe. It was legislative power, not military might, that finally conquered Maori. The government copied the Irish rebellion laws of the United Kingdom to declare Maori to be in rebellion. This allowed them to enact the New Zealand Settlements Act, 1863, designed to promote peaceful settlement through confiscation of land from Natives deemed to be in rebellion.[7] To add insult to injury, land was given to so called "loyal" Natives, who had little or no traditional right to the land returned. The effect of this legislation was to create a second level of grievances between various parts of the Maori community. These microdisputes still influence the resolution of Maori claims today.[8]

In summary, there are many historical bases for grievances and disputes between Maori and the Crown. These have resulted in protest by the Maori in one form or another over the last 160 years. This anger found new expression in the 1970s and coincided with movements such as Black Power in the United States and the rise of indigenous consciousness globally. The actual effectiveness of the Treaty of Waitangi for Maori was made plain in the courts in 1877 by Judge Prendergast, adjudicating on a land claim between a Maori chief and the Church of England. He made the telling observation that "the Treaty of Waitangi was a simple nullity."[9] It remained a simple nullity, legally and politically, until the enactment of the Treaty of Waitangi Act, 1975.[10] From this act the Waitangi Tribunal was born and with it, by degrees, the whole treaty settlement process. It has grown into a very significant industry in New Zealand.[11]

The Waitangi Tribunal: The First Step in Resolving the Macrodisputes

The Waitangi Tribunal was established under the Treaty of Waitangi Act, 1975. Its main function is to inquire into, and make findings and recommendations to the Crown on, claims submitted by Maori on matters relating to the Treaty of Waitangi. Although the tribunal is a standing commission of inquiry and as such is independent, it is nonetheless an important component in the government's strategic policy of making significant progress toward the negotiation of fair and affordable settlements based on well-founded grievances under the Treaty of Waitangi. The tribunal has now registered over 800 claims, and over 150 have been reported and/or settled in negotiation with the government.[12]

Social and Political Context of Tribunal Operations

Maori have consistently articulated grievances relating to failures on the part of the Crown to implement and honour the Treaty of Waitangi. In particular, the grievances have related to the loss of Maori land and resources, and the desire for *tino rangatiratanga,* or authority and control over resources. Prior to the establishment of the Waitangi Tribunal in 1975, these grievances remained largely unresolved. The first ten years of the tribunal's operations were restricted to contemporary claims directed at legislation and actions of the Crown that were seen to be contrary to the principles of the Treaty of Waitangi. However, in 1985, the Treaty of Waitangi Amendment Act gave the tribunal powers to look at historical claims dating back to 1840.[13]

Although not a court, the tribunal is often viewed by Maori as one. It is perceived by many Maori as engaged in the delivery of substantive justice in areas where Maori claims are not otherwise justiciable and have not been so throughout history. The tribunal is also seen to give effect to the

Treaty of Waitangi, which, though generally not part of domestic law, is seen by Maori as the fount of it.

Tribunal claims are heard within the social context of Maori overrepresentation in negative statistics such as those relating to health problems, social welfare, imprisonment, and mortality. There is also a widening gap between Maori and non-Maori in terms of educational achievement, economic advancement, and employment.[14] Many Maori have made appeals to government to increase their ability for self-development through more equitable access to land and other natural resources. The effects of the loss of land over the last century, with its associated loss of viable economic bases for Maori tribes, is exacerbated by losses in employment over the last thirty years. This has all contributed to the impoverishment of Maori. However, balanced against these negative statistics are increased recognition of the importance of *te reo Maori* (Maori language), higher levels of Maori cultural awareness and pride, and the blossoming of Maori theatre and arts. The number of young Maori becoming fluent speakers and well versed in the culture is also growing in a way unmatched in the twentieth century. The recognition of Maori language, culture, and history by non-Maori is also increasing, especially among school children. Maori business has also seen growth that is unprecedented in modern times.

Maori grievances generally originate from the attitudes and actions of past generations. However, the grievances are passed down to current generations, both through stories and histories and through the social, cultural, and economic conditions in which many Maori live today. The focus on past grievances is diverting the energies of many Maori from pressing social and economic needs, and preventing Maori from taking control of their own futures. It is difficult to move beyond a historical grievance if that grievance is not acknowledged. In this respect, the Waitangi Tribunal provides an important forum in which grievances can be acknowledged and recommendations for resolution made. Acknowledgment of grievances is a key step toward their resolution.

While the present focus of the tribunal is on historical claims, an increasing number of claims arise from contemporary government actions and/or are claims relating to ownership and development of natural resources. In the course of an inquiry, and especially when conducting remedies hearings, the contemporary situation often becomes the focus. Contemporary grievances are more keenly felt, as they affect people's everyday lives in a very direct sense. At present, however, contemporary claims are heard only if an urgent need arises from an irreversible action that would prejudice a claimant. Priority is given to investigation of historical grievances based on the treaty.

The settlement of treaty claims not only recognizes the validity of historical claims but also provides certainty necessary for development of

New Zealand's economy. The tribunal process of investigation and reporting provides society with a clear basis for settlement of grievances, allowing the settlement negotiation process to move ahead progressively. In the longer term, the land and resources used in treaty settlements can also help form an economic base for the Maori and address some of the social problems affecting their communities. In this way, the successful historical settlement of claims benefits both the claimant group and, indirectly, the non-Maori community in that area. For these and other reasons, non-Maori New Zealanders are becoming more aware of the treaty and the implications for New Zealand society of resolving claims. The tribunal has a significant role in influencing the wider community through its inquiry into and reporting on claims, and it also engages in other informational initiatives.

The Waitangi Tribunal has attracted international interest as a mechanism for the development of human rights law as it relates to indigenous people. It is a forum in which issues such as land and cultural rights can be addressed and information made widely available. Conversely, the international arena has been an important influence in the development of thinking about the Waitangi Treaty. Developments such as the Draft Declaration of the Rights of Indigenous Peoples 1993 and the overturning of the doctrine of *terra nullius* in the *Mabo* decision in Australia reflect significant ideological shifts in other countries.[15] Such developments generate a need for us to continuously review New Zealand's approach to the rights of indigenous peoples and treaty issues. Even international trade agreements such as GATT are the subject of Treaty of Waitangi considerations and may well generate associated "side agreements" to deal with these issues.[16]

On a national level, the Waitangi Tribunal is only one of the key mechanisms the government can draw on to resolve treaty claims. However, its role in the process is significant, and it is often the body that has the longest contact with claimants. Most claims are registered, extensively researched (by contracted historians in the main), and then subject to an inquiry by the tribunal. Some are negotiated directly between the claimant group and the Crown through the Office of Treaty Settlements, and a small number of others go through a tribunal mediation process, as a result of the matter being referred by a tribunal to mediation. However, the current policy is that all claims are received initially by the tribunal. The tribunal makes first contact with the claimants and sets the claim in the proper context and process. Nearly all well-founded claims, except those settled in mediation, are ultimately negotiated directly with the Crown, through the Office of Treaty Settlements, usually after the completion of the tribunal process. The exceptions are the claims in which the tribunal exercises its powers to hold a hearing on remedies and to make recommendations that in time bind the Crown.

As well as researching the claims, the tribunal provides funding for claimants to research their claims. Other potential sources of claimant funding are the Crown Forestry Rental Trust, established under the Crown Forest Assets Act, 1989, and civil legal aid through the Legal Services Board.[17]

General Procedures
Inquiries on historical claims generally proceed through two stages. The first is an inquiry on the facts and a full report of the results of the inquiry by the tribunal. If the claim is held to be well founded, the parties may then elect to negotiate a settlement. The second step in the tribunal process is activated only if negotiations are not preferred, or if negotiations fail. The parties are then heard on remedies and the tribunal reports its recommendations. This process assists in any subsequent negotiations by clarifying valid aspects of the claim and ensuring that all parties are well prepared for the negotiations. The tribunal sees the maintenance of an effective negotiations policy as crucial to the resolution of claims. The Minister of Maori Affairs receives the tribunal's reports and the Ministry of Maori Development monitors and reports on the implementation of the tribunal's recommendations.

The tribunal also has the power to refer claims to mediation. A tribunal member, the director of the tribunal, or some other person can be appointed as mediator. Claimants can request that a mediator be appointed if they believe that the whole or major parts of their claim can be settled by mediation. If a claim referred to mediation cannot be settled in this way, it can go back to the tribunal for a full hearing. Filing a claim with the Waitangi Tribunal does not prevent claimants from opening or continuing negotiations with the Crown over any matter in the claim.

As claims are against the Crown, it is necessary for the Crown to present its position before the tribunal, and it does that generally through the Crown Law Office (CLO). The CLO staff draw on the expertise of contracted historical researchers and specialists from government departments. CLO lawyers present the Crown case. For claims under negotiation, the Office of Treaty Settlements coordinates the Crown side and prepares the Crown case, with advice from CLO.

The seventeen members of the Waitangi Tribunal constitute a bicultural mix of senior Maori and people of equivalent *mana* (standing or prestige) from the non-Maori community. The tribunal members receive administrative support from the Department for Courts and are also supported by approximately fifty staff from a variety of disciplines.

Structure of the Waitangi Tribunal
The Waitangi Tribunal is a specialist body whose members are appointed for their knowledge and experience. The total membership reflects the

partnership in the Treaty of Waitangi through an approximately equal representation of *Pakeha* (non-Maori) and Maori. Unlike court judges, tribunal members are expected to bring with them a range of skills and previous knowledge of the matters likely to come before them. For example, in a hearing on historical claims there is at least one professional historian. Maori members of the tribunal not only bring knowledge of Maori history and traditions but often contribute to decisions concerning processes appropriate to the Maori. The chairperson of the tribunal is currently a High Court judge appointed for five years. Other members are appointed for renewable three-year terms. Appointments are made by the governor general on the recommendation of the Minister of Maori Affairs in consultation with the Minister of Justice.[18]

Members constitute a pool from which between three and seven are drawn for any one inquiry. As most members work for the tribunal on a part-time basis only, many have limited availability to hear a number of claims per year. The current chairperson, Justice E. Durie, is the longest-serving tribunal member, having been in this position since 1980. Judges of the Maori Land Court, while not members of the tribunal, may preside at any tribunal inquiry. The chief judge of the Maori Land Court is the deputy chairperson of the tribunal. Any member of the tribunal with at least seven years' standing as a barrister and solicitor of the High Court may also preside at an inquiry. A full-time permanent staff of fifty, with nearly half of that number being qualified historians, serves the tribunal.

Tribunal Functions

The Waitangi Tribunal is, in essence, inquisitorial. It is not a court, but is an independent commission of inquiry with some ability to make binding recommendations. The principal function of the Waitangi Tribunal is to inquire into and report on claims by Maori, that "any statute or regulation, or any past or present Crown policy, practice, act or omission is, or was, inconsistent with the principles of the Treaty of Waitangi and is prejudicial to an individual Maori or group of Maori" (s.6).[19,20] Where a claim is well founded, the tribunal may recommend appropriate relief or the action required to prevent similar prejudice arising in the future (s.6(3)(4)).

The tribunal generally makes recommendations that are non-binding on the Crown under s.5(a) of the Treaty of Waitangi Act. However, since 1988, the tribunal has been able to make binding recommendations for the transfer to Maori of certain state lands assets (principally state enterprise and education assets, forest lands, and certain railway land), including those sold to third parties (ss.8B and 8HC).[21] These recommendations effectively mature as orders. In addition, Parliament may refer bills to the tribunal to report on their consistency with the treaty, although this has yet to happen (s.8). The tribunal also has exclusive authority to determine the "meaning and effect" of the Treaty of Waitangi (s.5).

Claims Management and Research

The tribunal's approach to managing and researching claims has developed over time and continues to develop to find the most efficient way to get through the large number of historical claims now registered with it. The claims received by the tribunal can be classified as historical (arising from past government actions), contemporary (arising from current government actions), and conceptual (generic claims mostly relating to "ownership" of natural resources). Historical claims may be further divided into major claims (large tribal losses) and specific claims (particular losses). Historical claims include the confirmation of pre-treaty purchases, Crown (and some private) purchases to 1865 under Crown-Maori negotiations, Crown and private purchases under the Native Land Court system, land confiscations and expropriations (including Public Works), title arrangements and land development under the Native Land Court system, and tribal autonomy. One tribal claim may encompass all or many of these issues. Historical and natural resource claims may also be dealt with separately.

Given the large number of claims before the tribunal at any one time, it is essential that priorities are set. Large historical claims currently take precedence over contemporary claims. The tribunal has adopted the practice that claims will be heard when the prerequisite research has been completed to a proper standard. The tribunal, through its allocation of research funding, nonetheless influences the order in which claims are heard. It is aware that the seriatim hearing of claims has created inequities, advantaging those claims first heard and reported.

An integrated approach is required to effectively manage and research claims. In response to the large number of claims, and the need for an integrated approach, the tribunal developed three initiatives to assist in the efficient management of claims. The first was the *Rangahaua Whanui* (to research broadly) program, set up in 1993 and completed in 1997. The purpose of this program was to establish a broader context for considering issues arising from claims. The program's focus was on loss of Maori land. For purposes of the program, the country was divided into fifteen geographical districts, and the research needs for each district were determined. In addition to research on these districts, eighteen national themes were also identified and researched. The national themes covered ranged from "Inland Waterways: Lakes," through "The Trust Administration of Maori Reserves, 1840-1913," "Goldfields and other Mining Policy and Legislation, Foreshores," and "Public Works Takings through to Tino Rangatiratanga: Maori in the Political and Administrative System." The objectives of this program were to provide equal research time to all historical claims, to explore issues germane to several claims, to avoid research duplication, and to obtain a national overview of the claims position.

The second initiative was implementing the casebook method. Research related to a claim is compiled into a casebook filed with the tribunal and made available to all parties. The casebook method aims to avoid situations in which the tribunal commences its inquiry into claims but further research is still required. Where this occurs, the hearing process is interrupted and delayed until the research is completed. The casebook method is aimed at improving the efficiency of the claims process by ensuring that all claims are adequately researched in advance of the hearings.

Further, to comply with the rules of natural justice, and for reasons of efficiency and economy, the tribunal also groups for concurrent inquiry all claims that affect, or relate to, the assets of a particular area. For example, historical claims involving tribal resources are heard with all claims relating to those resources. Under the casebook approach, research for claims with a common set of interests and issues in an area is completed prior to the first hearing. This approach increases the efficiency of hearings, as it avoids delays that may be caused if additional research needs are identified at the hearing stage.

The third initiative was to establish a report-writing team within the tribunal. Creation of a team of report writers, one of whom is attached to each tribunal panel, addresses the problem of lack of time by tribunal members to prepare reports at the conclusion of hearings. Using report writers also avoids the problem of potential conflict of interest if researchers who have been involved in the hearings are also involved in assisting in the writing of reports.

The total number of claims on the tribunal's register is not an accurate indicator of workload. The register includes a mixture of major and small claims, most of which can be grouped for concurrent inquiry. Neither does the claims register accurately convey progress made to date on addressing claims. The tribunal has heard and reported on 90 percent of the South Island of New Zealand, which, by area, accounts for nearly half of the landmass of New Zealand. In terms of the Maori population, however, probably little over 20 percent have completed the tribunal process. Only 8 percent of those have received a settlement. Fishing claims (which have been reported on by the tribunal) cover the entire coastline of New Zealand, and there are few tribes without a coastline. Other areas, such as the Waikato, with the large Tainui tribe's settlement, have already been settled, along with the South Island tribe of Ngai Tahu.[22]

The tribunal has many requests for urgent contemporary hearings. In these cases, claimants and the Crown may be heard on whether urgency should be granted. The tribunal endeavours to hear cases where the contemporary government action complained of may have some irreversible consequence. Requests for urgency are submitted on a regular basis and a determination is made on each to see if it gets heard. Some have been declined. The tribunal does not grant urgency to accommodate illegal occupations and will not generally intervene on matters that are, or could be, the subject of court proceedings.

Historical research is a vital part of the treaty claims settlement process. The inquiry into claims involves considerable historical interpretation. It is therefore important that the tribunal has the benefit of competent competing arguments. The maintenance of the tribunal's own research capacity and a strong research unit within the Crown Law Office is seen as essential, as is the maintenance of the Crown Forestry Rental Trust's large research capacity. As noted above, the tribunal also funds claimants to conduct their own research. This has produced work of uneven quality, generating extra auditing costs. On the other hand, the engagement of professionals, while more cost efficient, has left claimants rightly complaining of the capture of their claims by academics. Research to date suggests there is not one tribal group without a valid claim of one sort or another. This was apparent to the tribunal as early as 1987 and led the tribunal to conjecture whether the most practical course was to concentrate on positive programs for the restoration of the economic base of the tribes according to appropriate tribal groupings. Nothing in subsequent research has caused the tribunal to draw back from that opinion.

Customary Representation
An issue currently faced in the management of claims is that of getting mandated representatives for tribal groups to negotiate settlements. This has been a major impediment to the resolution of claims. Three interrelated aspects to this issue are customary representation, level of representation, and modern representation. The issue of customary representation raises the further issue of which *hapu* (subtribe) or *iwi* (tribe) has customary rights to a particular area of land. The level of representation raises the question of what matters are appropriately settled at the *hapu, iwi,* and national levels. The question of modern representation raises the issue of what modern bodies or associations should represent Maori and non-Maori groupings.

Two statutory mechanisms currently assist the tribunal in its consideration of this issue. These are s.6A of the Treaty of Waitangi Act, 1975, which enables the tribunal to state a case to the Maori Appellate Court on the question of customary representation, and s.30 of the Ture Whenua Maori Act, 1993, which enables the chief judge of the Maori Land Court to refer to the court a question of modern-day representation.[23] The current tribunal feels that it would be more helpful if customary issues were referred to the Maori Land Court in the first instance and to the Maori appellate court only on appeal. The tribunal also believes that, as with references under s.30, the court should sit with additional members with expertise in Maori custom when hearing customary issues.

The question of customary representation is a most vexed issue that is spawned by the claims resolution process itself. Representation issues would be simplified if it were clear to claimants that all groups with proven claims are entitled to some compensation, and that compensation need not depend upon the definition of boundaries. Issues concerning the level of representation could be resolved by assuring adequate protection for, and recognition of, subgroups in the settlement structure. The question of customary representation might also be alleviated by the staged restoration of tribal endowments within economically sustainable limits.

In response to this and other issues, the tribunal is exploring the development of facilitation and mediation processes. These processes are described later in this chapter.

The Hearing Process

Any Maori, either as an individual or on behalf of a group of claimants, may lodge a claim. Once a written claim is lodged, the registrar assesses whether the requirements of the Treaty of Waitangi Act, 1975, have been satisfied. These requirements include first ascertaining that the applicant is a Maori,[24] *and that the applicant specify the act(s) or omission(s) of the Crown on which their claim will rely*. If these requirements have not been met, the claim is referred back to the claimants for further information. Otherwise, the tribunal issues a direction that the matter be registered as a claim by allocating it a number and placing it on the tribunal's register of claims.

Once all issues arising in all related claims have been researched, compiled into a casebook, filed with the tribunal, and made available to all parties, the claim is ready for hearing. If necessary, the claim can be amended once this research has been completed. This process usually takes a number of years. Both the claimants and the Crown then have the opportunity to select the venue for the hearing of their respective submissions. The presiding officer of the panel hearing the claim and legal counsel also hold conferences before and during the hearing to determine procedural matters such as the order in which submissions will be heard.

The hearing normally proceeds as follows: the claimant group(s) state(s) their claim; claimant and/or tribunal researchers speak to the main themes of their reports; the tribunal receives submissions from other interested parties that have requested to be heard; the Crown responds to the submissions and claimant evidence; the claimants reply. The tribunal may commission further research, make further inquiries, or commission an opinion on the evidence heard to that point, as it sees fit. Then the Crown and claimants present closing arguments. Throughout the hearing, the tribunal and other parties have the opportunity to question the submissions made.

Although bound by the rules of natural justice and subject to High Court review, the tribunal is not limited to the evidence and argument of the parties. It may receive material that would not be accepted as evidence by the courts. Cross-examination is permitted and is usual, though it is not encouraged for those giving traditional evidence (usually elders). It is usually the case that the evidence of *kaumatua* (elders) is in the nature of contextual evidence and should not be subject to legal argument. If in fact the evidence does go to the particular issues of a claim, it may be subject to cross-examination, as would the expert evidence of historians.

Claims must fit the broad parameters of the tribunal's jurisdiction but need not have the specificity of court pleadings. Nor is the Crown obliged to file a statement of defence. Issues generally emerge during the inquiry and are collated prior to final legal submissions. However, a practice is developing whereby issues are identified earlier in the process. Because the tribunal is a commission of inquiry, anyone who has an interest greater than that of members of the public at large may be heard. Public notices are given and members of the public regularly make submissions at hearings. Those with special interests may be treated as third parties.

The tribunal is able to set its own special procedure. It may adopt Maori hearing protocols, and hearings are generally held on the *marae*.[25] In practice, the tribunal tries to balance the legal domain and the Maori domain. Although Maori protocol precedes the start of each week of hearings and concludes them, much of the hearing process itself is like a court, with presentation and examination addressed through counsel representing the parties; the tribunal often hears evidence given in Maori accompanied by *waiata* (song). The tribunal may also state a case to the general courts on a question of law and to the Maori appellate court on questions of custom.

When the hearing is complete, the tribunal considers whether the claim is well founded. Sometimes it issues an interim report on its findings. When an interim report is issued, the tribunal may recommend that the Crown and claimants negotiate a settlement of the claim. The tribunal can also offer to assist the negotiation by holding further hearings on remedies. Where the tribunal issues a final report, including detailed recommendations on remedies, the Crown decides whether to put recommendations into effect, and if so, how. There is no further tribunal involvement in the claims settlement process following the final report.

Claims Facilitation and Dispute Resolution of Competing Microclaims

The establishment of a claims facilitation and dispute resolution process is a relatively new innovation in the resolution of Treaty of Waitangi claims.

However, it builds on provisions that have been in the Treaty of Waitangi Act for nearly twenty-five years. The process is an adjunct to the processes for the settlement of claims carried out by the Waitangi Tribunal and the Office of Treaty Settlements. Both processes are expected to reduce the overall costs associated with the hearing and settlement negotiation processes by reducing the indirect costs of duplication and delay and the direct costs of disputes to claimants and the Crown.

Both the Waitangi Tribunal hearing process and the Crown's direct negotiation process involve the grouping of claims. The tribunal groups claims by district, while the negotiation process seeks to deal with all the claims of an *iwi* (tribe) collectively. In the *Tauranga moana* tribunal inquiry, for example, well over fifty-five claims are grouped for concurrent inquiry in one district. One of the benefits of the casebook method of district inquiries discussed earlier is that it reduces duplication of research, hearing time, legal representation, and associated costs for all these processes. Nonetheless, over 800 claims are registered, with inquiry into some 650 claims still to be made. Despite grouping these claims into approximately thirty-six district inquiries, as the Waitangi Tribunal has done, it will take an estimated seven to ten years of hearings to deal with all the claims.

The Crown also aggregates claims. The Crown requires claimant groups to produce a mandated representative group to negotiate treaty claim settlements with the government. The Crown has an explicit policy preference to negotiate with *iwi* rather than *hapu* or other groupings of claimants. However, these may or may not be the natural or customary aggregations for the claimant groups. Inevitably there are disputes among them when they are required to work together and to harmonize or compromise their approaches to negotiations and desired outcomes from settlement.

There are three main categories of dispute between and among tribes:

1   *Intra-iwi*, where two (or more) large groupings exist with similarly sized constituencies within one *iwi* (e.g., Muriwhenua, a tribal group in the far north of New Zealand).
2   *Intra-iwi*, where one large group exists with one or more smaller dissenting groups, possibly *hapu/whanau* (e.g., Tainui, a large tribal confederation in the middle of the North Island and Ngai Tahu, a tribal group occupying a large part of the South Island).
3   *Inter-iwi*, where there are competing claims either by way of overlapping interest or challenge for representation (e.g., Wellington Tenths/ Te Whanganui a Tara Te Atiawa tribe from Wellington).

No effective process exists to bring multiple claimants together into the aggregations with which the Waitangi Tribunal and the Crown prefer to deal. Further, the Office of Treaty Settlements currently has no formal process for intervention in disputes between claimant groups regarding mandating or cross-claim issues. There have been some attempts by the Crown Forestry Rental Trust to rationalize representation through *kaumatua* (elders), with some success. However, generally it has been the practice to leave the matter for the tribal claimant groups themselves to resolve, or for the Maori Land Court and Maori appellate court. In some cases where there have been disputes between *iwi* and *hapu* with overlapping interests, legally trained mediators have been used with limited success. At least one attempt has been made to mediate an intratribal dispute using legally trained mediators; the attempt was unsuccessful in resolving the issues in dispute.

The Maori Land Court's s.30(b) procedure under the Te Ture Whenua Maori (Maori Land Law) Act has produced results, but, as discussed earlier, it is designed to identify the appropriate representatives for tribal groups rather than bring aggregations of groups together.[26] Court hearings also tend to be protracted and consequently expensive. Although the court ultimately provides a decision, it does not heal rifts in tribal groups and is adversarial in nature. Further, the court-imposed solution is not one generated by the people. For these reasons, more appropriate methods to determine groupings are required.

Settlement Mediation

Although settlement mediation of substantive issues by processes with legally trained mediators has had little success, the mediation process can be modified to assist in bringing multiple claimants together to prosecute their claims collectively and to resolve disputes between groups seeking to represent a group of claimants. This has been the experience of the bicultural and bilingual mediation processes offered by the tribunal.

The development of settlement mediation processes originates in provisions in clause 9 of the Second Schedule of the Treaty of Waitangi Act, 1975. The actual mediations are conducted by independent mediators from a mix of practice backgrounds. Matters referred to mediation by the tribunal can be mediated by almost anyone the tribunal chooses. In practice, the tribunal has tended to select co-mediation. One mediator bringing general mediation skills is paired with a *kaumatua* (elder) skilled in *tikanga* (traditional Maori practices) and *te reo* (the Maori language). This combination allows a bicultural and bilingual process – almost an absolute necessity for these types of dispute. The mediations contribute to both government and claimant goals for treaty settlement by constructively assisting diverse Maori claimant groups to resolve their differences and achieve the strength required for effective negotiation of a "macro" treaty claim directly with the government.

The mediations operate on the basis of these principles:

- Disputes should be resolved at the earliest point and at the lowest level possible.
- Consensual or interest-based processes are usually preferred over positional bargaining or adversarially oriented processes.
- Methods used should be cost effective and strategies designed to limit the time involved in the dispute process.
- The system should be culturally aware and empowering for all parties.
- Confidentiality for the parties should be protected and media protocols established, although this is difficult in practice given the size of claimant groups and the need for the Crown to be instructed by a minister of the Crown.

The objectives of the mediation process are:

- to provide a process that will assist Maori to come together as an effective body (or bodies) to prosecute and settle their historical treaty claims with the Crown
- to maintain an affordable, expert, and independent group of facilitators and mediators to achieve the first goal and to have that group available to groups of claimants as they move through the claim resolution process
- to improve the efficiency and credibility of the treaty claims settlement process by assisting groups to better self-manage their affairs, especially eventual treaty settlements.

Currently, the mediation process is independent from the tribunal's inquiry operations. It is available at any time after the start of tribunal hearings on a claim. A current proposal is that both facilitation and settlement mediation be provided throughout the life of an inquiry on an ad hoc basis, according to demand.

Facilitation and Dispute Resolution Process
The Waitangi Tribunal is currently exploring the desirability of a combined facilitation and settlement mediation process. It is expected that the proposed process will have a role in every inquiry handled by the tribunal where multiple claims or parties are involved. The aim of facilitation is to work with claimant groups to identify areas of conflict and anticipate disputes, rather than waiting for disputes to develop. It will also assist claimants who choose to go directly to negotiation at any stage in that process. This process would be similar in form to settlement mediation but would be based on consensus building and would not normally include legal counsel. Unlike mediation, the facilitation process would not extend to development of representative structures for tribal groups or the identification

of actual representatives by mediators. Rather, the tribal group would create the representative structure once key areas of dispute are identified and resolved. Producing mandated claimant groups as required by the government for negotiations would not be a specific goal of this process, but claimants who had accessed the process would be more likely to satisfy the mandating requirements of the government. The facilitators would not provide advice but would facilitate consensual decision making. Because the process has no commercial or other interest and does not give advice, it should be able to work effectively with the claimant groups to establish their collective views.

Facilitation could be provided at the initial identification of the hearing district. At this stage, the Waitangi Tribunal itself determines the geographical extent of a hearing district and adopts a firm strategy for the completion of research into the claims in that district. The Waitangi Tribunal has the authority to do this under its Waitangi Act and the criteria it applies in selecting districts are set out in its *Guide to Practice*.[27] A facilitator under the proposed process could meet with the various claimants to discuss the possibilities and advantages of their coming together initially at the tribunal phase. This process could work in tandem with the tribunal's research staff mandate. A facilitator would have to be well briefed on the common history of the claimants; a series of individual meetings with the claimants, followed by at least one joint meeting of all claimants, could start the process.

Facilitation could also occur at completion of the casebook and readiness for hearing. As historical research is completed and the casebook is being prepared, there will be greater awareness of the claim issues and common histories of the parties. This process culminates in the tribunal calling a conference to determine when the hearing process should start. At this time the claimant groups need to have agreed on legal counsel and applied for legal aid. They should also begin to consider how they will meet the requirements of the government for mandated representatives to negotiate settlements. The facilitation process can assist the parties and the tribunal during this stage.

If one or more parties choose to withdraw or not take part in the process when it is a multiparty facilitation and the matter is not yet in hearing, a decision would need to be made as to whether further attempts should be made to bring about some reconciliation, or whether to allow the matter to proceed through the hearing process with further facilitation attempts being made later. If there is a dispute that threatens unity between two parties, mediation could be initiated, provided there is support from the parties.

Facilitation could also occur once hearings are in progress with the Waitangi Tribunal and at the conclusion of hearings. At the conclusion of the substantive hearings, the claimants could discuss claim settlement strategies and options, including various forms of representation and the best ways to negotiate a settlement of their claims. The tribunal could also hear claimants on how they wish the claims to be settled and with whom it should be settled. The facilitation process could assist the claimants to resolve these issues.

Facilitation could also occur at the pre-negotiation stage. The next step would usually be to await the tribunal's report and recommendations prior to starting into the negotiation process proper. This is the time when mandated representatives are sought in accordance with the government's criteria. If the facilitation has been effective up to this point, that step should not be a major hurdle. However, if mandated representatives cannot be appointed at this stage, the facilitation processes can be continued.

There is no formal direction under the Treaty of Waitangi Act to use this process. The incentive comes from those bodies that play key roles in the claims process. The first of these are the various claimant parties and the Crown. Others include the Waitangi Tribunal, the Crown Forestry Rental Trust (CFRT), the Legal Services Board, and the Office of Treaty Settlements (OTS). However, the tribunal has powers to formally refer a matter to mediation, and in some cases facilitators would act as mediators once areas of conflict were identified. For example, when the tribunal starts to research claims for a district inquiry, facilitators would discuss the issue of the aggregation of claims with the claimants before disputes arise. However, before obtaining funding approval for research, every effort must be made by claimants to resolve disputes and to aggregate the claim. If the claimants are not able to achieve aggregation through their own devices, they could seek the assistance of the facilitation process. At the point where an inquiry casebook is being assembled, the tribunal can again advise that claimants consult with the facilitation process. If claimants seek legal aid, the committee assessing applications could also question whether they have participated in a facilitation mediation process or have attempted to combine their claims with similar claims.

One of the benefits of the facilitation process would be to reduce the overall costs of the treaty claims settlement processes. The claimants themselves would benefit by a reduction in overall costs and would be in a much better position when it came time to start negotiations of a settlement. There would also be a net saving in time for them, with the gap between the completion of tribunal hearings and the start of negotiations being reduced.

The time delay and cost of tribal groups getting a mandate to enter the claim settlement negotiations process are evident. Although there are considerable benefits from avoiding or reducing costs for various parts of the claim settlement process, the facilitation process would provide other direct short- and long-term benefits. There is considerable division in Maori society, and the treaty claim process, rightly or wrongly, shoulders much of the blame for this division. The process could go some way to dealing with division caused by the claims process. This may well have a spinoff for other divisions in Maori society.

To ensure cultural integrity and achieve the goals of the facilitation process, these principles would be followed:

- Where possible and practicable, two co-facilitators would be used. At least one would be Maori, capable of maintaining Maori protocol. Consideration would be given to having a mixed-gender team.
- Maori protocol would be observed, along with some rules on participant speaking, to allow all participants reasonable time to speak (i.e., each speaker may speak only once, until all have had a chance to speak).
- The facilitation *hui* (tribal gathering) would allow each group to bring a maximum of two (non-legal) representatives and usually would be held in a neutral venue within the district of the inquiry.
- Costs for each party would be met by the respective parties, with the tribunal providing the venue and any facilities required and covering the cost of the facilitators and mediators.
- Facilitators and mediators would be neutral and would be there to assist the parties to reach a written agreement. All parties and the facilitators would sign the agreement. The agreement would bind the parties.
- Substantive matters of a tribunal inquiry or the claims negotiation processes with the government would be outside this process.

Conclusion

Since its creation under the Treaty of Waitangi Act, 1975, the Waitangi Tribunal has participated in the resolution of many Maori claims. Although tribunal hearings of inquiry are flexible and procedures are designed to accommodate Maori culture, more work is being done to promote resolution of claims outside the inquiry process, based on a model of consensus. Mediation by co-mediators with cultural expertise has been used to help resolve intra- and inter-*iwi* disputes and disputes among *hapu* so that aggregate claims can be brought in to the tribunal inquiry or government claims settlement processes. To facilitate claims at the microlevel, the tribunal is also in the process of reviewing a new facilitation and dispute resolution process. Although similar to mediation, this process will not involve lawyers in the process and will be invoked at different stages, and by different means, in the inquiry and negotiation processes. It is hoped this new process will both save costs and help facilitate more satisfactory outcomes.

Notes

1 *Te Tiriti o Waitangi* (the Treaty of Waitangi) was signed first at Waitangi in the Bay of Islands in New Zealand on 6 February 1840. This original version in Maori is held at National Archives in Wellington. Several versions were signed around the country by some 550 chiefs through 1840, one being in English. Three versions are now used for official reference and are included as Appendix 1 of the Treaty of Waitangi Act, 1975.

2 Claudia Orange, *The Treaty of Waitangi* (Wellington: Allen and Unwin, Port Nicholson Press, 1987), 6-11.

3 Orange, *Treaty of Waitangi*, 51-53: "By Thursday morning, 6 February, the chiefs had come to the decision that the treaty business should be concluded immediately so they could return home ... There was confusion on the Thursday morning as Hobson had set the 'public meeting' for Friday 7. In the end he consented that only signatures would be accepted; no discussion would be allowed."

4 *Waitangi Tribunal Report,* The Ngai Tahu Report (Wellington: GP Publications, 1991).

5 South Island Landless Natives Act, 1906 (N.Z.), 1906, c.17.

6 David V. Williams, *"Te Kooti Tango Whenua": The Native Land Court 1864-1909* (Wellington: Huia Publishers, 1999), 65.

7 See the preamble to the New Zealand Settlements Act, 1863.

8 See the New Zealand Settlements Act, 1863, ss.5 and 6.

9 *Wi Parata* v. *Bishop of Wellington* (1877) 3 N.Z. Jur. R. (N.S.) S.C. 72. This case was between Wi Parata (a legislative councillor) and the Bishop of Wellington. For some time, efforts had been made to have a land grant revert to its former Maori owners because the terms of the original grant (that was to be used for educational purposes) were not being fulfilled. In giving his decision, Chief Justice James Prendergast declared that the treaty was a legal "nullity" because it had not been incorporated in domestic law.

10 Treaty of Waitangi Act, 1975 (N.Z.), 1975, c.114.

11 Alan Ward, National Overview Volume I, Waitangi Tribunal Rangahaua Whanui Series, Waitangi Tribunal 1997. The above section has of necessity been a very compressed summary of the history of the treaty. More comprehensive expositions are available including the research reports produced by the Waitangi Tribunal called the National Overview of the Rangahaua Whanui Series.

12 *Annual Report of the Department for Courts, 2000,* 103.

13 The Treaty of Waitangi Amendment Act, 1985 (N.Z.), 1985, c.148 (to amend s.6 of the Treaty of Waitangi Act, 1975).

14 Ministry of Maori Development, Te Puni Kokiri, "Progress Towards Closing Social and Economic Gaps Between Maori and Non-Maori," in *A Report to the Minister of Maori Affairs,* 1998.

15 United Nations, Draft Declaration on the Rights of Indigenous Peoples 1993; the Draft Declaration was agreed upon by the members of the Working Group on Indigenous Populations (WGIP) established in 1982. The Working Group is a subsidiary organ of the Sub-Commission on the Prevention of Discrimination and Protection of Minorities, itself a subsidiary of the Commission on Human Rights; *Mabo* v. *Queensland (No 2)* (1992) 107 A.L.R. 1.

16 *General Agreement on Tariffs and Trade (1947)* (Geneva: World Trade Organization, 1999).

17 The Crown Forestry Rental Trust (CFRT) was established by agreement between Maori litigants and the Crown to enable the Crown to sell cutting rights to plantation forests but get a rental for the lease of the forests to assist Maori claimants to research, present, and negotiate claims before the Waitangi Tribunal. The CFRT operates on the interest gained from the investment of the annual rentals for the forests, which now yield some $18 N.Z. M. per year. CFRT was established under the Crown Forest Assets Act, 1989 (N.Z.), 1989, c.99.

18 Treaty of Waitangi Act, 1975, s.4(2)(b).

19 Treaty of Waitangi Act, 1975, s.5(1)(a).

20 The references in brackets in this and the following paragraphs are to sections of the Treaty of Waitangi Act, 1975.

21 Treaty of Waitangi Act, 1975, ss.8B and 8HC.
22 Ministry of Justice, *Annual Report for the Year Ended 30 June 1999.*
23 Te Ture Whenua Maori Act, 1993 or the Maori Land Act, 1993 (N.Z.), 1993. c.4, s.30(1)(b).
24 For the purposes of the Treaty of Waitangi Act, 1975, a Maori is defined as being the descendant of a Maori.
25 Marae refers to the collective of buildings and land that have formed the centre of each Maori community from pre-European times. They generally include a large meeting house (*Wharenui*) where hearings are conducted and forecourt (*marae atea*) where ritual greetings are performed prior to starting hearings.
26 Te Ture Whenua Maori Citation for the Act, 1993.
27 Waitangi Tribunal, *Draft Guide to Tribunal Practice,* December 2000.

9

Commentary: Indigenous Dispute Settlement, Self-Governance, and the Second Generation of Indigenous Rights

Jeremy Webber

The three chapters in this section, by Larissa Behrendt, Morris Te Whiti Love, and Chief Justice Robert Yazzie, explore approaches to dispute settlement grounded in three widely varying indigenous contexts: Aboriginal Australia, Aotearoa/New Zealand, and the Navajo country of the southwestern United States. They address different types of dispute: Love and Behrendt focus on disputes crossing the indigenous/non-indigenous divide (although disputes among Maori can also arise in proceedings before the Waitangi Tribunal); Yazzie focuses on the resolution of disputes among Navajo by indigenous methods according to indigenous law. They also speak to a range of institutional forms:

- in Love's case, the Waitangi Tribunal of Aotearoa/New Zealand, with its highly institutionalized – and innovative – set of processes;
- for Yazzie, the courts of the Navajo Nation, which were at one point modelled on non-indigenous institutions and applied a set of laws that reflected, at least in form, non-indigenous codes, but which have recently turned back toward indigenous methods and which may now, as Yazzie tells us, be ceding those methods back to the communities from which they sprang; and
- in Behrendt's chapter, the processes of mediation, in whatever institutions they take place.

In this chapter, I will consider what the chapters together have to tell us about salient features of dispute settlement in the indigenous context. I will then explore how this reflects a significantly enhanced conception of what indigenous rights demand, one that involves an integral mediation of normativity and due process, not merely the application of specific indigenous rights by non-indigenous institutions.

Features of Dispute Settlement in Indigenous Contexts

These three chapters, despite the different peoples and types of disputes they address, reveal a number of elements common to indigenous dispute settlement.

At the simplest level they make clear that indigenous dispute settlement cannot be approached as though it were simply a matter of mediational or adjudicative technique. Indigenous disputes are not merely another field within which mediation or arbitration can be deployed. Indigenous dispute settlement, to be successful, must come to terms, in both its design and execution, with the broader context of colonial interaction, a context that has had such a profound impact on the relationships and institutions in issue. This is expressed in the chapters in different but broadly compatible ways. Love and Behrendt, for example, stress the need to begin with an acknowledgment of indigenous experience of violence and breach of faith through, for example (in the Australian case), the making of an apology. All three emphasise the need to take full account of widespread alienation of indigenous people from the institutions of the societies in which they find themselves, an alienation both prompted by and manifest in the high rates of incarceration for indigenous people.

The broader colonial context impinges upon dispute settlement regimes through its impact on the relative starting points and power of the parties in negotiations. This is an impact common across many areas of mediation, where the propensity for power differentials to be mirrored in, not displaced by, consensual dispute settlement processes has been widely noted and strategies for guarding against that propensity proposed (with greater or lesser success).[1] But in the indigenous context there are two additional concerns. The colonial experience affects indigenous parties' trust of state-sponsored mechanisms, generating deep suspicion of all institutions devised through the unilateral exercise of state authority. To be legitimate – to secure willing indigenous participation – the very structure of dispute settlement may have to be negotiated, either expressly or through mechanisms of consultation that result in hybrid forms, combining indigenous and non-indigenous elements. It also affects the cultural appropriateness of the means of dispute settlement – for example, the extent to which settlement mechanisms pay due attention to the authority of elders, or the extent to which social solidarity forms an important aim of the process. The greater the clarity and agreement about the historical conjuncture – the more sustained the attempt to incorporate indigenous concerns and modes of interaction – the greater the likelihood that mechanisms will produce outcomes acceptable to the parties.

These chapters also suggest features that contribute to successful mechanisms for indigenous dispute settlement. One is resistance to what might be termed the detached professionalization of non-indigenous dispute settlement. Most mediational or arbitral theory focuses on technique, not on the personal stature of the person seeking to resolve the dispute. By contrast, these chapters emphasize the importance of the peacemaker's intrinsic standing, prestige, and moral authority – the individual's *mana*, in the Maori term used by Love. That prestige flows from the person's long experience and wisdom, his or her deep acquaintance with the community and its customs, not from a course of professional training or the conferral of official imprimatur. The experience of the Waitangi Tribunal in Love's account seems particularly instructive in this regard. There, professional mediation had not been successful, leading the tribunal to turn toward facilitation by two intervenors, one indigenous and the other non-indigenous. It thereby developed a solution that seems especially appropriate for a process designed to bridge the indigenous/non-indigenous divide. The new approach combines a person of experience and wisdom, anchored in the indigenous context, with a person of non-indigenous professional expertise, possessing knowledge of the non-indigenous methods and institutions within which any settlement will also have to be comprehensible.

It is significant that Love uses the term facilitation, not mediation, to describe this process. All three chapters emphasize the extent to which the entire community tends to be implicated in dispute settlement. The process is not one that seeks to settle an isolated difference between individual parties, but rather one concerned with the reaffirmation of community and the restoration of peace. Yazzie emphasizes that the restoration of social solidarity, mutuality, and reciprocal obligations is one of the aims of Navajo justice. Similar themes appear in the chapters of Behrendt and Love, even though they are primarily concerned with disputes that cross the indigenous/non-indigenous divide.

Dispute settlement therefore takes a different cast from that generally assumed in the non-indigenous literature. Settlement is not merely a matter of calculated give and take between parties, with each party deciding, self-consciously, to trade off some of its private interests in order to obtain an acceptable outcome. Rather, it has much more the air of collective deliberation and discussion. The best non-indigenous analogy is not the negotiation of a business deal but the process of collective deliberation typical of a community meeting or legislative assembly. And indeed, this has tended to be the form of discussions dealing with indigenous land claims up until today. It was, for example, the form adopted in handling land disputes under the Royal Proclamation of 1763 and in the nineteenth-century treaty process in Canada. Indigenous peoples gathered together in council to discuss the proposals for a treaty, debating those proposals, making amendments, requiring clarification, and ultimately deciding whether or not to accept them. That sense of the process as a solemn deliberative occasion – a constitutive event in the life of the community and in its relations with others – has much to do with the sanctity of historical treaties today, both in Aotearoa/New Zealand and in Canada.[2]

The deliberative character of land claims processes is especially evident when the process is concerned not just with the determination of rights to land but also, simultaneously, with the creation of indigenous coalitions and representative processes to handle land claims negotiations, and with the construction of institutions to manage the land long into the future. This is the ordinary case, not the exception. Land claims generally involve the simultaneous development of community structures and political institutions. This is evident in Love's description of facilitation as a means of encouraging multiple claimants to build coalitions during the Waitangi process, both to prosecute their claims and to manage the land once granted. It was true of the development of the land councils in the Northern Territory of Australia during the Woodward inquiry of the 1970s and of the emergence of regional agreements and Native title representative bodies under the Australian Native Title Act today.[3] It was true of the creation of Cree and Inuit political institutions and Inuit land corporations during the negotiation of the James Bay and Northern Quebec Agreements in the 1970s.[4] We should not be surprised that land claims are as much about governmental development as about the confirmation or transfer of title. Land claims seek fundamentally to achieve autonomy, self-government, and the resources necessary to support that autonomy. They necessarily involve a political process of coalescence and reconstitution.

This emphasis on collective deliberation, on developing the institutions of community, on collective healing and reconciliation makes clear why indigenous dispute settlement is concerned with the values of the community, their renewal and reaffirmation. And in this process, it is the values of the *particular* community that are in cause, not a generic set of indigenous values (whatever those might be). Individuals who attempt to settle indigenous disputes need to be alive to the particular traditions and concerns of the specific people. Yazzie emphasizes, for example, the importance of specifically Navajo values to the courts he describes. Love makes clear the value of having Maori ways manifest in the proceedings of the Waitangi Tribunal.

Cultural reassertion and renewal are integral, then, to the successful processes of dispute settlement described in these chapters. Those processes are not simply about achieving land or self-determination; they are about doing self-determination. They involve the community laying hold of the processes (at least in part), remaking them in a manner that incorporates (to some degree) indigenous forms, and then deploying them to achieve acceptable outcomes. The settlement of disputes is itself a kind of practical self-determination.

A Second Generation of Indigenous Rights

It is instructive that each of the chapters argues for the refashioning of settlement mechanisms so that dispute resolution takes on forms very different from those of the general legal system. They do not seek to resolve indigenous disputes simply by having courts make the correct decision. They argue that indigenous dispute settlement should operate, in many ways, "without the law"[5] through its own hybrid procedures, with only partial regard for non-indigenous legal institutions and authority.

This represents a significant development beyond what might be termed the first generation of indigenous rights: the attempt to have indigenous interests recognized as rights within the general legal system. In this second generation, the institutions and processes of legality themselves are put into question, so that the very mechanisms of public order and of norm formation might be refashioned.

This development runs against the first instincts of most non-indigenous jurists, even those supportive of indigenous claims, who tend to think of indigenous rights in relatively simple terms: an injustice has been done, a species of property has been denied, a wrong cries out for correction; the law should respond by righting that wrong. There is an implicit assumption that the wrong should be righted within the general legal system, so that judges begin to recognize and enforce the indigenous interest. It is the general legal system that has perpetrated or perpetuated injustice. It should get its house in order.

This well-meaning approach can have perverse effects. The Australian recognition of indigenous title in the 1990s is a good example. Non-indigenous Australians had long assumed that there was no indigenous title within Australian law. This assumption was overturned by the landmark decision of the High Court of Australia in *Mabo* v. *Queensland (No 2)*[6] and a process for vindicating indigenous title was provided by the Native Title Act, 1993. Both *Mabo* and the Native Title Act tended to presume, however, that indigenous title should be considered simply another form of proprietary interest, conferring specific rights to specific tracts of land, recognized within the general structure of Australian land law. Claimants bring their claims before non-indigenous courts (or, under the Native Title Act, before the National Native Title Tribunal in first instance). Those courts hear evidence on the requirements of indigenous law and on the application of that law to the particular facts. They then rule upon the existence and nature of the right. Thus, the system acknowledges that there is Native title but proceeds to make non-indigenous judges the exclusive adjudicators of that title, ruling not only upon the common law's ability to make room for indigenous title but also upon the intricacies of each people's indigenous law. Indigenous peoples may obtain vindication of specific interests, but they do so only by losing control over the law that governs those interests.[7]

The three chapters discussed here point toward a more profound understanding of the demands of indigenous rights. They suggest that those
rights should be achieved not merely by a more sympathetic interpretation of the general law by the general courts. They argue for mechanisms
of adjudication and adjustment that take fundamental account of indigenous methods of social ordering, often through processes that combine
indigenous and non-indigenous features. This is the sense in which they
represent a second generation – concerned not merely with the recognition of specifically defined interests by non-indigenous institutions, but
with the refashioning of the institutions themselves.

Of course, like all second generations, this one had precursors. The logic
of the relationship has often compelled more fundamental accommodations. The treaty relationship so important in North America or New
Zealand – indeed, the very recognition of indigenous title in these societies – emerged out of a process of trial and error and had genuinely intercultural features. This is not to suggest that it was marked by a spirit of
pure equality. Like all other aspects of the relationship, it was affected by
the inequalities and brutalities of indigenous/non-indigenous interaction.
But it was not simply a one-time, limited acknowledgment of a particular
right. Instead, it set in place a structure of interaction that provided for
adaptation and adjustment across the normative divide.[8]

Similar allowance for adjustment and accommodation has been evident,
at least between the cracks, in courts' and governments' grappling with
indigenous title in recent times, for the very good reasons that indigenous
peoples have insisted on a more integral participation in the definition
of their rights, and non-indigenous actors have sometimes recognized, at
least implicitly, the incongruity of their presuming to rule on the fine
details of indigenous law. This is true, for example, of the development of
co-management structures for the regulation of natural resources. It is also
true of the Canadian courts' reluctance to make detailed findings on the
precise distribution of indigenous title within indigenous communities,
ruling instead on the title's existence and encouraging the parties to negotiate the details.[9] Recent developments in the field of criminal law have
moved from a first stage concerned principally with issues of misunderstanding in the courtroom (problems of translation, the comportment of
indigenous accused, the value of having elders present to interpret issues
of context and culture)[10] to a second stage of more fundamental adjustments to process (such as circle sentencing or lay tribunals) and even the
norms applied (through the recognition, albeit halting, of customary law).[11]

Given the presence of such elements in our practice from the very beginning, the "second generation" may represent more a change in understanding than in the substance of the relationship – though with important

implications for our ability to engage in that relationship successfully. The logic of the relationship may always have implied more fundamental accommodations than non-indigenous participants tended to recognize. And that logic may have shaped our institutions and our practice in ways that we are only now beginning to understand and build upon.[12]

There are many reasons why we non-indigenous jurists should be open to the creation of such hybrid processes and institutions. All have to do with the participation of indigenous people – and the reflection of indigenous culture – in the institutions that will govern their lives. The three chapters discussed here emphasize the value of indigenous agency in the resolution of indigenous disputes. Moreover, we should not underestimate the extent to which indigenous peoples distrust non-indigenous institutions.

Non-indigenous jurists tend to be quite nimble in their understanding of the law. They work with and for the law's evolution, and one of the ways they do so is by seizing upon principles or themes in the law, suggesting how they are best developed. In doing so, they often state that the law requires this and that, using the language of description – language that purports to say what the law *is* – in a manner that is really meant to exhort – to affirm how the law *should be* interpreted.

There is nothing wrong with this way of proceeding. The law evolves through argument about its central principles, what those principles are, what they mean, and their implications for new issues or unresolved challenges. One of the forms that that argument takes is an assertion that a certain interpretation is the best view of the law – that it is the interpretation most compatible with a commitment to justice taken to be inherent in the law. But although we all engage in those kinds of arguments, we should be careful not to fall into the trap of thinking that such assertions are an accurate description of the way in which the law has been applied in the past. We should not confuse exhortation with true description.

When we do focus on description, we often find that the law has earned well the distrust of indigenous peoples – even if we would now agree that the occurrences that generated that distrust were the product of a poor understanding of the law or indeed plainly unlawful conduct by state actors. Like all human institutions, the law never lives up to its best aspirations, and certainly did not live up to the aspirations that we now, retrospectively, ascribe to it. When dealing with state institutions, indigenous people naturally want to pay attention to the law as it has been in practice, not merely to its best image of itself.

That realization explains the vehemence in many indigenous peoples' suspicion of the law and its institutions. After all, the abuses of the past (if they are past) are often covered by a remarkably shallow layer of earth, especially for those on the receiving end. The realization reinforces the desirability of having indigenous peoples involved in the resolution of their own disputes, through mechanisms that provide for their substantial participation.

Final Comments

The sheer variety of the mechanisms of dispute settlement canvassed in these three chapters is indicative of the range of experimentation now occurring in indigenous communities and in institutions designed to cross the indigenous/non-indigenous divide. There are many issues still to be resolved, as those mechanisms are tried, adjusted, retained, or rejected. One, raised by Chief Justice Yazzie's invocation of non-punitive means for dealing with family violence cases, is whether some kinds of disputes are more appropriate than others for consensual, community-based resolution. There has been disquiet among some Aboriginal women in Canada with the submission of family violence cases to processes such as circle sentencing because of the pressures that often arise in small communities, where victims may be very vulnerable.[13] Forms of indigenous justice may have to be modulated to different issues in different contexts.

This must happen, however, through active indigenous involvement in the design and operation of dispute settlement mechanisms, to ensure the cultural responsiveness of those mechanisms, to ensure indigenous participation in decisions central to their communities, and to ensure that the institutions that result do a better job of delivering justice than the wholly non-indigenous institutions of the past.

Notes

1 For an excellent introduction to what is now a voluminous literature, see Hilary Astor and Christine Mary Chinkin, *Dispute Resolution in Australia*, 2nd ed. (Sydney: Butterworths, 2002), chap. 5.
2 See the description of the treaty process in Canada in Alexander Morris, *The Treaties of Canada with the Indians of Manitoba and the North-West Territories* (Toronto: Belfords, Clarke and Co., 1880; facsimile edition published in Saskatoon, SK: Fifth House Publishers, 1991); and in New Zealand in Claudia Orange, *The Treaty of Waitangi* (Wellington: Bridget Williams Books, 1987).
3 Native Title Act, 1993 (Cth). For the link between land claims and organizational development in the Australian case, see Peter Yu, "Multilateral Agreements – A New Accountability in Aboriginal Affairs" in Galarrwuy Yunupingu, ed., *Our Land is Our Life: Land Rights – Past, Present and Future* (St. Lucia: University of Queensland Press, 1997); Patrick Sullivan, "Dealing with Native Title Conflicts by Recognising Aboriginal Authority Systems" in Diane Smith and Julie Finlayson, eds., *Fighting Over Country: Anthropological Perspectives* (Canberra: Centre for Aboriginal Economic Policy Research, 1997), 129; Mary Edmunds, ed., *Regional Agreements: Key Issues in Australia*, vols. 1 and 2 (Canberra: Australian Institute of Aboriginal and Torres Strait Islander Studies, 1998).
4 The Cree dimension of this process is well described in Ignatius LaRusic et al., "Negotiating a Way of Life: Initial Cree Experience with the Administrative Structure Arising from the James Bay Agreement" (Department of Indian and Northern Affairs, October 1979) at 9ff.

5 The phrase is taken from H.W. Arthurs, *"Without the Law": Administrative Justice and Legal Pluralism in Nineteenth-Century England* (Toronto: University of Toronto Press, 1985), who in turn adapted it (at v) from William Hutton: "If the Commissioners cannot decide *against* the law, they can decide without it. Their oath binds them to proceed according to good conscience."
6 *Mabo* v. *Queensland (No 2)* (1992) 175 C.L.R. 1.
7 Jeremy Webber, "Beyond Regret: *Mabo's* Implications for Australian Constitutionalism" in D. Ivison et al., eds., *Political Theory and the Rights of Indigenous Peoples* (Cambridge, UK: Cambridge University Press, 2000), 62-63, 73, 83ff.
8 Richard White, *The Middle Ground: Indians, Empires, and Republics in the Great Lakes Region, 1650-1815* (Cambridge, UK: Cambridge University Press, 1991); Royal Commission on Aboriginal Peoples, *Partners in Confederation: Aboriginal Peoples, Self-Government, and the Constitution* (Ottawa: Minister of Supply and Services, 1993), 5-27; Jeremy Webber, "Relations of Force and Relations of Justice: The Emergence of Normative Community Between Colonists and Aboriginal Peoples" (1995) 33 Osgoode Hall Law Journal 623.
9 See Webber, "Beyond Regret," 70-73.
10 See, for example, *Royal Commission on the Donald Marshall, Jr., Prosecution: Commissioners' Report-Finding and Recommendations* (Halifax: Province of Nova Scotia, 1989), esp. 161ff.
11 In the Canadian context see, for example, Jean-Paul Brodeur et al., *Justice for the Cree: Final Report* (Grand Council of the Crees [of Quebec] and Cree Regional Authority, August 1991); Inuit Justice Task Force, *Aqqusiurniq Sivunitsasiaguniqsamut: Blazing the Trail to a Better Future: Inuit Justice Task Force Final Report* (Inuit Justice Task Force, 1993); Royal Commission on Aboriginal Peoples, *Bridging the Cultural Divide: A Report on Aboriginal People and Criminal Justice in Canada* (Ottawa: Minister of Supply and Services, 1996). An early and extensive consideration of the incorporation of indigenous customary law into criminal proceedings is found in Australian Law Reform Commission, *Report No 31: The Recognition of Aboriginal Customary Laws* (Canberra: Australian Government Publishing Service, 1986), vol. 1, 58-59, 279-398.
12 This is the central argument in Webber, "Beyond Regret."
13 See, for example, Teressa Nahanee, "Dancing with a Gorilla: Aboriginal Women, Justice and the Charter" in Royal Commission on Aboriginal Peoples, ed., *Aboriginal Peoples and the Justice System: Report of the National Round Table on Aboriginal Justice Issues* (Ottawa: Minister of Supply and Services, 1993), 359; Royal Commission on Aboriginal Peoples, *Bridging the Cultural Divide*, 269-75. See also the excellent discussion of responses to family violence in the Inuit villages of northern Quebec in Susan Drummond, *Incorporating the Familiar: An Investigation into Legal Sensibilities in Nunavik* (Montreal: McGill-Queen's University Press, 1997).

Part 3:
Canadian Contexts

The previous section showed broad challenges of establishing mechanisms of dispute resolution able to do justice to Aboriginal perspectives and interests, given differing national contexts. Part 3 sharpens our sense of these challenges by focusing on how Aboriginal interests and perspectives might best be asserted in negotiations and legal reforms in Canada. Each chapter in this section focuses on some particular set of tensions between mainstream Canadian ways and Aboriginal law (between Western scientific paradigms and Aboriginal wisdom, for example, or between understandings of reconciliation); each then offers a vision of how dispute resolution mechanisms could more adequately addresses Aboriginal needs and ways.

10
Weche Teachings: Aboriginal Wisdom and Dispute Resolution
Elmer Ghostkeeper

Those engaged in the practice of "dispute resolution appreciate that different cultures have different and equally complex approaches to resolving disputes. Culture is important not only in understanding what is meant by conflict but also in how parties to a dispute and dispute resolution prac-titioners approach, process, and resolve conflicts. There is also increased awareness about the importance of communicating across cultures, being sensitive to learned behaviours, and respecting difference. However, those of us involved in dispute resolution also need to be more aware of the different knowledge systems, concepts, and assumptions of fact that inform the content of our communications. Our focus is often on adopting appropriate patterns of behaviour, rather than understanding and respecting the knowledge, wisdom, and value that form our communications with each other about conflict.

The purpose of this chapter is to introduce key concepts and values based in Aboriginal knowledge systems. In particular, I explore the potential partnership between Aboriginal wisdom and Western scientific knowledge through the concept of *Wechewehtowin*, a Woodland Cree word meaning "partnershipping," and *Weche*, meaning a "partnership." I use *Weche* here to refer to a partnership of Aboriginal wisdom and Western scientific knowledge. To demonstrate my theory of *Weche*, I focus on Metis values, my experiences in the forest industry, and my experience as president of, and part of the negotiating team for, the Federation of Metis Settlements. I conclude by looking at the Metis settlements legislation and raise some questions I think Aboriginal people must consider in any dispute resolution process or design.[1]

I tend to approach complex issues as puzzles rather than problems. By starting off with one or two pieces of a puzzle, a person is more likely to find positive solutions and to successfully piece together a whole picture. If, on the other hand, complex issues such as land conflicts between Aboriginal and non-Aboriginal people are viewed as problems, it is hard to move forward from this negative position. *Weche* is best understood as a partnership between different belief systems that can be used to analyze and resolve such complex puzzles. I see it as a path for Aboriginal people to find pieces to puzzles that have been challenging us for quite some time.

Aboriginal Wisdom

I grew up as a Metis on the Paddle Prairie Metis Settlement in northern Alberta. Although the phrase "traditional knowledge" is often used at universities and other institutions of learning to describe the type of belief system that influenced my learning, I describe it as "Aboriginal wisdom." By Aboriginal wisdom I mean the body of information, rules, beliefs, values, behavioural and learning experiences, which made existence possible and meaningful for the Metis before we became "overwhelmed by the influence of foreign codes."[2] I reject the phrase "traditional knowledge" because it suggests old and aging. As people we are just as contemporary and creative as others. We do have old traditions, but we also have current practices that form part of our wisdom. The phrase "Aboriginal wisdom" captures this notion of being.

A fundamental concept in Aboriginal wisdom is the need to respect and balance the four aspects of self. In Cree, my first language, *neyo seniw neya* means I am a person with four aspects of self: mind, body, emotion, and spirit. These are depicted in Figure 10.1.

Many Aboriginal people believe if we balance these four aspects of self

Figure 10.1

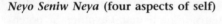

Neyo Seniw Neya (four aspects of self)

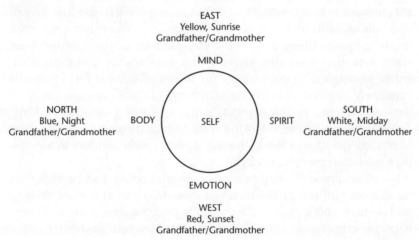

EAST
Yellow, Sunrise
Grandfather/Grandmother

MIND

NORTH   BODY   SELF   SPIRIT   SOUTH
Blue, Night   White, Midday
Grandfather/Grandmother   Grandfather/Grandmother

EMOTION

WEST
Red, Sunset
Grandfather/Grandmother

in everything we do, we will be healed, whole, happy, and healthy. However, if one of these aspects of self is repressed or impaired, we are no longer in harmony with ourselves or our world. This can lead to disease and sickness. For example, grief negatively affects the physical aspect of health. If the emotional aspect of grief is not allowed to run its course, it can also adversely affect the mental and spiritual aspects of self. In the context of land claims negotiations, balance means we must consider our emotional, spiritual, and physical connection to our traditional territories. We cannot abandon these aspects of self and focus solely on Western intellectual paradigms of legal rights and scientific fact. We must balance all aspects of ourselves in order to maintain happiness and wellness as individuals and as a people.

Another belief we have is that every day that we live is a gift from the Creator and Mother Earth. We live moment to moment, and this moment is our past, present, and future all in one. Everything is one as created by the Great Spirit. Consequently, every living thing on earth has the same four aspects of self that we do. This understanding of ourselves and our connection to nature is what we call a holistic worldview. Everything, even objects Western culture may view as inanimate, has a soul; in our worldview, this means all life is sacred.

Aboriginal wisdom is an ancient form of knowledge derived from experience with nature. It is usually passed down through generations and taught by wise people who have acquired wisdom through a lifetime of learning. However, this form of wisdom is often undervalued, especially by non-Aboriginal people. For meaningful communication to occur between Aboriginal and non-Aboriginal peoples in the land claims context, or any other negotiation, Aboriginal wisdom must be accepted in partnership, fellowship, and equity with other knowledge systems. In particular, it must be treated with respect and given equally serious consideration as Western scientific knowledge, which is often used to measure the nature of Aboriginal attachment to land and the legitimacy of their claims to it.

Aboriginal Wisdom and Western Scientific Knowledge
Modern science emerged as an important stream in Western thought approximately five hundred years ago. It is a Western belief system and nothing more. It is one way of organizing thoughts and ideas about the physical aspects of nature. However, it is given a place of priority and infallibility in Western hierarchies of knowledge. It is mostly about measurement of physical reality by mathematics and deductive reasoning. It has clear rules about what is real, what contributes to knowledge, what is excluded, what is myth, and what is fact. For example, scientists still debate whether inductive reasoning based on our personal experiences

is a reliable source of truth and knowledge, yet 80 percent of the decisions we make in our daily lives are based on inductive reasoning. It does not make sense to Aboriginal people to exclude our daily experiences of nature, and our stories about those experiences, from the realm of fact. However, this is what science would have us do.

Scientists argue that science is really about trying to discover or prove what we call laws of nature. Scientists tend to package these laws into theories, principles, models, and paradigms. Ironically, at the same time, science often denies or excludes our understandings of the world based on our experiences with nature. In this way, science promotes what I view as a "culture/nature dualism." The word "culture," as I understand it, is linked to the word "cultivate." The more Europeans cultivated nature and transformed the land to their use, the more they thought they acquired culture. The farther and farther removed they became from cultivating and dominating nature on a daily basis, the more cultured they became in the eyes of their own societies; the farther they moved away from daily experiences of nature toward thinking about and rationalizing laws of nature, the more cultured they became. Understood in this way, "culture" is an attribute of European people. It represents, in their worldview, domination over, and separation of identity from, nature.

I ask myself what pieces of the puzzle are missing from this European picture of knowledge and culture. I would like to share with you the answer that came to me in a dream in December 1996. I woke up with a new picture in mind that I call my circle of knowing. I realized that over time, science has repressed wisdom derived from personal learning experiences and connection with nature. Science has difficulty measuring things that cannot be quantified. It cannot quantify the spirit, emotion, and personal experiences with nature. It cannot plot these things mathematically on the Cartesian split of the x and y axis. It cannot recognize many individual rules and theories in its search for universal truths and laws of nature. Yet, in Aboriginal wisdom, a fundamental source of truth is our daily experience with nature. In my opinion, this means there is no wisdom in science itself, but there is significant wisdom in the experiences of scientists. Science is a system of knowing that contributes to wisdom, but science alone is not the equivalent of wisdom. This understanding of wisdom is reflected in my circle of knowing, depicted in Figure 10.2.

The question arises: How do I take this circle of knowing and my understanding of the relationship of science to wisdom and apply this to everyday thought puzzles that we as Aboriginal people face? Figure 10.3 represents the way that I have come to work with this circle of knowing and how I have attempted to understand the differences and relationships between Aboriginal wisdom and Western scientific knowledge.

It is clear that Aboriginal and scientific belief systems have two different foundations for truth and procedures to ascertain truth, but both are valid. Aboriginal wisdom is viewed by Aboriginal people as sacred – a gift from the Creator. It is sacred because it is holistic and it ensures that we retain all four aspects of our self. Aboriginal wisdom is also reciprocal in the sense that we believe that everything is one. For example, when we are born, we are about 98 percent water, and if we live to be a bright old age, we might leave Mother Earth with about 66 percent water content. We are nature. We are the environment. We are one. We observe and analyze everything holistically using our mind, spirit, emotion, and body. Our wisdom views experiential interactions as the primary learning process. Wisdom sits in our personal experience and the experience of others. It is both old and current knowledge primarily passed on through oral histories and stories that contain many teachings and lessons in many forms. Ceremonies, rituals, and sacrifices communicate and celebrate our wisdom. These stories and ceremonies are an integral part of our communication with each other and the world. Performing proper protocols is also an essential part of the communication process. We must be true to these beliefs in all our communications about our lands and our life on those lands to remain balanced as individuals and as a people.

Science is fragmented because it represses emotion and spirit and cannot measure them on the x and y axis. As René Descartes put it, "I think therefore I am."[3] People grounded in this knowledge system sometimes have difficulty understanding the relevance of what we need to communicate as Aboriginal people about our relationship to land. They listen to a story and try to discern a scientific fact, rather than personal, spiritual, or emotional connection, or they ask us to reduce our teachings to what we can

Figure 10.2

My circle of knowing

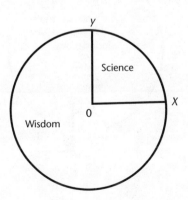

prove by Western scientific methods. There is little room at many negotiation tables for spirituality, emotion, or experience that is not also supported by scientific fact.

Weche Teachings

What I call *Weche* teachings is a partnership between these two belief systems. I first began to think about the two knowledge systems in this way when I was working in the forestry industry. I worked for a major forest company, Alberta Pacific Forestry Industries (Alpac), for five years. Alpac initiated cultural land-use studies in areas where logging was to take place. They studied how Aboriginal people living in the northern boreal forest used the land because they did not want their forestry activities to have a significant negative impact on cultural land-use activities, such as berry picking. I was part of a team asked to help ascertain how many edible berries existed within the areas we intended to log. I answered the question by seeking the wisdom of people who gathered the berries and who felt confident enough to eat them without fear of poisoning. When I asked them how many types of edible berries were in the area, those who still made a living by working the land named seventeen without hesitation.

Figure 10.3

Aboriginal wisdom and Western scientific knowledge

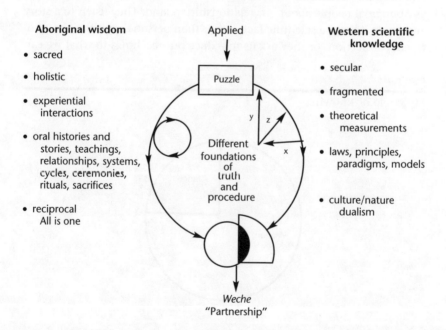

When I asked the same question of the chief forester and the biologist also on the team, the forester was able to name six and the biologist five. It was clear to me that there was more Aboriginal wisdom on the existence of edible berries than there was expert scientific opinion. We know more about what is edible and what is not in the northern territories where we live. We have acquired that knowledge through our experience. We have more knowledge because biologists have not studied every part of the North. This is one example of Aboriginal wisdom.

Another issue we examined at Alpac was the impact of forestry on wildlife, such as moose populations. As part of this process we had to consider the many uses of *moosewa* and why Aboriginal people valued the moose. When I approached Aboriginal people in northern Alberta to ask these questions, it was interesting how many uses they were able to describe. Aboriginal people who made a livelihood with the land identified sixty-three ways to use *moosewa*. However, when I asked the same questions of the chief forester and the biologist, they came up with only two uses. Again, this demonstrates that Aboriginal wisdom can be a great source of knowledge based on experience with the land.

Weche teachings can also be used to understand the Metis settlements legislation and to analyze what was accomplished by the Federation of Metis Settlements. I was very fortunate to be a part of the constitutional process when Aboriginal rights were included in the Canadian Constitution. In the 1980s, the Federation of Metis Settlements was struggling with a number of disputes we wanted to resolve with the provincial government of Alberta. In most of our meetings, we spoke Cree. The majority of the Metis at that time spoke Cree as their first language and English as a second language. So, when we discussed land, we always spoke in Cree. It was in this language we were best able to express our relationship to the land and its importance to us as the people. From our perspective, land was a gift from the Creator. We viewed ourselves as part of the land, nature, and the environment. As Adrian Hope, a Metis wise man, often said, "we belong to the land and the land does not belong to us."[4] I have described this relationship to the land as part of Aboriginal wisdom in my book *Spirit Gifting* in this way:

> This knowledge involve[s] a sacred worldview in which the Great Spirit, who can also be conceived as our Creator, our Father, or our Mother, created spirit helpers and messengers, referred to as our Grandfathers and our Grandmothers. Our Creator also created the land as a gift, referred to as Mother Earth. Plants, people, and other animals [are] also viewed as gifts because they [are] part of the land. Relationships between people and other gifts [are] characterized by spiritual exchanges which continually renew the body, mind, emotion and spirit.

Our [traditional] way of making a living was *with* the land. The land was used for basic subsistence with small surplus, rather than for profit, and the use of land was marked by an ongoing round of ceremonies, rituals, and sacrifices. The gifts from Mother Earth were viewed in concrete terms, and ownership was viewed as collective stewardship. The essence of holistic livelihood was sharing, giving and receiving in an attempt to keep body, mind, emotion and spirit in balance. To the extent this was done, the individual existed in a spiritual state, and was happy and healthy.[5]

This concept of land, our relationship to it, and its relationship to our spiritual and physical health was difficult for the government people to understand. To this day I am not sure that they understand completely, but they did come to understand that land was integral to our mental, physical, spiritual, and emotional well-being as a people and as individuals. Unlike the people we were negotiating with, we viewed ourselves as working *with* the land rather than *off* the land. It is a subtle but important distinction that connotes a relationship of equality rather than dominance. Our relationship to land is based on spirituality in the sense of sharing, giving, receiving, and repaying. This was the essence of our subsistence way of life taught to us by our elders and celebrated in our ceremonies. It is what I refer to as "spirit gifting" or the concept of spiritual exchange. Every time we harvest a living being, like a plant or an animal, we must ask it to sacrifice its life for our sustenance. Sacrifice means giving from the heart. This can be contrasted to the Western concept of land, which emphasizes productive land use and economic development *of the land,* rather than relationship *with the land.* People, and their uses of land, evolve over time. People are viewed as separate from, and dominant over, nature. Indeed, as I explained earlier, under the Western concept of culture, the more you cultivate and dominate nature, the more removed from the land you become and the more culture you acquire. This is working *off* the land, not *with* the land.

Capitalism is the main economic paradigm within which we are forced to negotiate and talk with non-Aboriginal people about our land. When this is combined with our different understandings of land and concepts of knowledge, many barriers to meaningful communication and agreement arise. I recall, for example, the difficulty we had communicating issues of economic land development in our negotiations with the province. We as Aboriginal people fear placing priority on technology and development. People rely so much on technology that it threatens to lead us, rather than us leading the uses of technology. There is a tremendous dependence on technology to cultivate nature. However, we also recognized that the province needed the benefits of our land and that we had to adapt aspects of our relationship with the land to a certain extent in order to survive in today's economy. Survival in Alberta is based on economic growth, participation in a currency-based economy, and financial stability. To survive as an Aboriginal people, we must also sustain economic growth, since we participate in the money economy. We must be concerned about jobs, keeping up with rates of inflation, and the increasing cost of living. However, for us this does not mean that ownership of land and resources brings with it the right to dominate land and resources; this is what ownership in the Western world is primarily about. It also does not mean capitalism should be the only paradigm within which we define our relationship to the land. Although we understand the need for economic development, our relationship to the land must continue to be collective stewardship so that all four aspects of ourselves, including our spiritual relationship with the land, can survive. Figure 10.4 illustrates how the *Weche* teachings helped me approach this puzzle.

When we negotiated the Metis settlements legislation, we tried to keep the fundamental principles, what I call "Metism," in place. When I talk about Metism, I am talking about the Metis way of doing things and Metis wisdom. I first articulated this notion of Metism in a paper I wrote for Professor Thomas Flanagan. I took his course, The Development of Radicalism

Figure 10.4

Weche and economic development

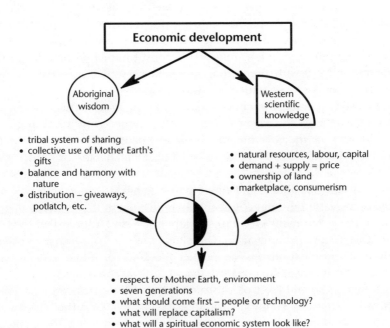

in Western Canada, at the University of Calgary. Louis Riel was one of the main characters of discussion. Professor Flanagan's thesis was that Louis Riel was a rebel and a radical. The word "radical" comes from the Latin *radix,* which simply means "root"; "radical" means "going to the roots." However, the term "radical" is often used in a pejorative way and invoked together with notions of resistance, difference, and change. Louis Riel was trying to change the existing system of government, or lack of government, to serve the need of Metis people and others in western Canada. In my opinion, he was not a radical in any pejorative sense of the term, but a hero. I wrote my paper "Metism: A Canadian Identity" to express my opinions. Riel was simply about change – a change for the betterment of the Metis. This essay later became the foundation for the position of the Federation of Metis Settlements at the national constitutional level. We called it *Metism: A Canadian Identity.*[6]

Metism: A Canadian Identity explains our historical relationship to our lands, and how the system of ownership and government of settlement lands needed to change to meet the needs of Metis people on settlement lands. It also explains our relationship to the land in a way that governments could understand in the legal language of the day; that is, we articulate our connection to the land in terms of a claim for Aboriginal title. We also call for the federal government to become involved in our negotiations with the province to protect our lands. However, it refused to do so. It is beyond the scope of this chapter to go into details of the constitutional discussions. The rights of the Metis people were the subject of national debate, and we did not want the progress that we had made with the province to be lost in the debate at the national forum.[7] Consequently, we focused our negotiations outside the constitutional process. This culminated in 1990 with the signing of the Metis Settlements Accord and enactment of the Metis settlements legislation.

The first legislation we wanted enacted was the Metis Settlements Land Protection Act. At the time we were very concerned with protecting the Metis land from the government. The government could dissolve the settlements if it thought the land was no longer suitable for, or needed by, Metis people. In the past, the government had taken back four settlements; it did not understand the importance of our connection to that land or, at least, it did not consider our connection to that land as important as the government's need to develop it. It was very important to prevent this from happening again. Our elders stressed that our number one priority in negotiations was to protect the land for future generations because it was integral to our wisdom and survival as a people.

Another important piece of legislation is the Metis Settlements Act.[8] This act provides greater autonomy for Metis people living on the settlement land. It recognizes three institutions of Metis government: the General

Council, settlement councils, and the Metis Settlements Appeal Tribunal. The General Council is composed of representatives from all the settlement governments. It makes policies affecting collective interests of the settlements, such as mineral and resource development. The settlement councils also have bylaw-making powers over matters of a more local nature that must be consistent with General Council policies. In this way the General Council and settlement councils act as the legislative arm of Metis settlements government. The tribunal, discussed later in this volume, is the dispute resolution arm.[9]

Weche teachings can be applied to help understand what we achieved through this legislation and what happened during the negotiation process. Collective ownership and stewardship of land is retained by us, and in this way our spiritual connection is maintained. However, we also include the Western concept of fee simple land ownership. The General Council has legal title to settlement land. However, there is still collective ownership by settlement councils through Metis title. Individual Metis and settlement councils cannot sell or devise land to non-settlement members. A partnership is developed between Metis concepts of land and Western concepts of ownership. There is also co-management of subsurface resources, another form of partnership. Although the province retains ownership of subsurface resources, Metis people control access and share in profits. They can also deny access and prevent development of land because of potential negative cultural or environmental impact.

One of the major disputes that we had to resolve was natural resources litigation we commenced in the late 1970s. In a way, the settlements legislation can be viewed as the conflict resolution agreement. The settlements argued that we were entitled to money from subsurface resources based on the negotiations and terms of the 1938 Metis betterment legislation.[10] However, the province disagreed. We relied on our understanding of an Order-in-Council establishing the Metis population trust fund, which provided that "all monies derived from sale of natural resources" would be "deposited into the population betterment trust fund."[11] However, the Crown interpreted this as meaning surface resources only. We also discovered that it was diverting monies intended for the fund into the provincial general revenue. Although we were not successful at acquiring ownership of all subsurface resources, we did gain significant control over land development and participation in profits. This was key because the importance of economic development and resources to Alberta could always threaten our relationship to land.

In terms of maintaining our identity, we acquired the right to define who is a Metis person for the purposes of entitlement to membership on Metis settlement land and for the purposes of being members of our community. However, the legislation does not expressly recognize Metis self-determination or Metis Aboriginal title. Although we talked about these things in the 1980s, our subsequent negotiations focused on communicating the central role of land in our lives, our relationship to it, and why we needed greater control over it to maintain our livelihood and survival as a people. We did not focus on proof of Aboriginal title using scientific methods as measurements of our rights. We found a common understanding and mutual goal in the concept of well-being. Catherine Bell suggests that the settlements legislation might be construed as satisfying claims to Metis Aboriginal title.[12] However, I do not think so. I think there are still tremendous opportunities for the Metis settlements to take our progress one step farther and to have our Aboriginal rights recognized under s.35 of the Constitution Act, 1982.[13] Indeed, as Professor Bell points out, our legislation states expressly that there is no intent to affect s.35 rights.

Section 35 provides that the Aboriginal people of Canada include the Indian, Inuit, and Metis, and that existing Aboriginal and treaty rights are recognized and affirmed. The word "existing" was proposed by then Alberta premier Peter Lougheed. I agreed with the inclusion of this word because I felt that the Metis people were an existing people and had existed since before Confederation. In my mind, the inclusion of the word "existing" did not affect the Metis Aboriginal title or Aboriginal rights. However, the provincial government wanted to avoid any mention of Aboriginal rights in the provincial negotiations and legislation. There were many reasons for this; one being debated was whether the provincial government had jurisdiction to pass legislation affecting Aboriginal people. Consequently, the provincial view is that our rights flow from the Metis settlements legislation. Although we disagree, we accepted this legislative framework because we were able to develop a relationship of mutual trust and respect with the province. We also found ways to protect our land outside the constitutional Aboriginal rights process. We were after results, not recognition of legal rights. My argument was that Metis Aboriginal title and provincial Crown ownership were mirror images of each other. One people did not have the right to extinguish or terminate rights of another, but only to recognize and respect them. In my opinion, we simply had to find a way to understand each other in order to make the changes that were necessary to meet our mutual concerns about survival and well-being.

It should be mentioned that most of the credit for the accomplishments of the Metis settlements goes to the fathers of the Federation of Metis Settlements: Adrian Hope, Richard Poitras, Sam Johnson, Maurice L'Hirondelle, and Lawrence Desjarlais. Four of these leaders have passed on into the spirit world. The only living member of the original leaders is Lawrence Desjarlais from the Elizabeth Metis Settlement.

Not all aspects of our legislation reflect our traditional values. Even though we grew to understand each other and respect each other's wisdom, both sides had to make compromises. We as the Metis people also had to make choices about what was necessary to move into the future, what we were able to change, and what we needed to keep the same. For example, under this legislation the provincial government has veto over our law-making power. I think this is wrong. Although the provincial government has never questioned a policy that the General Council has enacted, the potential for conflict is present if the relationship of trust, cooperation, and understanding breaks down. On the other hand, we now own our land in collective fee simple title: we can control its development and our relationship with it. Ultimately, I think the Canadian Constitution should be the authority on the question of Aboriginal rights, not the provincial government. Aboriginal people should have control over their own spirituality. We have taken significant steps in protecting our wisdom and spirituality with the protection of our land. Our title has not been extinguished, nor has our spirituality or our identity as the people.

Conclusion

What have I learned from these experiences and my reflections on the *Weche* teachings? I have learned that when you participate in any type of dispute resolution process, there are some key factors to consider. One factor is the language for negotiations. Will you use an Aboriginal language, and whose concepts are you going to adopt? Aboriginal language may be necessary to communicate Aboriginal concepts. Are you going to use the European concept of culture? You must remember that culture is only a concept and concepts exist in our minds. We can use our own concepts, and help others to understand our systems of knowledge, with time and patience. We can also build on our knowledge and relationships through a partnership of Aboriginal and Western concepts and values. This is the lesson of the Metis settlements legislation and the *Weche* teachings.

We must also think about the terminology we have been using in dispute resolution practice and literature. For example, some of the elders I work with do not use the word "culture" because they say it is not properly applied to Aboriginal people. We do not believe that we are separate from nature. Consequently, I even question if it is an appropriate concept to use in describing communications between Aboriginal and non-Aboriginal people or in trying to describe our worldview. I also question the label "intercultural dispute resolution." This is the language of Western science, not the language of Aboriginal wisdom or *Weche*.

Years ago I stopped using the word "cross-cultural" because I do not really know what it means. Even though I have studied culture for years as an anthropologist, the more I think about it, the more I realize this term does not apply to me. Let me conclude with an example. While I was teaching at McGill University, I met one of the top scientific researchers in the basement of the MacDonald Stewart Building. I asked him, "Tim, what are you doing down here?" He replied, "I am down here to check my cultures." I said, "Oh, I am interested in cultures as well." I was thinking human cultures. Tim said, "Well let me show you mine." He took me over to a big fridge and opened the door. "I have 200 cultures in here," he said. He was growing fungus cultures in petri dishes. I said to him, "Thank you very much, because you just put the culture in context for me." And that is the proper context for the concept of culture. It is to cultivate nature. It is scientific. I do not think it applies to people, to ideas, and to experiences. However, as social scientists we grab concepts from other disciplines, such as biology, and call them our own, rather than think up our own, more appropriate, terminology.

I have similar problems with the term "political science." This suggests to me that the study of politics alone is not an academic discipline. One has to tack on "science" to make it a legitimate field of study. We also create other studies, such as "environmental science." The use of the word "science" suggests these fields are not good enough to stand on their own; they must be propped with the belief system of science to acquire legitimacy.

We have resolved a number of major disputes with the Metis settlements legislation. Some of the major puzzles we encountered in our relations with the provincial government of Alberta were solved by partnering Aboriginal wisdom and Western knowledge, rather than adopting a hierarchy of knowledge and value systems. However, there is still a lot of work for us to do. We now have to link the Metis legislation to the Canadian Constitution. In my view, we are recognized in the Constitution, but we need to articulate why we are there and to guide non-Aboriginal people, especially those sitting across the table from us, in an understanding of what we are about as Metis. We are not about taking anything away from Canada, but rather, adding to Canada. We are not about taking anything away from nature, but rather, maintaining our relationship with our land. We are about being nature. We have tremendous opportunities as we head into this new millennium if we can work together in a partnership of Aboriginal wisdom and Western scientific knowledge and respect.

Notes

1 In 1990 the Province of Alberta enacted four pieces of legislation to implement a land, resource, and government agreement between the Federation of Metis Settlements and the Province of Alberta. From 1980 to 1984 I was the president of the Federation of Metis Settlements and helped to negotiate this agreement. See the Metis Settlements Act, S.A. 1990, c.M-14.3; the Metis Settlements Accord Implementation Act, S.A. 1990, c.M-14.5; the Metis Settlements Land Protection Act, S.A. 1990, c.M-14.8; and the Constitution of Alberta Amendment Act, S.A. 1990, c.C-22.2 (collectively referred to as the Metis

settlements legislation). For further discussion of the history and government of the settlements see Catherine Bell, *Alberta's Metis Settlement's Legislation: An Overview of Ownership and Management of Settlement Lands* (Regina, SK: Canadian Plains Research Centre, 1994); Cathy Bell and MSAT, *Contemporary Metis Justice: The Settlement Way* (Saskatoon, SK: Native Law Centre, 1999); F. Martin, "Federal and Provincial Responsibility in the Metis Settlements of Alberta" in David Hawkes, ed., *Aboriginal Peoples and Government Responsibility: Exploring Federal and Provincial Roles* (Ottawa: Carleton University Press, 1989), 243; and Tom Pocklington, *The Government and Politics of the Alberta Metis Settlements* (Regina, SK: Canadian Plains Research Centre, 1991).

2 Elmer Ghostkeeper, *Spirit Gifting: The Concept of Spiritual Exchange* (Calgary, AB: Arctic Institute of North America, 1996), 48. In this publication I use the term "traditional knowledge," as it is a concept understood in academia and I was completing my master's degree in anthropology at the time. However, as explained in the text, I now prefer to use the phrase Metis "wisdom."

3 See René Descartes, "Meditation Two: Concerning the Nature of the Human Mind: That It Is Better Known than the Body," *Meditations on First Philosophy,* trans. John Cottingham (Cambridge: Cambridge University Press, 1986), 25-26.

4 I recall Adrian often sharing these words of wisdom in our discussions and at community gatherings.

5 Ghostkeeper, *Spirit Gifting,* 48.

6 Elmer Ghostkeeper and Federation of Metis Settlements, *Metism: A Canadian Identity* (Edmonton: Alberta Federation of Metis Settlements, 1982).

7 For greater discussion see the commentaries on the Metis settlements legislation noted at 1, and Catherine Bell, "Metis Government: The Alberta Metis Settlement Model" in John Hylton, ed., *Aboriginal Self-Government in Canada,* 2nd ed. (Saskatoon, SK: Purich Publishing, 1999).

8 The role of the tribunal and dispute resolution in the settlements is discussed in Bell and MSAT, *Contemporary Metis Justice.* The federal government did not agree to amend the Canadian Constitution to protect our land. Consequently, we negotiated an amendment to Alberta's constitution to protect our land and government. See Bell, *Alberta's Metis Settlement Legislation* and Martin, "Federal and Provincial Responsibility."

9 See Catherine Bell's chapter in this volume.

10 Pursuant to this act, O.C. 1785/43 was promulgated, providing for the creation of a Metis Population Betterment Trust Account. This and subsequent regulations provided that various revenues for resource development were to be put in the trust account. The provinces argued it did not include subsurface resources. See Bell, *Alberta's Metis Settlement Legislation,* 1.

11 O.C. 1785/43.

12 See Bell, *Alberta's Metis Settlement Legislation,* 78-81.

13 Schedule B of the Constitution Act, 1982 (U.K.), 1982, c.11.

11
Who Gets to Say What Happened?
Reconciliation Issues for the Gitxsan
Val Napoleon

> The truth is validated by the majority, they say. Or you bring
> your own version of the truth to the merciless arena of the past –
> only in this way does the past become thinkable, the world
> become habitable.
>
> – Antjie Krog, *Country of My Skull: Guilt,*
> *Sorrow, and the Limits of Forgiveness in the New*
> *South Africa*

If reconciliation for Aboriginal people in Canada is ever going to move beyond rhetoric, reconciliation discussions must include substantive societal and structural changes that deal with power imbalances, land, and resources.

The term "reconciliation" pervades the political discourse of indigenous nations around the world, but different people in widely disparate circumstances give it numerous meanings.[1] Presently in Canada, there is no common understanding of what reconciliation might mean for Aboriginal people and the Canadian state, nor are there any agreed reconciliation goals. Questions about who should reconcile, what should or can be reconciled, and how reconciliation should take place loom large on the political landscape.

The Gitxsan, along with their neighbours, the Wet'suwet'en, undertook the *Delgamuukw* Aboriginal title action.[2] Following the Supreme Court of Canada's 1997 decision, the Gitxsan resumed their negotiations with the Province of British Columbia, but this time ostensibly to implement the court's findings.

The purpose of this chapter is to review the several ways that reconciliation has been defined and applied, and to explore some of the reconciliation issues facing the Gitxsan nation.[3] I provide a brief background and description of the Gitxsan negotiation process for lands and resources and human services, a cursory exploration and critique of how reconciliation has been defined and applied in four different contexts, a description of reconciliation issues from a Gitxsan perspective, and preliminary recommendations for future action for the Gitxsan and the Canadian state as represented by the provincial and federal governments.

Background

In its 1997 ruling on *Delgamuukw* v. *British Columbia,*[4] the Supreme Court of Canada recommended that the reconciliation of the pre-existence of Aboriginal peoples with Crown sovereignty be negotiated between the Aboriginal parties and the Crown. Chief Justice Lamer wrote that, "ultimately, it is through negotiated settlements, with good faith and give and take on all sides, reinforced by the judgments of this Court, that we will achieve what I stated in *Van der Peet* ... to be a basic purpose of s.35(1) – 'the reconciliation of the pre-existence of Aboriginal societies with the sovereignty of the Crown.' Let us face it, we are all here to stay."[5]

The Gitxsan Nation and the Province of British Columbia signed a Reconciliation Agreement on 15 September 1998.[6] Its purpose was to resume negotiations on Aboriginal rights and title that the province suspended in 1996 to precipitate the resumption of the *Delgamuukw* appeal to the Supreme Court of Canada. To facilitate implementation of the terms of the Reconciliation Agreement, the Gitxsan and the province established two negotiating tables:

- *Ts'eetix*[7] *(lands and resources)*: This table was responsible for the bilateral lands and resource issues outlined in the Reconciliation Agreement. As part of this work, the Gitxsan established nine watershed tables as a way to organize and facilitate *wilp*[8] *(house)*, involvement.
- *Lippgyt*[9] *(human services)*: This table was responsible for the human resources issues arising from the Reconciliation Agreement. Its intent was to directly involve the houses as well as representatives from local community agencies working with education, training, social services, health, and justice.

For the Gitxsan, the reconciliation process with the province to date has been fraught with difficulty.[10] Too few resources, lack of political will, and bureaucratic stumbling blocks have meant little meaningful progress for negotiations. At a practical level, the lack of government political will has produced a common bureaucratic obstacle called "stove-piping," where government ministries function strictly independently and hierarchically, as if inside a vertical stovepipe. In this configuration, it is the Aboriginal group that must organize the ministries and make the necessary horizontal connections between the bureaucrats to enable holistic planning and resource sharing – an enormous, frustrating, and essentially unprofitable task for Aboriginal groups with too few resources.

Another practical problem created by the void in government commitment and direction is the inability of ministry bureaucrats to move beyond procedural change to substantive discussions. They limit negotiations to managing and financing the lowest operational levels of programs and services rather than addressing issues of overall design, social change, or the root causes of the massive social problems.

Exploring Reconciliation

Antjie Krog wrote: "And if you believe your own version [of the past], your own lie, how can it be said that you are being misleading? To what extent can you bring yourself not to know what you know? Eventually it is not the lie that matters, but that mechanism in yourself that allows you to accept distortions."[11]

In 1996, the film documentary *Blockade* premiered in Hazelton, British Columbia.[12] *Blockade* is about the Gitxsan peoples' struggle to protect their land and resources, and to assert ownership and control of their territories in northwestern BC. The film also tells the stories of the settlers and loggers who live on Gitxsan territory, who are dependent on primary resource extraction for their livelihood, and who are directly affected by Gitxsan direct political action.[13] Following the film presentation, director Nettie Wild facilitated a spirited discussion with the full-house audience of Gitxsan, settlers, and loggers. During this session, a settler expressed some bewilderment about all the conflict and referred longingly to the days of his grandparents when whites and Indians used to "get along" without any problems. A Gitxsan woman responded with, "I don't know what was going on in your grandparents' living room, but I know what was going in the living room of my grandparents, and they weren't experiencing any 'getting along.' They were in pain about losing their land."

This section explores how the concept of reconciliation has been defined and applied in policy and legal contexts in four areas, including Aboriginal title. For the Gitxsan, there are important lessons to be drawn from the reconciliation struggles around the world.

I use a law dictionary definition of reconciliation to provide a starting point. *Reconciliation,* as defined in *Black's Law Dictionary,* is "the renewal of amicable relations between two persons who had been at enmity or variance; usually implying forgiveness of injuries on one or both sides ... It means something more than mere resumption of cohabitation and observance of civility, and comprehends a fresh start and genuine effort by both parties to avoid pitfalls originally causing separation."[14] While this definition contemplates individuals in conflict, some elements of it can usefully be extended to large groups of people. It implies a historic relationship, conflict, injury, mutual commitment and effort, acceptance of responsibility, a common future, and most importantly, memory. It is memory that holds the truth of our experiences – the content of reconciliation – and what we do with our memories determines our capacity to imagine our future. This is the reason to reconcile. Part of reconciliation is about reconciling our memories – who gets to say what happened.

Restorative Justice

Restorative justice is simply a philosophical basis for thinking about crime and conflict, rather than a distinct model or system of law. Within the restorative justice framework, crime is a violation of people and relationships, and justice is a creation of obligations involving the victim, offender, family, and community to promote reparation and rehabilitation. In contrast, crime as viewed by the current system is a transgression of moral order and a violation of state rules. The overall goal of restorative justice is to create safe, peaceful communities and self-governing citizens.

In the restorative justice field, reconciliation is the concept usually applied to less serious crimes where there can actually be a righting of the wrong and a restoration of relationships.[15] Regarding the often criticized concept of relationships in crime situations, Howard Zehr writes, "crime also represents a ruptured relationship between the victim and offender. Even if they had no previous relationship, the crime itself creates a relationship. And that relationship is usually hostile."[16] Victim Offender Reconciliation Projects (VORPs) usually consist of a face-to-face encounter between the victim and the offender in cases that have entered the criminal justice process, and where the offender has admitted to the offence.[17] The majority of VORPs deal with young offenders, and the reconciling intervention is usually at the pre-sentencing stage in order to influence sentencing outcomes.

When the crime is more serious, involving murder, serial rape, aggravated sexual assault, armed robbery, and so on, the process is one of mediation rather than reconciliation, and sentences are not affected. In cases involving serious or violent crime, there is no bringing back of a murdered loved one or undoing of a rape, but a mediation process can enable victims and offenders to come to terms with the crime constructively, and in whatever way they need to, so that they can get on with their lives in the best and most productive way possible. Victim Offender Mediation Projects (VOMPs) are usually not related to the sentencing process but become involved during or after the offender's incarceration.[18] VOMP processes are not predicated on written agreement or restitution between victim and offender. Ordinarily, the VOMP process is considerably more in-depth and takes place over a longer time, with very careful facilitation of any face-to-face meeting.

According to the William Head Restorative Justice Study Group, restorative justice could play an important role for those inmates sentenced to two years or more, including those with life sentences.[19] At the 1999 Symposium on Restorative Justice and Serious Crime, held at William Head Institution, convicted bank robber John Lamoureux reminded his listeners that he came from a community, and when he has served his time, he will go back to a community. He went on to say, "I am the son of a mother and father. I have two daughters who are married to good men and I have grandchildren. I did not come from Pluto. The 'us and them' system does not work because it does not provide a bridge."[20]

At the same symposium, Phil, another inmate, said, "in our society, we [the offenders] are protected from the impact on the victim [by being incarcerated]."[21] As these quotes indicate, in the restorative justice context, reconciliation moves from the abstract realm to a profound, human level inside the very lives of victims, offenders, and their families and communities.[22]

There are many lessons to be learned from the human, face-to-face reconciliation in restorative justice, because the experience of colonialism has been violent and this violence has been internalized by many Aboriginal peoples. The imploding violence of many Aboriginal communities is a consequence of recent history, so on an external level, how does collective human dysfunction factor into discussions about reconciliation with Canada? On an internal level, Aboriginal peoples must deal with the experiential human level of reconciliation so that people who have hurt others, and those who have been hurt, can figure out how to live with one another peacefully, safely, and with dignity in Aboriginal or non-Aboriginal communities.

The accumulated experience and wisdom of national and international restorative justice initiatives constitutes an extensive and rich resource for the Gitxsan as they move beyond theory to begin addressing the human aspect of reconciliation. This work is about restoration of humanity, because as long as we perpetuate violence upon one another, we are lacking our essential humanity and are not yet whole.

Aboriginal and Crown Sovereignty

In his paper "Kindreds and States: Using Anglo-Saxon and Gitxsan Law to Help Reconcile Aboriginal and Crown Sovereignty,"[23] former *Ts'eetix* researcher Richard Overstall suggests using the theoretical device of structural essentialism to explicate the social and legal systems of Anglo-Saxon and Gitxsan societies for comparison. Structural essentialism assumes that deeper patterns can be discerned from observable social phenomena. It is these intrinsic patterns, or social structures, that mould the evolution of society and individual behaviour within it. Overstall suggests that such basic structures are limited in number and that similar structures form a template that produces similar practices in the people who live under them.[24]

Overstall identifies two basic social structures in the evolution of early Anglo-Saxon and Gitxsan societies.

The first of these is the kinship structure seen in Gitxsan society and in early medieval Anglo-Saxon society.[25] Through kinship relations, the family was extended into the broader social, political, and spiritual institutions so that family bonds also formed community and societal bonds.

The second basic structure is the warrior structure as it developed and separated in later medieval Anglo-Saxon society. Relationships of command and obedience organized the broader social, political, economic, and spiritual institutions that became separated from family life. During this period, English society changed from a kinship-based structure into a bureaucratized hierarchy with a sovereign monarch, the church, the military, and independent courts.[26] In direct contrast to the Anglo-Saxon divergence at this time, Gitxsan society remained kinship-based and decentralized. It is against this historical backdrop that Overstall places the *Delgamuukw* ruling and, specifically, Chief Justice Lamer's urging of Aboriginal parties and the Crown to negotiate their reconciliation. Gitxsan and other Northwest Coast societies have a basic social structure fundamentally different from that of the state as represented by the federal and provincial governments. These differences are felt most acutely in discussions on land rights, self-government, and the administration of justice.[27]

Overstall concludes that, given the nature and structure of Northwest Coast Aboriginal societies, the modern Anglo-Canadian common-law system, with its emphasis on equity roots and informal alternative dispute resolution processes, would be useful in reconciling Aboriginal and state jurisdictions. This is a more process-centred approach than the rule-centred approach of legal codes and colonial treaties.[28] He also suggests that the courts take a more proactive role in applying the principles of the law of equity in judicial reviews regarding consultation and infringement of title (beyond maintaining the commercial status quo).[29]

In the next chapter of this volume, Overstall also suggests that the equity device of the legal trust could serve as a creative buffer between a centralized state system and kinship-based Aboriginal systems.[30] This latter suggestion of the legal trust merits further exploration and testing. The trust is potentially a model capable of practically aligning Aboriginal legal orders with Western common law without undermining either, and it can sidestep the polarized issues of sovereignty and ownership. Furthermore, the trust is a flexible legal instrument that can be organized on different scales for small or large groups to deal with natural resources and land management.

Australian Council for Aboriginal Reconciliation

Some efforts at reconciliation appear to have been caught up more in the drama of public performance than in achieving any depth or substance. One example of this might be the 1991 Australian Council for Aboriginal

Reconciliation which was established by the federal Parliament.[31] The council envisioned "a united Australia which respects this land of ours; values Aboriginal and Torres Strait Islander heritage and provides justice and equity for all."[32]

The decade-long Australian reconciliation process principally focused on the education of non-Aboriginal Australians about the cultures of Australia's indigenous peoples and the causes of division, discord, and continuing injustice to Aboriginals and Torres Strait Islanders.[33] Eight key issues of the council's strategic reconciliation plan were framed around the need to

- understand the importance of the land and sea in Aboriginal and Torres Strait Islander societies;
- improve relationships between Aboriginals and Torres Strait Islanders and the wider community;
- value Aboriginal and Torres Strait Islander cultures in wider society;
- instill a sense of shared and owned history in all Australians;
- understand the disadvantages causing Aboriginals and Torres Strait Islanders to have poor health, housing, education, and employment;
- understand the underlying causes that give rise to high levels of custody of Aboriginal and Torres Strait Islander children;
- provide opportunities for Aboriginal and Torres Strait Islander peoples to control their destinies; and
- reach an agreement on whether the process of reconciliation would be advanced by a document of reconciliation.[34]

The Australian Council of Aboriginal Reconciliation held community consultations, hosted a national "Sorry Day," and convened a national convention before its term expired on 1 January 2001. The convention endorsed a "Call to the Nation" to translate the convention's energy and goodwill into Australian homes, schools, work places, and parliaments. According to the council, the phenomenon of the Bridge Walks for Reconciliation in capital cities and towns across Australia has demonstrated community support for reconciliation. Furthermore, over a million people have signed the "sorry books," tens of thousands have signed the council's "pledge books," and hundreds of local reconciliation groups across the country have taken action to promote reconciliation and address particular issues within their own communities.[35]

During the spring of 2000, shortly after one march by over 55,000 people, the Australian government expressed enthusiastic support for reconciliation. In response, the Native Title Unit manager, Mr. Parry Agius, suggested that more practical examples of reconciliation were necessary, "such as the scrapping of the State Government's proposed Native Title bill, and support for a treaty."[36] The council was obviously predicated on the belief that the conflicts in current-day Australia are caused by a simple lack of information and lack of understanding on the part of non-Aboriginal Australians about Aboriginals and Torres Strait Islanders and their cultures. Substantive issues relating to land and resources had remained outside the Australian reconciliation process.

The real problem is the dispute over land ownership and the marginalization of Aboriginals and Torres Strait Islanders because of the theft of their land. At issue, among other things, is the disastrous impact of recent history and the continued exclusion of Aboriginals and Torres Strait Islanders from decision making regarding lands and resources, and from revenue sharing. Dr. Larissa Behrendt argues that even when indigenous rights are recognized under the law, they are valued less than the property rights of other property holders.[37] To change this, Aboriginal property would have to be valued as non-indigenous property is valued, and Aboriginal title would have to be conceptualized as a valuable property right, similar to other property rights. Behrendt suggests that future interpretations of indigenous property must acknowledge the vulnerability of Aboriginal people to the potential abuse of power by the majority, and furthermore, that broad interpretations and protections are needed to counter power imbalances.[38] She writes: "'Property is a set of social relations among human beings.' The legal definition of those relationships confers or withholds power over others. Failure to assign protective property rights leaves people at risk, vulnerable to the will of others. Property rights held by indigenous Australians had no status under law and now have an uncertain legal status – uncertain because so many areas are left unclear in the *Mabo* case, and uncertain because the legislative [assembly] has sought to limit the scope of the legal decision and to extinguish certain native title rights."[39]

What appears to be missing from the Australian Council for Aboriginal Reconciliation's strategic plan is any substantive goal or process to deal with the real issues at the heart of the dispute: How will Aboriginal title be expressed in land and resource decisions? How will Aboriginal peoples and Torres Strait Islanders participate in those decisions? Finally, what real authority will Aboriginal peoples and Torres Strait Islanders be able to exercise in the decision making?

I also criticize the council and its mandate in that it was not reciprocal. There was no suggestion in the written materials that non-Aboriginal Australians explain *their* culture, or *their* relationship to land and sea, government policies, collective racism, or anything else. All the explaining and self-reflection took place in the Aboriginal and Torres Strait Islander communities. In the non-Aboriginal communities, the non-Aboriginal peoples had their awareness increased, but not about themselves. Instead, it is a one-way street, another example of the "Aboriginal people under glass" phenomenon.[40]

The reconciliation work undertaken in Australia was far-reaching and impressive. The Australian Reconciliation Council's website reveals many serious criticisms, as well as volumes of praise.[41] At the end of the day, however, Aboriginal and non-Aboriginal peoples must review what has been accomplished in the name of reconciliation because the work is far from complete. One issue yet to be explored is how the relationship between Aboriginal people and the Australian state (which represents the Australian citizenry) has been influenced or changed by the reconciliation decade. This should include an examination of how the changes are playing out in the political, legal, and social environment regarding treatment of land and resource issues and conflicts.

Ceremony and Ritual
In British Columbia, the instrument of public ceremony has been proposed as a means of signifying reconciliation in the Ministry for Children and Families' Strategic Plan for Aboriginal Services.[42] The section on reconciliation reads: (1) "Undertake discussions with Aboriginal communities toward participation by Ministry for Children and Families officials, at all levels, in reconciliation ceremonies, when and if desired by the local Aboriginal community," and (2) "Ensure all ministry staff acquire an understanding of the history and cultural values of Aboriginal communities in their regions. This may include ministry participation in reconciliation ceremonies."[43]

The BC approach may be partly influenced by recent work in the dispute resolution field that promotes ritual as a conflict resolution tool. For example, referring to the writing of Victor Frankl, Professor Michelle LeBaron lectures about how the search for meaning is a central human need: Human beings find meaning by (1) creating something, (2) encountering something or someone, or (3) exercising an option of interpreting an event.[44] She explains that ritual can be a way for people to find meaning. Further, if ritual is a structured part of a conflict resolution process, it will move the participants beyond the linear, intellectual, interest- and outcome-based model to an experiential, human way of working. LeBaron suggests that if people are unable to find meaning in a decision-making or conflict resolution process, the results will be superficial, unable to bring about social change.

Aboriginal communities will have to guard against substituting ceremony or ritual for substance. In the desire to solve problems or resolve conflict, there is a danger of simply superimposing a ceremony or ritual over serious, underlying issues (power imbalances, jurisdictional or ownership disputes, revenue sharing, and so on). When this happens, the ceremony is reduced to rhetorical window dressing – or a pretty band-aid on a gaping wound. At the end of the day, the underlying issues continue to cause social destruction because issues such as power imbalances do not disappear without someone deliberately doing the very difficult and terrifying work of dismantling them.

The other problem with the Ministry for Children and Families' Strategic Plan appears to be that it is another one-way street. As with the Australian Council for Aboriginal Reconciliation, the emphasis is on the non-Aboriginal nations' ministry learning about Aboriginal nations' history and cultural values. There does not appear to be an opportunity for Aboriginal nations to learn about non-First Nations' or even the ministry's history and cultural values. Unfortunately, this serves to perpetuate the myth of the cultureless ministry with cultureless bureaucrats, whereas it is precisely our own understanding of our own cultures that provides the mental scaffolding through which we understand the culture of another. That is, we cannot know how others are shaped by their cultural experiences until we understand how we have been shaped by our own cultural experiences.[45] Cultures are not static, nor are they isolated from the dynamics and forces surrounding them. Rather, culture is understood within its historic, economic, social, political, and geographic contexts. Most importantly, culture cannot be confused with symptoms of poverty or dysfunction created by loss of power.[46] Michael Jackson has written about a particular and distinctive historical and political process that has made Aboriginal people poor beyond poverty internationally.[47]

Arguably, the 1998 Canadian Statement of Reconciliation delivered by the then Minister of Indian Affairs and Northern Development, Jane Stewart, fits the "public drama and ceremony" category of reconciliation.[48] The statement positively bristles with good intentions, even as it recounts the disruption and dispossession of territories, the legacies of physical and sexual abuse, and the erosion of the political, economic, and social systems of once self-sustaining Aboriginal nations. In the statement, the Government of Canada "formally expresses to all Aboriginal people in Canada our profound regret for past actions of the federal government which have contributed to these difficult pages in the history of our relationship together."[49] The statement includes references to reconciliation being an ongoing process, requiring partnerships, and ensuring that past mistakes are learned from; it is topped off with an announcement of a $350 million fund for community-based healing to support Aboriginal people's recovery from residential schools. Unfortunately, the statement is passive and thereby devoid of any real sense of responsibility or meaning – terrible things happened (beyond our control) and we are sorry. Jane Stewart's focus on the healing fund rather than on land and resources is also telling. All this provokes the question, has the relationship between Aboriginal people and Canada changed since the release of the Reconciliation Statement, and if so, how?

Defining Reconciliation from a Gitxsan Perspective

External Reconciliation

Reconciliation is a complex and onerous international dilemma. Two presenting authors at a conference entitled *Dilemmas of Reconciliation* held in Calgary in the spring of 1999 suggest that reconciliation must be understood as the building or rebuilding of trust in relationships that have been seriously ruptured by actual or perceived wrongdoing.[50] Furthermore, there is no arrival and no final state of union, harmony, or total and lasting agreement. Instead, the authors argue that reconciliation should be regarded as a coming together where parties learn to trust each other and seek to manage their relationship and inevitable future conflicts.[51]

David A. Crocker suggests that there are at least three types of reconciliation: (1) minimal reconciliation, which is about basic co-existence without violence; (2) democratic reconciliation, in which citizens can respectfully disagree and work together on common goals; and (3) comprehensive reconciliation, which allows mutual healing and restoration.[52] Practical reasons usually limit international truth and reconciliation commissions to the first and second types because commissions usually have a limited time frame and are also unable to force agreement about the past, forgiveness, or love (which would be morally repugnant anyway). According to Crocker, trying to get adversaries to seek and deal with forgiveness is part of a transformative justice process that takes generations. The hope of comprehensive reconciliation lies with future generations who will not have experienced the conflicts their forebears did.[53] Perhaps the true task of reconciliation is to work toward freeing the next generation from the anchor of current conflicts.

The issue of reconciliation is no less complex or onerous for the Gitxsan nation, which must discuss and explore several on-the-ground, practical questions: (1) How will the concept of reconciliation, as framed by Chief Justice Lamer in *Delgamuukw*, extend beyond land and resources (assuming it even gets that far) to broader social concerns? (2) What will be the terms and measure of reconciliation as they apply to human services, and to land and resources? (3) How will reconciliation be defined from inside a Gitxsan cultural and experiential perspective? (4) What are the politics and ethics of reconciliation for Gitxsan people? (5) Are Gitxsan people imagining mere coexistence with non-Gitxsan and external governments, cooperative goals and future building, or transformative justice with mutual healing and restoration? Similar questions will have to be discussed and explored by non-Gitxsan communities and the broader society.

What becomes clear at the outset of these discussions is that reconciliation will not be achieved by simply measuring against the status quo and then figuring out how achieve "parity" for Gitxsan people. For example, it is entirely inadequate to suggest that reconciliation within education is simply a matter of trying to achieve non-Gitxsan graduation rates for Gitxsan children. True reconciliation in education would mean Gitxsan people having the opportunity to define citizenship and their nation's goals and determine how education will develop Gitxsan citizens to fulfill the nation's goals. As with the rest of Canada, education for the Gitxsan would be about identity, citizenship, nationhood, and taking a place in the world. Not until this ideological foundation is in place will the Gitxsan be able to go on and meaningfully define education, its goals, and its standards of success, as well as equivalent graduation rates for their children and adult learners.

Another issue that emerges is forgiveness. The Gitxsan must explore what they need to forgive, both as individuals and collectively as a people, and they must decide how they can forgive. It is useful to draw an analogy with some of the more critical restorative justice work regarding forgiveness because of the great discomfort involved in talking about and hearing about pain and injury. M.A. Miller, a Mennonite writer, observes that, "too often survivors are silenced with the remark, 'Forgive and forget,' which actually says the speaker is unwilling to listen to the survivor. Those of us who wish to be helpful must examine our own motives for hurrying through the excruciating process of recovery. We must learn to stay with the pain ... We must support survivors as they learn to live with the memories of their experiences."[54]

Instead of attempting to elicit Gitxsan people's forgiveness as part of a reconciliation process, it would be more appropriate for all parties to acknowledge painful social injustices and then go on. Forgiveness cannot happen in a vacuum outside human relationships any more than love, trust, or power can. Given this, forgiveness ultimately means seeing the transgressor as a human being and reclaiming all the memories – both good and bad. There is no such thing as forgiveness in the abstract. Gitxsan people must seek a balance between, on the one hand, becoming immobilized by the pain, and on the other, minimizing it. Either extreme creates a complete dead end insofar as positive social change is concerned. For example, during the early reconciliation discussions between the province and the Gitxsan, a provincial official made incendiary remarks about how the Gitxsan situation should not be compared with other conflicts in the world. The ridiculous implication was that suffering could somehow be quantified and qualified to allow for a comparison and evaluation. Apparently, having done this, the speaker determined that Gitxsan suffering was not severe enough to warrant the same level of serious consideration and analysis necessary elsewhere in the world.

Internal Reconciliation

The Gitxsan nation needs an internal reconciliation process to parallel the external process. This internal process will enable Gitxsan people to come to terms with the consequences and changes wrought by recent history since contact.

The first step of this work is to identify and articulate changes to the Gitxsan kinship system, communities and governance, relationship to land, roles and responsibilities, internal and external relationships, citizenship and membership, and intergenerational cultural transmission and bonding.

The second step involves an explicit internal reconciliation process according to Gitxsan law. For example, there are clanless, landless ethnic Gitxsan (born of non-Gitxsan mothers) who must be adopted or dealt with according to Gitxsan laws of house membership and nation citizenship. As well, there are geographically and culturally disconnected Gitxsan who must be given an opportunity to integrate themselves in some meaningful and participatory way with the Gitxsan nation. Finally, there are non-Gitxsan residents who are active in Gitxsan families and communities, and whose place and role must be formalized in the kinship system.

The work involved with any one of these internal reconciliation issues is massive and further complicated by the results of recent history and the incorporation of colonial institutions. With the governance issue, for example, American author Russell Barsh writes that the extent to which tribal governments are structurally Western, or American, has deterred the evolution of indigenous institutional adaptations to contemporary realities.[55] Similarly, in Australia, William Tyler suggests that the concept of community is inseparable from structures of the post-assimilationist administration.[56] This is because community was a public instrument in Australian Aboriginal policy development during the 1960s and 1970s, and was associated with a positive rediscovery and restoration of Aboriginal identity and citizenship rights. According to Tyler, this concept of community offers a "politically acceptable, culturally appropriate expression of the new order of self-management and self-determination." Whether or not the community concept makes sense to traditional Aboriginal regimes is a question that is largely ignored.[57]

Consequently, indigenous governance and legal systems, including the Gitxsan's, have been largely in stasis. The Gitxsan system has remained intact, but its function with regard to house group management and protection of their territories has been seriously undermined. Many Gitxsan laws have been violated by both Gitxsan and non-Gitxsan, and this contributes to cultural paralysis, a kind of cultural cognitive dissonance. Reconciliation here would mean either an explicit acknowledgment of, and agreement to, the changes to Gitxsan law to fit contemporary circumstances, or application of Gitxsan laws to deal with transgressions – for example, specific environmental degradations caused by roads, logging, and other developments. It would be difficult to force participation by the transgressor, but nonetheless, the process of dealing with transgression through the Gitxsan system, even without the transgressing parties, would be healthy and constructive for the Gitxsan.

Furthermore, there is conflict and tension between the Indian Act-imposed band council structure[58] and the Gitxsan kinship system, because it is the band council structure that receives government recognition, legitimacy, and resources, not the houses. In recent years, the infernal and pervasive confusion between band, community, and nation has been magnified and increased by the BC treaty process.[59] Essentially, the BC treaty process and many bands have advocated treating bands as if they were nations. So, according to some Indian Act leaders, each band is supposed to be self-contained and self-sufficient, and able to provide for all the needs of its members. This is patently ridiculous because no community – Aboriginal or non-Aboriginal – is ever isolated and self-contained. For example, a modern city like Victoria is neither self-contained nor self-sufficient. The precontact communities of the North Coast Aboriginal nations shared all kinds of kinship connections because kinship ties (clans) extended far beyond community boundaries (and through marriage, there were kinship ties between nations). These clan connections enabled the nation to be a dynamic political unit. The resolution of a conflict in a community, through kinship networks, involved people from outside the community.

There are two critical aspects to this arrangement.

First, the interest group was kept larger than the community. Depending on the type of conflict situation, one didn't just deal with the house members and clan members of one community, but rather with house members, closely aligned house groups, clans from the other villages, and sometimes clans from other nations. This ensured enough "disinterest" and distance between citizens, families, and kinship groups that decision making had to consider the public good beyond the matter in dispute.[60] In other words, there were always enough people involved who were sufficiently removed from the conflict that they had no (or less) personal vested interest in its resolution and could take a broader view of the problems.

Second, the size of the group created healthy competition among families, communities, and kinship groups, and this kept everyone accountable. It is difficult to hold the people closest to us accountable, but we can demand accountability from those who are some distance from us. This is especially true when such driving factors as prestige, honour, and competition are involved.

Given this, justice initiatives must be designed on the basis of nation, not of band. For example, when Gitxsan people designed their justice program, Gitxsan Unlocking Aboriginal Justice (UAJ), they had to figure out how to practically and effectively compensate for this lack of scale in the six Gitxsan small communities. The Gitxsan had to ensure that there was some disinterest and distance, some competition and accountability. They had to consider what other measures were necessary to prevent unhealthy social insularity. The reality is that UAJ works best for the houses that are strong and organized, but less effectively for the weaker, dysfunctional houses. To date, the difficult problems and contradictions of UAJ have not been overcome completely, and this work remains part of the internal reconciliation homework.

Another internal reconciliation issue is the safety of Gitxsan women and children in dysfunctional communities that have adopted patriarchy. Some Aboriginal societies were sexist and less than ideal, and a return to traditional practices would be oppressive to women. However, there is an underlying assumption in mainstream society that Aboriginal societies and Aboriginal women are either frozen in time and locked into some pre-contact way of being or are trapped in a dysfunctional colonial time warp. The former assumption suggests that without the civilizing restraints of the Charter, the Criminal Code, the Indian Act, and other Western laws, Aboriginal people would revert to oppressive sexist practices in a quantum leap back across the centuries, and nothing could be done about it, because the sexist practices are traditional and therefore sacred and therefore unchangeable. The second underlying assumption suggests that Aboriginal people can overcome paralyzing social dysfunction only by adopting the Western liberal framework.

Some Aboriginal societies had sexist practices and many still do. However, no society is static; all viable societies are evolving. Just as all the societies that now constitute Canadian mainstream society have evolved and must continue to struggle to overcome sexism, so too must Aboriginal societies. Traditions can change, and the potential for growth and strengthening of the Gitxsan nation – specifically Gitxsan women – should not be underestimated. Gitxsan women, however, were in a much better position historically than in post-contact times. This is another piece of reconciliation homework.

The internal reconciliation issue also concerns citizenship. Aboriginal nations can choose the ideals and behaviours of a nation-strengthening approach – some form of civic nationalism – or they can choose the ideals and behaviours of a nation-diminishing approach – ethnic nationalism.[61]

A nation-building model is one wherein citizens are invited and welcomed, wherein a nation keeps all its citizens, because a nation's citizens are the source of its strength and ability to create political power, stability, wealth, and civil society. In the nation-building model, diversity and difference are power, leading to natural alliances with other nations. Applying this nation-building model to Aboriginal nations today means reclaiming all those members who are geographically and culturally disconnected through marriage, adoption, or parentage. It follows that reclamation must also include those who form the incarcerated inmate population, the gangs, and the inner-city poor.

In contrast, a nation-diminishing model is one that limits and excludes from membership according to ethnicity and blood. It is this model that the Indian Act has fostered within Aboriginal nations and that has been internalized through membership codes,[62] modern treaties, and self-government agreements. There is ample evidence of the long-term effects of these mechanisms and the enormous human cost – the fracturing of Aboriginal nations and the creation of a huge population of culturally dislocated and geographically dispossessed Aboriginal people. At issue here is not the authority of Aboriginal nations to define their own citizenship and nation, but the exclusionary ethnic nationhood model being adopted by Aboriginal bands. For the Gitxsan, membership is determined by the mother's lineage, and citizenship is formed by a series of reciprocal kinship relationships. Adoption practices make the Gitxsan system inclusionary. This system is in conflict with the Indian Act-modelled band membership systems presently employed by the six Gitxsan bands. Issues of membership and citizenship are about belonging and are therefore emotionally volatile for communities. They remain an unresolved internal reconciliation issue.

Ideally, non-Gitxsan citizens would have the support and opportunity to undertake a similar journey. Were this the case, local discussions of co-management would become truly productive and positive. However, decentralized citizen participation goes against Anglo-Canadian cultural roots and history. According to Richard Overstall, "local decision making has not been a part of Anglo-Canadian constitutions for a millennium, and redirecting the focus of the reconciliation on local arrangements may yet be another path to imaginatively implement a *Delgamuukw*-based agreement."[63]

Recommendations

To begin the reconciliation discussions with the province, the Gitxsan offered a preliminary set of recommendations for (1) design and development of an internal Gitxsan reconciliation process; (2) implementation of a meaningful participation process for the local non-Gitxsan communities to work with the Gitxsan on regional reconciliation; (3) investigation of various international reconciliation initiatives (e.g., South Africa, Northern Ireland, Yugoslavia, Rwanda, Guatemala, Cambodia, Australia); and (4) drafting of reconciliation statements for each of the human service areas: education, health, child welfare, social services, and justice. A fifth recommendation was that the provincial ministries explain their culture, including values, myths, legends, spiritual places, and traditional practices.

Interestingly, the major stumbling block to the discussions has been the fifth recommendation. This was of course compounded by the problems listed earlier (bureaucratic stove-piping and procedural focus versus substantive issues) and the lack of political will demonstrated by both the federal and provincial governments. The issues listed in the internal and external reconciliation sections in this chapter have not been discussed with either level of government.

Conclusion

> And so, if the truth is to be believed in this country, it must perhaps be written by those who bear the consequences of the past.
>
> – Antjie Krog, *Country of My Skull: Guilt, Sorrow, and the Limits of Forgiveness in the New South Africa*

None of these issues is simple. Each is complicated, difficult, and highly charged emotionally. For the Gitxsan nation, the reconciliation process must be grounded in Gitxsan experience and contextualized by Gitxsan sovereignty. There is no mileage in negotiating or accepting agreements that do not allow the future to be different – or at least imagined. Anything less than true reconciliation leaves the underlying issues intact beneath a veneer of liturgy. Anything less is a rerun of the same old, same old – a tinkering at the edges of what is possible.

Notes

1 For a broader international perspective regarding reconciliation and indigenous peoples, see Ian McIntosh, "Visions of the Future: the Prospect for Reconciliation" (winter 1999) 23 Cultural Survival Quarterly 4.
2 *Delgamuukw* v. *British Columbia,* [1997] 3 S.C.R. 1010.
3 There are profound differences between Western (European-originating) and Aboriginal constructs of nationhood, so care must be taken not to simply impose a Western definition. Different histories and cultures have produced different ways for large groups of people to define themselves and relate to others, non-human life forms, space, and the land. The key divergence between Aboriginal and non-Aboriginal constructs of nationhood lies in the structures of the hierarchies in social and political regimes (e.g., decentralized vs. centralized). To emphasize the different social constructs, some authors deliberately use the term "peoples," rather than "nations," when referring to Aboriginal groups. A critical cosmological difference is that Aboriginal nations make no fundamental separation of the history of humans from the history of the world, and human power

is fused with the power of the land. For more information, see Richard Overstall, "Encountering the Spirit in the Land: 'Property' in a Kinship-based Legal Order" (paper presented at Property Rights in Colonial Imagination and Experience, a colloquium of the Faculty of Law, University of Victoria, February 2001).

4 *Delgamuukw.*

5 *Ibid.,* 1123.

6 The Gitxsan have other agreements in place with various provincial and federal ministries that cover a range of political, social, and economic programs and services. They are also currently negotiating with the federal government.

7 In the language of the Gitxsan, the literal meaning of *ts'eetix* is "dirt" or "of the earth."

8 Every Gitxsan person is born into his or her mother's house, which is a subgroup of one of the four, larger Gitxsan "clans." In the past, each house had its own cedar "big house." These houses sheltered extended kin and affines, oral histories, regalia, songs, dances, and family and clan crests. Actual house members do not all live in one village, and never did. The chiefs and wing chiefs lived in the home village generally, but their members were, and are, widely scattered by marriage, occupation, age, and the seasonal round; they even lived, and live, among other First Nations. The house shows its corporate muscle only at times of crisis, particularly death, when invited guests formally witness the passing of family names. Each house member has rights in, and duties toward, other houses through marriage, clan affiliation, collateral lines, and affinal ties. For more information, see Overstall, "Encountering the Spirit in the Land," 4.

9 When used to apply collectively, *lippgyt* means "free people." When used to apply to an individual, *lippgyt* means "to be my own person." The meaning of the term, as translated for application to the Lippgyt Table, is "self-determining people" or "people free of central government."

10 Author's work experience with the Gitxsan Lippgyt Table.

11 Antjie Krog, *Country of My Skull: Guilt, Sorrow, and the Limits of Forgiveness in the New South Africa* (New York: Times Books, 1998).

12 *Blockade* (Vancouver: Canada Wild Productions, 1996) documentary film.

13 Of course, many Gitxsan people are also dependent on primary resource extraction for their livelihood.

14 *Black's Law Dictionary,* 6th ed., s.v. "reconciliation."

15 It is important to acknowledge that however the crime is classified, the consequences for the victim can be devastating. People often suffer loss of their sense of autonomy and post-traumatic stress disorder from break-ins and other property crimes.

16 Howard Zehr, *Changing Lenses* (Waterloo: Herald, 1990), 181.

17 Tim Roberts, Focus Consultants, "Evaluation of the Victim Offender Mediation Project, Langley, BC: Final Report for the Solicitor General of Canada" (1995), 2. I do agree that offenders bear personal responsibility for their decisions and actions, but I think there is a parallel collective, societal responsibility that must be correspondingly accepted and expressed in the work of restorative justice. In other words, do we believe that crime is simply a matter of personal failing? How are societal problems such as structural power imbalances, oppression, exploitation, and colonialism part of the crime? Exploration of this issue is beyond the scope of this paper.

18 *Ibid.,* 2-3.

19 The William Head Restorative Justice Study Group is a unique inmate initiative that meets weekly with volunteer citizens interested in discussing complex restorative justice issues as they apply to serious crime.

20 T.K. Demmings, "Searching for Justice at William Head," *Saanich News,* 29 January 1999, 5.

21 *Ibid.*

22 This was the first annual William Head Symposium of Restorative Justice and Serious Crime. Over one hundred people from all walks of life attended the two-day event, including corrections staff, inmates, students, politicians, reporters, chapel volunteers, lawyers, and other citizens. Unless an inmate identified himself as such, an observer could not distinguish between "them" and "us." After all, every man, woman, and youth incarcerated in Canada is related to someone.

23 Richard Overstall, "Kindreds and States: Using Anglo-Saxon and Gitxsan Law to Help Reconcile Aboriginal and Crown Sovereignty" (course paper for the Faculty of Law, University of Victoria, 1998), 5.
24 *Ibid.*
25 *Ibid.,* 38.
26 *Ibid.,* 39.
27 *Ibid.,* 40.
28 *Ibid.,* 41.
29 *Ibid.,* 42.
30 Also see Richard Overstall's chapter in this volume.
31 Council for Aboriginal Reconciliation, *Making Things Right: Reconciliation after the High Court's Decision on Native Rights* (Canberra: Council for Aboriginal Reconciliation, 1993). The Council comprises twenty-five members, including twelve Aboriginals and two Torres Strait Islanders. The council is divided into the rural, mining, industry, and consultative committees, whose mandate is to improve relations within the pastoral, mining, and industrial sectors.
32 *Ibid.,* 1.
33 *Ibid.,* 3.
34 *Ibid.,* 2.
35 For more information and the Australian Council of Reconciliation final report, see its website <www.reconciliation.org.au>.
36 Native Title Unit, Aboriginal Legal Rights Movement, South Australia, "The March for Reconciliation" (2000) 9 Aboriginal Way 6, 7.
37 Larissa Behrendt, "White Picket Fences: Recognizing Aboriginal Property Rights in Australia's Psychological Terra Nullius" (winter 1999) 10 (2) Constitutional Forum 52.
38 *Ibid.*
39 *Ibid.*
40 "Aboriginal people under glass" often occurs in so-called cross-cultural sessions where the only cultures explained or on display are the Aboriginal cultures. This perpetuates the myth that there are "normal" (non-Aboriginal) people who are cultureless, and "other" (Aboriginal) people who have cultures. The assumption is that an awareness of Aboriginal culture among the normal people will solve whatever problems are the focus of the exercise. This doesn't stand up. Cross-cultural sessions have been going on for over thirty years in Canada, but the basic disputes of Aboriginal title and sovereignty remain unresolved, as do many other major social injustices.
41 See <www.reconcilitation.org.au>.
42 British Columbia, Ministry for Children and Families, Aboriginal Relations Branch, *Strategic Plan for Aboriginal Services* (Victoria, BC: 1999), 10.
43 *Ibid.*
44 Michelle LeBaron (lecture at the Faculty of Law, University of Victoria, 15 June 1999).
45 G.W. Storytellers' Foundation, "Cultural Dialogue Project" (workshop presented locally by a Hazelton, BC, group and funded by Heritage Canada, spring 1998).
46 Cecil Helman, *Culture, Health and Illness* (Bristol: John Wright, 1984).
47 Michael Jackson, "In Search of the Pathways to Justice: Alternative Dispute Resolution in Aboriginal Communities" (1992) University of British Columbia Law Review 147, 154.
48 Native Law Centre, University of Saskatchewan, "Canada's Statement of Reconciliation with Aboriginal Peoples" (spring 1998) 3 (1) *Justice as Healing: A Newsletter on Aboriginal Concepts of Justice* 1.
49 *Ibid.,* 2.
50 Trudy Govier and Wilhelm Verwoerd, "Re-Building Trust: Toward an Account of Reconciliation Between Large Groups" (lecture given at the Institute of Humanities, University of Calgary, June 1999), 12.
51 *Ibid.*
52 David Crocker, "Truth Commissions, Transitional Justice, and Civil Society," in Robert Rotberg and Dennis Thompson, eds., *Truth v. Justice* (Princeton, NJ: Princeton University, 2000), 108.

53 *Ibid.*
54 Melissa A. Miller, *Family Violence: The Compassionate Church Responds* (Scottsdale, PA: Herald Press, 1994), quoted in *Mediation and Facilitation Manual: Foundations and Skills for Constructive Transformation* (Akron, PA: Mennonite Conciliation Service, 1995), 33-34.
55 Russell Barsh, "Aboriginal Self-Government in the United States: A Qualitative Political Analysis," in *Royal Commission on Aboriginal Peoples* (Ottawa: Minister of Supply and Services, 1993), 7.
56 William Tyler, "Community-Based Strategies in Aboriginal Criminal Justice: The Northern Territory Experience" (1995) 28 (2) *Australian and New Zealand Journal of Criminology* 139.
57 *Ibid.,* 130.
58 Indian Act, R.S.C. 1985, c.I-5.
59 For a discussion of bands versus nations, see Canada, "Report of the Royal Commission on Aboriginal Peoples," 2 (part 1), *Restructuring the Relationship,* 1996, 182-235.
60 John Ralson Saul, *The Unconscious Civilization* (Concord, ON: House of Anansi, 1995), 68. Saul argues that a healthy nation can create organized mechanisms that make it possible for citizens to share a level of disinterest (as opposed to self-interest) that is known as the public good.
61 Michael Ignatieff, *Blood and Belonging: Journeys into Nationalism* (Toronto: Penguin Books, 1994).
62 Larry Gilbert, *Entitlement to Indian Status and Membership Codes in Canada* (Toronto: Carswell, 1996). This book provides an overall detailed history and description of Indian Act machinery and membership code excerpts from a cross-section of Canadian indigenous communities.
63 Overstall, "Kindreds and States," 42.

12
Reconciliation Devices: Using the Trust as an Interface between Aboriginal and State Legal Orders
Richard Overstall

> Bureaucratic law is positive as well as public. The crucial condition
> for the emergence of positive law is what one might call the
> disintegration of community ... Positive law remains superfluous
> as long as there is a closely held communion of reciprocal
> expectations, based on a shared view of right and wrong. In this
> setting the normative order will not surface as formulated rules;
> indeed, it may remain almost entirely below the threshold of
> explicit statement and conscious understanding.
>
> – Roberto Unger, *Law in Modern Society*

According to the Supreme Court of Canada, the basic purpose of s.35(1) of
the Constitution is to reconcile "the pre-existence of Aboriginal societies
with the sovereignty of the Crown."[1] It is this pre-existence that the Court
in *Delgamuukw* recognizes as Aboriginal title. In its view, reconciliation
will ultimately be achieved "through negotiated settlements, with good
faith and give and take on both sides, reinforced by judgments of this
Court."[2] Earlier in *Delgamuukw,* Chief Justice Lamer held that title could be
proved either by establishing physical occupation under the common law[3]
or by establishing legal occupation under Aboriginal law.[4] Courts in Australia have gone farther by recognizing that "Australian law can protect
the interests of members of an indigenous clan or group ... only in con-
formity with the traditional laws and customs of the people to whom the
clan or group belongs and only where members of the clan or group
acknowledge those laws and observe those customs."[5]

In a formal sense, the negotiated settlements recommended by the
Delgamuukw court are about bringing together two distinct legal orders –
on the one hand, Unger's "communion of reciprocal expectations" and
on the other, the positive or prescribed law of the nation state. This chapter's thesis is that formal reconciliation can occur only through legal
devices that provide effective interfaces between the laws and governance
structures of the two orders while preserving the integrity of each. Three
areas of reconciliation are examined. The first I call external reconciliation. It is the type referred to by the chief justice – negotiated settlements
between an Aboriginal people and the Canadian and relevant provincial

governments. These negotiations have commonly been about treaties, rarely about interim measures agreements and, less formally, about Aboriginal rights and title consultation arising out of the Crown's fiduciary duty. At its least formal but most important level, external reconciliation brings together the Aboriginal community with those non-Aboriginal people who live within its territories. The second area I call internal reconciliation. It takes place within Aboriginal societies. In order to realize all the benefits and assume all the responsibilities of the wider reconciliation, communities will have to talk about which elements of their social institutions and legal order they will need to deal with the dysfunctions and internal changes resulting from two centuries of colonialism. The third area of reconciliation looks ahead. It reconciles the current generation with their children and grandchildren by managing their land territory to maintain its spiritual, biological, and physical processes. This is future-use reconciliation.

In the following sections, the chapter outlines the institutional issues that arise at each of the three areas of reconciliation in British Columbia. It then proposes the trust as a legal instrument that could provide the required interface between Aboriginal and common law. I discuss constraints imposed by each legal order on the various types of trust. The concept is described in terms general enough that it could be applied to governance issues ranging from housing, health, and child welfare, to forestry and fisheries co-management. The chapter concludes with a hypothetical example of a community salmon fishery management trust in a typical Northwest Coast watershed.

External Reconciliation

In both treaty agreements and lower court decisions on consultation, the Canadian legal system has made a concerted effort to push Aboriginal people away from their own governance structures and toward Western models. Two examples will demonstrate this tendency. In the Nisga'a Final Agreement, the legal body that will hold the Nisga'a treaty rights is the "Nisga'a Nation."[6] This is a corporation whose governance structure closely follows the Nisga'a Tribal Council, itself modelled on the utopian Christian villages established in the Nass by William Duncan's Anglican missionaries in the late nineteenth century. The village councils under the Final Agreement will be replicas of the existing Indian Act band councils. Nisga'a governance by the houses and clans through their hereditary chiefs is given only a token mention in the treaty – an omission that may undermine one of its main purposes. Under the *Delgamuukw* Aboriginal title test, the only Nisga'a institutions that can prove title using Aboriginal law are the Nisga'a houses – groups of related families. Without the consent of each Nisga'a house through its chief, the Nisga'a Nation would appear to have no legal authority to reach the "full and final settlement" of rights and title that it purports to in the Final Agreement.[7]

The second example of the effort to assimilate traditional governance comes from one of the many cases where an Aboriginal group sought to enjoin a government-approved activity on its territories because of inadequate consultation on potential infringement of Aboriginal rights or title. Government agencies see consultation as a process they have to follow in order to protect the Crown from potential judicial review or injunction litigation. They use consultation as a pre-trial information collecting process,[8] thus blocking its purpose to "substantially address the concerns of Aboriginal peoples."[9] Most such injunction applications have been brought by Indian Act band councils. The lower courts have sometimes challenged a band's legal capacity to bring the injunction, not because it was usurping the real right and titleholders, but because the court considered that even more centralized Aboriginal organizations had a stronger claim. Thus in one of the numerous Kitkatla injunction cases, Hutchison J. indicated he did not favour a single band bringing injunction petitions: "This court should be slow to accept the submissions of one band when it is not joined by its umbrella organization authorised to negotiate treaties on their [sic] behalf."[10] He went on to say that treaty settlements would be helped by trade union style "solidarity forever."[11] The source of the judge's reluctance to grant an injunction to a small Aboriginal group is clear: "I fear that if this court starts enjoining each individual band's claim pressed on by the *Delgamuukw* decision, the floodgates discussed in the *Meares Island* case may very well open. And I am not prepared to be the one that allows the first olive out of the bottle."[12] Partly because he perceived no support from an "umbrella organization," Hutchison J. denied the injunction application.

The lower courts appear to be attempting to enforce assimilation of Aboriginal people into Western organizational shells – a process begun by the missionaries, continued by Indian Agents, and now being enthusiastically pursued by treaty negotiators and government agencies. The impetus for maintaining these colonial relationships is the threat of economic disruption to vested interests if exercise of Aboriginal rights by decentralized kinship groups is allowed to influence resource extraction in local communities. For example, in another northwestern British Columbia Aboriginal injunction case, an appeal court judge said, "the court should not grant an injunction if the economic consequences of doing so would have a serious impact upon the economic health of the province, the region, or the logging company."[13] Courts have held that Aboriginal groups forfeit the right of consultation if they put conditions on the process such as requiring selection logging methods and consent of the appropriate kinship groups.[14] Government pre-conditions are apparently permitted.[15] Robert

Williams describes this stressing of Indian difference – such as different conceptions of governance – as a continuing colonial strategy to "place inherent limitations on tribal sovereignty."[16] Patrick Macklem sees both difference and similarity being selectively applied to invalidate Aboriginal law.[17]

Thus, while the Supreme Court of Canada establishes clear, if general, tests to justify title infringement, the lower courts in British Columbia have generally refused Aboriginal people any effective remedies when governments fail to meet the tests. In their groundbreaking article on remedies in contracts, Fuller and Perdue point out that while the language of law suggests that choice of remedies flows from decisions about the parties' rights, the process of selecting remedies to protect interests "is really part of the process of creating them."[18] The same conclusion can be applied to Aboriginal rights law. In injunction cases, judges apply a "balance of convenience test" whereby they weigh the inconvenience to the party seeking the injunction of not granting it against the inconvenience to the responding party of granting it. Through their particular use of this test, BC courts have effectively created a private corporate right to extract resources that is superior to the right of Aboriginal groups to "choose to what ends a piece of land can be put."[19] Aboriginal rights and title thus remain, as they have for over two centuries, largely a legal fiction.

Internal Reconciliation

While the courts and treaty negotiators are beginning to signal which institutions they will recognize as legitimate Aboriginal rights and titleholders, the failure of those institutional models among Aboriginal peoples is readily apparent. People's marginalization in their own communities and in urban areas is well documented – life expectancy, accidental death, suicide, incarceration, welfare dependency, and unemployment are more than double and triple the national average, while income and formal education levels are half those of the rest of Canada.[20] The standard response to these statistics is to advocate more money and more social services, despite their failed record. Accounts that get behind the numbers and the personal tragedies they cumulatively record show not only inept government agencies with a colonial mind set, but an inability of local band councils to effect change.[21]

Tom and Sarah Pocklington identify the moral dilemma facing elected band officials:

> Most Aboriginal people are members of extended families which are ... closely knit. A person is deemed to owe to kin not only special affection but also partiality ... For example, if he is an Indian band councillor and if the band has in its possession two new houses this year, and if one of the several eligible applicants is his sister-in-law's son, the course of duty is

clear: nepotism is obligatory. But he has a competing duty, that is, to distribute benefits without prejudice according to objective standards of need
or merit ... nepotism is impermissible.[22]

The Pocklingtons rightly reject the view that the parochial obligations
occupy an earlier, and lower, stage of moral evolution – "vestiges of a tribal
past."[23] They also say the dilemma is misunderstood if only the kinship
obligations are seen as authentic Aboriginal responses. The authors conclude that the political ethics of Aboriginal and non-Aboriginal political
institutions are not very different, and that the similarity is rooted in the
inherent tension between individualistic and collectivist concepts in both
political systems. This conclusion is flawed in that it fails to take into
account either the scale or the structure of the political institutions within
which the dilemma is played out. For example, the authors report how
consensus decisions were made by Dene hunting parties in the Northwest
Territories,[24] and then go on to describe how consensus later failed as a
decision-making process for the Dene Nation, especially in its attempts
to influence territorial and federal government policies.[25] On the one
hand, the hunting parties were small and made up of persons who were
closely related and had hunted together many times in the past. The Dene
national assemblies, on the other hand, were large annual events and made
up of Indian Act band chiefs and councillors, who would not have daily
contact with each other, who would likely be replaced by new faces from
year to year, and who themselves headed hierarchical and rule-governed
institutions. This suggests that a political process that appears to function
well on a certain scale, with a certain institutional structure, and with a
certain closeness of relatedness among its members, will not function well
at a different scale, structure, and consanguinity.

The point is not whether the paramountcy of kinship obligations is
"authentic" or not, but whether it is the most appropriate form of governance in the circumstances. Given the widespread failure of the alternatives, indigenous kinship institutions should be seen not as mere cultural
preferences but as the only institutions able to govern small communities
of closely related people. This is not to say that an instantaneous switch to
traditional or reconceived kinship authority structures will solve governance problems in Aboriginal communities. Too much has been taken
away for too long to tolerate a quick fix. Rather, I suggest such structures
should be diligently explored as part of a longer-term strategy for both
external and internal reconciliation.

Future-Use Reconciliation

One of the more imaginative findings in *Delgamuukw* is that Aboriginal
title land cannot be used in ways that are "irreconcilable with the nature

of the occupation of that land and the relationship that particular group has had with the land which together have given rise to Aboriginal title in the first place."[26] Excluded uses are those that would destroy the lands' value, either for the physical activities that define the group's occupation or for the bonds that define the group's culture. Land possession and spiritual bonds also form the legal basis of land holdings under Aboriginal laws.[27] This is the first time that the Court has devised a limit to rights that reinforces Aboriginal legal concepts rather than arbitrarily contradicting them[28] – a change in policy the Court appears to recognize by calling the limit inherent.[29] The Court does not preclude irreconcilable use, but says the Aboriginal title must be surrendered first.[30]

As the irreconcilable use limit applies to the Aboriginal group and, I would argue, the Crown,[31] the question arises as to who would have standing to enforce this limit if a government and an Aboriginal group agreed on a pre-surrender land use that Aboriginal title does not permit. A clue to this question's answer might be found in the Court's analogy between the limit and the common law doctrine of equitable waste.[32] The doctrine states that a person with a life interest cannot ruin the property by "wanton or extravagant acts of destruction."[33] In English common law or equity, the person who will assume ownership when the life tenant dies may sue for an injunction and for either rehabilitation or damages.[34] The equitable waste doctrine appears to apply also to an estate that can be transferred only to an owner's descendants.[35] This kind of transfer restriction, known as a fee trail, better approximates the land and succession law of those Aboriginal peoples where a specific territory is held by a kinship group and is transferred only within that group.[36] In the classic English case on equitable waste, *Vane* v. *Lord Barnard,* the chancellor granted an injunction on the life tenant's destruction of Raby Castle and ordered him to pay for such repairs as a court-appointed commission determined were needed.[37] The court also ordered an independent master to oversee the rehabilitation on behalf of the reversioner to the life interest. In a case of equitable waste or irreconcilable use by an Aboriginal titleholder, it is unclear who would bring the action on behalf of future generations and who would implement any court orders.

One legal concept that could both provide an interface between the communitarian kinship of Aboriginal societies and the liberal democracy of Crown sovereignty, and provide legal standing to future titleholders, is the trust. This is a legal device inherited from the English law of equity which is a discretionary power given to judges since medieval times to do justice in particular cases where application of the strict rules of the common law would cause unfair hardship. Today, equity's principles of justice and of acting according to conscience have themselves often evolved into quite technical rules.[38] Within the law of equity, a trust arises when a property is owned by a person, called a trustee, who is obliged to hold and manage it for the benefit of others, called the beneficiaries. The beneficiaries' interests are usually established in a document that creates the trust, in which case it is an express trust. If the beneficiaries' interests are imposed by law, it is a constructive trust.[39]

The next two sections of this chapter explore both the theory and practice of applying the trust to the external, internal, and future-use reconciliation issues outlined above.

Co-Management Trusts

Trust-like relationships have been extensively surveyed by the courts as a means of characterizing the relationship between the Crown and Aboriginal peoples.[40] In *Guerin,* the trial judge found the federal government was a trustee,[41] while the majority of the Supreme Court of Canada, after canvassing various trust-like obligations, held it was a fiduciary.[42] A fiduciary is someone who has unilateral, discretionary power over the interests of vulnerable others and is thus obliged to act in the others' best interests. The Court based the fiduciary obligation on the requirement to surrender Aboriginal title to the Crown before the land can be alienated.[43] It found that the purpose of the surrender requirement was to prevent, in the language of the Royal Proclamation, the "great Frauds and Abuses [that] have been committed in purchasing Lands of the Indians."[44] In this chapter, I suggest that the issue now, as in 1763, is as much a clash between two economic and institutional cultures as it is misfeasance by settlers or breach of confidence by governments.

Since *Guerin,* the Court has expanded on the sui generis or legally unique nature of the Aboriginal interest so that the Crown's fiduciary obligation applies both before and after any title surrender.[45] The concept I propose here, however, is neither to rename an existing legal relationship, nor to legislate the management of an Aboriginal group's affairs. Rather, it is to create a legal device that can form an interface, a permeable membrane, between federal and provincial jurisdictions on the one hand and Aboriginal jurisdictions on the other. It would allow information and obligations to flow both ways, ensuring mutual accountability without imposing inappropriate Western governance structures on Aboriginal communities. At the same time, space would be created to allow community members to develop their own governance structures, particularly those that historically have proved durable and useful. The proposed legal entity to form this membrane is a co-management trust, whereby an Aboriginal group, with or without other governments, could collectively assume the obligation to manage land, resource, and other rights for the benefit of present and future generations.[46]

What is proposed is a fixed, express trust, settled by the titleholding

Aboriginal group, either alone or in conjunction with others, including the Crown. The beneficiaries would be the Aboriginal group members, either directly or as the "public" benefiting from a charitable trust. Conflicts of interest would be avoided by the fixed and express terms, and by the recommendation that the trustees not be members of the benefiting group. The group would set out in the trust instrument, either by themselves or in agreement with others, terms that would help implement their laws and institutions. The reasons for proposing this type of trust are summarized below, together with discussion of the political and legal issues raised.[47]

Settlor

A settlor creates a trust by transferring an interest to the trust, setting out the trust's terms, and appointing the trustees. For the co-management trust being proposed here, the settling entity would have to include the Aboriginal titleholding group, such as a clan, a house group, or other political authority under Aboriginal law. This is because the transferred interest would be derived from Aboriginal title as recognized under both common law and Aboriginal law.

The joint source of Aboriginal title is explained in *Delgamuukw* where Chief Justice Lamer held that a title claim required proof of exclusive occupation prior to the Crown's assertion of sovereignty.[48] This can be done either by establishing physical occupation under the common law,[49] or by establishing legal occupation under Aboriginal law.[50] To prove pre-sovereignty physical and legal occupation using post-sovereignty evidence, Lamer held that "there must be 'substantial maintenance of the connection' between the people and the land."[51] As biological descent would be difficult to trace and involves unacceptable racial criteria, and Indian Act bands are post-sovereignty and were rarely established socially or geographically congruent with Aboriginal institutions, it follows that proof of Aboriginal title is held by those Aboriginal institutions that were extant at the Crown's assertion of sovereignty. Where such an institution is said to be extinct, an organization claiming successor rights would have to prove the extinction and demonstrate direct transfer of authority from the extinct institution under Aboriginal law. As hereditary Aboriginal governance systems are more alive than many government officials and some Indian organizations will publicly admit, a settlor under the trust arrangement proposed here would not normally be a band council, a tribal council, a treaty association, or some other post-sovereignty entity.

In situations where the primary objective was internal reconciliation or where Crown agencies were unwilling to participate, a trust might be settled by the Aboriginal group on its own. But where the objectives include external reconciliation and the Crown was contributing some of its legal interests, it could be a joint settlor with the Aboriginal group. In that case, the trust likely would be established as part of a treaty, interim measure, or other agreement.

Type of Trust

For a set of aspirations to be considered as a legally binding trust, there must be three certainties: certainty of intent, certainty of subject matter, and certainty of objects (beneficiaries or purposes). To meet its reconciliation objectives, a co-management trust would be an express trust where the intent of the settlor would be set out in a deed or an agreement that would identify the particular interests that were to be the subject matter. The trust would be an executed fixed trust in that the settlor would completely set out the terms of the beneficial interests with no discretionary powers vested in the trustees. The terms will reflect the indigenous laws and decision-making pathways of the Aboriginal group that settles the trust.

On the other hand, because the beneficiaries cannot instruct or bargain with the trustees once the trust has been constituted, there can be no day-to-day political pressure on the trust administration. The groups could manage their lands and economies in ways best suited to their small, closely-related communities, insulated by the trust from the centralized administration and information-gathering demanded by government and other institutions of the dominant society. In this way, the moral dilemma of band and tribal council leaders identified in the first part of this chapter would be ameliorated. To take up the housing allocation example, an Aboriginal people might settle a trust with provisions to allocate housing units to each of its kinship groups in proportion to non-discretionary criteria such as group population. Each kinship group would then reallocate among its members according to the people's own laws. As the power of a kinship group depends on its cohesion, there would be an incentive for it to form consensus decisions.

Trust terms would also constrain use of trust interests for purposes irreconcilable with the nature of the group's Aboriginal title, particularly uses that would restrict future land-use options. Trustees would be given powers to bring legal proceedings on behalf of minor and unborn group members if they perceived the group's land was planned to be used for irreconcilable purposes. In this aspect, the proposed trust could be compared with the American "public trust doctrine," which imposes a fiduciary obligation on the state to protect and to ensure access to certain public lands.[52]

Trust Property

The need for certainty of subject matter requires clear identification of the trust property or interest. Here, it would need to be defined so as to preserve the integrity of both Canadian common law and the Aboriginal group's law. Canadian law sees Aboriginal title as a sui generis burden on the Crown's underlying title.[53] Similarly, Aboriginal law sees Crown sovereignty as a sui generis burden on the Aboriginal group's underlying relationship with the land. As the Court in *Delgamuukw* put it, Aboriginal title "is *sui generis* in the sense that its characteristics cannot be completely explained by reference either to the common law rules of real property or to the rules of property found in Aboriginal legal systems."[54] The proposed trust would not encroach on either of these jurisdictions but would hold as trust property only the sui generis burdens and not the respective underlying or allodial titles. Thus, the Crown would not surrender its perceived sovereignty and the Aboriginal group would not surrender its perceived legal relationship with its territories. So defined, the trust property may include consultation and information-sharing rights, consent mechanisms for certain land uses, co-management regimes, transfer payments, and financial mechanisms to interface Aboriginal reciprocity with the market economy.

Beneficiaries
The third certainty, that of trust objects, may create some difficulties. Usually, the requirement means that the beneficiaries of the trust be clearly defined so the trustees can properly distribute the benefits of the trust. In this case, the beneficiaries would be the members of the Aboriginal group that settled the trust working under their own laws and institutions. The group would be the autonomous legal and social entity that holds the Aboriginal title under both common law and Aboriginal law. For Northwest Coast societies, that would be the house group – an extended family of between 50 and 200 persons who are biologically related through their mothers to a known common ancestor. For each society or people there is no higher land-owning or legal authority, although there is a complex weaving of reciprocal obligations through the clan, village, and tribe which is mediated through the feast or potlatch.

The two main difficulties are these. First, for the fixed trust proposed here, the trustees must be able to ascertain every object and make a complete list of all beneficiaries.[55] This would require the trustees to maintain genealogical charts of all group members and would involve the trustees in disputes about who was and who was not a valid group member. Alternatively, the trust instrument could specify an authority within the group, such as a chief or matriarch, who would determine who qualifies. This, however, would put such a person back into the conflict of interest that the trust was designed to avoid.

Second, in order to meet the proposed objective of future-use reconciliation and especially to bring an action on behalf of future generations, a trust for persons would have to include as objects all future group members. Such a term would contravene the rule against perpetuities, which limits both the duration of the trust and the period within which an interest in property must vest.[56] In both cases, the limit is either a period of the lives of its existing members plus twenty-one years (s.10) or a period of eighty years (s.7). The policy behind this rule is to prevent persons from retaining control over their property from the grave for too long into the future.[57] Part of the content of Aboriginal title recognized by the courts, however, is that an Aboriginal community's relationship with its land "should not be prevented from continuing into the future."[58] Therefore, a strong argument could be made that trusts relating to Aboriginal title lands should not be subject to the rule against perpetuities. It may also be possible to get exemption from the perpetuity rule by statute,[59] but this may involve unacceptable legislative control of the terms and operation of the trust.

The problems with ascertaining beneficiaries and the rule against perpetuities can be avoided by making the device a charitable trust – a purpose trust that does not have persons as objects but, rather, defined charitable purposes. The perpetuity rule against indefinite duration does not apply to charitable trusts and the rule against remoteness of vesting does not apply so strictly. Charitable trusts are also advantageous for tax purposes and for receipt of grants from charitable foundations. Courts generally qualify organizations as charitable using fairly rigid tests that date back to Tudor England. In *Native Communications Society of B.C.* v. *M.N.R.*, however, the Federal Court of Appeal relaxed the test for Aboriginal groups. It took into account "the special legal position in Canadian society occupied by the Indian people"[60] and found that the Society's purposes "are beneficial to the Indian community of British Columbia within the spirit and intendment of the preamble to the Statute of Elizabeth and, therefore, they are good charitable purposes."[61] For the trust being considered here, the purposes would have to be framed in terms that could reasonably be described as for the advancement and betterment of the specific Aboriginal group.

Trustees

The trustees and the trust administrators would require the confidence of both the Aboriginal group and any participating government and other agencies. Their qualifications therefore would need to be based solely on their reliability, knowledge, and skills, not on their authority within the Aboriginal group or within government. In most cases, to avoid conflicts of interest, it may be preferable that they not be members of the benefiting group. In some instances, however, the work of the trust may require specialized knowledge or training that is available only from a group member. Conflict can be mitigated by making it one of the trust terms that its administration be as transparent and open as possible, with accounting of information, funds, and other disbursements being widely circulated both within and without the community.

Having outlined some of the objectives of a trust as an interface between communal and nation state legal orders, and described some of the legal constraints imposed on it by both orders, the chapter concludes by describing a potential practical application to the management of a hypothetical Aboriginal salmon fishery.

Fishery Co-Management Trust: An Example

The main elements of the scheme can be seen in Figure 12.1.

Figure 12.1

Salmon management models

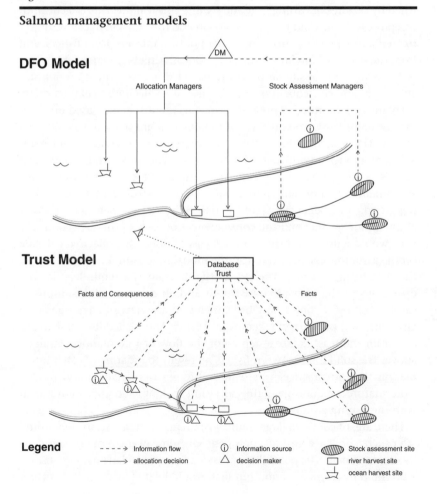

DFO Model

Allocation Managers   Stock Assessment Managers

Trust Model

Database Trust

Facts and Consequences   Facts

Legend

- - - -> Information flow
——> allocation decision
ⓘ Information source
△ decision maker
▨ Stock assessment site
▢ river harvest site
⟱ ocean harvest site

Figure 12.1 (top) conceptually shows the present salmon management model used by the federal Department of Fisheries and Oceans (DFO). The diagram is a combination of a sketch map and a conceptual institutional organizational chart. The map shows a coastline with a river and two tributaries. The oval shaded areas represent salmon ocean migration areas, river migration areas, and spawning areas where stock assessment data can be gathered. The boats represent ocean fishing areas and the rectangles are river fishing areas. In the organizational chart, the circles are data-gathering points, the dashed lines show the flow of data, and the triangle is the point at which information from the data assessment is received and the decision maker (DM) determines harvest size and its allocation using rules found in legislation, regulations, and policy. The decision is then communicated down through the structure to the various fishers and the harvest proceeds. Fishing is policed by specialized bureaucrats and violations are punished by seizures of fishing gear and by fines. In real life, this is a continuous process throughout the fishing season and the decision maker is subject to conflicting pressures from his or her political masters, from fishers, and from the stock assessment scientists. Historically, in every major fishing area of the world, this or similar processes have led to overestimation of available stocks and consequent overfishing and stock declines or extinctions.[62]

Figure 12.1 (bottom) represents a management scheme based on a co-management trust. The outlines of the diagram are the same as the DFO model. The principal difference is the presence of a database and management model administered by the trust. The trust would have two functions. First, it would operate the computer-based model using stock assessment data and self-reported catch data and would advise each fishing group – as a beneficiary – of the harvest strategies open to him or her at any point in time and the consequences of each of them. Second, the trust would request all fishing groups – as settlors – to collectively decide on the assumptions needed to run the model that cannot be derived from the data being received. The eye in the diagram is a reminder that the operations of the trust are transparent and all data and all assumptions can be seen by anyone at any time, including the harvest advice given to any fisher and the harvest taken by any fisher. The dashed lines flowing to and from the trust database represent the flow of information described above. The solid lines between fishers represent the sharing of catch information that, in practice, would flow through the database and model. Note that information gathering, decision making, and allocation are all with the fishing groups.

There are, of course, a large number of unanswered questions remaining after such a brief account of a new concept. Some of them can be summarily discussed here. The possibility of free-loading, particularly by those fishers who could intercept a salmon run first, would be met by the self-reporting and a system of checks by the trustees. The trustees, however, would merely publicly report catches by each fisher and not arrest or punish those who exceeded any suggested catch limit. In the absence of bureaucratic enforcement, the existence of community is essential to the social control that discourages freeloading. It is not clear at this stage of the inquiry to what degree a state of community, if any, would have to already exist among fishing groups before a scheme like the one suggested here became viable or to what degree such a scheme would create community after some time in operation.

This example of applying the trust concept to a problem of salmon fishing politics, economics, and ecology draws, of course, on knowledge of harvest management by the Aboriginal peoples of the Northwest Coast. Leaving aside the model's use of computers and other modern technology, the first difference from those communities' past experience is that the design and functioning of the proposed scheme will be quite explicit rather than implicit. The effect of this transparency is not clear at this stage. The second difference is that today's catches are much closer to the theoretical maximum sustained yield than in the past and it is for this reason that the more intense stock monitoring is required. The level of monitoring can be self-regulating by having the trust's operations funded by a levy on fish sales. As catches approach sustained yield levels, the intensity of monitoring rises exponentially and soon reaches a point where its increased incremental cost to the fisher exceeds his or her incremental returns.

The trust model differs from the bureaucratic command and control model in that it draws on historically observed institutional and ecological conditions to design a self-organizing system that is sufficiently robust and flexible to meet a reasonable range of possible futures. In effect, the trust creates a community property right distinct from the so-called common property right that has failed as a basis of past state fisheries management and the private property right – the individual transferable quota – that is currently failing.[63] The model shifts the locus of power from the nation state to the community and shifts the focus of change and experiment from positivist legal rules to equitable legal structures.

Conclusion
A predominant theme of modern treaty making in British Columbia has been the demand for certainty. While certainty is an elusive, if not unobtainable, quality in the real world, it pervades the rhetoric and express provisions of treaties.[64] The source of the demand is not hard to find. It comes from resource corporations, whose need to raise capital requires them to promise financiers that specific future events, such as the company processing a given amount of trees, minerals, oil, or fish at a given

cost, will for sure take place. One uncertainty perceived by BC resource companies has been unsettled land claims, and that perception has prompted them to pressure governments to sign treaties. As a result, treaties have tended to assume the legal form of commercial promises – the contract.

While the contract may be an appropriate positive law device for the simple, short-term, and strictly enforced requirement of business, it appears ill-suited for the complexities of social and natural systems that are the usual subject matter of treaties. The trust, on the other hand, originated as an equitable device for the more nuanced management of family matters – a context more reminiscent of Aboriginal practice. This chapter has offered the trust as an alternative legal form that may provide a more appropriate basis for the political and cultural reconciliation that the Supreme Court of Canada says the constitution requires.

Notes
1 *Delgamuukw* v. *British Columbia,* [1997] 3 S.C.R. 1010 at 1124 (quoting *R.* v. *Van der Peet,* [1996] 2 S.C.R., 539).
2 *Ibid.,* 1123.
3 *Ibid.,* 1101.
4 *Ibid.,* 1100.
5 *Mabo* v. *Queensland (No 2)* (1992), 107 A.L.R., 43.
6 Nisga'a Final Agreement, Canada, British Columbia, and the Nisga'a Nation (4 August 1998, reprinted December 1998) c.19, s.3. The treaty has been ratified by the Nisga'a Nation and enacted by the BC legislature as the Nisga'a Final Agreement Act, S.B.C., 1999, c.2.
7 Richard Overstall, "One Common Brotherhood: Utopian Communities and Present Governance in the Nisga'a Final Agreement" (Faculty of Law, University of Victoria, 2000).
8 Sonia Lawrence and Patrick Macklem, "From Consultation to Reconciliation: Aboriginal Rights and the Crown's Duty to Consult" (2000) 79 Canadian Bar Review 254.
9 *Delgamuukw,* 1113.
10 *Kitkatla Band* v. *British Columbia (Minister of Forests),* [1998] B.C.J. No. 1616 at para. 51 (B.C.S.C.) (Q.L.), affirmed, *Kitkatla Band* v. *British Columbia (Minister of Forests),* [1998] B.C.J. No. 1600 (B.C.C.A.) (Q.L.).
11 *Ibid.,* para. 52.
12 *Ibid.,* para. 59.
13 Esson J.A.'s concurring opinion in *Westar Timber* v. *Ryan* (1989), 60 D.L.R. 453 at 472 (B.C.C.A.).
14 *Ryan* v. *Fort St. James Forest District et al.* (1994), 40 B.C.A.C. 93.
15 For example, the acceptance of government policies as constraints on consultation in *Halfway River First Nation* v. *Ministry of Forests* (1999), 64 B.C.L.R. (3rd) 206 (B.C.C.A.).
16 Robert A. Williams Jr., "Documents of Barbarism: The Contemporary Legacy of European Racism and Colonialism in the Narrative Traditions of Federal Indian Law," in Richard Delgado, ed., *Critical Race Theory: The Cutting Edge* (Philadelphia: Temple University Press, 1995), 98 at 99.
17 "Native difference is denied where its acceptance would result in the questioning of basic premises concerning the nature of property, contract, sovereignty or constitutional right. Native difference is acknowledged where its denial would achieve a similar result." Patrick Macklem, "First Nations Self-Government and the Borders of the Canadian Legal Imagination" (1991) 36 McGill Law Journal 392.
18 Lon Fuller and William Perdue, "The Reliance Interest in Contract Damages" (1936) 46 Yale Law Journal 52.

19 *Delgamuukw*, 1113.
20 See, for example, James Frideres, *Native People in Canada: Contemporary Conflicts* (Scarborough, ON: Prentice Hall, 1983), c.6; Michael Jackson, "Locking Up Natives in Canada" (1989) 23 University of British Columbia Law Review 5.
21 See, for example, Peter Cheney, "How Money Has Cursed Alberta's Samson Cree," *Globe and Mail*, 24 April 1999, A1; Cheney, "Judge Lays Blame for Reserve Suicides," *Globe and Mail*, 22 September 1999; and K. Charleson, "Finger-pointing and Feuding Hinder Aboriginal Advances," *Vancouver Sun*, 25 March 2000, A23.
22 Tom Pocklington and Sarah Pocklington, "Aboriginal Political Ethics," in John Langford and Allan Tupper, eds., *Corruption, Character and Conduct* (Toronto: Oxford University Press, 1993), 51.
23 *Ibid.*
24 Such nuanced decision making by hunters is vividly described in Hugh Brody, *Maps and Dreams: Indians and the British Columbia Frontier* (Toronto: Douglas and McIntyre, 1988), c.5.
25 Pocklington, "Aboriginal Political Ethics," 59-61.
26 *Delgamuukw*, 1089.
27 For the basis of the land holding laws of the Gitxsan and Wet'suwet'en plaintiffs in *Delgamuukw*, see Gisdaywa and Delgamuukw, *The Spirit in the Land* (Gabriola, BC: Reflections, 1987), 25-26, 35.
28 Examples of such arbitrary limits on s.35 rights include the "food, social and ceremonial purposes" for fishing rights in *R. v. Sparrow* (1990), 70 D.L.R., 403 (S.C.C.); the "practice, custom or tradition integral to the distinctive culture" test for Aboriginal rights in *R. v. Van der Peet*, [1996] 9 W.W.R., 27 (S.C.C.); the "modern equivalent of sustenance: food, clothing and housing, supplemented by a few amenities" for the Aboriginal trade right in *R. v. Gladstone*, [1996] 2 S.C.R., 816; and the "moderate livelihood" for a treaty trade right in *R. v. Marshall* (1999), 177 D.L.R. (4th) 513 (S.C.C.). All Aboriginal rights and title are further limited by Crown infringement for "compelling and substantial objectives" (*Delgamuukw*, 1107), which can be justified using a test similar to the *Oakes* test for infringement of Charter rights under s.1.
29 *Delgamuukw*, 1089. By establishing an inherent limit to Aboriginal title, the Court in *Delgamuukw* is adopting the "internal limit" to Aboriginal rights proposed by McLachlin J. in dissent in *Van der Peet*, 92.
30 *Delgamuukw*, 1091.
31 In *Delgamuukw*, Lamer C.J. said that if the Crown wishes to put Aboriginal title lands to a use that infringes on Aboriginal title, the Crown's fiduciary duty is invoked. He uses examples that show that even infringing uses requiring the group's full consent would clearly be within the irreconcilable use limit (*Delgamuukw*, 1111-14). If an Aboriginal group wishes to put title lands to an irreconcilable use, it would have to surrender them to the Crown (*Delgamuukw*, 1091), which would again invoke the Crown's fiduciary duty to deal with the lands in the best interests of the group (*Guerin v. R.*, [1984] 2 S.C.R., 376). These overlapping fiduciary duties would put such a burden on the Crown that neither it nor the Aboriginal group could breach the irreconcilable limit without the consent of the other.
32 *Ibid.*, 1090.
33 *Ibid.*, quoting Edward Burn, *Cheshire and Burn's Modern Law of Real Property*, 14th ed. (London: Butterworths, 1988), 264.
34 Burn, *Cheshire and Burn's Modern Law.*
35 *Williams v. Williams* (1810), 12 East, 222 (Eng. K.B.).
36 For example, for the Gitxsan and Wet'suwet'en plaintiffs in *Delgamuukw*, this would be joint tail female, given their matrilineal succession and communal land holdings by each extended family house group.
37 *Vane v. Lord Barnard* (1716), 2 Vern. 738 at 739 (Eng. Ch.).
38 R.H. Maudsley, *Hanbury's Modern Equity*, 9th ed. (London: Stevens and Sons, 1969), 4.
39 *Ibid.*, 86.
40 Brian Slattery argues that the fiduciary relationship between Aboriginal peoples and the Crown is a special instance of a general doctrine of collective trust that animates the Canadian Constitution as whole (B. Slattery, "First Nations and the Constitution: A Question of Trust" (1992) 71 Canadian Bar Review 261).

41 *Guerin* v. *R.*, [1984] 2 S.C.R., 371.
42 *Ibid.*, 387.
43 *Ibid.*, 376.
44 *Ibid.*, 383.
45 *R.* v. *Simon,* [1985] 2 S.C.R. 387; *R.* v. *Sioui,* [1990] 1 S.C.R. 1025; *Sparrow,* 29; *Delgamuukw.*
46 This suggestion is not novel. Maitland claimed trusts were the main agent of English "social experimentation" and shielded groups from the "assaults of individualistic theory." Trusts, he said, provided the legal framework for the Inns of Court, Lloyds insurance company, the London Stock Exchange, various nonconformist churches, and the London clubs; F.W. Maitland, "Trust and Corporation," in H.A.L. Fisher, ed., *The Collected Papers of Frederick William Maitland* (Cambridge, UK: Williams and Norgate, 1911), 371. At about the same time, historian Ernest Barker wrote, "It may indeed be urged that the trust has sheltered group-life more fully than any legal recognition of the "real personality" of groups could ever have done. Hidden behind their trustees, groups have thrived and grown unnoticed." Ernest Barker, "The Discredited State: Thoughts on Politics Before the War" (1915) 2 Political Quarterly 107.
47 The discussion here focuses on the current issues arising out of the reconciliation of Aboriginal and Crown rights and title. The trust model described can also be used to reconcile Aboriginal and non-Aboriginal land use at the community level. See, for example, Cheri Burda, et al., *Forests in Trust: Reforming British Columbia's Forest Tenure System for Ecosystem and Community Health* (Victoria, BC: Eco-Research Chair of Environmental Law and Policy, University of Victoria, 1997).
48 *Delgamuukw,* 1097.
49 *Ibid.*, 1101.
50 *Ibid.*, 1100.
51 *Ibid.*, 1103.
52 D.W.M. Waters, "The Role of the Trust in Environmental Protection Law," in D.W.M. Waters, ed., *Equity, Fiduciaries and Trusts* (Toronto: Carswell, 1993), 384. Under a public trust, the state has a fiduciary obligation to ensure that public coastlines and rivers are continuously available to the public at large. This concept has been expanded in some American courts to include protection of the public from pollution and other environmental threats. Dr. Waters links public trusts with the English common law principle of *parens patriae* and the Roman law principle of *bonus paterfamilias,* "he who cares for and tends to the best interests of his family" – an apt precis of the role of a chief in Aboriginal law.
53 *Delgamuukw,* 1098.
54 *Ibid.*, 1081.
55 This is known as the class ascertainability test.
56 Perpetuity Act, R.S.B.C. 1996, c.358.
57 E.E. Gillese, *The Law of Trusts* (Concord, ON: Irwin Law, 1997), 59.
58 *Delgamuukw,* 1089.
59 For example, the Inuit obtained exemption for the Nunavut Trust through special federal legislation (Agreement Between the Inuit of Nunavut Settlement Area and Canada, 25 May 1993, article 31.1.5, ratified and given effect by Canada under the Nunavut Land Claims Agreement Act, S.C. 1993, c.29).
60 *Native Communications Society of B.C.* v. *M.N.R.* (1986), 86 D.T.C., 6357 (F.C.A.).
61 *Ibid.*, 6359. The "Statute of Elizabeth" still used by courts today refers to An Acte to Redress the Misemployment of Landes, Goodes and Stockes of Money heretofore Given to Charitable Uses, 1601, 43 Eliz. 1, c.4. This act was passed along with the first English Poor Laws, and Aboriginal people in Canada today might find some irony in using a statute designed to contain the social and economic dislocation caused by the enclosure of communal fields and common lands by the dominant segment of society.
62 Anthony Scott, "Moving Through the Narrows: From Open Access to ITQs and Self-Government" (paper presented to the FishRights 99 Conference, Fremantle, Australia, 18 November 1999).
63 Evelyn Pinkerton, "Factors in Overcoming Barriers to Implementing Co-Management in British Columbia Salmon Fisheries" (1989) 3 Conservation Biology 2.
64 See, for example, "Preamble" to *Nisga'a Final Agreement.*

13
Parallel Justice Systems, or a Tale of Two Spiders
Dale Dewhurst

Recently, attempts have been made to modify or create systems of justice to respond to Aboriginal rights and values. One such attempt is the establishment of Canada's first Aboriginal Court, the Tsuu T'ina First Nation Court.[1] Staunch advocates of the adversarial system of justice may complain that the First Nation Court gives Aboriginal people too much power; or, they may complain that it breaches fundamental principles of justice by providing separate justice systems for Aboriginals and non-Aboriginals. However, it is my position that where the court model is weak it is because Aboriginal people have too little control.

My concern is that attempts to introduce Aboriginal justice systems into the "adversarial system" (the term used to designate the current Canadian justice system) are prone to fail where the two systems have differing levels of authority. If Aboriginal systems are considered to be alternative, preliminary, of lower authority, or unofficial, their opponents will resort to the more "final" or "official" adversarial system in controversial cases. Instead, Aboriginal justice systems must be designed as authoritative and parallel models of justice. To discover some of the principles necessary to achieve this end, I will critically examine the rationale and structure of the Tsuu T'ina First Nation Court and I will draw out three useful comparative points from the historical development of the courts of common law and equity. This critique and comparison will show how we may take further steps toward achieving truly authoritative and parallel Aboriginal justice models. But first of all, for those who want a shorter route, the problem and its solution are revealed in the tale of the two spiders.

A Tale of Two Spiders
Once upon a time there were two spiders in a lodge, sitting on the roof, discussing the web of justice. After a very long time they both agreed there was injustice in the world that needed to be fixed. And, because spinning webs is what spiders do, they both agreed that they had to spin a better

web. But, sadly, they could not agree on how the new web should be spun. So, each spider decided to try to solve the problem in the best way she could.

The first spider continued to sit on the roof thinking about how to build the complete and perfect web. She sat and she sat without moving, without spinning, thinking about all the things that could go wrong. If she moved too fast she might make a misstep, destroy the web, or fall to her death far below. If the creatures that sometimes lived in the lodge with her didn't like her web, or if it got in their way, she would be frustrated and hurt by building her web only to have it smashed. The more she thought, the more problems she discovered. To try to head off these disasters, she thought about the best place to start her web. While many places seemed beneficial, none seemed perfect. So, she thought about where her web should end. Again, there were too many possibilities. She couldn't sort through them all. So then she thought about the exact design of her web. There were just too many things beyond her control that might affect the web's shape, like the wind and the movements of the other creatures. She finally decided that she could not predict exactly how her web should turn out. When the other creatures saw her sitting there and offered to give her a helping hand, she refused for fear that the hand might crush her or be snatched away, leaving her to fall. So there she sat, without a web to sustain her, and there she died.

The second spider crawled across the roof of the lodge looking for a place to spin her web. In a little while she found an opening where no webs had been built. Although she wasn't sure exactly how her web would turn out, she felt that it had to begin with the first strand. So, anchoring the first strand of her web securely to the framework of the lodge around her, she dropped into the empty space. There she hung, suspended in midair. She wasn't sure where the wind or the other passing creatures would take her but she placed her faith in the forces of nature to take her to a spot where she could tie off her first strand. The wind blew her back and forth. Finally, it blew her to a place where she could tie off her first strand and she quickly did so. Then she started the whole process over again. On and on she worked, and her web took shape: sometimes through her own efforts, sometimes redirected or assisted by those around her, sometimes guided by the forces of nature. As she spun, some of the old strands were cut or broken, and she replaced them or resecured them. She never knew in advance what the final shape of her web would be. As her web developed she took time to appreciate what she had done and a pattern began to emerge. In the end, after long effort, she had spun something unique and beautiful. Her web was firm and flexible, it filled the openings that she had found, and it was able to sustain her in a way that nothing had before.

The Development of the Tsuu T'ina First Nation Court

The Tsuu T'ina First Nation Court is the result of a proposal made by the Tsuu T'ina Nation of Alberta and the report of a review team established to look into the proposal (hereafter the "report"). Before the review team prepared the report, Tsuu T'ina representatives gave a presentation to the team.[2] Some of the essential aspects of the presentation follow.

Generally, First Nations people see the adversarial system as based on fear, intimidation, partiality, unfairness, and bias against First Nations' perspectives.[3] In fact, First Nations' concepts of justice were rejected wholesale by the colonizers and little concession was made to Aboriginal cultural, social, or governmental structures.[4] While First Nations people do not desire the return of a pre-colonial state, they do insist upon becoming empowered and taking responsibility for creating a justice system that addresses justice issues with Aboriginal values.[5]

Essential to Aboriginal justice is a focus on "restoration of harmony (healing)" as opposed to the over-emphasis on deterrence and punishment in the adversarial system.[6] While the differences between the approaches are numerous, the Tsuu T'ina Nation believes the two approaches can accommodate each other and work together.[7] Unfortunately, to this point, most of the accommodations in cases of conflict have been made by sacrificing Aboriginal values.[8]

Because of this value schism, and ongoing Aboriginal compromises, the First Nations people have understandably seen the adversarial system as one that was forced upon them.[9] Their initial response was an adverse reaction to the adversary system; the secondary result, "chronic *over-representation* of First Nations people in the current justice and corrections systems and under-representation before agencies such as the National Parole Board."[10] For example: in Alberta, Aboriginal people make up 5 percent of the population and account for 39 percent of sentenced admissions to custody; in Manitoba, Aboriginal people make up 12 percent of the population and account for 58 percent of sentenced admissions to custody; and, in Saskatchewan, Aboriginal people make up 11 percent of the population and account for 74 percent of sentenced admissions to custody.[11] The only meaningful ways to resolve these problems seem to require substantial changes in the justice system to incorporate Aboriginal values and accommodations being made by the adversarial system in favour of the Aboriginal system where the two conflict.[12] To allay the fears of a non-Aboriginal population unwilling to undergo such change, the Tsuu T'ina representatives pointed out that the Aboriginal traditional way is compatible with Christian principles and the Canadian Charter of Rights and Freedoms.[13]

Based upon the Tsuu T'ina First Nation proposal, the presentation made by its representatives, and the report, a Tsuu T'ina First Nation Court was established. Because of the desire not to isolate First Nations people from the surrounding population, the review team concluded that the court should work within the adversarial system, not as a free-standing institution.[14] Initial thoughts about developing a separate *Criminal Code* were rejected: (1) to avoid duplication, (2) to avoid a focus on identifying criminal behaviours, and (3) in favour of a change in emphasis away from defining offences toward consideration of how to deal with offences.[15] In the view of the review team, theft is theft, and assault is assault, no matter which perspective they are viewed from.[16] And, undoubtedly, there is a practical problem in expecting the Tsuu T'ina Nation to put in all the upfront work that would be required to recreate an entire criminal code and the case law that interprets it.

As a result, the court was designed to be an enhancement to the adversarial system and not a separate system.[17] In keeping with this vision, the First Nation Court was instituted as a full-fledged provincial court. It has the full jurisdiction of any other provincial court but its operation is limited to offences committed on the reserve.[18]

To more adequately respond to Aboriginal values, the report required a First Nations prosecutor and judge to be appointed. Both were to be aware of Aboriginal cultural values and fully qualified as members of the bar.[19] In the case of the judge, he or she was to have resided on a reserve and ordinarily qualify for the bench.[20] Additionally, Aboriginal court administration was to be established and a peacemaker component was to be added.

The report provides that when the judge renders decisions, full records are to be kept and reported.[21] Beyond administering justice in the adversarial system, the judge is to "bridge the cultural divide between the First Nation community and the non-Aboriginal community and justice system."[22] The review team believed that the judge having resided on a reserve would ensure that he or she had the necessary cultural awareness.[23] However, it was conceded that the appointment of the judge remains a provincial responsibility and that "the discretion inherent in that responsibility must not be fettered by any proposal."[24] Why this principle was considered to be untouchable was not explained. The report also acknowledges the independence of the chief provincial court judge and the assistant chief judge in approving venues and scheduling judges to sit in various provincial court locations, including the First Nation Court.[25] The line drawn by the review team was to say that if the authorities did not find it appropriate to appoint an Aboriginal judge, then the First Nation Court should not proceed.[26]

As for the prosecutor, the review team envisioned Aboriginal values coming into play when prosecutorial discretion is used to decide what charges to lay and which charges to proceed with.[27] Where healing and restorative justice can bring a suitable resolution, laying formal charges is not required.[28] In making these decisions, the prosecutor works closely with the peacemakers.[29] However, the prosecutor remains, at all times, under the authority of the chief Crown prosecutor of Alberta.[30]

While the judge and prosecutor work within the adversarial system, modified by Aboriginal values where no prohibitive conflict exists, peacemakers have a different role. Peacemakers focus on healing, incorporation of Aboriginal values, and the desire to mend breaches between offenders and their community.[31] They work with elders, the accused, victims, the community, and all people relevantly connected to the problem behaviour.[32] They become involved at the outset, providing traditional and nontraditional dispute resolution. They make recommendations for sentencing. And they deal with pre-charge and post-charge diversion.[33] The peacemakers' role may involve "traditional circles, sweat lodges and spiritual healing techniques"[34] or any other method of problem solving they consider helpful.[35] Their goal is to address as many problems as possible in the community[36] and restore healthy family relationships.[37] In fulfilling this role, the peacemakers look for underlying causes of criminal behaviour and attempt to address them.[38] Unlike the neutral mediators operating in the shadow of the adversarial system, the peacemakers take an active role to promote and teach traditional Aboriginal values.[39] *"Restoring healthy relationships grounded in spirituality* is of paramount importance" to the peacemakers.[40] But, in the final analysis, where there is disagreement about the cases to be handled by the peacemakers, the decision of the prosecutor is final.[41]

Finally, the costs of the Aboriginal justice system are to be borne by the provincial and federal governments.[42]

Critique of the Tsuu T'ina First Nation Court

Although the Tsuu T'ina First Nation Court represents a step forward for Aboriginal justice systems, further steps need to be taken if a truly authoritative and parallel justice model is to be realized. As indicated above, one of the major desires of the Tsuu T'ina Nation was to find a way to address the chronic overrepresentation of Aboriginal people in sentenced admissions to custody. Here, the new court is deficient in at least two ways.

First, there are a large number of indictable or hybrid offences where either provincial court judges cannot have jurisdiction or accused may elect trial by a judge, or judge and jury, in a superior court of criminal jurisdiction.[43] As a result, a large number of offences committed on the reserve will not be dealt with by the First Nation Court. Any negative impact from this may be modified by the accused electing, where possible, to remain within the jurisdiction of the provincial court. But to really address this concern, the judicial authority of Aboriginal justice systems must be expanded to include the judicial authority of superior courts of criminal jurisdiction.

A second problem which gets in the way of addressing overrepresentation of Aboriginals in sentenced facilities is that a large number of convictions which result in incarceration of Aboriginal people are the result of offences committed off the reserve. To address this issue, the geographical authority of Aboriginal justice systems must expand to include all areas in which Aboriginal accused are charged with criminal offences.

Heated objections to these suggestions can be anticipated. Those opposed to Aboriginal justice systems will certainly not want to grant them even more power. As well, there is the concern of setting up separate justice systems for Aboriginals and non-Aboriginals. In response to the first objection, it must be remembered that even if Aboriginal justice systems were given the power of superior courts of criminal jurisdiction, they would still be bound by the law and procedural rules that apply to superior courts.

As to the second objection – the concern about separate justice systems – those voicing it may be genuine or not. If their concern is that the new systems will not do justice in Aboriginal hands, it is hard to find a supporting reason that is not based in condescension or prejudice. Such a position must either be based on the argument that there is a flaw in the system or a flaw in the people running it. If it's the people who are the concern, the objection is likely motivated by prejudice. For there can be no objective evidence that Aboriginal people are naturally incapable of running a justice system or that they are likely to excuse the serious criminal behaviour of other Aboriginal people. If it's the new system that is the concern, the objection is likely motivated by condescension and the assumption that Aboriginal justice systems cannot possibly be as good as the adversarial system. Factually, the record of the adversarial system in dealing with Aboriginal people is not strong evidence for its superiority – just the opposite. Philosophically, there is strong support for the values underlying Aboriginal justice systems and only time will tell how effective the Aboriginal approaches are in practice.

A stronger way to phrase the second objection is that with two systems, Aboriginal and non-Aboriginal accused may receive different treatment for the same crimes; this would offend fundamental principles of fairness. This may be addressed by allowing all accused, Aboriginal and non-Aboriginal alike, to elect the system under which they would be tried.[44] Under the Aboriginal justice system, the accused would be held accountable to their victims, their family, and their community, instead of being held accountable to the court and to the state, as under the adversarial system. The offenders would be required to take responsibility for their behaviour, and the community would become more responsible for policing the accused and helping them to change, grow, and avoid re-offending. Also, with two cooperating systems, the peacemakers would be able to redirect Aboriginal and non-Aboriginal offenders back into the adversarial system if they concluded that the offenders were not serious about making amends or addressing the underlying causes of their criminal behaviour. Equal treatment and equal opportunity would be ensured by the accused's election, and the system that proved to be most beneficial to the joint interests of society and accused would be enabled to develop.

Another problem with the First Nation Court is that the adversarial system remains the default position in cases of conflict. A concern of Aboriginal people is that they see the adversarial system as based on fear, intimidation, partiality, unfairness, and bias. The new model does take steps to address this by involving peacemakers and by attempting to ensure that all accused, victims and others relevantly connected, are aware of their rights before they go through the system. However, the central processes of the adversarial system do not change. Peacemakers may intervene to avoid the system, or the accused may be better informed within the system, but the adversarial system remains fairly stable. Because there is no power to create offences or modify existing ones, convictions will continue to be based on offences promulgated in accordance with non-Aboriginal value systems.

While the authors of the report dealt with this concern by indicating that theft is theft and assault is assault, when viewed from either perspective, this may not be accurate. For example, Aboriginal people do not traditionally view property and land ownership in the same way as it is viewed in the English law tradition. Accordingly, offences created with an English law perspective on land and property rights are not necessarily the same as the offences that would have been created under Aboriginal traditional laws. Looking directly at the offence of theft, the Criminal Code states: "Everyone commits theft who fraudulently and without colour of right takes, or fraudulently and without colour of right converts to his use or to the use of another person, anything whether animate or inanimate, with intent, (a) to deprive, temporarily or absolutely, the owner of it, or a person who has a special property or interest in it, of the thing or of his property or interest in it."[45]

Even if the wording of the offence is acceptable from both perspectives, there is no guarantee that the case law interpreting such terms as takings or convertings "without colour of right" would have developed in similar ways. And, because case law is an equally authoritative element of criminal law, it is oversimplifying to state that "theft is theft."

To clarify this point, I wish to share three teachings that were given to me by an elder.[46] First, with regard to Aboriginal property, there were many instances where it was considered acceptable to take an item without anyone else's express permission, providing something of equal or greater value was left in its place. Anyone who tried to take advantage of this customary way by leaving nothing, or by leaving goods of inferior worth, would be punished or tormented by the spirits, the community, or both. From a non-Aboriginal perspective, the initial taking would be theft. It would be addressed by the law or directly by the original owner.

A second example involves a sacred bundle located on the Blood Reserve. This bundle is known as The Many Peoples Bundle. Originally it was a Cree bundle that was taken by the Blood. Over time, ceremonies were given to the Blood in connection with the bundle and it remains in Blood possession. It is not really correct to say that it is Cree property, nor is it really correct to say that it is Blood property. It is not really correct to say it is property at all. It has found it own place, where it is supposed to be. From a non-Aboriginal perspective, the Blood stole the bundle from the Cree.

A final example relates to a traditional man by the name of Manygrey-horses. Manygreyhorses had dreams and visions about a sacred bundle that had come into the possession of a museum. Manygreyhorses had never been to the museum or physically seen the bundle before. Not being sure what to do about the dreams and visions, he consulted with the other traditional people in his community. After much prayer it was decided that the bundle was calling to Manygreyhorses and that he should go get it. If he did not, he would be offending traditional law and his family and those close to him would suffer as a result. The rest of the traditional people said they would help him by staying on the reserve and praying for him while he completed his task. So, Manygreyhorses went to the museum, went directly to the bundle, and took it from its resting place. No one stopped him. He took the bundle outside, prayed to the four directions, and then took the bundle home. At some later time, a man from the museum came to see Manygreyhorses. He demanded the return of the bundle. Instead, Manygreyhorses built a teepee, put out many valuable offerings, and asked the man from the museum whether the offerings were sufficient exchange. The man from the museum agreed they were. A transfer ceremony was conducted and the matter was concluded. All was done according to traditional law. However, from a non-Aboriginal perspective, Manygreyhorses was guilty of theft;[47] perhaps the other traditional people who advised and helped him were guilty of aiding and abetting a criminal offence.[48]

What these examples tell us is that theft has not been traditionally viewed the same way from both perspectives; that is, theft is not theft. Either the wording of the offence, the case law interpreting its application, or both require amendment to comply with Aboriginal laws.

A further concern with the First Nation Court is that, because the court is only a provincial court, it is bound by all the decisions of all the superior courts. Even though its own decisions are recorded, they are not binding authority for any other court, not even for other provincial courts. While other courts may consider the First Nation Court decisions as persuasive authority, no other court is bound to follow them. Additionally, as the provincial court is the lowest level of court, its decisions are readily subject to being overturned on appeal. Therefore, any other court that disagrees with the decisions of the First Nation Court can ignore them or overturn them.

The ability to subvert the intention of Aboriginal justice systems does not stop with the procedural functioning of the legal system. Under the structure of the First Nation Court, the peacemakers have a wider range of authority, and are more able to incorporate Aboriginal values into the administration of justice, than any comparable position in the adversarial system. However, the peacemakers are free to act under the guidance of Aboriginal cultural values and laws only until they come into conflict with the values and laws that the prosecutor is required to enforce. In such cases, the prosecutor has final say.

Similarly, the prosecutor can exercise his or her discretion, to either proceed with charges or send the case to the peacemakers, only within the prescribed limits imposed upon the prosecutor by his or her superiors in the Chief Crown Prosecutor's Office. While there may be no reason to assume that the Chief Crown Prosecutor's Office will act in bad faith, the overrepresentation of Aboriginal offenders in sentenced facilities tells us that bias and prejudice are realities of the current system. Even if this bias and prejudice cannot be directly attributed to the Chief Crown Prosecutor's Office, it is unavoidable that the office's decisions will be grounded in non-Aboriginal conceptions of justice. Aspects of Aboriginal justice of which the office is unaware, does not understand, or which make the office uncomfortable, will be easily overridden.

These problems may continue with the judge. Because the judge must be someone ordinarily qualified for the bench, he or she is trained in the adversarial system of justice, expected to follow the adversarial system of justice, and subject to scrutiny or removal by the chief provincial court judge if there is a perceived failure to comply. The judge may temper his or her rulings with Aboriginal cultural values and laws, but only until there is conflict. Even if the judge does not act in a way that would justify his or her removal from the bench, the chief provincial court judge can simply schedule another judge to sit. Again, there may be no reason to assume bad faith on the part of the chief provincial court judge, but the same problems of lack of understanding and unease come into play here as they did for the decisions of the Chief Crown Prosecutor's Office. Because the Aboriginal community is not interested in proceeding without an Aboriginal judge, this could lead to the downfall of the court. The point is that decisions which could lead to the downfall of the court are entirely within the discretion of the chief provincial court judge.

Finally, the fate of Aboriginal justice systems can also be sealed by determinations of the provincial and federal finance departments. If funding is withdrawn, the systems will collapse. The Aboriginal community, without its own powers of taxation and revenue generation, will be unable to support them alone.

So, to this point we have seen that Aboriginal people wanted to be responsible for the creation of their own justice system but that the adversarial system is still the default position. Where the First Nation Court model is most effective is in avoiding the adversarial system in the first place: for example, by the peacemakers diverting the process from the courts or the prosecutor choosing not to lay charges. But, as was discussed, even with the continued goodwill of all involved, the First Nation Court can only bring in Aboriginal values when dealing with less serious criminal offences, committed on the reserve. Offences considered more serious under the Criminal Code will be dealt with by the courts of superior criminal jurisdiction; or, if the offences are important and controversial, (1) they can be taken out of the peacemakers' hands by the prosecutor; (2) they can be taken out of the prosecutor's hands by the chief Crown prosecutor; (3) they can be taken out of the judge's hands by the binding principles of the adversarial system, including the precedent-setting decisions of the superior courts; (4) they can be taken out of the judge's hands by the chief provincial court judge; (5) they can be overturned on appeal; or (6) Aboriginal justice systems can be shut down by withdrawing provincial or federal funding.

In a cynical nutshell, it could amount to saying the following: "We (the politically more powerful supporters of the adversarial system) respect you (the politically weaker supporters of Aboriginal justice systems). Accordingly, we will *let* you deal with your own justice matters when they are of little significance to us and don't unduly disrupt our adversarial model of justice. However, in the event of disruption or excessive cost, our system and our values must prevail. Even though our system hasn't worked for you, and even though we know little about your system, we know ours is better. So, we reserve the right to intervene in our sole discretion when we consider a matter to be too important to let you deal with it on your own." The Aboriginal people wanted to have the adversarial system and Aboriginal justice systems work together without having all accommodations being made by sacrificing Aboriginal values; this has not been fully achieved.

Comparisons with the Development of the Courts of Common Law and Equity

In this section I propose to show how the expectations of the Aboriginal people are neither unreasonable nor unique in the historical development of systems of justice. Aboriginal requests to have their cultural norms, and their traditional and spiritual laws, incorporated into the justice system are very similar to the demands placed upon the courts of common law and the courts of equity as the English law developed.

The first point of comparison is between the inclusion of English secular values in the development of the courts of common law and the Aboriginal requests for the development of a justice system based upon Aboriginal cultural values. The common law, in its development, has been described in numerous general ways. It is the non-ecclesiastical or secular development of the law. It originally began its development in the Anglo-Saxon and Norman times (somewhere between the sixth and eleventh centuries) and has been described as "the commonsense of the community, crystallised and formulated by our forefathers."[49] It can be distinguished from statute law, promulgated by kings and legislators; and from equitable law, deriving originally from the ecclesiastical courts. The common law is considered to be organic, unfolding over time as decisions are made.[50] Given its early beginnings and that the common law is still evolving, we have a development period of over fourteen hundred years without perfection yet being achieved.

More specifically defined, the common law is the written record of court decisions that set out, preserve, and enforce the secular customs of a community. As such, judicial decisions and judge-made maxims are critical in recognizing and codifying a culture's secular values. Over time, as the culture's secular values become more completely enshrined in the case law, direct resort to custom is replaced by resort to case law alone.[51] If judges are unaware of a culture's values, the values cannot be incorporated into the court's decisions or find their way into the system as principles of law. Or, if cultural values are incorporated in judgments that are not binding on other courts, again, the culture's values cannot find their way into the system as principles of law. Thus, for the development of the common law, three elements are required: (1) recognition and inclusion of secular cultural values in court decisions, (2) a system where these principles become binding legal principles for future decisions, and (3) a gradual transformation in the principles' status from the realm of cultural wisdom to legal principle.

The problem, in the case of the First Nation Court, is that these three requirements are not met. While the judge of the First Nation Court may recognize the secular cultural values of the Aboriginal community, the judge is unduly limited in his or her ability to include them in the court's decisions. Accordingly, the first condition is not met. Because the First Nation Court's decisions are not binding on any other court, the second condition is not met. Finally, because the principles cannot enter into the system in the first place, they cannot undergo a gradual transformation from the realm of cultural wisdom into legal principle; therefore, the third principle is not met.

This conclusion may be further supported with a bit more analysis on how the procedures under the criminal law can work to subvert Aboriginal cultural values. As stated by the Tsuu T'ina representatives, a focus on harmony and healing is critical to Aboriginal justice systems. The First Nation Court addresses this to some extent by involving peacemakers, and by having Aboriginal court administrators, prosecutors, and judges. But, when the judge reviews the peacemakers' sentencing recommendations, the judge is still legally bound to impose a sentence in keeping with the range established by statute and cases involving other accused in similar circumstances. The Aboriginal desire to sentence with more emphasis on rehabilitation or restitution may, at times, be overridden by the adversarial system's emphasis upon principles of deterrence and retribution.

Also, to summarize what was stated in the critique above, because the First Nation Court is only a provincial court, its decisions are not a binding authority for any other court. Any other court that disagrees with the decisions of the First Nation Court can ignore them or overturn them. While the peacemakers have a wide range of authority, the prosecutor has the final say in regard to their decisions. The prosecutor, in turn, can be overridden by the Chief Crown Prosecutor's Office, which may be unaware of Aboriginal cultural values. The judge is bound by the laws and precedents of the adversarial system and can be overridden or transferred by a chief provincial court judge who, again, may be unaware of Aboriginal cultural values.

The second point of comparison is between the inclusion of English ecumenical/spiritual values in the development of the courts of equity and the Aboriginal requests for the development of a justice system based upon Aboriginal spiritual values and traditional laws. In the development of the courts of equity in the English tradition, these courts sought to apply moral standards that the common law had ignored.[52] Equity refers to "ideas of that which is just or right, or that which is derived from the exercise of the conscience or from the doctrines of so-called 'natural justice.'"[53] In its development, equity took on a strange role, being both "separate from, and yet a part of, the general [common] law."[54] In some cases equity developed beside the common law, supplementing its gaps; at other times, equity overrode the common law, based on a claim to the "superior sanctity inherent in these [equitable] principles."[55]

The development of equity in England can be clearly traced to the twelfth century. For example, in 1180 the chancellor spoke about the duties of the court of Chancery as including the duty to fulfill equitable commandments and make good the evil laws of the realm.[56] When a person was "without remedy in the common law, therefore he requireth the Chancellor according to equity and reason to provide for him and to take such order as to good conscience shall appertain."[57] Relief was often sought with an appeal for "charity in God's name" and a request for remedies based in reason, right, and conscience.[58]

Accordingly, the rules of equity emerged out of the ecclesiastical courts. These courts were initially presided over by bishops, who applied the residual powers of the king to do justice. Where common law decisions were not in keeping with natural law, the ecclesiastical courts made appropriate corrections. As a result of the ecclesiastical background of the chancellors, decisions in equity took on a spiritual or natural law flavour.[59] As with the common law, judicial decisions and judge-made maxims were critical in recognizing and codifying the culture's spiritual values. If judges were not aware of the culture's spiritual values, the values could not be incorporated in court decisions or find their way into the system as principles of equity.

One problem as equity developed was its unpredictability. In the courts of equity, relief was not restricted to "rules of strict of logic or by analogy to prior decisions."[60] Different interpretations of natural law by various chancellors (or even the same chancellor at different times), or a different exercise of conscience, resulted in decisions that were irreconcilable.[61] Over time, "predictability became almost impossible."[62] Eventually, this problem was dealt with by legislative acts and changes in procedure that drew out and explicitly stated the nature of the equitable principles that were emerging.[63]

A second problem in the development of equity was the ongoing struggle to survive the challenges for supremacy made by the courts of common law. Notably between 1485 and 1615, there was much rivalry between the two courts.[64] This rivalry ended with an initial victory by the Chancery (acting in equity), and then with the fusion of equity and common law under the powers of a single court as a result of the Judicature Acts in the late 1800s.[65] Under the Judicature Acts, where any conflict remained, the principles of equity took priority.[66]

Thus, for well over eight hundred years (between the twelfth century when equity was clearly established and the nineteenth century when the Judicature Acts fused equity and common law), equity and the common law struggled side by side and often came into conflict. But, despite the sometimes overt struggles for supremacy, equity most often functioned as a supplement to the common law, filling in holes the common law had left.[67] With the fusion, it is now difficult for new principles of equity to emerge. Now equitable relief depends almost exclusively on precedent, as with the common law, rather than on spirituality and natural law.[68]

This general merging of equity and common law "has been the normal course of legal evolution throughout most of the world."[69] Principles of equity tend to appear in justice systems which no longer correspond to the needs of a society and attempt to correct the deficiencies in the current system.[70] Equity supplements or interferes with the common law to bring about natural justice; equitable decisions initially cover a broad area and are often irreconcilable; common principles begin to appear and become codified; finally, the principles of equity and the common law merge and a system remains somewhat dormant until the society, or an element within the society, is no longer receiving justice at the hands of the common law; equity then re-emerges.

Turning to the equitable demands of the Aboriginal community, when you talk to Aboriginal elders about the nature of law, it is not long before you'll be told that it is not sufficient to take an inadequate system and simply attempt to paste Aboriginal spirituality on top of it. Granting Aboriginal justice systems more of the common law powers of the courts of superior jurisdiction will bring Aboriginal cultural values and laws into play but will continue to leave out Aboriginal spiritual values and Aboriginal conceptions of the laws of nature. The true spirit of Aboriginal law can be achieved only when traditional spirituality provides the foundation for the law and the rest of the structure of the justice system is then built upon that foundation.[71] In short, elders will tell you that the supporters of the adversarial system have forgotten what the courts of equity recognized long ago. Spiritual laws, traditional moral standards, and cultural conceptions of the natural law must have a part to play in the development of the legal system. From an Aboriginal point of view, it is time for Aboriginal conceptions of equity to appear in a justice system that does not currently address the needs of Aboriginal society.

The objections to inclusion of Aboriginal conceptions of equity into the legal system will be numerous. First of all, Aboriginal spiritual values are not commonly shared by the majority of the country, unlike the case in England during the development of the laws of equity. However, forcing English or European values onto Aboriginal people is a colonial approach that has been far from successful in the past. It has been drastically unsuccessful in many ways for Aboriginal religious and social life, and colonial missionaries have been forced to reassess the usefulness of such an approach. It is now time for supporters of the adversarial justice system to rethink the usefulness of a colonial legal approach that denies Aboriginal conceptions of law.

It will also be objected that it is a mistake to see Aboriginals in Canada as a homogeneous whole. While this objection is undoubtedly true, it is not fatal for the inclusion of Aboriginal spiritual values in the justice system. First of all, there are some protocols or laws that are generally applicable among all Aboriginal nations.[72] Second, it must be remembered that the English laws of equity were initially unpredictable, as numerous interpretations of natural law were stated. In time, these various strands became consolidated by further judicial decisions or legislative acts. There's no reason to believe, at least at this time, that a similar result could not be expected from the inclusion of Aboriginal spiritual values and conceptions of natural law.

A further objection to including Aboriginal conceptions of equity in the legal system is that it will lead to too much conflict between Aboriginal justice systems and the adversarial system. Undoubtedly, there will be much conflict. Undoubtedly, there will be times when the adversarial system seeks to retain its power and overrule Aboriginal justice systems. This was the case in England, where the conflict between equity and the common law raged for centuries. However, this is the price that must be paid if we expect meaningful change. In England, especially in the period from 1485-1615, rivalry between equity and common law was intense. However, equity prevailed and the entire legal system was the better for it. In cases of conflict between Aboriginal values and adversarial values, it is time to have Aboriginal values prevail (at least in criminal cases where Aboriginals are involved or other accused elect to be tried in the Aboriginal justice system); the entire legal system will be the better for it.

To summarize, we have seen that Aboriginal justice systems need more powers akin to those employed in the development of the courts of common law and equity. With an expanded geographical and judicial scope, Aboriginal cultural and spiritual values and laws can be applied in more cases where Aboriginal people are involved. The ability for all accused, Aboriginal and non-Aboriginal alike, to elect the court system in which to be tried will grant Aboriginal values a broader role in shaping the nature of the entire justice system and, at the same time, preserve the principles of fairness and equal treatment under the law. As well, the benefits to be derived from an emphasis on restitution and rehabilitation will receive a greater test in society as a whole.

As the representatives of the Tsuu T'ina Nation indicated, they want to have a hand in developing the legal system without always being the ones to compromise. For supporters of the adversarial system to assume that justice cannot possibly benefit from Aboriginal input shows an unwarranted regard for the perfection of the adversarial system, or perpetuates an outdated colonial attitude that is condescending, prejudicial, or both. Ultimately, the fundamental values of Canada will be protected by the Charter, and the truly valuable principles of the adversarial system will survive because of their proven usefulness in the promotion of justice.

The third, and final, point of comparison is a brief one having to do with the time frames that can reasonably be imposed for the development of Aboriginal justice systems. In the development of the adversarial system (through its roots in common law and equity), the fact of the matter is that it has had over 1,400 years for its systems to develop and its principles to be discovered, and perfection still has not been achieved. Aboriginal justice systems need a similarly lengthy opportunity to shape the justice system with Aboriginal cultural and spiritual values and laws. While it will not take 1,400 years, since Aboriginal systems can build upon the adversarial system where desirable, it is not reasonable to expect Aboriginal justice systems to be complete and fully functioning in a short time frame. Undoubtedly, as is the case in the development of the common law and equity, there will be decisions that are later seen to be mistaken, but there's no reason to believe that Aboriginal justice systems will fail in their entirety if given the time, authority, and space they need to develop.

Conclusion: The Wisdom of the Spiders
Without doubt, the Tsuu T'ina court was the product of long and dedicated labour, negotiation, and compromise; it is a definite improvement on what came before it. Often, change comes slowly and we (Aboriginal and non-Aboriginal communities alike) must be satisfied with less-than-perfect incremental changes rather than holding out for complete and perfect change. That being said, the critical analysis and comparative points above reveal that further negotiations should take place and additional powers should be given to the Tsuu T'ina court (and other similar Aboriginal justice systems). Without additional powers, the Tsuu T'ina court is at risk of failing or, at least, of achieving something much less than the Aboriginal community and the non-Aboriginal community require.

The problem with the Tsuu T'ina First Nation Court is that too much of its effect depends upon others using their sole discretion in a way that is in keeping with the values, purposes, and intent of the court. This problem is compounded by the fact that the majority of those exercising this discretion may have little or no awareness of Aboriginal cultural and spiritual values and laws. First Nations people don't really have control over their own system of justice if, at any time, chief prosecutors, chief justices, attorneys general, courts of appeal, or federal and provincial departments of finance can pull the plug or overrule decisions with which they do not agree.

As with the spiders, there's no clear, predetermined path to perfect or certain success. Endless studies, pondering, inquiries, and commissions will amount to nothing if no actions are taken. Rationality and protracted reasoning will never tell us the answer in advance. It is time to build. We (and here I referred to all of us, Aboriginals and non-Aboriginals alike) must begin to build with genuine respect for each other, based upon the feeling that it is right and necessary, and based upon the faith that it will work out in the end. We must take the tools we have on hand, supplement them in some of the ways I have suggested, and simply start to build. If we like what is being created, we can foster it. If we are initially confused by what is being created, we can work to understand it. However, we must build something and resist the urge to tear it down just because it is being built in a way that we are not used to or had not foreseen. The input from Aboriginal spiritual and cultural values is needed to address the problem of over-representation of Aboriginal people in sentenced admissions to custody and to kick-start changes in a justice system that does not respect Aboriginal values and laws and no longer responds to the needs of society. All of us stand to gain, the Aboriginal community and the non-Aboriginal community alike.

Notes

1 As set out in *A New Direction: Report of the Review Team Established to Study the Tsuu T'ina Nation Proposal for a First Nation Court,* chaired by Karen Kryczka, M.L.A. Calgary West, Review Team: Harley Crowchild, Marsha Erb, Geoffrey Bickert, David Gillies, Richard Butler (Edmonton, AB: Alberta Justice Communications, 1988). The first judge of the court, Leonard (Tony) Mandamin, was sworn in 15 October 1999. Judge Mandamin is an Anishnabe from the Wikwemikong First Nation of Manitoulin Island and has been active in numerous aspects of Aboriginal law in Alberta since 1982. Also sworn in on 15 October 1999 were the first peacemakers, Harley Crowchild and Rodney Big Crow. The court became operational effective 6 October 2000.
2 *Ibid.,* 4.
3 *Ibid.,* 8.
4 *Ibid.*
5 *Ibid.*
6 *Ibid.*
7 *Ibid.*
8 *Ibid.*
9 *Ibid.,* 9.
10 *Ibid.*
11 Similar discrepancies are found in all other provinces and territories resulting in Canada-wide numbers of Aboriginals making up 2 percent of the population and accounting for 16 percent of the sentenced admissions to custody. *Ibid.,* 41 and Appendix VII, Figures 9 and 11.
12 *Ibid.,* 9.
13 *Ibid.,* 10.
14 *Ibid.,* 14.
15 *Ibid.,* 15.
16 *Ibid.*
17 *Ibid.*
18 *Ibid.,* 22-23.
19 *Ibid.,* 27-31.
20 *Ibid.,* 27.
21 *Ibid.,* 37.
22 *Ibid.,* 27.
23 *Ibid.*
24 *Ibid.*
25 *Ibid.,* 28.
26 *Ibid.,* 29.
27 *Ibid.,* 29-30.
28 *Ibid.,* 18.
29 *Ibid.,* 29.

30 *Ibid.*, 29-31.
31 *Ibid.*, 15.
32 *Ibid.*, 25-27.
33 *Ibid.*, 16-17.
34 *Ibid.*, 25.
35 *Ibid.*, 26.
36 *Ibid.*, 25.
37 *Ibid.*, 26.
38 *Ibid.*, 16, 25.
39 *Ibid.*, 17.
40 *Ibid.*, emphasis in original.
41 *Ibid.*, 27.
42 *Ibid.*, 46-51.
43 In Alberta the superior courts of criminal jurisdiction are the Court of Queen's Bench and the Court of Appeal. For further discussion on this point see John C. Martin, Ian Cartwright, and Edward L. Greenspan, *Martin's Annual Criminal Code, 2000* (Aurora: Canada Law Book, 2000), CC/921; and Criminal Code, R.S.C. 1985, c.C-46, as am., s.468 (jurisdiction of superior court of criminal jurisdiction to try indictable offences), s.469 (offences over which the superior court of criminal jurisdiction has exclusive jurisdiction), s.536(2) (accused's power of election of mode of trial), ss.555 and 567 (the powers of the provincial court judge to override the accused's election), s.568 (the Attorney General's power to override the accused's election), and related sections.
44 An additional benefit of requiring an election for all accused is that all practising criminal lawyers would be required to become familiar with the Aboriginal justice system so they could competently advise their clients of the available options. This expanded awareness would enhance the development of the entire justice system through the efforts of Aboriginal and non-Aboriginal lawyers, and would create a demand for Aboriginal (and Aboriginally aware) lawyers outside Aboriginal communities. The resulting overlapping legal expertise would facilitate understanding between the two systems and increase the chances that the two systems would work in harmony. Additionally, the growing base of Aboriginal (and Aboriginally aware) lawyers would provide an expanded pool of candidates for future appointments to the Aboriginal judiciary.
45 Criminal Code, s.322(1).
46 The teachings were given to me by Phillip Auger and it is with his permission that I relate them here.
47 My assertion that Manygreyhorses is guilty of theft is not so clear cut as I have stated. A finding of guilt would depend upon whether Manygreyhorses could successfully argue recaption. The principle of recaption is based upon Aboriginal rights to cultural property. Briefly, if you have a better claim to ownership or prior possession, the common law principle of recaption enables you to recover your property even if limitation periods would normally prevent resort to the courts. However, this is a complicated area, many things would have to be proven, and a full discussion of recaption is beyond the scope of this chapter.
48 With regard to aiding and abetting a criminal offence see Criminal Code, s.21.
49 L.B. Curzon, *English Legal History*, 2nd ed. (Plymouth: MacDonald and Evans, 1979), 57.
50 *Ibid.*, 58.
51 *Ibid.*, 61.
52 Ralph A. Newman, *Equity and Law: A Comparative Study* (New York: Ocean Publications, 1961), 30.
53 Curzon, *English Legal History*, 95.
54 Newman, *Equity and Law*, 11.
55 Curzon, *English Legal History*, 95.
56 *Ibid.*, 99.
57 *Ibid.*, 97, quoting Sir Thomas Smith.
58 *Ibid.*, 106 (Curzon); Newman, *Equity and Law*, 37-38; F.W. Maitland, *Equity, Also, the Forms of Action at Common Law; Two Courses of Lectures* (Cambridge, UK: Cambridge University Press, 1929), 8.

59 Curzon, *English Legal History,* 97.
60 Newman, *Equity and Law,* 28; and see Maitland, *Equity,* 8, where he points out that no real effort was made to even record the decisions of the court of Chancery until the mid-1500s.
61 Curzon, *English Legal History,* 129; Maitland, *Equity,* 9.
62 Curzon, *English Legal History,* 129.
63 *Ibid.,* 133.
64 *Ibid.,* 99.
65 *Ibid.,* 100.
66 *Ibid.,* 141.
67 William Geldart, "Introduction to English Law," 9th edition by D.C.M. Yardley (Oxford: Oxford University Press, 1984), 17-18.
68 Curzon, *English Legal History,* 100-10.
69 Newman, *Equity and Law,* 11, 14.
70 Curzon, *English Legal History,* 95.
71 Personal communications with Phillip Auger, Wes Fineday, and Frank LaRose.
72 Personal communication with Phillip Auger.

14
Commentary: Reconciling Our Memories in Order to Re-Envision Our Future
N. Bruce Duthu

The chapters in this section reflect a cautious optimism regarding the prospects for improved relations between Aboriginal and non-Aboriginal societies in Canada based, in part, on recently negotiated political arrangements obtained through non-adversarial approaches. Drawing variously upon the storehouses of Aboriginal wisdom, Aboriginal and Western legal traditions, and the accumulated knowledge from years in the praxis of intercultural exchanges, these chapters serve to underscore the notable, if limited, advances in Aboriginal and non-Aboriginal relations, while also providing potent reminders of the significant work that lies ahead. Reconciliation of Aboriginal and non-Aboriginal interests is a recurring theme in these chapters, an objective that includes the task of "reconciling our memories." As Val Napoleon notes, "it is memory that holds the truth of our experiences – the content of reconciliation – and what we do with our memories determines our capacity to imagine our future."

In their own distinctive ways, these writers call attention to at least three important elements that bear on the development of effective systems for conflict resolution. First, there is attention to what I call the "negotiating posture" of the involved parties. Second, there is consideration of the structural or systemic environment within which political and/or cultural discourse occurs. Finally, there is attention to the substantive content, language, and conventions of this discourse. I will discuss each of these elements briefly as reflected in the preceding chapters.

The "negotiating posture" of the involved parties relates both to their distinctive approaches to conflict resolution in terms of purpose (or objective) and to their views of the other party or parties in the process. For Elmer Ghostkeeper, effective models of conflict resolution must proceed from an understanding of and sensitivity to Aboriginal ways of knowing and relating to others, including the natural world. An ethic of respect for Aboriginal epistemology serves to counterbalance the often overwhelming hegemonic force of Western value systems and approaches to conflict resolution. This ethic finds expression in Aboriginal values such as "balance," (Ghostkeeper) and "harmony" or "healing" (Dewhurst). Dale Dewhurst's use of traditional narrative in his chapter powerfully demonstrates the effectiveness of storytelling to reveal what Ghostkeeper calls "Aboriginal wisdom," while also serving to critique and challenge the normative assumptions often embraced within the dominant society about its dispute resolution systems. Scholars such as Michelle LeBaron and Jim Potts have offered their own rich observations about indigenous storytelling which may serve to animate traditional values such as respect, cooperation, and balance, while also exposing the "fallacy of imposing processes or systems without an understanding and respect for traditional ways."[1] They offer the following story to illustrate the point:

A long time ago, this land was known as Turtle Island and all the animals were children. One day the Spirit of the Sky looked down, and he saw the geese flying in a V. The Spirit of the Sky did not like that very much. He thought to himself, "That is very inefficient and it certainly does not look very neat; from now on, the geese must fly in a straight line."

With that, the Spirit of the Sky went down and called all the children of the geese together and said, "I have been watching you fly in a V. As this is not neat or efficient, you will now fly in a straight line."

The children of the geese were shocked and they said, "But oh, Spirit of the Sky, we have always flown in a V. We do this because the goose ahead breaks the wind for the one behind and we do it so we can all watch each other so we know all are safe."

This response angered the Spirit of the Sky and he replied, "Enough of this! I said you will fly in a straight line, so that is what you will do. Now pick one leader and do as I say!" To this the geese replied, "But Spirit of the Sky, we do not have one among us who is strong enough to lead all the time. We all take turns being leader, gander or goose, it makes no difference. We follow the one who is strongest at the moment."

"If you do not have one who is strong enough to lead, then I will be your leader." With that, the Spirit of the Sky transformed himself into a large and powerful goose.

Soon, all the children of the geese were flying behind this powerful leader. As they flew they came to realize that the Spirit of the Sky was right. Flying in a straight line was more efficient. It was easier, for now the air was broken for both wings. They were traveling faster and actually did look a little neater in the sky. And so it went for many days.

One day, high above, an eagle appeared. When the eagle looked down and saw the geese, he said, "Ah-hah! The geese are flying in a straight line. Today I eat!" And with that, the eagle swooped down and took the last goose off the line. The second last goose did not even notice that the last was gone. And so it went as the days went by and more and more of the eagles came and kept picking the last goose off the line.

Eventually, the Spirit of the Sky reached his destination. He landed and turned around to talk to his flock only to find that he was all alone.

While all this was happening, the Creator was watching. The Creator became very angry when he saw what the Spirit of the Sky had done. He called the Spirit of the Sky to account for his actions, and he said: "Spirit of the Sky, I am very angry with you. You changed the way the children of the geese had lived for thousands of years and now they are gone. For that I hold you responsible."

In a trembling voice, the Spirit of the Sky said, "Oh, Creator, it was not me who destroyed the children of the geese. It was those eagles."[2]

LeBaron and Potts present this story to those involved in conflict resolution processes in order to have them reassess the "inclusivity and universality of their approaches."[3] Along with Ghostkeeper and Dewhurst, the story calls attention to the "negotiating posture" of the respective parties (and facilitators) involved in conflict resolution as a critical threshold inquiry toward the creation of effective, mutually satisfying arrangements.

The chapters in this section also call attention to the structural or systemic environment within which political and/or cultural discourse between Aboriginal and non-Aboriginal parties takes place. As Napoleon notes, these structures or mechanisms must be designed to support the heavy lifting of truly substantive matters (e.g., distribution of political power, land rights, and regulation of natural resources), not function as "window dressing" for the enactment of superficial dramas of public performance which merely suggest or mimic true efforts at reconciliation. Both Napoleon and Overstall are right to call attention to the necessity of creating structures that facilitate positive intergroup arrangements (as between First Nations and the provinces or the federal government, arrangements that both Napoleon and Overstall refer to as "external reconciliation"), as well as those that facilitate intragroup cohesion (which they term "internal reconciliation"). This recognizes the complex interplay among the elements of cultural (and personal) identity, legitimate political authority, and the distribution of rights within shared political spaces. It also acknowledges the evolving historical forces (contests over land, resources, political power) and dynamics of cultural change that influenced the nature of relations and arrangements between (and within) Aboriginal and non-Aboriginal societies.

Overstall's suggestion for the creation of a trust to function as an interface between Aboriginal and state legal orders may strike some as an overly "Westernized" structural arrangement in which indigenous values, interests, and aspirations may be too easily compromised or threatened. This observation follows from those commentators who express ambivalence (or outright hostility) about First Nations even employing rights-based and sovereignty discourse in relating to Western governments as a breach of traditional indigenous philosophies. For example, Taiaiake Alfred (Mohawk) notes that, "Native leaders have a responsibility to expose the truth and debunk the imperial pretense that supports the doctrine of state sovereignty and white society's dominion over indigenous nations and their lands. State sovereignty depends on the fabrication of falsehoods that exclude the indigenous voice. Ignorance and racism are the founding principles of the colonial state, and concepts of indigenous sovereignty that don't challenge these principles in fact serve to perpetuate them."[4] This criticism may suggest that the proper structural or systemic environment to help achieve "external reconciliation" must proceed along a higher axis, something akin to the forms of constitutional arrangements posited by Jeremy Webber.[5]

Overstall's proposal does, however, display keen sensitivity to those extant Aboriginal political structures that operate effectively and appropriately for their members given the scale and function of local government. In other words, with the trust serving as intermediary between the Aboriginal community and the state, there is minimal invasion or threat to those indigenous structures of self-government. This also opens the possibility for the continued operation of an indigenous government that is both structurally and operationally more consonant with tribal values and traditions. This notion of "internal reconciliation" has parallels in the literature relating to American Indian tribal efforts at stimulating local economic development. For example, research by Joseph Kalt and Stephen Cornell reveals that among the factors favouring sustained economic development in tribal communities is the degree of cultural "fit" between the governing institutions and the tribe's cultural norms relating to legitimate authority and governance.[6]

Finally, the chapters in this section call attention to the substantive content, language, and conventions of the political and cultural discourse between Aboriginal and non-Aboriginal parties. Ghostkeeper's analysis of "culture," for example, illustrates the importance of achieving clarity, understanding, or at least appreciation for distinctions among different peoples in any efforts directed toward conflict resolution. Taiaiake Alfred echoes similar views when he writes that "Nowhere is the contrast between indigenous and (dominant) Western traditions sharper than in their philosophical approaches to the fundamental issues of power and nature. In indigenous philosophies, power flows from respect for nature and the natural order. In the dominant Western philosophy, power derives from coercion and artifice – in effect, alienation from nature."[7]

A crucial decision from the United States Supreme Court, *United States* v.

Sioux Nation of Indians (1980),[8] illustrates the importance of achieving consensus on the substantive content, language, and conventions regarding the subject matter under dispute. The Sioux Nations sought the return of lands contained within the Black Hills in South Dakota that had allegedly been taken by the federal government in violation of extant treaty promises. Many traditional members of these tribes regard the Black Hills as a cultural and spiritual centre of their existence. Although the Supreme Court ultimately ruled in favour of the tribes, the court's legal analysis left considerable room for the federal government – as the tribes' legal guardian or trustee – to defend against future allegations of wrongful takings by demonstrating that the tribes received property of equivalent value. That is, in exercising its role as trustee, the government could "transmute" the tribal assets into other forms of property (e.g., land or money) and not incur legal liability to the tribes for a claimed unconstitutional taking of their property. This view belies the tribal understanding of property, which features a symbiotic relationship between tribal members and particular lands and an array of associated stewardship obligations. The Supreme Court's view essentially commodifies the tribes' real property interests into fungible assets that are then easily transmuted into other forms (such as monetary equivalents). One can readily see the potential for evisceration of the tribal connection and relationship to land. Thus, Ghostkeeper and others are right to demand clarity and, indeed, consensus on the substantive content, language, and conventions before Aboriginal groups proceed too far along the path of conflict resolution, particularly over finite resources like land.

The chapters in this section demonstrate well how the various processes for dispute resolution effectively function as crucibles for Aboriginal self-governance.[9] In that regard, it behooves all parties concerned, but especially the Aboriginal parties, to give serious attention to the range of issues identified in these chapters and addressed in this brief review. Throughout, it is worth restating Dewhurst's admonition about affording sufficient time for these processes, systems, and content elements to develop into effective, sustainable, and just mechanisms for conflict resolution. Perhaps then, Aboriginal and non-Aboriginal societies will be able to appreciate and enjoy what Napoleon calls "true reconciliation."[10]

Notes

1 Michelle LeBaron (Duryea) and Jim Potts, "Story and Legend: Powerful Tools for Conflict Resolution" (1993) 10 Mediation Quarterly 392.
2 *Ibid.*, 391-92.
3 *Ibid.*, 392-93.
4 Taiaiake Alfred, *Peace, Power, Righteousness: An Indigenous Manifesto* (New York: Oxford University Press, 1999), 59. See also, generally, Robert A. Williams Jr., *The American Indian in Western Legal Thought* (New York: Oxford University Press, 1990).

5 Jeremy Webber, *Reimagining Canada: Language, Culture, Community, and the Canadian Constitution* (Kingston and Montreal: McGill-Queen's University Press, 1994), 267: "Under a regime of self-government like that proposed in the Charlottetown Accord [1992], Aboriginal governments would be recognized as having the kind of status possessed by the provinces and Ottawa. They would be sovereigns, within their spheres, in the same way that Ottawa and the provinces are sovereign in their spheres. They would become, in the words of the accord, 'one of three orders of government,' having their own, original authority over matters falling within their jurisdiction. They would have a form of 'sovereignty,' but one that would not be absolute. And of course, the justification for a constitutional status independent of the will of the non-Aboriginal legislatures would be the inherent source of Aboriginal peoples' entitlement to govern themselves."

6 See, for example, David H. Getches, et al., *Cases and Materials on Federal Indian Law,* 4th ed. (St. Paul, MN: West Group, 1998), 721, 725-26.

7 Alfred, *Peace, Power, Righteousness,* 60.

8 *United States* v. *Sioux Nation of Indians,* 448 U.S. 371 (1980).

9 See Frank Pommersheim, *Braid of Feathers: American Indian Law and Contemporary Tribal Life* (Berkeley: University of California Press, 1995) for his reference to tribal courts as the crucibles for tribal sovereignty.

10 See Val Napoleon's chapter in this volume for a discussion of this concept of "true reconciliation."

Part 4:
Issues of Design and Implementation

The three previous sections have moved from theoretical explorations of culture, power, and dispute resolution to the broad national contexts in which Aboriginal and non-Aboriginal peoples may seek to craft dispute resolution mechanisms adequate to their respective ways and interests and to visions of how Canadian law and practice might be transformed to make greater space for Aboriginal perspectives and needs. Part 4 now turns to specifics of design and implementation in the Canadian context, looking at details of existing dispute resolution mechanisms in Aboriginal contexts, and drawing broader lessons for the future.

15
Indigenous Dispute Resolution Systems within Non-Indigenous Frameworks: Intercultural Dispute Resolution Initiatives in Canada
Catherine Bell

In its report *Bridging the Cultural Divide*, the Royal Commission on Aboriginal Peoples (RCAP) identifies three "root causes" that help explain Aboriginal dissatisfaction with, and overrepresentation in, the Canadian justice system: (1) cultural stress, (2) socioeconomic deprivation, and (3) the impact of colonization.[1] Increased awareness of the impact of cultural stress and pressure on Aboriginal communities has resulted in recent reforms designed to reduce the alienation Aboriginal people feel within the justice system and to make the system more accountable to Aboriginal communities. Often referred to as indigenization, these reforms rely on modifications to conventional litigation processes before Canadian courts and administrative tribunals. Examples include modification of court-annexed mediation programs to incorporate indigenous values, processes, and expertise; the creation of administrative tribunals with cultural and community expertise; the appointment of Aboriginal people as judges, court staff, and prosecutors; Native court worker programs; Aboriginal law student programs; and Aboriginal-focused court information kits. These reforms do not require drastic institutional change, recognition of the inherent right of Aboriginal peoples to self-government, or new jurisdictional arrangements between Aboriginal and Canadian governments. In many ways this is the strength of indigenization – structures, procedures, and decision makers that are culturally inappropriate can be altered and replaced quickly, and often effectively, as an alternative to the alienating adversarial system. However, for many Aboriginal peoples it is also important to locate justice reform within a broader understanding of the role played by poverty and the process of colonization in both creating conflict and destroying Aboriginal institutions of conflict resolution.

Conflict in Aboriginal communities has roots in "despair, dependency, anger, frustration and a sense of injustice ... stemming from cultural *and community* breakdown."[2] For this reason, some people are cautious about endorsing the process of indigenization. They fear that non-indigenous governments will view cultural modifications to Canadian institutions as an adequate response to cultural and community breakdown without examining how non-indigenous laws and legal culture play a role in the process of colonization and socioeconomic marginalization. For example, at a recent conference on violence against Aboriginal women, two hundred Aboriginal women emphasized the "need to recognize colonialism as a major source of the problem [of domestic violence] and to address violence against Aboriginal women in a manner which is holistic and deals with colonial laws, policies and practices as well as issues of poverty."[3] All agreed it was not enough to simply change the faces and procedures of current agents and institutions of justice. Rather, the substantive objectives of the legal system designed to address domestic abuse had to change from punishment to rebuilding and healing community and familial institutions.

Similar concerns about failures to address the impact of colonization were echoed by participants attending the national forum on Intercultural Dispute Resolution (hereafter, the "forum").[4] The purpose of this forum was to explore the cultural foundations of dispute resolution and to discuss mechanisms for making dispute resolution processes more inclusive of Aboriginal values and practices. Dispute resolution practitioners, people engaged in systems design in Aboriginal communities, and members of boards and tribunals established under land claims, treaty, and self-government agreements were invited to share ideas on how to incorporate culturally sensitive dispute resolution mechanisms into their operations. Speakers from Canada, Australia, New Zealand, and the United States presented and critiqued various justice models and facilitated group discussions on the real and apparent challenges of intercultural justice. Although participants discussed how alternative dispute resolution (ADR) processes such as mediation, arbitration, and delegation to expert administrative tribunals could be used to make the administration of civil justice more accountable to Aboriginal communities, an equally dominant theme was how to take advantage of the increased flexibility in the Canadian system offered by the ADR movement without furthering the project of colonization.[5]

In her opening address to the forum, Michelle LeBaron identified a number of factors important to consider when designing intercultural dispute resolution systems. She explained that there is "influence and power attached to the dominant culture way of doing things" which often "come to be viewed as 'right and necessary,' while other ways get labelled as 'alternative.'"[6] This can contribute to a "loss of confidence in traditional methods, or controversy about what these methods truly are and whom these methods serve."[7] Another concern is the impact of "internalized oppression" or the tendency in some "victims of colonization to regard their own knowledge as less when compared to that of the colonizer."[8] Combined with non-indigenous people having a "vested interest in believing that 'our way works,'" "differing cultural understandings of effective leadership," the difficulty of altering the legal culture of modified institutions (such as courts and administrative tribunals), internalized oppression, and colonization make the process of culturally appropriate dispute resolution design a challenge.[9] According to LeBaron, we must continually keep asking questions such as, "For whom do our processes work? How do our processes accommodate conversations about what is important, how it is important, and for whom? Whose values do our processes mirror and whose do they exclude?"[10]

Participants also questioned whether modification of popular ADR mechanisms would reinforce internalized oppression by adopting only those aspects of indigenous knowledge, values, and processes that do not conflict with Western values and laws.[11] As we work toward formalizing more culturally appropriate methods of dispute resolution through legislation and negotiated agreements, some participants wondered if we also risk promoting generalizations about indigenous cultures, thereby rendering alternative processes less flexible and culturally alive. As most intercultural tribunals and boards are funded by non-indigenous governments, others wondered how much risk tribunal and board members would be willing to assume in the interpretation of their procedures and quasi-judicial powers. These comments, concerns, and questions underscored the tension felt by many participants at the forum: the inability to change the institutional designs and laws under which they currently operate and the desire to create a climate in which Aboriginal people within their jurisdiction can participate in the resolution of disputes in a meaningful way. Although answers to questions remained elusive and the tensions unresolved, participants embraced many helpful suggestions and considered a spectrum of international perspectives on improving intercultural communication and dispute resolution.

Forum presentations and models of dispute resolution discussed below offer suggestions on how to improve intercultural communication and be more inclusive of Aboriginal values within the confines of conventional legal contexts. Suggestions range from taking advantage of ADR processes to codification of indigenous values and the creation of special indigenous courts. All suggestions have in common a broader philosophy of promoting healthy, strong, and independent Aboriginal communities. However, not all forum participants agreed that this could be accomplished through delegated dispute resolution authority and modifications to judicial process. Although this may be an important interim step, significant change to familiar institutions of dispute resolution, jurisdiction to enact and enforce indigenous laws, and the removal of non-indigenous laws and institutions that undermine the preservation and enhancement of Aboriginal culture are also required. Achieving justice for Aboriginal people requires looking beyond analysis of culture conflict to ask more complex questions such as:

- How is the existing regime of Canadian law undermining the cultural survival of Aboriginal communities?
- To what extent must indigenous laws be enacted and enforced through indigenous institutions to reduce conflict and sustain indigenous communities?
- Can the justice objectives of a given community be met through a blending of conventional and indigenous values and institutions, or must completely new institutions be created to avoid undermining indigenous knowledge and practices?
- How do we reconcile the jurisdictions of Aboriginal, federal, and provincial governments to establish and administer their own systems of justice, including the power to make law and resolve disputes?
- Given the diversity of indigenous peoples within Canada, the range of skills, and the human and financial resources required to implement new justice systems, what kind of practical interjurisdictional agreements must be negotiated?

For some indigenous peoples, such as the Inuit of Nunavut, the Nisga'a Nation of British Columbia, and the Metis of the Metis settlements in northern Alberta, the answers to these questions can be found by blending conventional and indigenous processes and by negotiating new jurisdictional arrangements within the existing constitutional framework. They adopt an incremental and collaborative approach to change by assuming jurisdiction to enact laws within defined areas of responsibility and developing multilevel dispute resolution processes that adapt "what is useful" in the Canadian legal system to a specific indigenous context.[12] Other indigenous people fear this approach threatens the cultural integrity of indigenous institutions and will promote, rather than guard against, further cultural assimilation. It is only when Aboriginal jurisdiction and dispute resolution systems are equal in authority and legitimacy to, rather than alternative to or delegated from, non-indigenous governments and processes that true Aboriginal justice can be obtained.

Although some discussions at the forum engaged in critical analysis of various approaches to justice reform, such an analysis is not the purpose of this chapter. Forum presentations and chapters exploring this theme are contained earlier in this volume. The purpose of this chapter is to review indigenous community-based dispute resolution processes negotiated within the broad parameters of the ADR movement – a movement that includes a vast array of consensual and command decision models of dispute resolution as an alternative to litigation. Examples are drawn primarily from models discussed at the forum and panel presentations.[13] I begin with reflections on the challenges and opportunities of developing contemporary dispute resolution processes based on community and cultural values. This is followed by a discussion of the ADR movement and some opportunities and challenges it offers for the inclusion of Aboriginal culture and values in the resolution of disputes. Bicultural tribunals and boards established under land claims and self-government agreements, dispute resolution mechanisms under the Nisga'a Treaty, and specialty First Nation courts are the main examples used to develop these themes. Also included are excerpts from forum presentations by Edward Allen (chief executive officer, Nisga'a Tribal Council), Phyllis Collins (former vice-chair, Metis Settlements Appeal Tribunal), Stein Lal (chair, Inuvialuit Arbitration Board), Michelle LeBaron (director of the Program on Dispute Resolution, Faculty of Law, University of British Columbia), Leonard (Tony) Mandamin (His Honour Judge Mandamin of the Alberta [Tsuu T'ina First Nation] provincial court), Stephen Mills (chair, Yukon Surface Rights Board), Judge Irene Toledo (district judge of the Navajo Nation), Rebecca Williams (former assistant deputy minister of Justice, Nunavut), and Robert Yazzie (chief justice of the Navajo Tribal Courts).[14]

Identification of Community Values and Processes

Traditional Values
A common message at the forum was that effective justice initiatives must be anchored in the values of the community they are intended to serve. For example, in 1985 the Navajo Nation reformed its court system to include a Navajo Peacemaker Division. Navajo peacemaking, described by Robert Yazzie earlier in this volume, is based on traditional Navajo dispute resolution values and practices in which peacemakers are used to resolve problems and restore relationships. The process of Navajo peacemaking is a procedure of "talking things over in groups."[15] The problem is described, Navajo values and laws are discussed, and an action plan to restore relationship and create harmony is developed by consensus. Peacemakers are people in Navajo communities who "show their spirituality through what they do. They demonstrate that they have the ability to plan, and get into a leadership position not by seeking it, but by being selected."[16] They are natural leaders who are not picked because of their formal education, but because "their life is a model of success."[17] Outlining some of the steps taken by the Navajo to revive the tradition of peacemaking, Judge Irene Toledo explained that it is Navajo-specific cultural values that generate

respect for the Navajo justice system by Navajo people. Similarly, it will be the specific cultural values of the various indigenous peoples in Canada that will make their systems effective and accountable to their citizens.[18]

In his presentation, Leonard (Tony) Mandamin (now the Honourable Judge Mandamin) emphasized that operating on traditional value systems is not a new concept to indigenous communities. Traditional ways have survived in many communities despite the imposition of foreign institutions under the Indian Act.[19] Relating information shared between him and a Siksika elder, Mandamin explained: "Our laws are agreement. The people make an agreement on what is to be, that agreement having been made, all follow that agreement. This actually has been in operation in Indian country (if you call it that) for a long time."[20] He elaborated this point with an example of how the traditional law of agreement, or broad community consensus, is the mechanism by which customary election codes and appeal processes are enacted into law, even though writing of codes is a creation of the Indian Act. In his opinion, "members are the driving force behind the custom" and these codes, which must be approved by the community, are a tool that can be used to formalize custom and recognize "what has been going on ever since reserves have been established."[21] Provisions and appeal processes in these codes reflect "the will of the people that are members of that community;"[22] some processes include appeals to elders and community referendum. Federal courts have been reluctant to substitute their opinion for decisions that issue from these appellate processes and to treat an indigenous process as flawed or biased simply because a decision maker is related "in some way to a disputant when the reality is that everybody in the community is somehow related or interconnected."[23] These examples are not "high profile" examples of "Aboriginal law making mechanisms," but they "carry on what was an ancient right of the First Nations people."[24] Other areas identified by Judge Mandamin that reflect the law of agreement include adoption of band membership and land management codes, and appeal mechanisms under those codes.

Traditional Values and Contemporary Justice Initiatives

Navajo Peacemaking
Despite the tenacity of core indigenous values and processes, such as the law of agreement, identifying community values for a contemporary indigenous justice system is a complicated task that requires more than looking to values that were dominant prior to colonization. Culturally specific values now include a blend of Western and indigenous ideas of law and conflict. Consequently, difficult questions emerge about how to balance the desire to revive and protect traditional values and processes and, at

the same time, be accountable to those in the community who have become separated from traditional ways. Philmer Bluehouse, director of the Navajo Nation Peacemaker Division, explained at a recent conference on criminal justice that the Navajo approach to this problem was to look at historical practices, spiritual leaders, creation stories, ceremonies, and other sources as a way to bring traditional values back into contemporary life (not to *replace* contemporary life); to assist offenders, victims, and others to resolve internal psychological and spiritual conflict; and to reach an effective balance of the sacred and contemporary in healing communities and resolving disputes.[25] Important questions asked during the design of the Navajo peacemaking process were aimed at respecting traditional values, not imposing them, and included:

- Do peacemakers meet the human expectations and values within the community?
- Do policies, rules, and regulations for the resolution of disputes complement traditional minds and narratives?
- Do the songs, stories, prayers, ritual objects, and ceremonies developing as sources of law identify who we are as a people and where we are going?

Each of these questions reflects the goal of the Peacemaker Division to apply Navajo knowledge and values to the resolution of a dispute. Peacemakers guide those in conflict with the law, or each other, on a journey to discover their perfections and imperfections and what it means in Navajo law to lead "a good life."[26] At the core of this journey are Navajo creation stories. As Bluehouse explained:

> Peacemaking is the practical application of knowledge and reason to a situation of dispute. The source of Navajo knowledge and reasoning is contained in the Native Origin and Journey Narratives. These narratives lay the foundation of Navajo relationships with self, family, others, the world, and the universe. This relationship is called K'e. K'e is a Navajo word that describes respect and relationships in Navajo society.
>
> K'e is metaphorically described in the origin and journey narratives. The description is a lengthy oration revealing details, in the Navajo language of policy, procedure, rules and regulations about life and its purpose – to maintain a good life using and understanding respect and relationships.[27]

Alberta Metis Settlements

The complexity of developing contemporary institutions based on respect for indigenous traditions, such as respect for the law of agreement and creation stories, is illustrated in community consultations preceding the signing of the Alberta Metis Settlements Accord – a bilateral agreement between the Federation of Metis Settlements and the Province of Alberta concerning ownership and governance of Metis settlements lands.[28] Metis tradition required the leadership to respect principles of democracy and operate through consultation and consensus. Ken Noskey, past president of the Metis Settlements General Council, explains the tradition of consensus this way:

> Consensual decision making may be difficult, but we believe it is funda-
> mental and part of our tradition. Unless the institutions which we are
> developing as vehicles for self-government incorporate at their heart the
> practices and processes that have been used by our people and which are
> familiar to them, we will not be able to create any popular base upon
> which these institutions can build. Without the popular base, Aboriginal
> self-government will simply be the imposition of yet another form of out-
> side control upon the people of our communities.
>
> There are circumstances, of course, where consensus need not mean
> unanimity. On such issues there will also be division of opinion. All com-
> munities, no matter how highly they value consensus, require some
> mechanism by which division of opinion will not bring all decision mak-
> ing to a halt. What that mechanism will be will vary from community to
> community and we in the Metis settlements are currently confronting this
> issue. I cannot predict what the outcome of this examination will be, but
> I also know that whatever the result may be, I know that it will not jeop-
> ardize our fundamental commitment to consensus seeking.[29]

Given the importance of consultation and consensus in Metis communities, it is not surprising that extensive consultations preceded the implementation of the accord. During these consultations it became clear that
settlement members and leaders did not agree on the dispute resolution
role of elders and traditional knowledge. The requirement of community
consultation and a desire to reach consensus meant that differing contemporary opinions on the role of elders' knowledge had to be resolved
at the community level. While some identified the need to distinguish
between "genuine elders" and "elders who might be old, but have not
earned respect of the community," others feared elder knowledge lacked
"the insight and foresight to bring traditional ideas to bear on new
problems and opportunities."[30] However, despite these differing attitudes,
the majority agreed that elders should have a formal role in Metis government and dispute resolution. Indeed, the original vision for dispute
resolution offered by Metis negotiators was the establishment of elders committees on each settlement, appointed by elected settlement governments.

Like administrative tribunals, these committees would be appointed by government (although in this case by Metis government), hear appeals of controversial government decisions, have power to resolve disputes within delegated areas of jurisdiction (such as land and membership), and advise settlement government on other controversial issues. Elders would establish their own procedures to exercise this function, which could include traditional methods, knowledge, and practices.[31]

For many people, independence, impartiality, fair process, and neutrality are an integral part of their concept of justice. Looking within small communities for decision makers raises fear of nepotism and bias, particularly when decision makers are appointed by local governments or community processes dominated by extended families. The Metis responded to this phenomenon in two key ways. The first was to ensure that community members participated in the creation of the laws subject to the jurisdiction of the elders committees. Consultation and consensus decision making was incorporated into the processes for debating and enacting settlement bylaws and the collective policies of the regional government, the Metis Settlements General Council. Second, Metis negotiators proposed that disputants lacking confidence in the outcome of the elders committee be able to exercise a right of appeal to a Metis arbitrator, or panel of arbitrators, agreed to by the parties, or in the event of disagreement, appointed by the General Council. However, as negotiations developed and Metis government acquired greater power, it became apparent that the Metis dispute resolution process would extend in its jurisdiction beyond local lands and settlement members, particularly in the areas of membership and oil and gas disputes. Consequently, the original Metis proposal for dispute resolution was altered to accommodate Metis jurisdiction over non-Metis people.

The end result of the consultation and negotiation on dispute resolution arising from implementation of the accord was the creation of the Metis Settlements Appeal Tribunal (MSAT) – a bicultural tribunal with a chair and majority membership from the Metis settlements designed to serve as "a practical, inexpensive and culturally sensitive justice system for the Metis Settlements."[32] The emphasis on creating specific roles for elders gave way to the inclusion of elders through vehicles such as alternative dispute resolution processes promoted by MSAT, appointments to MSAT, participation in general community consultations on settlement laws, and expert advice on matters such as Metis ancestry and traditional land-use practices. Elder opinion is also viewed as important evidence by MSAT in the assessment of the cultural impact of resource development on Metis land, the resolution of family and estate matters, and identification of traditional Metis practices relevant to the resolution of contemporary disputes. Despite these avenues for elder participation and consideration of traditional

knowledge, the decision not to include specific institutions of Metis elder-
ship in the legislation implementing the accord indirectly acted as a cata-
lyst for the decline of the traditional role of elders in dispute resolution.
This is one reason why Phyllis Collins, former vice-chair of the Metis Settlements Appeal Tribunal, supports the increased use of mediation by
MSAT.[33] Mediation is one method MSAT is exploring to address the need
to increase the role of elders and traditional dispute resolution values in
the current system.[34]

Nisga'a Youth Justice Initiative
The Nisga'a Nation have encountered similar challenges in the design and
implementation of their youth justice initiative, which is based on the traditional approach of counselling, guiding, and supporting individuals,
and recognition that all individuals are part of larger extended family. It
is a process based on resolution within and respect for nuclear families
and their members, and members and leaders (hereditary chiefs) of the
extended families (also known as houses). Sharing an example offered by
the president of the Nisga'a Nation, Edward Allen explained the traditional practice this way: "Our president (of the Nisga'a Tribal Council) was
saying that even when he was in his 50s ... his father would say: 'You will
now sit and listen to what I have to say as we sit and eat dinner. You will
eat the words that I say and you will carry them in you.' His father would
make that statement as hereditary chief and our president (of the Nisga'a
Tribal Council) would sit and listen."[35]

Reviving respect for the family and asking extended family members
to guide and support youth is at the heart of the Nisga'a youth justice
initiative. An offender, family, and house group may, with the help of a
facilitator, be involved in developing a plan of education, healing, and
restitution for the offender. However, the success of this approach varies
with the strength of the family groups involved. As Mr. Allen explained,
"because of the imposition of the *Indian Act* and the residential school
system and the damage that has caused to some families in our communities, some families are not really in a position to fully utilize this [pro-
cess]."[36] Consequently, the youth justice strategy remains an alternative to
the Canadian youth justice system and is dependent on voluntary participation and the strength of the nuclear and extended family. The creation
of a Nisga'a Court (discussed below) will help ensure that prosecutors,
judges, and other actors in the legal system are not reluctant to utilize this
alternative.

Tsuu T'ina Nation
Affinity with, and reformulation of, traditional processes is also influenced
by factors such as geography and economic and social interdependency.

For example, the Tsuu T'ina Nation is surrounded by the city of Calgary. Many members of that Nation work in the city and carry on business there. As a result of close relationships with the non-indigenous community over a long period and the desire to maintain positive economic and political relationships, the Tsuu T'ina decided to "work within the current justice system and not to create a free-standing separate court which could isolate the people from their neighbours."[37] Although consideration was given to developing a separate criminal code based on Tsuu T'ina laws and values, this approach was "abandoned because it was determined that the focus should not be on identifying behaviour and duplicating the criminal law of the land," as many actions prohibited by the Criminal Code would also be prohibited according to traditional and contemporary values of the Tsuu T'ina people.[38]

Emphasizing that the Tsuu T'ina "live in both cultures" and "are the first to say that the clock cannot be turned back completely," Marsha Erb (general counsel to the Tsuu T'ina Nation) explained at a recent conference in Edmonton that "ownership" of the justice system, in particular the process and values for resolving criminal and civil disputes, became the key issue in consultations with the Judiciary, the Federal Department of Justice, the Alberta Department of Justice, and other stakeholder groups.[39] A consistent message was: For the justice system to work, people must take responsibility and become empowered to "deal with justice issues in their own way, that is, based on their own value systems."[40] The Tsuu T'ina value system is one that seeks to heal and restore relationships through promotion and teaching of values grounded in spirituality. Although there was some discussion around the compatibility of traditional values and Christian principles now adopted by many First Nations people, the focus on managing justice issues through healing and spirituality was ultimately viewed as accommodating both religious systems.[41] Ultimately, the Tsuu T'ina proposed an enhancement to the current system, consisting of five main elements: (1) a First Nations judge, (2) a Peacemaker Office (similar to the Navajo Peacemaker Court), (3) administration of the court by First Nations people, (4) an Aboriginal prosecutor, and (5) location of the court on Tsuu T'ina land. These elements are discussed throughout this chapter.

Other values incorporated into the Tsuu T'ina proposal are those that inform the Canadian Charter of Rights and Freedoms.[42] This was not viewed as an imposition by the Tsuu T'ina leadership, who appreciated the importance of these values to those who live in both cultures. As in non-indigenous communities, members of the Tsuu T'ina Nation value independence, neutrality, knowledge (cultural and legal), and impartiality in decision making; the right to be heard; and freedom of choice. The reconciliation of Charter values with those informing the traditional process of healing and restoration is demonstrated in the rationale for judicial appointment. The Tsuu T'ina call for a First Nation judge to preside over their court who has "an innate understanding of the cultural sensibilities of First Nations people through direct personal involvement with the culture, [has] resided on a reserve and [has] worked with Aboriginal people."[43] Selection of an indigenous judge is intended to result in serious and consistent consideration of more traditional dispute resolution processes offered by the peacemaker component of the court. Judicial familiarity with indigenous culture, language, and protocol is also expected to increase comfort levels of indigenous people involved in the adversarial court process. At the same time, the importance of impartiality, legal education, and independence of the judiciary are reflected in the preference of the Tsuu T'ina Nation to appoint a "highly qualified member of the First Nations Bar from outside the Treaty 7 area to avoid community pressure and to set the tone of 'non-interference.'"[44]

Justice in Nunavut
Geography also plays an important, but different, role in the Nunavut system of justice. In her presentation to the forum, Rebecca Williams explained that the legal and political framework in Nunavut is significantly influenced by the remoteness of many Nunavut communities.[45] As the Inuit form 85 percent of the population in Nunavut territory, they felt they would be able to maintain sufficient control over their life and land through a public government structure that enables both Inuit and non-Inuit to participate in elections and public life. Consequently, values and beliefs informing the justice goals and priorities of Nunavut are informed by different cultures within the territory of Nunavut. As Rebecca Williams explained: "The creation of Nunavut government means that we [Inuit] have the opportunity, authority, and responsibility to do things for the people of Nunavut ... We have set our goals and priorities according to our values and beliefs. Now when I say values and beliefs, I am talking about everybody who is living up there [in Nunavut]. Not just Inuit values, but anybody who lives up there ... Inuit values and cultures will be strengthened by government from the people and together Inuit and non-Inuit people of Nunavut will run our own affairs."[46]

However, a Cabinet dominated by Inuit members, the policy of hiring a public service that reflects a majority Inuit population, Inuit cultural and education programs, the requirement that all laws be enacted in Inuktitut, and the wide use of community justice committees are some of the ways in which the Nunavut government is ensuring that Inuit values remain embedded in the decision-making process and structure of Nunavut government.

Remoteness of Inuit communities, socioeconomic issues common to isolated communities, the presence of active and respected community justice groups in most of these communities, and a positive relationship between existing justice committees and the territorial court have made issues such as access to justice and prevention of conflict the justice priorities in Nunavut. Creation of the Nunavut Court of Justice and increased decision making at the local level by community justice committees and justices of the peace are initiatives designed to address these priorities. The Nunavut Court of Justice consists of judges appointed in consultation with the Nunavut government and exercises the combined jurisdictions of what were formerly the territorial and Supreme Courts of the Northwest Territories. An important result of this change is that a judge can deal with both minor and major criminal offences and civil justice matters in a single visit to a community, thereby simplifying scheduling and travelling. As Iqaluit is currently the only community with a resident judge, and judicial services are offered to 26,000 people in twenty widely dispersed remote communities, it is hoped that these changes will also decrease the current delays inherent in the circuit court system. In communities other than Iqaluit, justice committees and elders committees are expected to have an increased role. However, according to Rebecca Williams, although justice committees and sentencing circles are "very active in smaller communities," they are not as active in Iqaluit.[47] In her opinion, this is likely the result of the presence of lawyers and a formal court in the community of Iqaluit, which make local people feel more isolated from the decision-making process. This is one area the Justice Department is addressing in cooperation with other Departments of Nunavut government, such as Culture and Education.

Common Themes
The above discussion underscores that no uniform initiative has been adopted or recommended by indigenous communities that have researched values in their communities and assumed increased control over the administration of justice based on those values. The dynamic nature of value systems and contemporary factors affecting cultural identity ensure this diversity. However, a uniform theme that emerges from all models echoed at the forum is that, despite the challenging nature of the value identification process, identifying core community values and strengthening community traditions is essential for the success of indigenous justice initiatives. An equally dominant theme is that core indigenous values have survived the process of colonization and, in some cases, simply need to be brought to the surface and utilized more frequently to be appreciated for what they are. The following section explores some of the trends in Canadian justice that create space for Aboriginal justice initiatives based on community-specific conflict and dispute resolution values.

Opportunities and Challenges

The ADR Movement

History and Rationale
Three major trends in the administration of Canadian justice create opportunity for the implementation of community-specific dispute resolution processes:

- dissatisfaction by the Canadian public as a whole with the adversarial process, including complicated judicial procedure, cost of litigation, reliance on lawyers to communicate and translate legalese, and lack of meaningful input into the outcome of a dispute
- acceptance by federal and provincial governments that the power to resolve some disputes should be removed from judges and delegated to individuals with more factual expertise, including community and cultural expertise
- increased awareness of the impact of discretion on the administration of justice and how factors such as cultural difference affect the exercise of that discretion.

General public dissatisfaction with judicial process and increasing costs of litigation have resulted in more and more alternative dispute resolution (ADR) processes being incorporated into the conventional court structure. These processes range from replacing courts as the forum of first complaint with expert administrative tribunals and arbitrators, to annexing participatory dispute resolution processes, such as facilitated negotiation and mediation, to existing judicial and administrative processes. Participatory processes are based on a more consensual approach to problem solving that encourages parties to look beyond legal rules to discuss underlying interests and other dimensions of the conflict. However, all ADR processes share the search for more accessible, efficient, user-friendly, and affordable ways for resolving disputes. The fiscal cost of developing and experimenting with these systems is increasingly viewed by non-indigenous government as a reasonable alternative to the fiscal and human costs of the expensive and time-consuming litigation process. In the context of Aboriginal justice initiatives, developments in Aboriginal rights law, and numerous studies demonstrating the overrepresentation of Aboriginal people in the justice system and the lack of accountability of the system to Aboriginal people, add to the reasons to support the development of Aboriginal community-based ADR processes.[48]

The proliferation of ADR over the last fifteen years suggests that it is no longer appropriate to use the term "alternative" to describe non-judicial processes. The term "alternative" suggests that these processes are peripheral and inferior to judicial processes when in fact they may be more "appropriate" methods for resolving the conflict in issue. Further, the term "alternative" is increasingly becoming a misnomer as processes of dispute resolution other than litigation are becoming more mainstream. This point was emphasized by Michelle LeBaron in her presentation to the forum and in the chapter included in the first section of this volume.[49]

Culture and Conventional Conflict Restitution
Although not an initial focus of the movement, the relevance of culture in ensuring meaningful access to, and survival of, non-litigious processes has become an important issue in the development and design of new dispute resolution training programs and processes. As LeBaron explains:

> Culture came to be understood as a broad construct, extending far beyond the ethno-cultural group association that often fetters it. Attention was shed on the multiple influences that shape individuals and processes, as well as on the centrality of power to the conversation about culture. Awareness grew of the truism that dispute resolution processes reflect cultural assumptions of those who design them. For example, a process designed to focus on "facts" may reflect a cultural bias against the expression of emotions. A process designed with values and efficiency and cost savings in mind may screen out what some participants see as critical relationship building steps.[50]

For these reasons, LeBaron suggests that in the design of dispute resolution processes, one must ask questions that take into account the influence of culture.

Awareness of cultural styles of participation and communication also helps us appreciate how conventional ADR techniques and processes are similar to, or different from, traditional indigenous community processes. For example, in mediation, the mediator often takes a neutral role and tries to bring the parties to agreement. In an indigenous system, an elder or some other person with natural authority in the community may take a more interventionist approach by promoting traditional values, evaluating behaviour, and fashioning solutions, rather than leaving the affected parties to fashion solutions for themselves.

The potential differences between conventional ADR mechanisms and indigenous processes, and the need to address both cultural understanding and styles in the development of indigenous dispute resolution processes, is illustrated in the composition and philosophy of the Office of the Peacemaker that will operate in conjunction with the Tsuu T'ina provincial court. The mandate of this office is to "resolve problems, [and] investigate and discover the root causes of behaviour which have translated into criminal activity or disharmony in the community or among families."[51]

At present, peacemakers deal only with criminal and youth matters, and jurisdiction is limited geographically to matters arising on Tsuu T'ina lands. However, as the provincial court component assumes more jurisdiction over civil and family matters on Tsuu T'ina lands, so too will the Office of the Peacemaker.[52] Although trained to facilitate conventional participatory dispute resolution processes, peacemakers are also individuals highly regarded in the community as knowledgeable in traditional ways and values. Peacemakers were selected by asking each member in the community who, including family members as well as those not related by blood, they felt would be fair in resolving disputes. Of the fifty names gathered, the first third were trained in conventional dispute resolution, traditional dispute resolution, addictions, and child welfare matters. The intent is to train all of the fifty members recommended as the peacemakers who will not only deal with referrals from the coordinator of the Office of the Peacemaker, prosecutors, court workers, and judge, but will also eventually have a function in helping resolve issues that arise in the community that are not before the court. As the jurisdiction of the Tsuu T'ina court is defined by geography and extends to indigenous and non-indigenous peoples, so will the services offered by the Office of the Peacemaker. However, entitlement to these services is not automatic. If the coordinator of the Peacemaker Office does not think peacemaking will work, then the matter will be dealt with by the Tsuu T'ina court, or by other appropriate institutions if the issue is not before the court.[53]

Although peacemakers are trained in conventional dispute resolution practices, these methods may not always be utilized or deemed appropriate for the dispute and participants affected by the dispute. Contrasting the Office of the Peacemaker to other ADR initiatives such as mediation, the report of the review committee established to consider the Tsuu T'ina justice proposal elaborates on this important point:

> While disciples of ADR take a neutral role and work to bring the parties to consensus, the role of the Peacemaker is to *actively promote* and *teach traditional values* as well as determine *why* an individual is out of harmony with the community and to *restore* harmony.
>
> *Restoring healthy relationships grounded in spirituality* is of paramount importance in this system as opposed to simply balancing conflicting interests. Those who have breached community trust must find the way toward healing and acceptance in the community. Those involved must be well informed as to what the cultural values of the community are and how to appropriately express those views to others and to guide them.[54]

Complementary Processes: Adoption and Adaptation
A fundamental goal of consensual ADR processes is to create a process that is meaningful to the parties and improves relationships, participation, responsibility, and satisfaction; this goal is shared by many traditional and contemporary indigenous dispute resolution mechanisms. This point was illustrated by Edward Allen in his presentation on the Nisga'a Treaty to the forum. Noting that the "Nisga'a Treaty in and of itself is a form of dispute resolution in that it represents a reconciliation between the [Nisga'a] existence as an Aboriginal people and the arrival of the British Crown," Allen reviewed the various dispute resolution mechanisms adopted under the treaty and their relationship to contemporary and traditional Nisga'a justice values.[55] These values include respecting the individual, acknowledging wrongs, making restitution, achieving reconciliation and harmony, and respecting the wisdom of elders, chiefs, and matriarchs. The Nisga'a Constitution reflects these and other values, such as respect for the unique spirit of each individual and government accountability to the people. Allen advised participants that the Nisga'a started and remained consistent with these values in taking "what [was] useful in terms of the language of the Canadian legal system" and modifying it under the treaty.[56]

Dispute Resolution under the Nisga'a Treaty
A number of processes developed under the Nisga'a Treaty illustrate that ADR rationales are consistent with traditional Nisga'a values. Consider the system and rationales for resolving disputes among Nisga'a, provincial, and federal governments involving issues of treaty interpretation, implementation, and breach. The rationales are articulated in the treaty as a common desire:

1   to co-operate with each other to develop harmonious working relationships
2   to prevent, or alternatively, minimize disagreements
3   to identify disagreements quickly and resolve them in the most expeditious and cost-effective manner possible
4   to resolve disagreement in a non-adversarial, collaborative and informal atmosphere.[57]

These rationales, and the three-stage process created to respect and implement them, reinforce the importance of respect, acknowledgment, harmony, and reconciliation in the Nisga'a justice tradition.

Stage One: Collaborative Negotiations The three phases to the process are collaborative negotiations, facilitated processes, and adjudication (or arbitration). If consensus cannot be reached through informal discussion, disputes over treaty terms are to be resolved through these stages. Subject to limited exceptions, parties to the treaty process cannot refer a disagreement to adjudication or arbitration in stage three without first proceeding through stages one and two.[58] In stage one the emphasis is on how the parties "understand the language of the treaty" and on reaching consensus.[59] Unlike a judicial process, parties not directly affected by the disagreement can participate in this discussion. Appendix M-1 to the Nisga'a Final Agreement provides greater detail on matters such as timing and content of the notice required to invoke collaborative negotiations, stages of the collaborative negotiation process, confidentiality, withdrawal, recording, and termination. The recording and confidentiality provisions are designed to encourage full and free discussion. For example, negotiations are closed to the public, transcripts and electronic recording are prohibited, and parties must keep confidential the information disclosed in negotiations. Further, oral and written information, including documents, views, admissions, suggestions, and "willingness to make or accept a proposal for settlement" cannot be introduced in evidence in any proceeding "whether or not that proceeding relates to the subject matter of collaborative negotiations."[60]

Section 9 of Appendix M-1 underscores an understanding of conflict that looks beyond legal dimensions of a dispute to restoration of harmony through adoption of an interest-based negotiation model. Section 9 reads:

The parties will make a serious attempt to resolve the disagreement by:

a   identifying underlying interests;
b   isolating points of agreement and disagreement;
c   exploring alternative solutions;
d   considering compromises or accommodations; and
e   taking other measures that will assist in the resolution of the disagreement.[61]

Stage Two: Facilitated Processes   If agreement is not reached through collaborative negotiation, stage two is implemented. This stage enables the parties to invoke a range of facilitated processes, including mediation, a technical advisory panel, early neutral evaluation, and an elders advisory council. Again, the focus is on restoring relationships through discussion and consensus. The details for each of these processes, such as appointment procedures, terms of reference, conduct of mediators or other third-party facilitators and fact finders, procedural stages, confidentiality, referral of issues to other processes, withdrawal, and termination are outlined in Appendices M-2 to M-5 of the Final Agreement. Of particular interest are the technical advisory panel and the elders advisory council. The former is designed to assist parties in disputes involving technical or scientific subject matter. The example given by Allen at the forum was a dispute relating to fishing. Parties could select a panel of people with the authority to make binding decisions like a judge, but unlike a judge, panel members would have a broader base of expertise in the non-legal dimensions of the dispute, such as the importance of fishing to the Nisga'a culture, economy, and environment. Elders would be appointed to this panel depending on the subject matter in issue. Panels may have three or five members – either one appointed by each of the parties and the third by the panel members, or two by each of the parties and the fifth by the other four panel members.[62] The panel's terms of reference are limited to the subject matter and nature of assistance the parties seek. This can include "giving advice, making determinations, finding facts, conducting, evaluating and reporting on studies and making recommendations."[63] The panel may also hold a hearing, but transcripts are not to be kept, and the legal rules of evidence do not apply.[64] Within twenty-one days of receipt of the panel's final report, the parties must make an effort to resolve the disagreement with or without assistance of the panel.[65] If they cannot agree, the matter can go to arbitration or the courts.

The Elders Advisory Council is included as an alternative facilitated process to ensure elder expertise and traditional processes are considered in matters such as "language and culture."[66] Procedures of the council are to be flexible, informal, and determined by the council. Council may conduct itself in a manner analogous to that of a mediator, including "meeting with the parties together and separately, conducting informal interviews or inquiries and facilitating settlement negotiations."[67] In keeping with the Nisga'a tradition of decision making, "best efforts to reach consensus" by elders on the council must take place before the council gives advice or recommendations. In keeping with the equally important values of equal and fair representation, no action may be taken unless at least one elder appointed by each party agrees.[68]

An interesting aspect of the council is that all parties may appoint at least one and not more than three elders. Although it is anticipated that Nisga'a appointments will be from the Nisga'a Nation, appointments are not limited to members of the Nisga'a Nation. Rather, s.4 of Appendix M-5 to the treaty provides:

Preferably, the Elders will be individuals who:

1   are recognized in their respective communities as wise, tolerant, personable and articulate, and who:
    a   are often sought out for counsel or advice, or

    b have a record of distinguished public service; and
2   are available to devote the time and energy as required to provide the
    assistance described in the Appendix.[69]

Stage Three: Arbitration and Adjudication   If agreement cannot be reached at stage one or two, the parties may call for arbitration of the matter by an expert arbitrator or panel of arbitrators. This process of dispute resolution can be invoked only if attempts to resolve the disagreement through a collaborative process have failed. Some sections of the Final Agreement provide for final determination by arbitration, thereby eliminating the option of going to court as a dispute resolution forum of first resort. If judicial resolution is selected as an option, the Final Agreement also envisions the creation of a Nisga'a court (discussed in further detail below). Again, the details regarding appointments and the arbitration process are set out in an Appendix to the Final Agreement.[70] Not surprisingly, the arbitration process pays greater attention to procedural fairness and other administrative law concepts, as the arbitrator, or arbitral tribunal, may render final and binding decisions. For example, no presentation of oral information to the arbitrator may be given without all the parties present, and all written communications must be copied to the parties. Basic accessibility issues such as costs of travel and comprehension of proceedings are addressed by the input of the parties into selection of the arbitrators, empowering the arbitral tribunal to meet at any place it considers appropriate in British Columbia, and the ability to order translations and expert testimony where appropriate.[71] Decisions of the arbitrator or arbitration tribunal must be made in accordance with relevant provincial, federal, or Nisga'a law and the spirit and intent of the Nisga'a Final Agreement.[72]

Metis Settlements Appeal Tribunal (MSAT)
Drawing on her experiences as a member of the Metis Settlements Appeal Tribunal (MSAT) and its work to develop a "healing mediation process," Phyllis Collins also gave examples of how the values that inform the ADR movement can complement the justice goals of indigenous communities.[73] As explained earlier, MSAT is a bicultural administrative tribunal with a majority consisting of Metis settlement members. The role of MSAT is to interpret and enforce Metis settlements legislation and Metis laws enacted pursuant to that legislation. Although technically an administrative tribunal, MSAT's role in interpreting law is analogous to a court and is resulting in the evolution of a Metis settlements common law based on provincial legislation, Metis laws, settlement custom, and the Canadian common law. Like other administrative tribunals, MSAT must comply with principles of administrative law when holding a hearing and rendering a decision. MSAT members are trained on what this means and must

comply with a code of ethics that addresses issues such as conflict of interest, bias in law, and the role of tribunal members in the community. However, unlike many tribunals, MSAT also has jurisdiction over laws that are yet to be enacted under the framework legislation. It also has express statutory authority and significant flexibility to select among various dispute resolution processes, ranging from early neutral fact-finding by investigative and research officers, to mediation, to formal hearings attended by legal counsel.[74]

The concept of justice that informs all of MSAT's operations reflects both traditional Metis dispute resolution values and ADR rationales.[75] MSAT is concerned primarily with administering justice, not simply with enforcing law. Justice requires "an understanding of Metis law and custom as well as legal rules."[76] This can be achieved only if MSAT creates a comfortable atmosphere for resolving disputes and a relationship of trust and respect with those affected by its jurisdiction. This requires impartial decision making if necessary, but also an increased emphasis on "healing, reconciliation, consensus and Elder participation in the resolution of disputes" in circumstances where a consensual and facilitated process is preferred by the individual and community members affected.[77] In short, the primary goal is to dispense justice "in a manner which may depart from the ways of the non-Metis courts, but which respects the need for consistency, understanding of law and custom, and procedural fairness."[78]

Dispute Resolution Goals   The mission statement of MSAT, endorsed after settlement community consultations on its most recent three-year business plan, also links concepts of justice to the ADR movement. MSAT's mission is:

> To contribute to the self-sufficiency of Metis life by providing resolution of issues that would affect the progress of Settlements and Individuals. In providing this assistance the Tribunal believes that the following are fundamental:
>
> 1   The Tribunal's principal focus must be to ensure that justice is dispensed, using principles of law as a tool, not as an ultimate objective.
> 2   Alternative dispute resolution (ADR) mechanisms are incorporated into Tribunal processes so that disputes are settled in an effective and timely way, with the least possible disruption to Metis life and relationships.
> 3   Decisions of the Tribunal must be carried out using its own processes supplemented by those of external agencies.
> 4   To inform settlement Councils and members as to the role of the Tribunal so that appropriate issues can be brought to the attention of the Tribunal clearly and without fear.[79]

The Healing Mediation Process   In pursuit of this mission, MSAT is in the process of developing a healing mediation process with the expert assistance of consultant Cathy Sveen. The goals of this process are to "facilitate healing, promote harmony and build consensus decision making within the Metis community" in a voluntary, non-adversarial, and confidential environment.[80] The process is based on the traditional Cree belief system of a medicine wheel. The mediation proceeds through four phases, facilitated by a mediator: telling your story, finding yourself, finding balance, and opening your heart. As participants move through the phases of the circle, they become more in touch with themselves as they seek to hear and respect the voices of others and move from head-thinking to the heart. The mediation circle is depicted in the diagram designed by Cathy Sveen and depicted in Figure 15.1.

The process is intended to respond to concerns raised by community members concerning healing, fairness, and more local control over dispute resolution. In particular, it is based on the following principles:

1   using mediation as a process for healing relationships and restoring harmony and balance to individuals and the community;

Figure 15.1

Mediation circle

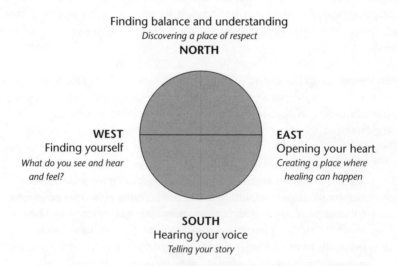

Source: From Cathy Sveen and MSAT, "Healing Mediation Process" (presentation to MSAT Mediation workshop, Edmonton, AB, 15 November 1997), reproduced in C. Bell and MSAT, *Contemporary Metis Justice: The Settlement Way* (Saskatoon, SK: Native Law Centre, 1999), 110.

2   respect for elders and seeking elders' wisdom in the healing mediation process
3   treating people with respect and dignity
4   the importance of spirituality
5   using the circle for healing as it signifies the wholeness and unity and equality
6   "speaking from your heart" [and] "speaking from your head"
7   using a form of consensual dispute resolution (mediation)
8   removing the constraints of time from the healing process
9   having a process that is simple and can be translated into Cree, and
10   using a mediator(s) who people trust and who is acceptable to all participants in the *healing gathering*.[81]

The role of the mediator is one of facilitator but may also involve more active intervention, such as making sure that an elder is present to provide cultural or community expertise. All tribunal members and research officers are offered mediation training, and some also act as voluntary mediators in the Edmonton court system, to develop and contribute their skills. MSAT supports greater settlement input into the resolution of disputes through settlement specific processes that can be adapted to the values and protocols of a particular community. For example, a mediation process based in Cree spirituality and the concept of the medicine wheel, which seeks to fashion solutions based on traditional Metis values and practices, may not be as appealing to a community or individual more influenced by Christian values and rule orientation. The latter may prefer to have a priest with expertise in Christian principles rather than a tribunal member trained in neutral facilitation or an elder with expertise in Metis tradition, facilitate the resolution of the dispute.

The Problem of Gatekeeping
One of the biggest challenges encountered in using the ADR movement to promote Aboriginal justice is unveiled by asking the simple question, Who are the gatekeepers?[82] Often it is a non-indigenous judge, lawyer, or prosecutor who lacks appreciation for traditional processes or who, schooled in the language of Western law, believes adjudication based on rights and rules is the best way to resolve disputes. This is one reason why indigenous people need to be able to be the gatekeepers to their own processes. Robert Yazzie makes this point forcefully in his contribution to this volume.[83]

The Tsuu T'ina justice initiative attempts to address the issue of gatekeeping by replacing important non-indigenous actors in the provincial court system with Aboriginal people. The proposal calls for a First Nations judge who has "lived" First Nation cultural values, as well as for First Nations administrative staff and prosecutors. It is often a prosecutor who decides, or convinces a judge, that an individual should be diverted from the conventional courtroom to an alternative process, or that an alternative process should be utilized in determining an appropriate sentence for criminal behaviour. The First Nations prosecutor is expected to "balance the traditional and contemporary approaches" to dispute resolution with an emphasis on "healing and justice as opposed to a punitive approach."[84] First Nations clerks, interpreters, and other staff will aid in procedures being handled in a more culturally sensitive and meaningful way. Further, emphasis on non-legalistic terminology, regular use of interpreters, incorporation of traditional ceremonies and symbols into court procedures and structure, and location of the court on the Tsuu T'ina reserve will make both the court and peacemakers more accessible.

Improving Eurocentric Institutions

The importance of changing the faces and cultural symbols of existing dispute resolution institutions was one of many suggestions offered by Stein Lal, chair of the Inuvialuit Arbitration Board, to make tribunal and court processes more inclusive of Aboriginal culture and to reduce cultural stress. Recognizing the Eurocentric origins of adjudicative tribunal and court processes and the need for these institutions to change "right down to the core," he emphasized the importance of making what are perceived by some as minor changes when more significant change is not readily available.[85] He emphasized this point by sharing the following hypothetical example he uses when trying to educate members of the Canadian judiciary about the alienating atmosphere of their courtrooms:

> I think one of the most important techniques that I was able to use was to say to all these white judges before whom I stood that they should transpose themselves to a country in Africa like Botswana. They were accused and when they looked around them all people were black. The judge was black. The court staff were black. The clerk was black. The jury of twelve men and women were black and on the walls were all kinds of insignia and all kinds of decoration that meant absolutely nothing to the accused and the accused perhaps understood anywhere from 20% to 80% of the language that was being spoken. The fate of that individual was then to be decided by the court that was established in such a good and democratic system as we claim to have in Canada. It become obvious very readily how an Aboriginal person feels when he or she stands in a courtroom, that we take for granted, as being representative [of the culture and values] of the criminal.[86]

Bicultural Boards and Tribunals

Bicultural boards and tribunals established under land claims and self-government agreements can be useful vehicles for implementing and respecting indigenous values, knowledge, and processes. However, principles of administrative and constitutional law operate to place some limitations on these models for dispute resolution. Of particular influence on the question of control, or "gatekeeping," are the rule against bias, the requirement of institutional independence, and the inability of a government to deprive a court of its supervisory jurisdiction. Under the Canadian Constitution, parliament and provincial and territorial legislatures are prohibited from diminishing the power of superior courts, including their supervisory powers over administrative tribunals.[87] However, legislatures can reduce the right to appeal tribunal decisions and limit scope of judicial review to jurisdictional errors and patently unreasonable errors of law.[88] Further, a court will often show deference to the opinion of tribunal members who are considered to have greater factual expertise with and more intimate knowledge of the agreement or legislation that creates it. However, the fact remains that the decisions of expert bicultural tribunals are subject to review by a non-indigenous judge and system of administrative law. This is one reason indigenous people object to delegation of authority to specialty tribunals as a final step in justice reform.

Equal or Majority Representation
Bias in law is different than actual bias. For example, it can arise if there is a reasonable basis to apprehend bias by parties subject to tribunal authority. The more a tribunal exercises judicial-like functions, the more concerned administrative law is with issues of bias, impartiality, and independence. The word "impartial" refers to a "state of mind or attitude of a tribunal" and connotes "absence of bias actual or perceived."[89] Independence refers to how the system of decision making is structured. If there is a "reasonable apprehension of bias on the institutional level, the requirement of impartiality is not met."[90] To safeguard challenge to tribunal decisions on this basis, most tribunals that affect both Aboriginal and non-Aboriginal populations have members appointed from both of these populations. Under contemporary agreements the standard formula is equal representation and a chair agreed to by the parties.[91] However, this is not the case under some of the earlier agreements. Among the dispute resolution bodies created under the Yukon Umbrella Land Claim Agreement are the Yukon Surface Rights Board, the Yukon Water Board, the Land Use Planning Council, the Fish and Wildlife Board, the Salmon Sub-Committee, the Renewable Resources Council, and the Development Assessment Board (which replaces the Environmental Assessment Board in the Yukon). First Nation composition varies among these different boards, ranging from majority to minority representation. Noting that the Yukon agreement was one of the first agreements negotiated in Canada, Stephen Mills cautioned those at the forum engaged in designing bicultural

administrative boards and tribunals to ensure, at a minimum, equal First Nation representation.[92] Being a minority often "makes it difficult to bring arguments into the operation of the Board."[93] As an example he discussed how some boards established under the Yukon Agreement are obliged to give traditional knowledge full and fair consideration. Nevertheless, scientific knowledge and other values held by a majority may influence how they interpret this obligation.

Representation and Effective Communication
According to Stein Lal, indigenous representation is important not only to address issues of control but also to ensure receipt and communication of issues in the way they are "intended to be conveyed."[94] Drawing on his experiences as chair of the Inuvialuit Arbitration Board, he shared the following story with forum participants:

> In one of our hearings at the Inuvialuit Arbitration Board, the issue before the Board was the cleanup of defense early warning sites. There was a dispute between the government of Canada and the Inuvialuit who alleged that work on cleaning up the sites had not been done properly. One of the issues critical in resolving the dispute was the meaning of the term "buried" because the Agreement said [Canada] would bury x number of used barrels of oil. So, evidence centred on the issue of whether [these barrels] were buried properly or not buried properly. There was a senior gentleman from the Inuvialuit group who was on site when the barrels were buried. In cross-examination the Government of Canada Counsel was trying to get at the real meaning of what burial meant. He asked [of the Inuvialuit gentleman] "well let me put it this way. Suppose I was going to church, just before entering the church I took my hat off and put it on the ground and I put two thirds of it into the ground and a third was left out. Would you say that was buried or not?" The Inuvialuit man looked at him and said "Why would you do a fool thing like that?" So here is an example that the way we approach [communication] is not necessarily the way it is being received. This individual was not relating to the analogy.
>
> It is very, very important to have Aboriginal people on tribunals and boards. Nothing changes the culture faster than having someone sitting next to you with a different perspective. You may read all the books you want, you may attend all the courses you want, but until you are that individual you can never have [the] 100% perspective that person has. I saw this time and time again in our tribunal when Inuvialuit members brought a perspective that was absolutely absent before. If you don't believe me, then just look at the Supreme Court of Canada. See what women judges have done to the Supreme Court. If that Court seems enlightened today when it comes to women's rights, it is because there are women on that Court.[95]

Tribunal-Annexed ADR

Many tribunals established under land claims agreements also incorporate indigenous values and processes through annexation of processes such as mediation and negotiation to tribunal procedures. The ADR powers of MSAT, and the complementary nature of values informing Metis and conventional alternative dispute resolution processes discussed earlier, illustrate this point. Another example is the requirement for negotiation, and option of mediation, articulated in the Yukon Surface Rights Board Act.[96] Participatory and consensual dispute resolution processes not only are part of the history of Yukon First Nations but are commonly annexed to non-indigenous surface rights dispute resolution bodies. Consequently, it is not surprising that disputes involving lands and resources subject to the jurisdiction of the Yukon Surface Rights Board must proceed through a negotiation phase before a hearing can be called. If negotiation efforts are unsuccessful, board procedure requires that it *must* offer the option of mediation to the parties.[97] Parties may elect mediation to be held in Whitehorse or other locations chosen by the parties, or, in the case of a hearing affecting settlement lands, in the traditional territory of the affected Nation.[98] Because of these provisions, the board has yet to meet for a formal hearing. As the Yukon Surface Rights Board promotes parties having direct input into the fashioning of solutions outside the hearing process, Mills considers its record of no hearings a record of success.

Other examples of provisions of the Yukon Surface Rights Board Act designed to address issues of cultural accountability identified by Mills include funding for cross-cultural education and language training for board members, the requirement that hearings be informal and held on traditional lands (where such lands are in issue), the requirement that half of the board members be appointed by the Council of Yukon Indians, and the ability of the board to create its own procedural rules, including the establishment of mediation processes. Mr. Mills also cautioned participants to take into account the intercultural issues that arise among various First Nation parties to an agreement in appointment provisions and in designing intercultural education programs for board members. In his experience of multination agreements, conflict can also exist among the indigenous signatories and members of the board who are from different Nations and have differing opinions on matters such as identification of territorial boundaries, conservation, and development. In his words: "Cross-cultural orientation is [normally understood] as telling white people how to think or how to understand native people. That is not necessarily what has to happen in order for Boards to work together in the Yukon for relationships to develop ... An awareness that has to take place is a good understanding [between] a First Nation and another ... Part of our process to resolve these [types of disputes] is to bring the groups and the Elders from the communities together and try to understand better what their needs are."[99]

Evidential and Procedural Flexibility
As administrative tribunals are not bound by the usual rules of evidence, greater emphasis can be given, with greater comfort by non-indigenous members, to arguments based on customary practice or the oral history of elders. For example, MSAT tribunal members can accept any oral, written, or other evidence in a hearing they consider to be relevant and proper. Parties are free to "tell stories of past traditions in the community, communicate information they have received from others not present at the hearing, and rely on documents which may not hold up under judicial scrutiny."[100] This does not mean that they accept all evidence as trustworthy. Although evidential flexibility enjoyed by MSAT and many other tribunals enables more voices to be heard and more perspectives to be considered, MSAT assesses the appropriate weight to be given to testimony and other evidence, based on factors such as "character and reputation of parties giving testimony, the existence of corroborating or contradictory evidence, and the opinion of witnesses considered to be experts."[101]

The importance of evidential flexibility is demonstrated in the exercise of MSAT jurisdiction over settlement land. For example, in the area of land transfer and devolution of estates, MSAT has been able to render decisions that uphold community custom and respect for elder opinion. Although not *expressly* obliged to consider matters of custom in these areas, MSAT feels obliged to do so. For example, in the decision of *Meyers and Blyan*, MSAT based its decision on custom and Metis values:

> Apart from considering the statutory and common law principles (such as the doctrine of part performance) it is also the Panel's obligation to examine any relevant traditional practices followed by members of the settlement. By examining the past and present practices of settlement members it is the Panel's hope that it can uncover important underlying community values that give rise to these practices in the first place. Once the underlying value is unearthed, it is the tribunal's duty to determine if it applies to the case at hand.
>
> The Panel recognizes that it was not uncommon practice, prior to Nov. 1, 1990, for transfers of land between settlement members to be done by way of verbal agreements. Though somewhat informal, a transfer of land between settlement members by way of verbal agreement was usually recognized as a valid transfer by the appropriate settlement council, and ultimately, the Metis Rehabilitation Branch.
>
> Based on the traditional land transfer practice alluded to above, the Panel is prepared to recognize the agreement for sale of land reached

between John Meyers and Joseph Blyan as valid and enforceable. This Panel is prepared to make this finding not only on the basis that it accords with past land transfer practice, but because such a finding falls in line with the underlying value that, in Metis culture, the spoken word is as important as the written word.[102]

Absence of a sound factual basis for decision making is grounds to challenge a tribunal decision under principles of administrative law. Members of the settlement community have expressed general satisfaction with this approach, and appeals have not been forthcoming. Over one hundred decisions have been rendered by MSAT, three have been appealed, and one challenged by judicial review. No decisions have been sent back to MSAT or overturned on the basis of insufficient evidence or lack of a sound factual basis. Indeed, tribunal notice of cultural and community factors has been recognized as appropriate, and indeed beneficial, in MSAT decision making by the Alberta Court of Appeal. For example, in the *Chalifoux* appeal, Madame Justice Picard noted that one of the primary objectives of the MSAT is to enable Metis people to deal with their own disputes relating to settlement land.[103] For this reason she refused to hear an appeal of a decision in which MSAT erroneously assumed jurisdiction over a land dispute under the wrong section in the Metis Settlements Act, when MSAT clearly had jurisdiction under other sections of the legislation and Metis government land policy. In reaching this conclusion, she noted the complex factual situation that MSAT had to analyze in the absence of a written land contract and concluded:

> There is no doubt that the nature of the contract between Mr. Chalifoux and Ms. Risdale was different in a number of ways: it started as a handshake; the consideration included a satellite dish, a truck, a camper, logs, bales, calves and cash; and family members of Ms. Risdale were involved. There was never any contract in writing setting out the terms. However, an examination of the written decision of the tribunal shows it heard from the parties and was made well aware of Mr. Chalifoux's position and of the nature of the arrangement made by the parties. It had ample evidence before it which supported its conclusions. The legislation was set up to allow this tribunal to deal with interests in land arising in a Metis settlement in whatever form they might arise. The tribunal had the benefit of understanding the parties, practices and community setting.[104]

Parties to land claims and self-government agreements can also require administrative boards and tribunals to consider unique factors not ordinarily associated with conventional decision-making processes. As Aboriginal people have direct input at the stage of conceptualization and design, they can require that decision making take into account the need to recognize cultural difference. For example, the Yukon Environmental Assessment Board is required to give equal weight to scientific and traditional knowledge in rendering its decisions. Unlike with provincial lands, the evaluation of compensation for access and damage to Metis settlement land by MSAT must also take into account "cultural value of the land for preserving the Metis way of life" and disturbance to the "physical, cultural and social environment."[105] Similar provisions in the Yukon Surface Rights Board Act enable the Yukon Surface Rights Board to consider the cultural and environmental impact of development on Yukon settlement land.[106] However, as Stephen Mills explained to the forum, if the board is not *required* to consider cultural impact, this can cause disagreement among members regarding the relevance of this factor to the dispute. Even if board members agree, the difficult question, how do we evaluate culture?, emerges.[107] Mr. Mills recalled a case before the Water Board concerning mining on lands considered traditional territories of a Yukon First Nation family for many years. Although the land had not been used for traditional purposes for a long time, the family had a hard time quantifying their loss. They questioned how the board could ask them to attach an economic value to interference with their right to exercise cultural activities on these lands now or at a later date. Some board members felt that development needed to be stopped, but the board had no jurisdiction to do that. Noting that the Yukon agreement is an early agreement, Mills suggested this example illustrates one reason why greater control over both surface and subsurface development by indigenous government is important.

MSAT faces similar challenges when it attempts to place an economic value on the potential impact of development on cultural activities such as berry picking, hunting, trapping, and fishing. Although Metis government can prevent development of subsurface resources, can participate in the development and profits from these resources, and can place conditions on development, these powers do not apply to subsurface agreements entered before the accord was negotiated in 1990.[108] However, regardless of when agreements were entered, MSAT must consider cultural impact in assessing compensation to surface rights holders when compensation is in issue. Settlement government is now attempting to address this question by enacting legislation establishing minimum compensation rates and hiring experts to assist in the evaluation process. In past situations where these measures were not available, MSAT established a minimum compensation rate and the assumption of minimal interference with Metis culture unless the occupants of the affected settlement land established "through oral or written testimony, that the impact on the social or cultural environment is such that greater compensation is warranted."[109]

For example, in the Husky Oil decision, the Land Access Panel of MSAT awarded $800 per annum for cultural impact based on the following reasoning:

> The Panel finds as a fact that oil and gas activity, however minimal, has an impact on the surrounding environment. Since hunting and trapping, which the Panel agrees is an inherent and vital part of Metis culture, is wholly dependent on the maintenance of a healthy physical environment, it follows that the introduction of oil and gas activity onto settlement lands has a corresponding impact on Metis Culture for which the existing mineral lease holder must pay compensation.
>
> ... The Panel did its best to heed General Council's call to keep in mind the cumulative effect of oil and gas activities on traditional Metis hunting and trapping way of life. The panel was particularly moved by the testimony advanced by Eugene Jensen about how the loss of even a single moose within the project area, especially if there are similar losses in other project areas, can have a serious impact on the maintenance of traditional Metis hunting and gathering way of life. The panel is also mindful, however, that Mr. Jensen's testimony was only allegorical, or symbolic, in nature. So, while the Panel agrees that the loss of even one moose, or equivalent game, in one or more project area would have a serious effect on Metis culture which would give rise to greater annual compensation, nothing was actually advanced by the occupants to show that such a loss has occurred.[110]

One of the main opportunities offered by boards and tribunals established under land claims and self-government agreements is increased accessibility. Most boards and tribunals established under these agreements can hold hearings in the community affected and in surroundings familiar to indigenous parties. Although legal counsel are permitted to appear in hearings, often this is not necessary given the location and informality of the process. Tribunals and boards can also take advantage of procedural flexibility to adopt more inclusive, familiar, comfortable, and culturally appropriate procedures. For example, prior to an MSAT hearing, members engage in informal conversations unrelated to the dispute with those present at the hearing and sometimes a meal is shared.[111] The hearing begins in a relaxed fashion with introductions of everyone present and explanation of the hearing process. Often all present and giving testimony are seated around a large table. The chair emphasizes the importance of everyone having a chance to speak without interruption. The hearing does not follow the standard adversarial format of applicant evidence followed by respondent evidence, rebuttal, and final argument. It flows more like a facilitated discussion emphasizing sharing of information, rather than proving one person's argument is better than another's. All parties are given an opportunity to tell their stories in full, with minimal interruption, before any witnesses are heard. Questions are put by tribunal members as they arise in a conversational tone, rather than the adversarial tone characteristic of cross-examination. Parties may also ask questions of each other and witnesses. The chair controls the order and flow of information and may shift the process to a mediation process if this is appropriate given the nature of the communications occurring.

Tribunal Flexibility and Cultural Stress

The general flexibility of the tribunal process and the opportunities this flexibility offers to address issues of cultural stress and communication were highlighted by Stein Lal in his presentation to the forum. In particular he offered these suggestions:

1   Remember "what is not prohibited is allowable ... Use all the imagination you have to make sure that you use what is not prohibited to create some new and innovative ways" to deal with the inability to change the law or design under which you operate.[112]
2   Relax the rules. "The rules are intended to facilitate arriving at a just and fair decision. The rules are not intended to put the process into a straight jacket. Very often we get so bogged down in rules that we forget that the purpose of the forum, or of the tribunal, is to render justice. It is not to score full points in foreign rules."[113]
3   Expand the use and role of "interpreters so that everyone knows what is going on. We have traditionally used interpreters to interpret, let us say on cross-examination between counsel and a witness. Most of the audience ... do not know exactly what is going on. Give the interpreters a free hand to explain what is happening."[114]
4   Create a climate for Aboriginal people to feel "welcome in a real and meaningful way and not feel that they are being patronized. You do that by making the forum sensitive to Aboriginal issues and what their requirements are."[115]
5   Enable communication to convey intended meanings: "There isn't a more powerful word than communication."[116]
6   Use expert evidence. "I don't think that there is any subject on this earth that a good expert ought not to be able to explain to a tribunal ... and if he or she is not able to do so, get a different expert." [Experts need not be] "highly educated individuals" with university degrees.[117]

Despite offering these words of advice, Mr. Lal acknowledged that one cannot "borrow perspective" and the only way to ensure consideration of

Aboriginal perspectives is for Aboriginal people to be involved in the design of administrative boards and tribunals and to sit as members of these boards.[118] He also emphasized that courts and tribunals that engage in more adversarial processes are not designed to resolve disputes but to determine who wins and who loses. This is the Anglo-Saxon legal culture upon which the whole Canadian justice system is based, and which non-indigenous people often fail to realize is also culturally specific. Lawyers involved in the design and implementation of these processes are not trained to resolve disputes but to "win cases for their clients."[119] Thus, if the concept of trying to resolve a dispute through more inclusive processes is to be accepted, "we need to make changes in how we train our lawyers who eventually become judges."[120] Although the goals and philosophies of ADR are being taught in law school, and law firms are offering ADR services, this is still peripheral to the adversarial and judicial decision-making processes that dominate legal education. Only "time will tell how fundamental this change is."[121] Lal argued that there is a need to change our system "radically and right down to the core" if we are serious about resolving intercultural disputes.[122] We need to be "sophisticated enough to recognize that there are several cultures in Canada" and our institutions need to address the distinct and specific values of these cultures for meaningful change to occur.[123]

Conclusion
Although the concept of delegated jurisdiction and reliance on trends in the administration of justice is offensive to some First Nations who view their right to administer justice as an inherent Aboriginal right, an important strategy in selling Aboriginal justice initiatives to the non-Aboriginal public has been to emphasize how they are similar to existing non-indigenous initiatives. This helps non-indigenous politicians address allegations of reverse discrimination and special treatment, even though such allegations may be unfounded. For example, specialty courts are not a new idea. We have traffic courts, small claims courts, family courts, youth courts, tax courts, and so on. The Tsuu T'ina court is like a specialty court in the sense that it embraces the philosophy that access to justice can be enhanced by streamlining certain types of cases to a judge, or judges, who have experience and expertise in a particular area. The specialization of the court, and the expertise of the judge, lie not only in the areas of law that are being administered but also in the cultural factors that limit the effectiveness of standard judicial process. Like other specialty courts in the country, such as family courts and small claims courts, an alternative dispute resolution process will be operated in conjunction with the court. The significant changes are Aboriginal control over discretionary decisions

at various levels of the administration of justice and anticipated increase in the use of alternative processes to address conflict with the law, not the content of the laws themselves.

The Nisga'a court goes a step farther in that it will be part of a judicial system *required* to address Nisga'a and non-indigenous laws in the resolution of disputes. As Edward Allen explained, the unique aspect of the Nisga'a court is not the ability to craft culturally specific procedures and processes into the administration of justice, but the constitutional protection that will be given to the court and the ability of the court to enforce Nisga'a law.[124] Under the Nisga'a treaty, the ability to enact Nisga'a law extends to a variety of areas not previously within First Nation jurisdiction under the Indian Act. Nisga'a government can create statutory offences and penalties in these areas and is responsible for prosecution of these laws. In the event of conflict with provincial or federal law, Nisga'a law prevails in designated areas such as elections, culture, and language, operation of business on Nisga'a lands, health services, child and family services, and education. Laws with respect to natural resources, wildlife, migratory birds, and the environment are to be negotiated with the Nisga'a and will be enforced by the Nisga'a court. Similar arrangements for the enactment and enforcement of indigenous laws can be negotiated by Yukon First Nations under the Umbrella Land Claim Agreement. Currently, non-indigenous courts and administrative boards and tribunals enforce laws enacted by Yukon First Nations under nation-specific self-government agreements.[125]

Although the strategies and initiatives discussed so far are extremely important in supporting the health and well-being of Aboriginal people and Aboriginal communities, they are limited in what they can achieve. In particular, these systems are subject to review by non-indigenous courts, and indigenous law continues to be applied only if those affected agree to an alternative dispute resolution process, or non-indigenous governments agree that indigenous law should be paramount. Only in recent agreements, and under limited circumstances, are indigenous laws made paramount to non-indigenous laws in their application. For this reason, many believe that although ADR models for justice reform may help address issues of cultural stress, they are unable to effectively address the issue of colonization. Rather, the hierarchy of decision making promoted by these processes, the dominant role of non-indigenous law, and the ability of non-indigenous government to alter many of these processes if they no longer have popular support, perpetuate Aboriginal dependency.

Nevertheless, many First Nations also accept an approach to justice reform that is gradual and pragmatic. Pitching gradual change through indigenization against the movement for separate Aboriginal justice is viewed as generating a "false dichotomy" and a "fruitless distinction" because for many it is not an "either/or choice."[126] This does not mean that separate civil or criminal justice systems that are immune from judicial review by non-indigenous courts and enforce indigenous law should be ruled out. It does mean that work needs to be done on capacity building within the community. In the opinion of Judge Mary Ellen Turpel-Lafond,

> Resisting colonialism means reclaiming by Aboriginal peoples of control of the resolution of disputes and the jurisdiction over justice, but it is not as simple or as quick as it sounds. Moving in this direction would involve linkages with the existing criminal justice system and perhaps a phased assumption of jurisdiction.
>
> ... Public security and gradual process of criminal justice reform is what people are looking for, not a sudden break and some completely isolated regime. Community members want lots of time for discussion, training (including training on relevant aspects of the Canadian legal system) and a phased in process of criminal justice reform implementation. They also require fiscal resources. There might be some aspects of the current criminal justice system that will never be taken on by Aboriginal justice systems. There will be many points of convergence between Aboriginal justice systems and the Canadian criminal justice system.[127]

The obvious danger of promoting reform through incremental change is that the steps taken toward reforming existing justice institutions may be confused with the end goal. Inherent limitations in the development and implementation of current Aboriginal justice initiatives suggest that this would operate to the detriment of Aboriginal people by failing to address the need for Aboriginal peoples not only to adopt their own procedures but also to control when those procedures will be used within their communities and what traditional laws need to be revived and enforced to ensure cultural and community survival. Progress may come to a standstill because of a perception by non-Aboriginals that procedural reform is sufficient to make the system more accountable to Aboriginal people. Even if existing reforms are sufficient to meet the concerns of some First Nation communities, shifts in public opinion could have a significant impact on how discretion within the existing system is exercised at a future date. For these and other reasons, many call for reform outside the ADR movement.

Notes

1 The Royal Commission on Aboriginal Peoples (RCAP), *Bridging the Cultural Divide: A Report on Aboriginal People in the Criminal Justice System* (Ottawa: Ministry of Supply and Services, 1996), 39. Although Canadian reports and inquiries have focused on the administration of civil justice, these issues also influence reforms in civil justice.
2 *Ibid.,* 50 [emphasis added].

3 Anna Pellatt, "Recommendations and Resolutions," in Catherine Bell and Anna Pellatt, *Gathering Our Strength: Conference Report on Violence Against Aboriginal Women* (Edmonton, AB: Institute for the Advancement of Aboriginal Women, 1998).

4 Intercultural Dispute Resolution: Opportunities and Issues (Faculty of Law, University of Alberta, Edmonton, AB, 8-10 July 1999) (referred to in notes below as Intercultural Dispute Resolution forum). The forum was by invitation only, and the program was designed to meet the needs of those directly involved with the design and implementation of dispute resolution mechanisms under Canadian land claims, treaty, and self-government agreements and the work of administrative tribunals and boards under those agreements.

5 The term "alternative dispute resolution" (ADR) is used in this chapter to refer to a continuum of processes that fall short of a judicial process and range from command processes such as decision making by expert administrative tribunals to processes in which parties to a dispute arrive voluntarily at a solution, such as mediation.

6 Michelle LeBaron, "Learning New Dances: Finding Effective Ways to Address Intercultural Disputes," Chapter 1, this volume, p. 23.

7 *Ibid.*, p. 23.

8 *Ibid.*, p. 23.

9 *Ibid.*, p. 22.

10 *Ibid.*, p. 26.

11 Intercultural Dispute Resolution forum. Comments are drawn from recorder's notes of questions to speakers and discussion groups on file with the editors of this volume.

12 Edward Allen, "Dispute Resolution and the Nisga'a Final Agreement," Intercultural Dispute Resolution forum, 9 July 2000 (transcript of presentation on file with editors).

13 Some examples are also drawn from presentations at a recent conference in Edmonton, AB, on criminal justice, *infra,* note 25, the texts of treaties and agreements discussed at the forum, and publications concerning models discussed at the forum.

14 I have been working with draft verbatim transcripts and recorders' notes with the exception of two conference speeches, one prepared by Michelle LeBaron and the other by Chief Justice Robert Yazzie. Consequently, I have taken the liberty to fix punctuation, grammar, and other technical problems in the verbatim transcript. However, a draft of this chapter has been reviewed by all the forum presenters quoted.

15 Judge Irene Toledo presenting a paper prepared by Chief Justice Robert Yazzie, "Navajo Peacemaking and Intercultural Dispute Resolution," in Chapter 6, this volume, p. 108.

16 *Ibid.*, p. 112.

17 *Ibid.*, p. 112.

18 *Ibid.*, p. 110-11.

19 Indian Act, R.S.C. 1985, c.I-5.

20 Leonard (Tony) Mandamin, "Appeal Boards Under the *Indian Act,*" Intercultural Dispute Resolution forum, 9 July 2000 (transcript on file with editors).

21 *Ibid.*

22 *Ibid.*

23 *Ibid.* See, for example, *Matsqui Indian Band* v. *Canadian Pacific Ltd.,* [1995] 2 C.N.L.R. 92 (S.C.C.) [hereinafter *Matsqui*].

24 Mandamin, "Appeal Boards Under the *Indian Act.*"

25 Philmer Bluehouse, "Navajo Peacemaking: Where Did It Start?" (speech presented at First Nations Justice Conference: Journey Towards Change, Yellowhead Tribal Council, Edmonton, AB, 11 November 1999).

26 *Ibid.*

27 *Ibid.*

28 The accord was implemented in 1990 by provincial legislation that outlines terms and protection of the land grant; the structure and jurisdictions of local and regional Metis settlement governments; the relationship between Metis laws and other laws; the creation, jurisdiction, and operations of the Metis Settlements Appeal Tribunal (MSAT); a co-management regime for the development of subsurface resources; a financial commitment to the settlements; and other elements integral to accord implementation. A condition precedent for the implementation of the Metis land and self-government agreement

was acceptance by the community. See, generally, C. Bell and MSAT, *Contemporary Metis Justice: The Settlement Way* (Saskatoon, SK: Native Law Centre, 1999).

29 Quoted in C. Bell and MSAT, *ibid.,* 48.

30 Tom Pocklington, *The Government and Politics of the Alberta Metis Settlements* (Regina, SK: Canadian Plains Research Centre, 1991), 58-59.

31 For more details on elders committees, proposed arbitration process, and the origins of the Metis Settlements Appeal Tribunal (MSAT) discussed in this and subsequent paragraphs, see C. Bell and MSAT, *Contemporary Metis Justice*. This volume also contains MSAT decisions.

32 MSAT, *1998 Annual Report,* quoted in Catherine Bell, "Metis Self-Government: The Alberta Settlement Model," in John Hylton, ed., 2nd ed., *Aboriginal Self-Government in Canada* (Saskatoon, SK: Purich Publishing, 1999), 340.

33 Phyllis Collins, "MSAT: Sharing Our Experiences and Success," Intercultural Dispute Resolution forum, 10 July 1999 (transcript notes of panel presentation on file with editors).

34 The MSAT mediation process is discussed later in this chapter. The Metis Settlements General Council has also hosted conferences to discuss concerns of elders and to recommend steps to increase their role and value in the community. See C. Bell and MSAT, *Contemporary Metis Justice*, 18, 109.

35 Allen, "Dispute Resolution and the Nisga'a Final Agreement."

36 *Ibid.*

37 Alberta Justice Ministry, *A New Direction: Report of the Review Team Established to Study the Tsuu T'ina Nations Proposal for a First Nation Court* (Edmonton, AB: Alberta Justice Communications, October 1998), 14.

38 Marsha Erb, "The Tsuu T'ina Nation Proposal for a First Nation Court" (speech presented at First Nations Justice Conference: Journey Towards Change, Edmonton, AB, 10 November 1999).

39 *Ibid.*

40 *Ibid.*

41 Alberta Justice Ministry, *A New Direction,* 10.

42 Part I of the Constitution Act, 1982, being schedule B to the Canada Act, 1982 (U.K.), 1982, c.11.

43 Alberta Justice Ministry, *A New Direction,* 27. His Honour Judge Leonard (Tony) Mandamin has been appointed to this position and was sworn in at a ceremony on the Tsuu T'ina reserve in August 1999. He is an Anishnabe from the Wikemikong First Nation, has been involved with numerous Aboriginal organizations and events, and is a highly qualified member of the bar. Also sworn in at this unique ceremony, drawing on Tsuu T'ina and legal traditions, were two peacemakers for the Office of the Peacemaker, discussed later in this chapter.

44 *Ibid.,* 10.

45 Rebecca Williams, "Opportunities and Issues in Nunavut," Intercultural Dispute Resolution forum, 9 July 1999 (transcript on file with editors).

46 *Ibid.*

47 *Ibid.*

48 See, generally, *Bridging the Cultural Divide.*

49 LeBaron, "Learning New Dances," p. 15.

50 *Ibid.,* 14-15.

51 Alberta Justice Ministry, *A New Direction,* 17.

52 Judge Mandamin, "Restorative Justice and the Tsuu T'ina Court" (speech presented at Aboriginal Awareness Days, Faculty of Law, University of Alberta, 5 February 2001).

53 *Ibid.*

54 See also the discussion of Navajo Peacemaker process discussed earlier in this chapter. Alberta Justice Ministry, *A New Direction,* 17.

55 Allen, "Dispute Resolution and the Nisga'a Final Agreement."

56 *Ibid.,* 14-15.

57 Nisga'a Final Agreement, Canada, British Columbia, and the Nisga'a Nation (4 August 1998, reprinted December 1998), c.19, s.3. The treaty has been ratified by the Nisga'a

Nation and enacted by the BC legislature as the Nisga'a Final Agreement Act, S.B.C., 1999, c.2.
58 *Ibid.*, s.13.
59 Allen, "Dispute Resolution and the Nisga'a Final Agreement."
60 Nisga'a Final Agreement, Appendix M-1, ss.13(c) and (d).
61 *Ibid.* The language used includes terms of art that point to the interest-based model of negotiation developed by Roger Fisher and William Ury of the Harvard Negotiation Project. See R. Fisher and W. Ury, *Getting to Yes* (New York: Penguin Books, 1981).
62 Nisga'a Final Agreement, Appendix M-3, s.6. See also, ss.4-13.
63 *Ibid.*, s.14(c).
64 *Ibid.*, ss.24 and 25.
65 *Ibid.*, ss.43 and 44.
66 Allen, "Dispute Resolution and the Nisga'a Final Agreement."
67 Nisga'a Final Agreement, Appendix M-5, s.11.
68 *Ibid.*, ss.24 and 25.
69 Nisga'a Final Agreement, Appendix M-5.
70 Nisga'a Final Agreement, Appendix M-6.
71 *Ibid.*, ss.62-64.
72 *Ibid.*, ss.95 and 97.
73 Collins, "MSAT: Sharing Our Experiences and Successes."
74 Both the Metis Settlements Act, S.A. 1990, c.M-14.3, s.188, and the Yukon Surface Rights Board Act, S.C. 1994, c.43, ss.39 and 40 provide for the annexation of mediation processes. MSAT powers are quite broad and include the power to establish "any means of dispute resolution that it considers appropriate including mediation, conciliation and arbitration processes."
75 C. Bell and MSAT, *Contemporary Metis Justice,* 100.
76 *Ibid.*
77 *Ibid.*, 101.
78 *Ibid.*
79 Quoted in C. Bell and MSAT, *ibid.*
80 Cathy Sveen and MSAT, "Healing Mediation Process" (presentation to MSAT Mediation workshop, Edmonton, AB, 15 November 1997). Discussion of this model is drawn from this presentation and from Bell and MSAT, *Contemporary Metis Justice,* 108-12. See also M. Huber, "Mediation Around the Medicine Wheel" 10 (1993) Mediation Quarterly 4, 355.
81 From C. Sveen and MSAT, *ibid.*, reproduced in C. Bell and MSAT, *ibid.*, 110.
82 *Ibid.*, 111.
83 Yazzie, "Navajo Peacemaking," 11.
84 *Ibid.*
85 Alberta Justice Ministry, *A New Direction,* 18.
86 Stein Lal, "Inuvialuit Arbitration Board: Sharing Our Experiences and Successes," Intercultural Dispute Resolution forum, 10 July 1999 (transcript on file with editors).
87 *Ibid.*
88 Constitution Act, 1867 (U.K.), 30 and 31 Vict., c.3, s.96, requires that the federal governor in council (Cabinet) appoint judges to superior courts. What constitutes a s.96 court is a question of law but does not preclude the province or federal government setting up bodies that carry out a judicial function, such as an administrative tribunal. Whether a tribunal is really a court in the eyes of the law depends on a number of factors but arguably, if the power it exercises is "necessarily incidental to the achievement of a broader policy of the legislature" and it is subject to some form of judicial scrutiny, it does not violate s.96 (Re Residential Tenancies Act of Ontario, [1981] 1 S.C.R. 714 at 735-36). See also, generally, David Jones and Anne de Villars, 2nd ed., *Principles of Administrative Law* (Scarborough, ON: Carswell Thomson Professional Publishing, 1994), 36-41. Tribunals that exercise judicial powers, such as MSAT, are viewed in law as exercising a quasi-judicial function.
89 Most legislation establishing administrative tribunals includes what is called a privative clause designed to limit the scope of judicial review. Allowing complete deprivation of judicial review would be viewed as a threat to the independence of the court, a violation

of s.96 and the rule of law. See, generally, *Crevier* v. *A.G. Quebec,* [1981] 2 S.C.R. at 236; and Jones and de Villars, *ibid.*

90 *Valente* v. *The Queen,* [1985] 2 S.C.R., 685.

91 *Ruffo* v. *Queen,* [1991] 2 S.C.R. 100 at para. 44.

92 Recent case law suggests that the fact that all tribunal members are derived from the community of people affected, or are related in some way, will not necessarily give rise to a reasonable apprehension of bias, especially when the reality is that everyone in that community is related. See, generally, *Matsqui* v. *Canadian Pacific.*

93 Stephen Mills, "Yukon Surface Rights Board: Sharing Our Experiences and Successes," Intercultural Dispute Resolution forum, 10 July 1999 (transcript on file with editors).

94 *Ibid.*

95 Lal, "Inuvialuit Arbitration Board."

96 *Ibid.*

97 Yukon Surface Rights Board Act, ss.26 and 40.

98 Yukon Surface Rights Board Rules of Procedure (30 April 1996), s.5. According to Mills, members decided not to make mediation mandatory for a number of reasons including concern about the proliferation of individuals claiming expertise in mediation and lack of a formal accreditation process.

99 *Ibid.*

100 Mills, "Yukon Surface Rights Board."

101 Bell and MSAT, *Contemporary Metis Justice,* 107.

102 *Ibid.*

103 *Ibid.,* 400.

104 *Paddle Prairie* v. *Arthur Chalifoux and Bernice Risdale and MSAT,* [1999] 1 C.N.L.R. 134 (Alta. C.A.).

105 *Ibid.,* para. 16.

106 Metis Settlements Act, s.118.

107 *Supra,* note 74, s.56.

108 Mills, "Yukon Surface Rights Board."

109 See, generally, Bell and MSAT, *Contemporary Metis Justice,* 87-97, 470-538.

110 *Husky Oil Ltd.* v. *Barrington Petroleum and Elizabeth Metis Settlement,* in C. Bell and MSAT, *Contemporary Metis Justice,* 513.

111 *Ibid.,* 512-13.

112 See, generally, Bell and MSAT, *Contemporary Metis Justice,* 106-8.

113 Lal, "Inuvialuit Arbitration Board."

114 *Ibid.*

115 *Ibid.*

116 *Ibid.*

117 *Ibid.*

118 *Ibid.*

119 *Ibid.*

120 *Ibid.*

121 *Ibid.*

122 *Ibid.*

123 *Ibid.*

124 *Ibid.*

125 Allen, "Dispute Resolution and the Nisga'a Final Agreement"; see, generally, Nisga'a Final Agreement, ss.30-52.

126 MSAT is also like a court in that it enforces Metis law generated within the framework of the Metis Settlements Act.

127 RCAP, *Bridging the Cultural Divide,* 79.

128 *Ibid.*

16

What's Old Is New Again: Aboriginal Dispute Resolution and the Civil Justice System

Diana Lowe and Jonathan H. Davidson

While ADR[1] is a relatively new phenomenon in Western legal systems, dispute resolution techniques have been used by Aboriginal people in North America for millennia.[2] In recent years, as dispute resolution has been adopted into contemporary legal systems, there has been a growing interest in traditional Aboriginal dispute resolution, especially in the area of criminal law. There has been comparatively less development toward applying Aboriginal dispute resolution in private, civil disputes involving Aboriginal peoples. In this chapter, we will first discuss traditional Aboriginal approaches to dispute resolution as well as other traditional dispute resolution programs that are working in combination with contemporary legal systems. We will then examine the work of the Canadian Bar Association Task Force on the Systems of Civil Justice and the Canadian Forum on Civil Justice, both of which are concerned with improving the civil justice systems in Canada. In this context, we will consider the opportunities that exist today to enable the incorporation of traditional Aboriginal dispute resolution into our civil justice systems.

Traditional Aboriginal Dispute Resolution

It is tempting to classify Aboriginal dispute resolution mechanisms in terms of contemporary ADR techniques; however, the apparent similarities must not be allowed to mask the dramatic cultural and philosophical differences that underlie Aboriginal and contemporary dispute resolution. One author, educated and experienced in both Aboriginal and contemporary dispute resolution techniques, comments that "the system of Aboriginal Dispute Resolution is fundamentally different from the system of Alternative Dispute Resolution. It has only been explained in terms of Western-based dispute resolution in order to achieve a common understanding of the different approaches."[3] Navajo tribal peacemaking, for example, is superficially very similar to Western-style mediation but it also has several important differences:

Although tribal peacemaking clearly departs from conventional Anglo-American adversarial justice, differentiating it from non-Indian alternative dispute resolution (ADR) is more subtle; non-Indian proponents of tribal peacemaking have only begun to explore such differences. Certainly informality, party control, and problem-solving orientations characterize not only tribal peacemaking but also negotiation and mediation, key forms of ADR. As Professor Bernard has pointed out, however, tribal peacemaking differs from mediation in two important and related ways. First, the tribal peacemaker usually knows the parties involved and is expected to employ that knowledge during the proceeding. The non-Indian mediator, in contrast, should be neutral and impartial. Second, the peacemaker can and should invoke community values as a guide to establishing a proper outcome. As Navajo spokesperson Bluehouse indicated above, tribal peacemakers invoke creation narratives as well as cultural ideals of proper conduct. In this respect, Bernard claims, tribal peacemaking more closely resembles arbitration than mediation. Yet arbitration still differs from peacemaking in other important ways; the arbitrator normally engages in principled decision making and articulates legal rights relating to the individuals directly involved in the proceeding, while the tribal peacemaker focuses on states of mind and patterns of conduct for the future well-being of the extended family and sometimes the community as a whole.[4]

Among the Coast Salish people of the northwestern United States, the role of elders has changed with the advent of elected tribal councils, formal tribal courts, and law enforcement. However, elders still play a key role in both formal and informal dispute resolution. Depending on the nature of the dispute and the parties involved, dispute resolution may involve elders from only one family or from the families of each of the disputants.[5] In the past, more significant disputes, especially those involving larger groups, were settled by payments intended to avoid violent revenge and to restore the status of all parties; "resolution was acknowledged in public at a potlatch or other ceremonial gathering." Today, these gatherings create an opportunity to hear both sides of a story.[6] Contemporary ADR has no equivalent to these processes.

Minor disputes among the Dene people of the Northwest Territories were settled by the head man of the particular camp. More serious matters were brought before a meeting of the senior members of the community, who would determine the appropriate way to settle the matter, usually through restitution. Both "civil" and "criminal" disputes were handled in this way.[7]

The Aboriginal peoples of Canada employ a wide variety of traditional dispute resolution techniques; all, however, share a basic emphasis and reliance on kinship and community and the desire to maintain (or restore) harmony in the community.[8] This is a significant, culturally based distinction between Aboriginal dispute resolution and ADR, and there are other differences as well. Unlike the dichotomy recognized by Western culture, no clear distinction is made between civil and criminal matters in traditional Aboriginal societies: the rehabilitation (or sanction) of the offender and the restitution of the victim are of equal importance.[9] There is also no separate "legal system"; rather law is an integral part of the social fabric: "non-Indian justice is rigorously segregated from religion; and the non-Indian social system does not establish a comprehensive, well-specified regime of individuals' social responsibility to extended kinship or other groups."[10] This is also observed by Mary Ellen Turpel:

> Aboriginal cultures are non-Anglo-European. We do not embrace a rigid separation of the religious or spiritual and the political. We have extended kinship networks. Our relations are premised on sets of responsibilities (instead of rights) among individuals, the people collectively and toward land. Our cultures do not embrace discipline and punishment as organizing principles in the same fashion as Anglo-European peoples' do. Aboriginal people live with a basic connection to the natural order, which we see as the natural law. This means that family connections, i.e. natural connections, are more important in controlling anti-social behaviour. The lessons offered by a family member, particularly if that person is an Elder, are more significant than any other type of correctional interaction. The personal, familiar interaction is the consensual social fabric of Aboriginal communities. It is this which makes Aboriginal communities distinct culturally and politically from Canadian social institutions.[11]

And while she was speaking of her own traditional Maori society, Moana Jackson's observations echo North American authorities on this essential difference in the organization of Aboriginal and European societies: "The system of behavioural constraints implied in the law was interwoven with the deep spiritual and religious underpinning of Maori society so that Maori people did not so much live under the law, as with it."[12]

The distinctive values and worldviews that give meaning to Aboriginal systems lead authors such as Carole Goldberg to caution against contemporary legal systems borrowing from Aboriginal dispute resolution. She notes that, "unlike a dispute resolution system based on sacred injunctions, a secular democratic system has few sources that command positive behavior," and "the population size, heterogeneity, dispersion and mobility of non-Indian America are real obstacles to achieving the kind of social accountability that Navajo communities experience ... Without sacred prescription of states of being, ritual practice, and specific intra-group obligations, it is difficult to make a peacemaking process work, at least a peacemaking process like that of the Navajo."[13]

The question this leads us to is whether it is possible or desirable to bring together Aboriginal dispute resolution and the contemporary legal system. We should clarify here that we do not disagree with Goldberg. We are not advocating the adoption of Aboriginal dispute resolution in all cases before our civil courts. To do so would simply be to commit the error of failing to recognize culturally appropriate practices, which already occurred when legal practices of the dominant culture were imposed on Aboriginal parties without regard for the cultural practices and beliefs of the parties. What we are suggesting is a multi-option dispute resolution system that enables our contemporary legal system to recognize, incorporate, and defer to culturally appropriate dispute resolution.

Fusion of Traditional Dispute Resolution and Contemporary Legal Systems

Perhaps the best-known adaptation of a traditional Aboriginal dispute resolution technique being used within the contemporary justice system is the use of sentencing circles for Native offenders.[14]

The first Canadian case to employ the concept of a sentencing circle was *R v. Moses*.[15] There, Judge Barry Stuart of the Yukon Territorial Court discussed the advantages of circle sentencing, including the opportunity it presents to merge Aboriginal and contemporary legal values:

> Because Aboriginal people use the same language, engage in similar play and work, western society assumes similar underlying values govern and motivate their conduct. Particularly within the justice system, this widely spread erroneous assumption has had a disastrous impact on Aboriginal people and their communities.
>
> Much of the systemic discrimination against Aboriginal people within the justice system stems from a failure to recognize the fundamental differences between Aboriginal and western cultures. Aboriginal culture does not place as high a premium on individual responsibility or approach conflict in the direct confrontational manner championed by our adversarial process. Aboriginal people see value in avoiding confrontation and in refraining from speaking publicly against each other. In dealing with conflict, emphasis is placed on reconciliation, the restoration of harmony and the removal of underlying pressures generating conflict.
>
> After extensive exposure to the justice system, it has been assumed too readily that Aboriginal people have adjusted to our adversarial process with its obsession on individual rights and individual responsibility, another tragically wrong assumption. Similarly, we have erroneously assumed by inviting their involvement in our system they will be willing

and eager participants. If we generally seek their partnership in resolving crime, a process that fairly accommodates both value systems must emerge.

The circle has the potential to accord greater recognition to Aboriginal values, and to create a less confrontational, less adversarial means of processing conflict. Yet the circle retains the primary principles and protections inherent to the justice system. The circle contributes the basis for developing a genuine partnership between Aboriginal communities and the justice system by according the flexibility for both sets of values to influence the decision making process in sentencing.[16]

In a later article written for *The National,* Judge Stuart observed that the circle involves not only the offender but the entire community:

> Circle sentencing fundamentally shifts the focus in searching for solutions from symptoms to causes. The discussion in circles, unlike courts, does not isolate the criminal act from the social, economic and family environment fostering crime. Further, unlike courts, the circle focus extends beyond the offender to include the interests and concerns and circumstances of offenders, their families, the victim and the community.
>
> Consequently, the sentencing plan (which includes elements of punishment, rehabilitation, healing and reconciliation with the victim and community) is based on greater knowledge. The sentence attempts to redress the causes of crime generally within the community and specifically those conditions prompting criminal conduct by the offender.
>
> Circle sentencing is just beginning to engage communities in a significant manner. Once fully engaged, once the potential of communities to work in concert with the professional justice system is realized, the cumulative savings in monetary and human terms will be enormous.[17]

In a companion article, Judge David Arnot of the provincial court of Saskatchewan described the process of designing the Saskatchewan model of sentencing circles, and noted that during this process there was a realization that through sentencing circles, the contemporary criminal justice system can be responsive to the needs of the Aboriginal community:

> "Katapamisuak" is a Cree word meaning "to take responsibility and control for oneself." The Katapamisuak Society was formed in 1992 as an equal partnership between the Battlefords Justice Advisory Council and the Aboriginal community in northwestern Saskatchewan ... Over the course of several meetings, we were exposed to the Cree perspective on many issues and gained a better understanding of Cree spirituality, traditional values, traditional celebrations and the Cree language. The most

compelling feature was a realization that the existing system is liberal and flexible enough to accommodate the needs and the concerns of the Aboriginal community.[18]

A fusion of traditional and modern dispute resolution techniques can also be seen in the operation of the Metis Settlements Appeal Tribunal. The tribunal is "a quasi-judicial body ... designed to provide practical and unbiased solutions to some of the day-to-day disputes facing the [Alberta Metis] settlements."[19] The tribunal has jurisdiction over private, civil matters, and its primary focus has been disputes involving land transfer and ownership. Tribunal members include a majority of Metis as well as non-Metis members, and decisions are reached by consensus, which ensures that the tribunal must consider and reconcile traditional Metis opinions in reaching decisions.[20] Disputes can also be settled by resort to arbitration or mediation, which has been designed to incorporate traditional values of healing and harmony.[21]

In Michael Jackson's article "Alternative Dispute Resolution in Aboriginal Communities," he describes a publicized custody dispute from British Columbia that provides another example of how traditional dispute resolution can be made part of the civil court process. This case involved a custody dispute between the aunt and father of a child whose mother had died, but who had expressed her desire that the child be raised by the aunt so that he would be taught Indian traditions and given privileged status in her band. Both the aunt and the father were Salish, but from different bands. Both wanted custody, and the case ended up before the provincial court. The South Island Tribal Council obtained intervenor status and successfully sought a six-week adjournment of the custody hearing, to enable a council of elders to mediate the dispute. The dispute was resolved by the council of elders and the agreement was written down and signed so that it could be incorporated into the order of the court. The provincial court ultimately issued a consent order, with the written agreement attached and the access provisions therein made part of the court order.

In his written judgment, Judge O'Donnel commented:

> Before dealing with the form of the actual Order, I personally would like to add a few words because of the historical significance of this process by which this agreement and this court judgment has been arrived at ... This method of resolving disputes has shown that traditional native methods and institutions can and do operate effectively in this day and age. The entire process has demonstrated that it is possible for the native institutions and in our courts to co-operate and work together for the benefit of all parties.
>
> In this case the application of Salish law and the invocation of its dispute resolution process avoided the hostility and pain usually associated

with custody battles. Both families will have the opportunity to contribute towards development of the child who is thus enabled to enjoy and benefit from the heritage and traditions of both families without having to choose between them. Nor is it likely that the same result could have been achieved by having each party call as witnesses elders from their respective families to give as it were expert evidence on Coast Salish law, leaving it with the Judge to take this into account in determining the best interests of the child. The successful outcome of this case is integrally related to the fact that all essential elements of the Aboriginal system of justice were invoked.[22]

Other Traditional Approaches to Dispute Resolution

Canada's Aboriginal people are not the only group to have developed a system of dispute resolution that reflects traditional beliefs and values. As with Aboriginal dispute resolution, Islamic models of conflict intervention draw upon a culture of interdependence and community. The individual is viewed as part of the community, and discord among individuals is seen to have an impact on the unity and harmony of the community. The community therefore has a valued and legitimate role in conflict resolution.[23] Whenever possible, decisions are rendered in accordance with the Islamic tradition of conciliation or amicable settlement, through the concept of *sulh,* a negotiated settlement that is facilitated by mediators or conciliators. In those cases where amicable settlement cannot be achieved, disputes are decided by a third party, whose decision is based on fairness and equity.[24]

These traditional values are manifest in the highly organized system of Ismaili Conciliation and Arbitration Boards (the "CABs"). Established in twelve countries by his Highness the Aga Khan in 1986, the mandate includes: (1) assisting in the conciliation process between parties with differences or disputes arising from commercial, business, and other civil liability matters, or from domestic and family matters, including those relating to matrimony, children of a marriage, matrimonial property, and testate and intestate succession, and (2) acting as an arbitration and judicial body to hear and adjudicate upon matters referred to in (1).[25] In Canada, there is the National Conciliation and Arbitration Board, as well as five regional boards. A regional board generally consists of five members, of which at least two are women and one must be a lawyer. Decisions are usually reached using conciliation or negotiation, but the parties can resort to arbitration if desired.

The Supreme Court of British Columbia recently dealt with a matrimonial case in which the concept of *maher* was considered.[26] The court in *Nathoo* v. *Nathoo* recognized the contractual obligation of *maher* as part of the marriage tradition of the Ismaili community, of which the parties were members.[27] The court concluded that the *maher* was a marriage agreement entered into in contemplation of marriage, and that the *maher* should be upheld. Dorgan J. held that "our [Canadian] law continues to evolve in a manner which acknowledges cultural diversity. Attempts are made to be respectful of traditions which define various groups who live in a multi-cultural community. Nothing in the evidence before me satisfies me that it would be unfair to uphold the provisions of an agreement entered into by these parties in contemplation of their marriage, which agreement specifically provides that it does not oust the provisions of the applicable law."[28]

The decision demonstrates sensitivity to the cultural practices of the Islamic community, and "also recognizes, albeit tangentially, the community interest by referring to the role of the elders in the process of arriving at the amount of *maher*. This signals a less "individualistic" approach and takes into account relationships, community interests and cultural contexts."[29]

The Jewish rabbinical courts provide another example of a culturally specific dispute resolution practice which is increasingly recognized and deferred to by our courts. While Jewish rabbinical courts have existed for centuries to settle theological issues and disputes, in recent years their scope has been expanded to encompass an increasing range of civil matters. Rather than existing as standing courts, the Beit Din[30] sit on an ad hoc basis as necessary.[31] Similar to arbitration tribunals, the "Batei Din are composed of three judges, where each party picks a judge, and the two judges agree on a third."[32]

A Beit Din can be used to resolve commercial disputes, provided that at least one of the parties is Jewish and both agree to be bound by the decision. Scottsdale Plaza Resort, for example, had a dispute with a company that organizes tours for observant Jews. Rather than resorting to litigation, the hotel agreed to take its dispute to a Beit Din. As well as being faster and less costly than the courts, the procedure was less formal. The hearing was described as "an open discussion with the rabbis and the parties jumping in to ask questions and rebut claims."[33] Decisions are based on traditional Jewish law but they must also be tenable in modern North American society.[34]

The use of Beit Din in Canada is not as widespread as it is in the United States or the United Kingdom, though it is common in both Toronto and Montreal. Canadian courts have shown a willingness to defer to the decisions of Beit Din where the procedural rules employed were fair and the judgment itself was considered fair and reasonable under Canadian law and natural justice. Decisions of the Beit Din have been deferred to as private arbitration decisions:[35] "There being, then, no evidence before me that the judgment of the Rabbinical Court was improvident, I would then hold that the parties, as is their right, have submitted to a forum of arbitration by which they had agreed to be bound, and that, therefore, it is appropriate to grant summary judgment upon the judgment of that arbitration forum."[36]

Indeed, in the matter of *Levitts Kosher Foods Inc.* v. *Levin,* the Ontario Superior Court of Justice held that the Beit Din was the appropriate forum to resolve a dispute between three Toronto rabbis and a Montreal company that produced and sold kosher meat and deli products. At issue was the certification that the food produced by the company met appropriate standards: "Having decided to operate its business within the orthodox community, and having for many years taken the benefit of the system, [*Levitts Kosher Foods*] can not now claim it is prejudiced by following one of its basic laws. Viewed in the religious context of the business world that the plaintiff chose to operate in and profit from, I cannot find that the plaintiff is prejudiced by following the rules of that system."[37]

Courts will concede jurisdiction to religious tribunals where "the essence of the issue ... pertained to internal church discipline or regulatory matters" and where "the Court was satisfied not only that the secular court was less able than the ecclesiastical court to determine the particular issue but also that depriving the plaintiff of access to this Court on that issue would not cause him or her an injustice."[38] It seems reasonable to assume, then, that the courts would give deference to properly constituted Aboriginal dispute resolution bodies.

Canadian Bar Association Task Force on the Systems of Civil Justice

In 1995, the Canadian Bar Association established the Systems of Civil Justice Task Force "to inquire into the state of the civil justice system on a national basis and to develop strategies and mechanisms to facilitate modernization of the system so that it is better able to meet the current and future needs of Canadians."[39] The task force identified a number of problems with the civil justice system as it currently operates – chief among these were delay, cost, and the public's lack of understanding.[40] While the task force did not specifically address concerns of Aboriginal persons or other distinctive groups in our society, a number of Aboriginal organizations were consulted.[41] The task force was concerned with public needs, and indeed recognized that

> the most important participants in the civil justice system are members of the public, both individuals and organizations, seeking to have disputes resolved. It is for their benefit and that of Canadian society as a whole that the civil justice system was created. It follows that the system should continue to exist, in its current or adapted form, only so long as it serves the needs of Canadians and is considered by them to be relevant, accessible and fair. Accordingly, the Task Force considered it essential that members

of the public have a direct role in the work of the Task Force from the outset and, further, that they have considerable voice in any recommendations made by the Task Force.[42]

The task force report set out fifty-three recommendations for change,
which respond to seven areas of concern:

1   Creation of a multi-option justice system
2   Reduction of delay in the courts
3   Reduction of costs
4   Improving public understanding
5   Preserving the integrity of the courts
6   Focusing on the needs of legal professionals
7   Increasing the focus on civil justice

The recommendations to create a multi-option justice system will result
in the incorporation of dispute resolution options into the procedures
available to the parties through our civil courts. The task force recommended that:

1   Every jurisdiction
    (a)   make available as part of the civil justice system opportunities for
          litigants to use non-binding dispute resolution processes as early
          as possible in the litigation process and, at a minimum, at or
          shortly after the close of pleadings and again following comple-
          tion of examinations for discovery;
    (b)   establish, as a pre-condition for using the court system after the
          close of pleadings, and later as a pre-condition for entitlement to
          a trial or hearing date, a requirement that litigants certify either
          that they have availed themselves of the opportunity to partici-
          pate in a non-binding dispute resolution process or that the
          circumstances of the case are such that participation is not war-
          ranted or has been considered and rejected for sound reasons; and
    (c)   ensure that individuals involved in helping litigants in non-
          binding dispute resolution processes have suitable training and
          support to carry out this function.
2   Each jurisdiction through its rules of procedure impose on all litigants
    a positive, early, and continuing obligation to canvass settlement pos-
    sibilities and to consider opportunities available to them to participate
    in non-binding dispute resolution processes.
3   Every court undertake studies or pilot projects to determine best prac-
    tices concerning the integration of non-binding dispute resolution
    processes in the post-discovery stages of litigation.[43]

Incorporation of Aboriginal Dispute Resolution
into the Justice System

This is an opportune time for the Aboriginal community and others who prefer the option of dispute resolution to the adversarial approach that has been predominant in our civil justice systems. One of the responses of Canadian courts and departments of justice to the recommendations to create a multi-option justice system has been the development of models of court-annexed dispute resolution. Aboriginal communities will want to ensure that the models adopted ensure processes that are both culturally sensitive and sufficiently flexible and broad as to include Aboriginal dispute resolution practices among the options available to the parties.

At the time of writing, four particular Canadian jurisdictions have been the most active in adopting dispute resolution processes as alternatives or prerequisites to the adversarial court process. They are all moving to integrate dispute resolution into the civil justice system; however, the priorities identified in each jurisdiction and their views about how best to integrate dispute resolution opportunities have resulted in a real variation in approaches.

In Ontario, mandatory mediation began as pilot projects in Ottawa and Toronto but has since been expanded across the province, where it is part of all civil non-family cases (Ontario R.24.1). The concerns that led Ontario to adopt mandatory mediation were primarily delays and backlogs in the trial system. Mandatory mediation was adopted, in conjunction with case management, to address these concerns. In recognition that the most effective time for resolution is at the start of an action, the parties are required to proceed to mediation within ninety days of the defence being filed unless the parties obtain a court order exempting them from mediation or extending the time. Parties may select their own mediators within thirty days after the defence is filed, failing which the local mediation coordinator will appoint a mediator from the roster. The parties share the cost of the mediator for one hour of preparation and three hours of mediation, at a rate set by the regulation under the Administration of Justice Act. The parties can negotiate the fees to continue beyond the three-hour mediation. The mediator files a report as to whether the action has been settled, narrowed, or remains unresolved, but further details are not provided, as the mediation is considered confidential and the mediator is not a compellable witness should the case continue to trial.[44]

Mandatory mediation also began as a pilot project in Saskatchewan and continues as a program in the judicial centres of Regina, Swift Current, Prince Albert, and Saskatoon. The program is available on a voluntary basis in the remaining judicial centres. Civil cases in the specified judicial centres do not proceed to examination for discovery until the parties have attended an initial two-hour mediation session. The mediation is administered by the Mediation Services Branch of the Saskatchewan Department of Justice and conducted by staff mediators or contract mediators hired by the branch. The mediations are provided to the parties without charge. Depending on the readiness of the parties, discussions can either address procedural planning (case management) or move into substantive settlement negotiations. If a party fails or refuses to attend, a Certificate of Non-Attendance may be filed with the court upon the request of the other party. A Certificate of Completion is filed with the court at the end of a mediation session.[45]

The Court of Queen's Bench of Alberta has developed a practice of judicial dispute resolution:

> In the pre-trial conference the judge urges the parties to consider settlement negotiations or to expedite the litigation. Judicial Dispute Resolution (JDR), which was introduced in 1994, attempts to build on the pre-trial conference. In JDR, a judge conducts a settlement conference which assists the parties in reaching an agreement. The Alberta Court of Queen's Bench incorporates dispute resolution weeks into its regular sitting schedules.
>
> Finally, another type of mediation is the mini-trial, which was implemented in Alberta in 1991. The mini-trial is a structured proceeding designed to encourage voluntary settlement negotiations. The presentation of evidence and arguments on behalf of the parties before a judge enables the parties to settle the dispute on the basis of a non-binding opinion rendered by the judge at the conclusion of the process. If there is no settlement, it is an established practice in Alberta that the judge who conducted the mini-trial does not preside at the trial. There is no specific authority for the mini-trial in the *Alberta Rules of Court*. There are three possible sources of legal authority. These sources include the broad wording of Rule 219 relating to pre-trial conferences, the inherent statutory jurisdiction of the court under the *Judicature Act*, and the inherent common law jurisdiction of the court.[46]

The approach in the BC Supreme Court has not been to establish mandatory mediation but to create a Notice to Mediate Program, under which any party to an action may require all other parties to participate in a mediation of the matters in dispute. Rather than creating a blanket requirement for mediation in all cases, the mediation becomes mandated only when one or more of the parties has made an informed assessment that mediation will be productive. After the Statement of Defence is filed, a party can serve a notice to mediate, and a mediator is selected from a mediator roster within sixty days. Parties share jointly the cost of the mediation, which generally lasts three hours. This process was originally introduced in April 1998 for motor vehicle actions under the Insurance

(Motor Vehicle) Act and then expanded in May 1999 to residential construction claims under the Homeowner Protection Act. On the basis of its success in these areas and following wide consultation, the Notice to Mediate Program was expanded in February 2001 to cover most civil, non-family cases in the BC Supreme Court.[47]

In most of these jurisdictions (except where the mediation is conducted by staff), the parties may select a mediator of their choice. Although there may be a requirement to select from a roster of mediators and, increasingly, the mediators may be required to meet certain standards, it is certainly possible in these systems for the parties to select a mediator who will conduct the mediation in accordance with Aboriginal dispute resolution practices. In this way, the civil justice system can recognize and adopt culturally appropriate practices that will enable the system to be more relevant, valuable, and effective to Aboriginal parties.

Arguably, dispute resolution practices should always result in a culturally appropriate and sensitive process, whether the parties select the mediator or not. A mediator should approach dispute resolution in a manner "respectful of not just the interests but the cultural values of all the parties involved. Rather than focussing on interests to the exclusion of values, it is suggested that a useful approach is to try to identify the values which are the root of the conflict and then attempt to define areas in which each party may exercise decision making in a manner which is respectful of their own cultural values while moving forward, where possible, towards common objectives."[48]

In addition to recommendations aimed at creating a multi-option dispute resolution system, Recommendation 27 of the CBA task force report proposes that "every court provide point-of-entry advice to members of the public on dispute resolution options within the civil justice system and available community services."[49] An example of this is found in the Los Angeles Superior Court, where

> an attempt has been made to provide a single point of access to a variety of ADR services through implementation of a system known as court-annexed mediation.
>
> The court-annexed mediation service offered by the Los Angeles Superior Court does not imply that ADR services are exclusively provided by sitting judges of the court. Rather, the term refers to the fact that litigants who voluntarily wish to engage in ADR, or who are required to engage in some form of ADR by the rules of court, may obtain all those services at a single location in the courthouse.
>
> Litigants filing claims in the Los Angeles Superior Court attend the office of the ADR Administrator to obtain a list of screened mediators and arbitrators. Litigants who are referred to mediation by a sitting judge in

Los Angeles court or who wish to access mediation on a voluntary basis may immediately attend at the office of the ADR Administrator in the courthouse and there be provided with a list of available mediators and arbitrators.

The list is previewed and approved by the ADR Administrator. There is a quality control process that is overseen by the court. Litigants receive the benefit of early referral to ADR.

The ADR Administrator in Los Angeles Superior Court, with the aid of a comprehensive software program, and the individual expertise of intake staff, is able to provide a broad-based expertise with respect to the type and style of hundreds of mediators in both the private and public sector in the greater Los Angeles area.

This comprehensive information base at a single site permits the ADR Administrator to offer litigants expert assistance with respect to the choice of mediator and type of ADR process best suited to their dispute.[50]

Courts that adopt this practice of providing point-of-entry advice on dispute resolution options will be in a position to help parties identify mediators who will approach dispute resolution in a culturally sensitive manner appropriate, relevant, and effective for Aboriginal parties.

A significant amount of change is occurring within our civil justice systems. Many of these changes are in response to recommendations such as those in the CBA *Report of the Task Force on the Systems of Civil Justice*. While those recommendations did not focus specifically on traditional Aboriginal dispute resolution, they do point to both a need to increase the dispute resolution capacity in the civil justice system and to be responsive to the needs of users. Those designing the new multi-option justice systems need to be made aware of the benefits of making Aboriginal dispute resolution available within that framework, and Aboriginal parties will ultimately need to be aware that this option is available to them.

The Canadian Forum on Civil Justice

The Canadian Forum on Civil Justice is a national institute created directly as a result of Recommendation 52 of the CBA *Report of the Task Force on the Systems of Civil Justice*. The goal of the forum is to "bring together the public, the courts, the legal profession and government to strive to ensure that civil justice is accessible, effective, fair and efficient."[51] The forum welcomes the membership and involvement of the public in its efforts to improve our civil justice systems and, in fact, depends on the contribution and participation of the public and those who work within the civil justice system. We provide a forum for discussions to take place about civil justice reform, are increasingly a resource of information about our civil justice systems, and are pursuing research projects designed to expand our knowledge and understanding.

The forum has begun its work by developing a database of published materials that touch on issues relevant to the civil justice systems in Canada and civil justice reforms. Efforts have also begun to incorporate the full text of unpublished or not widely available materials. The database is known as our Civil Justice Clearinghouse and is publicly available on the forum website.[52]

The forum has also begun its research mandate with a unique research program aimed at studying and ultimately improving communication between the civil justice systems and the public. We have established a large research alliance with partners from academia and the community, including the Aboriginal community. The three-year national research project began in April 2001 with an Alberta pilot. The project has continued at sites in Nova Scotia, Ontario, Quebec, and Nunavut. We will travel to BC in early 2004, and the analysis and dissemination will take place in 2005 and 2006. By working first to better communications between the civil justice system and the public(s) it serves, the forum hopes to increase the opportunity for public involvement in designing a civil justice system that is sensitive and relevant to all the communities it serves.

As with any information about the civil justice system and proposals to improve the system, the forum can facilitate the flow of information about the benefits of Aboriginal dispute resolution in a number of ways. Published and unpublished articles can be included in our Civil Justice Clearinghouse, which expands the audience with access to this information. Links can be made to relevant websites from our website. ADR and Aboriginal dispute resolution will be among the "best practices" that will be studied in our research on improving communication between the courts and the public. Our research results will be widely disseminated among the courts, governments, judiciary, legal professionals, and the public, and we anticipate that real improvements in communication practices will flow from our findings. The forum also participates in national conferences, publishes a newsletter, and has formal and informal partnerships with key contacts in our civil justice systems, which provide further opportunities to share information about the role that traditional Aboriginal dispute resolution can play in the civil justice systems being designed today.

Notes

1 "The abbreviation ADR, when it first appeared, was taken to mean *alternative* dispute resolution; that is, alternative to litigation. In recent years it has come to refer to *appropriate* dispute resolution. The change in language reflects a growing consensus that dispute resolution options should no longer be seen as alternative to, or as opposed to, the litigation process. From this perspective litigation is not seen as the starting or default option with mediation considered only as an alternative in the event that a litigation approach is rejected. Rather, selecting a dispute resolution process is a matter of considering all dispute resolution options equally and selecting the one most appropriate to the individual

case." M. Jerry McHale, "Uniform Mediation Act – Discussion Paper for the Civil Section of the Uniform Law Conference of Canada," August 2000 at 1 (paper on file with authors).

2 Michael Jackson, "In Search of the Pathways to Justice: Alternative Dispute Resolution in Aboriginal Communities" (1992) University of British Columbia Law Review (Special Edition), 187-88.

3 Mark Dockstator, "Alternative Dispute Resolution Experiences in Canada," in *Making Peace and Sharing Power: A National Gathering on Aboriginal Peoples & Dispute Resolution* (Victoria, BC: University of Victoria Institute for Dispute Resolution, 1996), 169.

4 Carole E. Goldberg, "Overextended Borrowing: Tribal Peacemaking Applied in Non-Indian Disputes" (1997) 72 Washington Law Review, 1010-1.

5 Emily Mansfield, "Balance and Harmony: Peacemaking in Coast Salish Tribes of the Pacific Northwest" (1993) 10 *Mediation Quarterly*, 344-45.

6 *Ibid.*, 347-48.

7 Joan Ryan, *Doing Things the Right Way: Dene Traditional Justice in Lac La Martre, N.W.T.* (Calgary, AB: University of Calgary Press, 1995), 33-34, 57.

8 Jackson, "Pathways to Justice," 166. See also Chester Cunningham, "Alternative Dispute Resolution Experience in Canada," in *Making Peace and Sharing Power: A National Gathering on Aboriginal Peoples and Dispute Resolution* (Victoria, BC: University of Calgary Institute for Dispute Resolution, 1996), 168; and Carolyn M. Buffalo, "Traditional Alternative Dispute Resolution in Aboriginal Communities: Possible Models for the Future" (essay, University of Alberta Law Library, 1994).

9 Jackson, "Pathways to Justice," 214.

10 Goldberg, "Overextended Borrowing," 1015.

11 P.A. Monture-Okanee and M.E. Turpel, "Aboriginal Peoples and Canadian Criminal Law: Rethinking Justice" (1992) University of British Columbia Law Review (Special Edition), 256.

12 Jackson, "Pathways to Justice," 164.

13 Goldberg, "Overextended Borrowing," 1015-16.

14 Sentencing circles were first used in 1992 in the Moses case (see note 15 below) and the practice increased until 1995, when we saw a decline in decisions where sentencing circles were used. Although still in use, the anticipated growth in the practice of sentencing circles has not occurred. This can be attributed to at least three causes: community-based projects were provided with three-year funding by the Federal Department of Justice and no further funding was made available at the end of that three years; the chilling effect of some court decisions which established requirements incompatible with traditional Aboriginal justice; and the reliance on judicial and Crown support. Thanks to Jim Robb, Q.C., for his insight and assistance on this point.

15 *R v. Moses* (1992), 71 C.C.C. (3rd) 347 (Y.T. Terr. Ct.).

16 *Ibid.*, 366-67. At least one author strongly disagrees with the idea of alternative sentences that return offenders to their community, as she feels that they are "actually more empowered by the system that supported and protected them as offenders, yet did nothing to alert the victims." Mavis Henry, "Resolving Differences within Aboriginal Communities and Public Governments," in *Making Peace and Sharing Power: A National Gathering on Aboriginal Peoples & Dispute Resolution* (Victoria, BC: University of Victoria Institute for Dispute Resolution, 1996), 189-90.

17 Barry Stuart, "Sentencing Circles: Purpose and Impact," *The National*, October 1994, 13.

18 David Arnot, "Sentencing Circles Permit Community Healing," *The National*, October 1994, 14.

19 Metis Settlements Appeal Tribunal (brochure), 1997, 1. See also <www.metis-settlements.org/MSAT.html>.

20 C. Bell and MSAT, *Contemporary Metis Justice: The Settlement Way* (Saskatoon, SK: Native Law Centre, 1999), 63.

21 *Ibid.*, 110-1, which discusses the "Healing Mediation Process" developed by the Metis Settlements Appeal Tribunal in consultation with Cathy Sveen.

22 Jackson, "Pathways to Justice," 204-6.

23 C.M. Nurjehan Mawani, "Community-Based Dispute Resolution – A Model for Consideration: The Conciliation and Arbitration Boards of the Ismaili Muslims" 2000, 6 (essay on file with authors).

24 *Ibid.*, 7.
25 *Ibid.*, 9.
26 *Maher* is part of the personal law applicable in a Muslim marriage whereby a sum of money is pledged by a man to a woman upon their marriage. The amount of *maher* varies depending on the circumstances. From time to time, a dispute may arise upon divorce, when the wife insists on the *maher* being paid and the husband argues that his obligations have been discharged upon meeting the divorce laws of Canada. *Ibid.*, 3-4.
27 *Nathoo* v. *Nathoo*, [1996] B.C.J. No. 2720 (Q.L.).
28 *Ibid.*, para. 25.
29 Mawani, "Community-Based Dispute Resolution," 5.
30 This is the term most commonly used in the American literature. British sources generally favour *"Beth Din"* and some authors use the two spellings interchangeably. Wren J. in *Weidberg* (note 32, below) uses the unique term *"Bet Din."*
31 Ron Csillag, "Faith in the Law," *Globe and Mail,* 7 February 2000.
32 Michelle Greenberg-Kobrin, "Civil Enforceability of Religious Prenuptial Agreements" (1998-99) 32 Columbia Journal of Law and Social Problems 359 at 368. See also, *Weidberg* v. *Weidberg,* [1991] O.J. No. 3446 (O.C.J.) at para. 2. "Batei Din" is the plural form of "Beit Din."
33 "Hotel Resorts to an Old-Fashioned Technique for Resolving a Modern Contract Controversy" (1996) 14 Alternatives to High Cost Litigation 11.
34 James Pasternak, "Tell It to the Rabbi: Under Jewish Law, One Jew Can Only Sue Another in a Jewish Court," *National Post,* 15 September 1999, B3.
35 Yechiel (Gene C.) Colman, "Ensuring Enforceability of Beis Din's Judgments" (1998) <www.jlaw.com/Articles/Beisdin1.html>.
36 *Weidberg,* para. 12.
37 *Levitts Kosher Foods Inc.* v. *Levin* (1999), 45 O.R. (3rd) 147.
38 *Gruner* v. *McCormack,* [2000] O.J. No. 789 (Ont. S.C.J.) para. 31.
39 Canadian Bar Association, *Report of the Task Force on Systems of Civil Justice* (Ottawa: Canadian Bar Association, 1996), iii.
40 *Ibid.*, 12.
41 *Ibid.*, 94 (Appendix E) where the list of Aboriginal organizations consulted includes the CBA National Aboriginal Law Section, the Native Women's Association of Canada, Pauktuutit (Inuit Women's Association), Assembly of First Nations, Metis National Council, Congress of Aboriginal Peoples, and the Inuit Tapirisat of Canada.
42 *Ibid.*, 3.
43 *Ibid.*, v.
44 The Honourable Mr. Justice James B. Chadwick, "What's New in Alternate Dispute Resolution and the Courts" (paper presented at the Canadian Bar Association National Meeting, Edmonton, August 1999); see also Ann Merritt, "Ontario Mandatory Mediation Program" (fall 1999) Canadian Forum on Civil Justice *Newsletter* (2) 5-7; and <www.attorneygeneral.jus.gov.on.ca>.
45 Ron Hewitt, Q.C., paper presented at the Canadian Bar Association National Meeting, Edmonton, August 1999; see also Ken Acton, "Saskatchewan Civil Mediation Program" (June 2000) Canadian Bar Association National Alternate Dispute Resolution Section Newsletter, 4-6.
46 Graeme Barry, "In the Shadow of the Rule of Law: Alternative Dispute Resolution and Provincial Superior Courts" (fall 1999) Canadian Forum on Civil Justice Newsletter (2) 11, in which Dr. Barry refers to the February 1999 "Annual Report of the Court of Queen's Bench" and the Alberta Law Reform Institute 1993 report, "Civil Litigation: The Judicial Mini-Trial."
47 The BC Attorney General's website <www.ag.gov.bc.ca/dro/bulletins2000/general.htm> links to a June 2002 bulletin which provides the following information: "The *Notice to Mediate (General) Regulation* applies to Supreme Court actions; it does not apply to originating applications. In addition, the following actions are excluded: family law proceedings, actions brought under the *Judicial Review Procedure Act,* claims for compensation for physical or sexual abuse, and actions to which the other Notice to Mediate regulations apply." See also Jerry McHale, "Notice to Mediate in British Columbia" (June 2000) Canadian Bar Association National Alternate Dispute Resolution Section Newsletter, 1, 5; Ron

Hewitt, Q.C., paper presented at Canadian Bar Association National Meeting, Edmonton, August 1999, and "Cross Country Snapshot of Dispute Resolution" (spring 2002) Canadian Forum on Civil Justice Newsletter (4), 13.

48 Peggy J. Blair, "Aboriginal Dispute Resolution: Conflicting Values in Co-Management Negotiations," *ADR and Aboriginal Rights: A Creative Solution for Complex Problems ... Or Just Another Trend?* (Toronto: Institute of Canadian Legal Education, Canadian Bar Association, Ontario Branch, 1998), 19.

49 Canadian Bar Association, *Report of the Task Force on the Systems of Civil Justice* (Ottawa: Canadian Bar Association, 1996), vi.

50 Judge Heather A. Lamoureux, "Multi-use Courthouse a Model for New Millennium" (20 October 2000) Lawyers Weekly 9.

51 CBA, *Report of the Task Force.*

52 <www.cfcj-fcjc.org>.

17
The Dispute Resolution Provisions of Three Northern Land Claims Agreements
Nigel Bankes

This chapter offers a preliminary survey of the dispute settlement provisions of three northern land claims agreements: the Inuvialuit Final Agreement, 1984 (IFA),[1] the Sahtu Dene and Metis Comprehensive Land Claim Agreement, 1993 (SA),[2] and the Agreement Between the Inuit of the Nunavut Settlement Area and Her Majesty the Queen in Right of Canada, 1993 (NFA).[3] In each case, the analysis reviews the overall scope of the different dispute settlement procedures but focuses on the arbitration provisions of each agreement. The analysis is preliminary in nature. I hope that others will be stimulated to carry out more detailed research on the implementation and dispute resolution questions associated with modern land claims agreements. Other chapters in this volume offer more extensive considerations of how these processes may be used to promote Aboriginal participation in, and control over, dispute resolution.

Each of these three agreements is a land claims agreement within the meaning of s.35 of the Constitution Act, 1982.[4] Thus, the rights created or recognized by such agreements are constitutionally protected by being "recognized and affirmed" by that section of the Constitution. In addition to their constitutional status, such agreements also create contractual entitlements[5] and statutory entitlements[6] insofar as each of the agreements is, in some measure, statutorily endorsed by federal ratification legislation.[7] The agreements are complex documents that are much too lengthy to summarize here, but it is important to note that, in addition to provisions dealing with land ownership and financial compensation, the agreements also create complex regulatory and administrative structures to deal with the management of land, water, and the environment and that these arrangements apply throughout the settlement regions and not just to the lands owned by the beneficiaries to the agreements.

The chapter is divided into four parts. Following this brief introduction, the chapter canvasses the range of dispute settlement provisions under the three agreements, pointing out the extent to which, in addition to the arbitration provisions of each agreement, other bodies established by each agreement have been endowed with dispute resolution functions. The next part of the chapter examines the arbitration provisions of each agreement under five headings: manner of appointment, jurisdiction, legal effect of decisions, parties, and the use of special procedural rules. The final part examines the experience to date of arbitration panels established under each of the three agreements and concludes with a review of the two arbitration decisions that have been handed down under the IFA.

The Range and Scope of Dispute Settlement Provisions

This part of the chapter describes some of the techniques the negotiators adopted to deal with the settlement of future disputes. The techniques include the courts, arbitration, the use of other specialized quasi-judicial tribunals established by the agreement, and, in some cases, unilateral decisions by one party.

The Courts

The parties to these three agreements clearly contemplated that the courts would continue to play a significant role in the interpretation and application of the agreements. Indeed, the continued jurisdiction of the federal and superior courts was part of the background jurisdictional and legal facts assumed by the parties in negotiating the agreement.[8] A board created by an agreement that is endorsed by a federal statute will be a federal board, commission, or other tribunal for the purposes of the Federal Court Act and subject to the supervision of that court unless, of course, the parties agree to confer exclusive supervisory jurisdiction on the territorial superior court.[9] All three agreements deal explicitly with the choice of supervisory court, but not always consistently. In some cases the negotiators have explicitly picked the Federal Court (presumably for greater certainty or perhaps because of a desire, at least in the case of the IFA, to stipulate for the Federal Court of Appeal rather than the Trial Division), whereas in other cases they have invoked the supervisory jurisdiction of the territorial superior court. For example, s.5.3.1 of the NFA accords supervisory jurisdiction over the Nunavut Wildlife Management Board to the Federal Court,[10] while s.38.3.12 of the same agreement accords supervisory jurisdiction over that agreement's arbitration panel to the territorial superior court.

The SA is more consistent and, in a general provision in the dispute settlement article, explicitly selects the territorial superior court as a competent court, not just for supervision of the boards or tribunals created by the agreement, but for all disputes.[11] The following paragraph goes on to extend this jurisdiction to the review of arbitration decisions on questions of law or jurisdiction. The IFA accords supervisory jurisdiction over decisions of the arbitration panel to the Federal Court of Appeal (IFA, s.18.31).[12] It is not clear why these three agreements should show such diversity of practice. One might perhaps have expected the Aboriginal parties to select the territorial superior court on the grounds that it was more likely to be better grounded in the conditions of the particular jurisdiction.[13]

In addition to any supervisory jurisdiction that the courts may have over statutory decision makers established by the agreements, the agreements are at pains to preserve the general legal rights and entitlements of the parties and the original jurisdiction of the courts subject only to the rules pertaining to the availability of a stay of proceedings where a matter has already been submitted to arbitration.[14] This suggests that the parties were not prepared to put all their faith in such alternative processes as arbitration. Indeed, I suspect that the Aboriginal signatories, in particular, wanted to be able to resort to the courts in the event of non-compliance by government.[15]

Quasi-Judicial Tribunals

All three agreements either establish or call for government to establish a series of bodies with co-management and regulatory jurisdiction over different matters, including land-use planning, surface access, water, wildlife, and environmental assessment. The agreements describe these bodies as institutions of public government and accord them general jurisdiction over all activities occurring within the geographical area covered by the agreement (i.e., as already noted, their jurisdiction is not confined to activities occurring on beneficiary-owned land and neither is it confined to the activities of beneficiaries). In some cases the agreements also accord such a tribunal specific dispute settlement jurisdiction over specific categories of disputes involving the parties to the agreement. This dispute settlement jurisdiction, especially with respect to surface access issues and wildlife compensation, extends to non-parties.

The NFA contains several examples:

1   Claims for compensation against government or private parties in relation to damages suffered by beneficiaries in relation to wildlife harvesting can be brought before the Surface Rights Tribunal (SRT) (article 6).
2   Determination of the need for access by government to Inuit-owned lands (IOLs) for sand and gravel purposes is to be determined by the SRT (s.21.6).
3   Compensation payable for the use of IOLs by private parties is to be determined by the SRT (ss.21.8 and 21.7.14).
4   Disputes as to eligibility to enrol as a beneficiary are to be determined by an appeals committee (s.35.5).

5   Disputes as to the location of recorded mineral claim boundaries located in whole or in part on IOLs are to be resolved under the Canada Mining Regulations (s.19.8).

The SA reveals a similar, but not quite so extensive, list:[16]

1   Determinations as to the absence of alternative sources of supplies of sand or gravel and as to the terms and conditions and compensation for access are to be made by the Land and Water Board (LWB) (s.19.2.3(b) and (c)).
2   Disputes as to water rights and the compensation payable are to be made by the LWB (article 20).
3   Disputes as to compensation for damage to Sahtu lands as a result of approved access are to be determined by the Surface Rights Board (SRB) (s.21.3.6). However, disputes as to the actual taking of the lands will be subject to arbitration (s.24.1.12).
4   Disputes as to amendments to existing rights of third parties on Sahtu lands to be resolved by the SRB.
5   Disputes as to enrolment may be appealed (i.e., not simply judicial review) to the territorial superior court (s.4.5).

Both the Sahtu and Nunavut Agreements reserve to the National Energy Board its specialized arbitration jurisdiction (with certain modifications) concerning takings of land required for pipeline purposes (SA, s.24.1.5, NFA, s.21.9.8).

Although the IFA calls for the creation of a number of similar structures, including environmental screening and review bodies with public government responsibilities, the IFA does not accord these bodies dispute resolution functions in the same way as the Sahtu and Nunavut Agreements confer authority on the surface rights board or tribunal. Instead, as we shall see, the negotiators of the IFA have accorded the arbitration board under the IFA a very broad and compulsory jurisdiction over all manner of disputes.

Arbitration

Each of the three agreements provides for the establishment of an arbitration board or panel to deal with potential disputes arising under the agreement. While detailed treatment of the arbitration provisions of the agreements is postponed to the third part of this chapter, it is important to make the preliminary observation that the jurisdictional scope of the panels varies dramatically across the three agreements.

In addition to arbitration between the parties to the agreement (and potentially others) by the arbitration panel established by the agreement, one agreement, the NFA, also envisages the use of more ad hoc arbitration to resolve disputes between the beneficiaries and others. Thus, article 40 of the NFA envisages referring disputes between the Inuit and other Indian peoples of Manitoba and Saskatchewan with respect to hunting cabins on IOLs to arbitration[17] and article 26 envisages using a single arbitrator to resolve the terms of an impact and benefit agreement between Inuit and a developer, very much a form of "interest arbitration."[18]

Other Procedures

While the agreements ordinarily contemplate that disputes between the parties will be resolved by reference to some third party in the absence of an amicable settlement between the parties, in some limited circumstances the agreements accord to the government party the right to make the final decision. Examples include the power accorded to the responsible minister under the SA and NFA to settle the terms of an impact and benefit plan or agreement for a park if the parties cannot reach agreement within a reasonable period[19] as well as the complex "disallowance" provisions affecting decisions of the wildlife management boards under both agreements.[20] While the minister's discretion is not unlimited under these provisions but is constrained by some severe disciplines (e.g., the duty to provide reasons) and may be subject to judicial review, these examples do serve to emphasize the inequality in bargaining power between the parties to the agreements.

All the above examples, even (and perhaps especially) the examples of unilateral decision making by government, deal with what happens when negotiations break down. They do not deal with how disputes should be *avoided*. In this context it is important to refer to the roles of the implementation committees that have been established under the two more recent agreements (the NFA and the SA). As a result of a new federal policy initiative,[21] the government has required the adoption of an implementation plan as part of the negotiation of any new land claims agreement.[22] While such plans or agreements do not form part of the land claims agreement (and therefore do not have constitutional status), they are referenced in the SA and the NFA.[23] Both agreements establish an implementation panel composed of "senior" federal and territorial government officials and officials from either the Inuit or the Sahtu/Metis as the case may be. The panels have the overall responsibility for overseeing implementation and monitoring the implementation of the plan, but are also accorded the responsibility to attempt to resolve disputes regarding implementation.[24]

The availability of the implementation panel has led to the adoption of at least one innovative model to resolve a dispute in the case of the NFA. One of the most difficult problems under both the SA and the NFA has proven to be the timely introduction of the various pieces of implementing legislation called for by the two agreements and the concordance of such legislation with the agreements. While there is a common concern that the legislation should faithfully reflect the agreements, the parties, not surprisingly, differ as to how best to attain this common objective. The result has been multiple drafts of the various bills and interminable responses and counter-responses. To try to cut through this process in the case of proposed legislation to implement two aspects of the NFA (the surface rights board and the water board), the parties (Nunavut Tunngavik Inc. [NTI], the Department of Indian Affairs and Northern Development [DIAND], and the Government of Nunavut [GN]) over the summer 2000 agreed to engage an agreed-upon "eminent person"[25] to facilitate a workshop on selected problem issues[26] and then provide a non-binding report containing recommendations.[27] One potential problem with the process was the non-involvement of the Department of Justice, a department with a significant interest in the development of any new legislation.[28]

Other opportunities to problem-solve have also arisen outside the agreements. One of the most significant in the case of the NFA is the practice of holding high-level meetings between senior officials from the territorial and federal governments and NTI.[29] These meetings occur twice a year. They began in 1993 as a way of dealing with the challenges posed by division of the NWT and the creation of Nunavut.[30] They have, however, continued since 1998 with Nunavut succeeding to the chair previously occupied by the NWT.

Conclusions

The three agreements reviewed offer a bewildering potpourri of dispute settlement provisions, and there is surprisingly little consistency either internally or between the agreements. For example, it is not clear why some compensation disputes are to be referred to a surface rights tribunal whereas others may be subject to arbitration. The same observation applies to land access provisions. The dispute settlement provisions throughout are characterized by their formality and their use of quasi-judicial procedures contemplating hearings, subpoena and examination of witnesses, and binding decisions supported by reasons, all making for winners and losers. This stands in marked contrast to more flexible procedures designed to help parties resolve their differences. There are extremely few references to mediation in the agreements, and, while negotiations may be required in some particular instances, there is no general requirement for collaborative negotiations or mediation before referring a difference to more formal dispute resolution mechanisms.

Further research would be required to ascertain the reasons for this variety as well as for the failure of the parties to emphasize more facilitative methods of dispute resolution, but I hypothesize that it is, in part at least, the result of incremental, chapter-by-chapter negotiations over a long period. In the course of those negotiations, dispute resolution issues may be dealt with on a subject-by-subject basis, on an as-needed basis. For example, in some cases it might be important to one party to establish agreed upon dispute resolution procedures in order to deliver "certainty" before that party felt able to initial the subagreement and move on to the next topic (for example, the dispute resolution provisions relating to land access). An alternative approach would be to park the issue with the intention of returning to all the dispute resolution matters at the end of the negotiations. I think that it may also be the case that general dispute resolution as an overall topic did not assume the importance that the parties attached to the more "substantive" parts of the agreement such as land and financial resources. Thus, while the diversity and multiplicity of the dispute resolution processes might well have been noticed by the parties as part of moving from an agreement-in-principle stage to a final agreement, neither party may have wished to invest time and effort in consolidating these provisions at the end of the negotiations which, in some cases, we should not forget, had already consumed the parties for more than a decade.[31]

Arbitration

In this section I review in greater detail the discrete arbitration provisions of the three northern agreements. Each of these agreements devotes a separate chapter or article of the agreement to the subject of dispute settlement through arbitration. I shall deal with the following topics: manner of appointment and composition, jurisdiction, legal effect of decisions, parties, and the adoption of special procedural rules.

Manner of Appointment

The Sahtu and Nunavut Agreements
The Sahtu and Nunavut Agreements offer broadly similar models for (1) the appointment of a panel (i.e., a pool) of arbitrators (eight for the SA, nine for the NFA), and (2) the selection of individual arbitrators for a specific dispute; the IFA (with eleven members) offers a quite different model. Both the SA and the NFA envisage that Canada, the territorial government, and the beneficiaries shall endeavour to agree on appointments to the pool. Failing that, appointments shall be made by a superior court judge in the case of the NFA or, in the case of the SA, by the beneficiaries (four members), Canada (two), and the territorial government (two). Appointments are for five-year terms. In both cases, the initial appointments to

the panels occurred with the agreement of all three parties, following a call for self-nomination published in newspapers with both national and local circulation. Notwithstanding similarities in the process, the composition of the two panels has proven to be quite different. The first appointments to the Sahtu panel were dominated by lawyers: five from the practising bar and two academics. Of the seven lawyers, three have an extensive commercial or labour arbitration background and two are of Aboriginal ancestry (but not Sahtu/Dene or Metis). The one non-lawyer is a professional geologist with an extensive background in the petroleum and hard-rock mining sectors. None of the members has been a resident of the settlement area, although one was a resident of Yellowknife for a number of years and several have northern work-related experience.

The Nunavut Arbitration Panel has much stronger representation from northern residents and beneficiaries. It includes only two lawyers, some former federal and territorial politicians, a businessman, and five persons of Aboriginal ancestry (including one of the lawyers who is an Inuk from Labrador) of whom four are also beneficiaries under the NFA. There is some evidence that the very "representativeness" of the panel may have posed an obstacle to the parties agreeing to use it. The Five Year Review Team[32] drew attention to the fact that the chair of the panel was an employee of NTI[33] and that "this is a potential barrier to its use,"[34] presumably on the grounds of an appearance of bias, conflict of interest, or lack of independence.

Actual disputes are to be heard and considered by either a single member of the panel (where the parties to the arbitration can agree) or by a panel of three, with one panel member nominated by the party initiating the reference, a second by the respondent, and the third appointed by the nominated members, or, failing that, by a superior court judge.[35] The judicially appointed member may be selected from outside the ranks of the standing panel under both agreements, but the SA also seems, in any case, to contemplate the possibility of selecting an arbitrator from outside the standing panel membership if the parties agree.[36] In the case of the SA, failure of the respondent to nominate an arbitrator is deemed to be consent to the applicant's nominee acting as sole arbitrator (s.6.3.3). This eventuality is not specifically dealt within the NFA, but s.11 of the Territorial Arbitration Act may cure this omission by according to a judge the power to make the appointment.[37]

The continuing expenses of the board, including panel honoraria, are the responsibility of government (NFA, s.38.1.7, SA, s.6.2.6), but the actual expenses of an arbitration, including the remuneration of the arbitrators, shall ordinarily be divided among the parties to the arbitration unless the panel decides otherwise (NFA, ss.38.3.8-38.3.10, SA, s.6.3.8).[38]

The Inuvialuit Agreement

The Inuvialuit Agreement calls for a standing arbitration board of eleven members, of whom five shall be appointed by Canada (of whom one shall be a nominee of Yukon and one a nominee of the Northwest Territories),[39] three by Inuvialuit, and three by industry. Unlike the Sahtu-Nunavut model, each member is to be remunerated (and replaced) by the appointing party.

Sections 18.12 and 18.13 of the IFA contemplate that arbitrations may involve two parties (Canada and the Inuvialuit or the Inuvialuit and industry) or three parties (Canada, industry, and Inuvialuit) and structures the panels for arbitration references accordingly.[40] Each party designates two members, with the panel chaired by either the chair or the vice-chair as designated by the chair of the board. Where one of the parties is Canada, one of Canada's designated members "shall be designated by the Territorial Government in whose jurisdiction the matter arose" (s.18.12). Where a party fails to appoint its members, the panel may proceed as if fully constituted (s.18.14).

The first two arbitrations under the IFA reveal the complexity of these appointment provisions. Both arbitrations related in part to the terms of a settlement agreement, which was itself negotiated in the shadow of an earlier and adjourned arbitration commenced in 1989. The settlement agreement referred to locations in both Yukon and the Northwest Territories. Pursuant to the provisions noted above, this allowed each territorial government to designate a panel member, but, since Canada could only appoint two members, this created a difficult situation in terms of Canada's "representation" on the panel as well as raising a potentially fatal jurisdictional issue as to the proper composition of the panel. The matter was resolved by the agreement of counsel for the Inuvialuit and counsel for Canada by structuring the dispute as giving rise to two separate arbitrations (and hence two separate decisions) and then proceeding in the following manner:

> It was agreed that both Yukon Government and the Northwest Territories Government designate a panel member. Both panel members would hear the evidence relating to both jurisdictions and could, if they so wished, excuse themselves from the Arbitration panel when the evidence related exclusively to matters within the other jurisdiction for which they were not designated. It was further agreed by counsel that both panel members would be present when the Arbitration Panel members considered the merits of the case at the conclusion of the evidence in respect of issues that transgressed [sic] the territorial boundary. However, when considering the merits of the case as they relate exclusively to one jurisdiction, the other panel member would be excluded.

It was the opinion of both counsel that this was the most prudent, efficient and expeditious method of proceeding and that it did not require
the introduction of the same evidence twice.[41]

Proceeding in this manner allowed federal as well as territorial representation and insulated the panel from a technical attack on its jurisdiction.

Jurisdiction

The three agreements display a tremendous range of choices when it
comes to the scope of the issues that may be referred to arbitration. The
IFA is the broadest, the NFA the narrowest, and the SA falls somewhere in
between. In making this observation I should be clear that the distinction
that I am making between the three agreements turns upon the scope of
what I term the "compulsory" jurisdiction of the panel or board. By this
term I mean the range of disputes that can be submitted to arbitration
without the consent of the other party in relation to that specific dispute.
The "voluntary" or "optional" jurisdiction of the Sahtu and Nunavut panels refers to the jurisdiction of a panel over any dispute that requires the
consent of both parties before the matter can be submitted to the panel.
As one might expect, the optional jurisdiction of the NFA and SA is much
wider than each panel's compulsory jurisdiction. In fact, each agreement
includes a clause to the effect that, in addition to the range of disputes
over which the panel has compulsory jurisdiction, it may be seized of any
further matter with the consent of the parties.[42]

The IFA contains the simplest and at the same time the most comprehensive clause conferring jurisdiction on the board.[43] Thus, s.18.32 simply
provides that "the Arbitration Board shall have jurisdiction to arbitrate any
difference between the Inuvialuit and Industry or Canada as to the meaning, interpretation, application or implementation of this Agreement."[44]

In addition to this broad conferral of jurisdiction, s.18.35 indicates that
the board *also* has jurisdiction to arbitrate differences in relation to a broad
range of matters, listed below:[45]

1   Any person denied enrolment as a beneficiary may "appeal" denial to
    the Arbitration Board (s.5.7).[46]
2   The Inuvialuit Land Administration (ILA), or any government or
    municipality may refer to arbitration a dispute as to the need to
    acquire Inuvialuit lands for the provision of government services
    (s.7.61). The scope of the dispute presumably may include a determi-
    nation of need, absence of alternatives, and the terms and conditions
    under which a taking might be permitted.[47]
3   Disputes between government and the ILA as to the location or
    amount of alternative lands to be provided for: (1) taking of lands for

a public road right of way (s.7.64), (2) to accommodate development needs in one particular area (De Salis Bay) (s.7.69), and (3) to compensate for lands to be included in the proposed Pingo Canadian Landmark (s.7.72) and the Nelson Head Landmark (s.7.79).

4   The board may be asked to establish a work program for Canada lands and Inuvialuit lands to protect their respective interests in the exploration or production of their respective resources in that same area (s.7.12).[48]

5   Disputes in relation to the sand and gravel provisions of the IFA. This might include disputes as to prices and as to the priority of access accorded to a particular project (ss.7.27-7.42) and presumably might be commenced by a private party or one of the parties to the IFA.

6   Disputes as to the compensation and terms and conditions associated with the use of Inuvialuit lands for meteorological and climatological stations (s.7.87).

7   Disputes as the expropriation of Inuvialuit lands, including disputes as to the availability of alternative lands, compensation available in the absence of alternative lands, and other matters, including costs (ss.7.50-7.58).

8   Disputes as to the terms and conditions of a participation agreement (PA)(s.10). A PA must be negotiated by a developer with the ILA where the developer owns Crown mineral rights but requires access to Inuvialuit lands in order to exercise those rights. A PA may cover a range of matters including rent (but not royalties), inspections and the costs associated with inspections, wildlife compensation, restoration and mitigation, employment service and supply contracts, education and training, and equity participation and other similar types of participatory benefits.

9   Disputes between beneficiary claimants and developers as to responsibility for and the amount of compensation for damages to wildlife harvesting activities (s.13).

The interrelationship between these two types of jurisdictional provision (i.e., the general provision of s.18.32 and then the specific heads of s.18.35) was the subject of some discussion in the first two arbitrations to come before the board in 1994.[49] Counsel for the Crown argued that the specific listing of jurisdictional grounds in s.18.35 required that a narrow reading be accorded s.18.32 and that therefore the board should not assume jurisdiction over a dispute relating to an agreement between the parties (the Settlement Agreement) that was designed to settle an earlier arbitration. The panel rejected that contention noting that s.18.35 by its express words confers an additional jurisdiction on the panel. In my view this conclusion is clearly correct, not so much because the subject matters listed in s.18.35 are so obviously *additive* to s.18.32 but because s.18.35 contemplates a broader range of potential parties to an arbitration.[50] While s.18.32 is confined to the Inuvialuit, industry, and Canada, a review of the specific list in s.18.35 referred to above suggests a broader potential range of claimants and respondents.

The dispute at the heart of these first arbitrations related in part, as noted above, to the interpretation of a settlement agreement that had been designed by the parties to resolve an earlier dispute as to the interpretation or implementation of the IFA. Did an arbitration on the terms of the Settlement Agreement fall within s.18.32? The panel answered in the affirmative: "The 1989 Settlement Agreement was entered into as a result of an arbitration commenced in respect of matters relating to the interpretation and implementation of the IFA. As a result of the 1989 Settlement Agreement, those matters have not ceased to relate to the interpretation and implementation of the IFA. The 1989 Settlement Agreement was a means adopted by the parties to attempt to resolve these differences; it did not thereby alter the nature or origin of their differences which continue to relate to the meaning and interpretation of the IFA."[51]

The compulsory jurisdiction of the arbitration panel under the NFA is not as broad as under the IFA. Section 38.2.1 of the NFA stipulates that the arbitration panel shall have jurisdiction to arbitrate in respect of "matters specifically designated in other Articles for resolution by arbitration under this Article." The list of such matters (below) is short by comparison with the IFA's broad conferral of jurisdiction:

1   Under s.19.9 of the NFA, Inuit have the right to swap existing Inuit Owned Lands (IOLs) for Crown lands containing deposits of soapstone. Disagreements as to the lands to be exchanged shall be referred to arbitration. There is a similar jurisdiction with respect to municipal land swaps under s.14.10.1.

2   Under 21.5.9, disputes as to compensation for damage caused by government agents while exercising rights of access to IOLs shall be referred to arbitration as shall disputes regarding procedures for government access (s.21.5.5) and disputes concerning the location of public easements across Inuit lands (ss.19.6.2 and 19.6.3).

3   Under s.21.7.15, where a person requires access to IOLs for commercial purposes, that person may apply for an entry order from *the SRT* where that person has convinced the *arbitration panel* that: (1) it has tried to negotiate access in good faith, and (2) access is essential to the commercial purpose and that it is physically or financially impractical to obtain access by other means, and the *arbitration panel* has determined a route that minimizes the damage and interference with Inuit use.[52]

4   Under s.21.9.8, where a person exercises a power of expropriation (as qualified by the agreement) to take Inuit lands, the amount of any compensation payable shall be determined by arbitration failing agreement between Inuit and the expropriating authority.
5   Under s.33.7.5, the arbitration panel is accorded jurisdiction over disputes between the Inuit Heritage Trust and a "designated agency" relating to the long-term alienation of archaeological specimens.[53]

The SA follows the same model as the NFA and does not confer general compulsory jurisdiction on the arbitration panel but confers such jurisdiction on a case-by-case basis through specific provisions of the agreement. That said, the list of matters on which a reference may be made to an arbitration panel is somewhat more extensive than is the case under the NFA. In addition, the arbitration panel also assumes jurisdiction on an interim basis for a number of matters that will be referred to a surface rights tribunal once such a body is established for the settlement area. The following list summarizes the specific heads of jurisdiction conferred on the panel:

1   Section 13.4 of the SA deals with the harvesting rights of beneficiaries and s.13.4.10 confers on beneficiaries a broad right of access to all lands within the settlement area for the purpose of harvesting wildlife. However, ss.13.4.12 and 13.4.13 contemplate that some future authorized uses of land by others may conflict with these harvesting rights and establish a mechanism for restricting the right of access in such a case. The procedure envisages that government or the interest holder may give notice of a proposal to restrict access in a particular area. Any Renewable Resource Council or an interest holder may refer the proposal to arbitration. The arbitration panel shall determine (1) whether the proposed use conflicts with harvesting, and, if so, (2) the nature, extent, duration, and conditions of restrictions on access for harvesting, including the establishment and maintenance of hunting, trapping, and fishing camps, required to allow the proposed use, and (3) any such restrictions shall apply only for so long as the land is in actual use and only to the extent necessary to permit the proposed use without conflict.
2   Section 18.1.4 accords the arbitration panel jurisdiction over wildlife harvesting compensations claims as between beneficiaries and developers.
3   Section 21.3.2 accords the arbitration panel jurisdiction to establish the terms pursuant to which government shall be able to occupy Sahtu lands for a term of more than two years.[54]
4   Under s.21.3.3(a) the arbitration panel may settle the terms of an agreement pursuant to which the Department of National Defence and the Canadian Armed Forces may access Sahtu Lands for manoeuvres.

5   Under s.23.3.4 the arbitration panel may settle a dispute between a local government and the beneficiaries over the municipal acquisition of Sahtu lands for municipal purposes. The panel may consider (1) the necessity of the acquisition, (2) the extent and location of the lands to be acquired, and (3) the value of improvements.

6   Under s.25.5.2 the arbitration panel has jurisdiction over disputes between the Government of the Northwest Territories and a designated Sahtu organization over changes in local government boundaries.

7   Under s.24.1.12 disputes between the Sahtu Tribal Council and an expropriating authority may be referred to arbitration but only as to the matter of compensation.

8   Section 27.3.1 accords the arbitration panel an interim jurisdiction over surface rights matters pending establishment of the Surface Rights Tribunal by legislation but only to the extent that such matters are not already provided for in the relevant minerals (including oil and gas) legislation.[55]

In summary, while the IFA confers broad compulsory jurisdiction on the arbitration body established by the agreement, the SA and NFA are much more tentative. As a result, the dispute resolution provisions of these latter two agreements are characterized by tremendous complexity. Complexity increases costs and somewhat ironically will, in all likelihood, create disputes over technical jurisdictional matters rather than facilitate the resolution of the substance of disputes.

Legal Effect of Decisions or References
None of the agreements has much to say about the type of award that a panel may give or the remedies that may be available. The IFA's general compulsory arbitration clause (s.18.32) is completely silent on the matter while the NFA (s.38.3.8) and SA (s.6.3.5), in somewhat similar (but, as usual, not identical) language, specifically refer to the jurisdiction of the panel to make an award, including interim relief and payment of interest and costs. The reference to interest suggests an implied jurisdiction to make a damages award. The NWT Arbitration Act is also relatively silent on the jurisdiction of arbitrators to make particular types of awards, such as an order of specific performance. For example, the act lacks a specific clause, common in other statutes based upon the UK Arbitration Acts of 1889 and 1950,[56] that gives an arbitrator the same power as a superior court to order specific performance of a contract unless otherwise stipulated in the reference to arbitration. Given the relative silence of the agreements and the applicable act, what rules apply?

The general rule and fundamental principle of arbitration law is that the jurisdiction to make an award and to make a particular order must be in accordance with the legal rights of the parties and must be based upon the arbitration agreement between the parties. In light of that principle one would, in any particular case,[57] need to examine the specific head of compulsory jurisdiction upon which the arbitration was based, along with any specific agreement between the parties in the event of a voluntary submission to arbitration. It would be helpful if these matters could be dealt with more specifically in future land claims agreements.

All three agreements describe the awards or decisions of the arbitrators as final or as conclusive and binding, and, in the case of the SA and IFA, not subject to appeal. All three agreements contemplate judicial supervision on jurisdictional grounds, in the case of the IFA by the Federal Court of Appeal (where the grounds include all the grounds stipulated in s.28 of the Federal Court Act) and, in the cases of the SA (s.6.3.7, point of jurisdiction or law) and NFA (s.38.3.12, jurisdiction only), by the territorial superior court. The IFA and NFA stipulate that an arbitration award can be enforced in the same manner as a judgment or order of the court, while the SA achieves the same result by stipulating that the territorial Arbitration Act shall apply to the extent that it is not inconsistent with the agreement.[58] Once again, close examination shows considerable and important variation as to the details of the three agreements.

Parties

The analysis of the jurisdictional provisions above shows that the jurisdiction of the arbitration panel is not confined to the parties to the agreement. This is no doubt consistent with the view of the agreements as not only contracts but also as statutory regimes that create rights and obligations for third parties. The question of who may be a party in any particular case, then, can be answered only in the context of the specific jurisdictional provision that has been invoked. However, perhaps in light of this, and in order to protect the interests of the parties in "their" agreement, two of the agreements provide that both governments and the beneficiary have a right to participate as a party, as of right in the case of the Sahtu (SA, 6.3.4), and if their interests are affected in the case of the IFA (IFA, s.18.16). In the case of the NFA, the parties themselves, unless made a party to the arbitration by its initiation, seem confined to seeking intervenor status (NFA, s.38.3.7) at the discretion of the panel on the basis that that party's interests may be affected. This may have several practical implications in terms, for example, of the right to seek judicial review, ability to appoint an arbitrator, and liability for costs.

Special Procedural Rules

The agreements contain all manner of special substantive rules that the arbitrators are to apply in resolving disputes under particular terms of the respective agreements in order to recognize the special subject matter of land claims agreements,[59] but they offer remarkably little in the way of guidance as to special procedural rules. In the case of the NFA and the SA, much of the procedure will be supplied by the territorial Arbitration Act,[60] while the IFA offers similar guidance in ss.18.21-18.25, dealing with such matters as the presentation of evidence and the compellability of witnesses and documents.[61] However, the IFA also contains some interesting procedural innovations. For example, two of the provisions of the IFA make use of some elements of final offer arbitration (IFA, ss.7.63 and 10.8 and 9) and one of the provisions according the board jurisdiction envisages a potential mediation role for the board.[62] Clearly the board will have to exercise considerable care in performing such a mediation role and, in particular, will likely need to ensure that different individuals are involved in the mediation and, if necessary, arbitration phases of dispute resolution. In addition, s.18.25(e) specifically contemplates that the board may commission a special study on an issue from the Research Advisory Council established by s.14.81 of the IFA.

The SA and the IFA content themselves with indicating that the process of arbitration is intended to resolve disputes submitted in an expeditious and, where appropriate, informal manner (NFA, s.38.3.2, SA, s.6.3.6) and that the panels may establish rules and procedures for the conduct of any references (NFA, s.38.3.1, SA, s.6.2.2).[63] These latter provisions offer the panels considerable scope for flexibility and the development of procedural rules that are more culturally sensitive and less hierarchical than courtroom procedures. All three agreements contemplate that decisions shall either always (in the case of the NFA, s.38.3.14, IFA, s.18.8) or ordinarily (in the case of the SA, s.6.3.10) be published. This is unusual in the context of commercial arbitrations where the possibility of confidentiality is an important consideration in influencing parties in their choice of arbitration rather than litigation.

Conclusions

In this part of the chapter I have considered a number of standard questions in relation to the arbitration procedures established by each of the agreements. The resulting analysis emphasises the variety and complexity of these procedures. Unfortunately, in my view, this offers great potential for unproductive disputes. On the most important question, that of jurisdiction, we saw a significant difference in the ambit of the compulsory arbitration provisions between the IFA on the one hand and the SA and NFA on the other hand. There were also significant differences on points of detail, but in each case the basic model of formal, quasi-judicial procedures is the same. It does not follow from this that arbitration panels cannot adopt more flexible and culturally sensitive procedures, but it does mean that the adoption of such procedures has not been prescribed by the agreements and that much will therefore turn on the actual practice of the panels. As we shall see in the next section, it is too soon to draw any conclusions from the very limited practice that is available.

In light of this review I shall now turn to consider the limited actual practice that does exist under the three agreements.

The Experience to Date

Use of the Courts and Arbitration

The experience to date under the three agreements (recall that the IFA was signed in 1984 and the SA and NFA in 1993) confirms that the parties have not made extensive use of the arbitration provisions. While the Inuvialuit Arbitration Board has handed down two decisions (effectively one; as we have seen the matter was dealt with as two disputes purely to deal with the jurisdictional problems resulting from sites in both Yukon and Northwest Territories),[64] no disputes have been submitted to the other two boards. At the same time, the beneficiaries under both these claims have commenced litigation against the Crown. In the case of the Inuit of Nunavut, this has taken the form of judicial review applications in relation to the allocation of groundfish quotas in the marine areas adjacent to Nunavut.[65] While the issue there might have been crafted as a dispute to be submitted to arbitration under the optional arbitration procedure (s.38.2.1(a)), it is clear that compulsory arbitration was not available with respect to the applicable article 15 of the NFA (which deals with marine areas).[66]

Similarly, the Sahtu commenced an action in the Federal Court Trial Division seeking a declaration that monies payable by Imperial Oil Ltd. to the Crown under the terms of the 1944 Norman Wells Proven Area Agreement constituted a royalty as defined in the SA and therefore subject to sharing under the terms of the SA.[67] Such a dispute might have been submitted to voluntary arbitration by the parties under s.6.1.5(b) of the SA but there is no provision for compulsory arbitration under the relevant s.9 of the SA.[68] The question remains: Why did the plaintiffs in each case elect to use the courts rather than arbitration?

Clearly this is an issue that merits further research and reflection, but it is my understanding, based on informal discussions with some of the participants, that arbitration was never seriously considered in either case. Although speculative on my part, the possible reasons for this include: (1) a sense that the issues raised were "pure" questions of law and in each case involved the interpretation of the agreement; (2) a sense, in the case of the *NTI Turbot* cases, that the issues presented themselves as standard judicial review fact patterns and were boxed that way by counsel who typically, and understandably, would not think of arbitration and judicial review as interchangeable possibilities (and, in any event, what remedy would an arbitration panel have had the jurisdiction to award?); and (3) a sense that, in the absence of compulsory jurisdiction, the submission to arbitration in each of these two cases would have to be negotiated, thereby depriving the moving party of the opportunity to frame its case in the way it wishes. As well, in the Norman Wells royalty case, it seems fairly clear from the interlocutory proceedings that the plaintiffs actually wanted to be able to rely upon technical rules of evidence relating to the non-admissibility of extrinsic evidence absent ambiguity;[69] the plaintiffs might well have concluded that a court, rather than an arbitrator, would more likely take a firm position on this point.

Since the two decisions of the Inuvialuit Arbitration Board represent the only decisions available to this point and since they are not likely broadly available, it seems useful to examine these decisions in some detail and, as well, to comment on the subsequent judicial review applications that ensued.

Arbitration under the Inuvialuit Agreement

The arbitrations involved three substantive issues. In summary they were (1) the implications of Canada's failure to notify the Inuvialuit of plans to seek bids on a proposal to clean up distant early warning (DEW) line sites within the Inuvialuit Settlement Region (ISR);[70] (2) the scope of Canada's clean-up responsibilities for the DEW line sites which responsibilities had been detailed in an earlier agreement between the parties; and (3) the alleged non-fulfilment of Canada's obligation to pursue adding one site, once cleaned up, to an existing national park.

In my earlier discussion of appointment and composition of arbitration panels, I also noted that the panel had to consider several preliminary issues prior to considering the merits of the application brought by the Inuvialuit. These were the issues of composition of the panel and the panel's jurisdiction to deal with matters arising out of the 1989 Settlement Agreement rather than the IFA proper. There was a third preliminary issue that seems useful to note at this point. Counsel for Canada raised the question of whether or not the arbitration was to be conducted in accordance with the terms of the Commercial Arbitration Act.[71] The panel answered no: "The IFA is an agreement in the nature of a treaty, it is comprehensive and its provisions deal with matters relating to all aspects of the claim of the Inuvialuit. As far as arbitration provisions are concerned, section 18 of the IFA provides a complete code for the conduct of arbitrations. The *Commercial Arbitration Act,* on the other hand, would seem to be designed to arbitrate disputes arising out of commercial matters and was not intended to apply to arbitrations that arise out of comprehensive claim agreements such as the IFA."[72]

Section 16 of the IFA sets out certain agreed economic measures designed to support full Inuvialuit participation in the northern Canadian economy. To that end, s.16(8) required government to notify the Inuvialuit of all government contracts that relate to activities within the settlement region (ISR). The federal government failed to notify the Inuvialuit of a request for proposals (RFP) for a contract to design and cost the decommissioning and cleanup of ten DEW lines sites in northern Canada, three of which fell within the ISR. The RFP also provided that a further contract (the second contract) for the cleanup of an additional eleven sites (three of which again were within the ISR) might be issued to the contractor without competition if its performance were satisfactory. Although the Inuvialuit did in fact find out about the RFP by other means and did submit a bid for the first contract after the government made some adjustments to the bidding process to take account of their failure to provide direct notice, the Inuvialuit bid was rejected largely because, as the panel acknowledged, it was almost double the successful bid. The successful bidder was also awarded the second contract without further competition.

The IFA contained different provisions to deal with (1) those cases in which government contracted for goods and services by public tender, and (2) those cases in which it contracted by using some other means. The difference for present purposes was that if the contract were awarded by public tender, the Inuvialuit would get the contract if they "offered the best bid" (s.16.8(b)), whereas if the contract were issued by a means other than public tender, the Inuvialuit should obtain a "reasonable share" of the contracts if the Inuvialuit were capable of supplying the goods and services on a "reasonable basis" (s.16.8(c)).

Canada argued, first of all, that it had no obligation to notify the Inuvialuit since the contract did not relate to activities within the ISR, because only three of the sites in each of the first and second contracts fell within the ISR. The panel rejected that contention drawing, *inter alia*, on the opening section of the IFA that sets out the basic goals and principles upon which the agreement was based. These principles included that of enabling "Inuvialuit to be equal and meaningful participants in the northern and national economy and society."[73] The panel went on to hold that "public tender" was not synonymous with a competitive procedure and that both contracts were issued by a means other than public tender and therefore governed by a duty to ensure that the Inuvialuit receive a reasonable share of the contracts provided that they could supply on a reasonable basis.

Given that there was a duty to notify (which duty had been breached), what were the implications of this breach? Here the panel, somewhat surprisingly, made nothing of the difference in the language of the IFA insofar as it dealt with contracting through public tender versus non-public tender, simply remarking that, in both cases, the intent of the paragraphs was "to give the Inuvialuit a preference in economic activities but only if they are competitive in their bids."[74] As a result, the panel concluded that the Inuvialuit would not likely have been awarded the first contract and therefore awarded only nominal damages. The panel treated the breach in relation to the second contract in the same manner, remarking that Canada had failed to provide the Inuvialuit with an opportunity to show that they were capable of supplying the services sought by Canada on a reasonable basis but equally, and without further reasons, declined to award anything other than nominal damages. Thus, in both cases, victory was hollow but perfectly consistent with the principles that an arbitrator must decide according to law, that contractual damages are designed to put the innocent party in the position that it would have been in had the contract been performed, and that punitive damages are only rarely available and then only in tort actions.

The second set of issues in each case related to Canada's alleged non-performance of certain obligations that it had assumed under the 1989 Settlement Agreement. The first such issue related to the timing of the agreed clean-up operations at two of the DEW-line sites, Horton River (NWT) and Komakuk Beach (YT). In both cases the panel found that there was an implied obligation that the clean-up operations should be undertaken within a reasonable time and that Canada's delay was unreasonable and that a declaration should issue to that effect, and to the effect that Canada was in breach of the terms of the Settlement Agreement.[75] The panel, however, declined to grant specific relief on the basis that the terms of the agreement were too vague and incapable of being supervised by the arbitration panel.[76] It also declined to award damages, as the claimants had been unable to show that they had been injured by the delay.

Second, Canada argued that the term "remove" as used in the Settlement Agreement allowed Canada the option of removing structures from their current surface location but then still burying them somewhere else on the site. The panel rejected that argument, holding that a reasonable person would interpret this as meaning removal from the site. That DND and DIAND might have had a different understanding between themselves was hardly to the point since this understanding had not been communicated to the Inuvialuit. The panel also made extensive comments on the importance of Inuvialuit approval of the restoration plan to be implemented for the various sites.

Third, the panel held that the Inuvialuit were entitled to a declaration that the clean-up obligations not only extended to the physical DEW-line sites but also included the surrounding areas where debris in those areas would have emanated from the site. Fourth, the clean-up obligations of the

Settlement Agreement bound all departments of government. Finally, and with respect to the Komakuk Beach site in Yukon, Canada had undertaken in the Settlement Agreement to use its best efforts to add the site to Ivvavik National Park either by proclamation pursuant to s.3.1 of the National Parks Act (NPA) or by amendment of the NPA "as the Minister of the Environment should determine to be most expeditious."[77] The panel held that Canada was also in breach of this undertaking, noting that even if it were to accept Canada's understanding that the undertaking was simply a commitment to begin the process without any guarantee of its outcome, there was still a breach since the proposed amendments had not even been discussed at the interdepartmental level. In this case, too, the panel declined to award specific relief or even the $10,000 nominal damages sought by the claimants.

In an unusual move, the panel awarded costs to the claimant on a solicitor client basis. In so ordering, the panel reasoned that the claimants were in the nature of public interest plaintiffs, that Canada had simply proceeded with the bidding process for the two contracts notwithstanding Inuvialuit Regional Corporation (IRC) complaints rather than taking more substantive measures to rectify its breach of the IFA, and finally that Canada had yet to fulfill its obligations under the 1989 Settlement Agreement.

The panel concluded its reasons with some general observations to provide guidance to the parties to help them "avoid arbitrations in the future."[78] In the course of these observations the panel was at a pains to emphasize that its decision was unanimous and that it was important to all to restore mutual respect and recognition between the parties. The panel also noted that the arbitration had, in effect, been caused by the lack of knowledge of the contents of the IFA within different departments of government. To the panel, that was unacceptable given the constitutional status of the IFA. The panel noted that the practice and procedures of the Department of Supply and Services needed to be revised to take account of the requirements of the IFA "and indeed any other present and future settlement agreements"[79] and urged DIAND to accept a mandate to inform and educate other departments of government about the IFA.

Canada sought judicial review of the panel's decisions and as a result we have three further decisions of the Federal Court of Appeal. In the first decision, the Appeal Court confirmed that it did indeed have original supervisory jurisdiction and that this had not been accorded to the Trial Division.[80] In the second and third decisions, the Court, in two very short judgments, simply ruled that the panel had not made any reviewable error.[81] The Inuvialuit were entitled to notice of the RFP, although to the Court it was immaterial whether this obligation arose under the public tender or non-public tender provision of the IFA. Finally, the Court ruled that the panel had full and unfettered discretion in the matter of costs

under s.18.30 of the IFA and could, "on the peculiar facts" of the present case, determine that special circumstances existed that justified awarding
costs on a solicitor and client basis.

The panel's decision was rendered in English using plain, non-technical
terms. Despite being faced with complex questions such as the availability
and appropriateness of specific relief and the interpretation of various
terms of the agreement, the panel's decision makes no reference to legal
texts and refers to only two judicial decisions, *Nowegijick* and *Horseman*.[82]
For each specific issue the panel seems to have taken a purposive approach
to the interpretation of the agreement rather than a more literal approach.
One can see this most specifically in the panel's references to s.1 of the IFA,
which lays out the governing principles, but also in its treatment of the
bidding provisions,[83] the interpretation of "removal," and in its finding
that cleanup of the sites should be completed within a reasonable period.

We can also see that the panel was moderately proactive. This is most
obviously the case with its concluding comments addressed to the parties,
but especially to Canada, with a view to having Canada take some internal measures so as to avoid future disputes. However, one can also see such
an approach in the award of solicitor and client costs to the Inuvialuit. In
monetary terms, this was of course a far more significant award than the
nominal damages and declaratory relief awarded by the panel elsewhere
in its decision. It also shows that the panel was prepared to be creative
in crafting what it considered to be a just solution. Less creative was
the panel's willingness to dismiss the availability of specific relief on the
grounds that such an order would be too difficult to supervise – this notwithstanding the panel's explicit statement that it was retaining jurisdiction to deal with any issues that might arise out of its award. While this
may be persuasive in the case of the commitment to include one of the
areas within Ivvavik National Park, this is less persuasive in terms of the
supervision of the clean-up commitments, although part of the explanation here might simply be the uncertainty surrounding the jurisdiction of
the panel to order specific relief.[84]

Conclusion
What lessons can we learn from the above?

First, there is a dramatic difference between the dispute settlement
model offered by the Inuvialuit Agreement and that offered by the SA and
the NFA. In the case of the Inuvialuit Agreement, arbitration attains preeminent status as the means for resolving disputes between the parties.
While the IFA does not preclude the parties to the agreement from electing to go to court rather than to arbitration (except of course where the
same dispute has already been submitted to arbitration), it does allow either
party to send a dispute to arbitration without the consent of the other

party. This is not the case under the NFA and SA, where only a relatively narrow range of matters may be submitted to arbitration by the unilateral act of one party. It is perhaps not coincidental that the beneficiaries under both the SA and NFA have initiated important litigation in the courts concerning the interpretation of their agreement and have not undertaken arbitration, whereas the Inuvialuit have not resorted to the courts but have invoked the arbitration provisions of the IFA.[85] The IFA also stands out for the role it accords to industry with respect to certain categories of dispute and for the manner in which the agreement's arbitration panel is systematically accorded jurisdiction over particular categories of dispute rather than other bodies established by the agreement.

Second, it is clear that the parties have certainly not lavished on the subject of dispute settlement the sort of attention accorded to the subject by some more recent agreements, such as the Nisga'a Agreement.[86] That agreement establishes a three-stage sequential procedure for resolving disagreements: (1) collaborative negotiations, (2) facilitated procedures using a neutral, and (3) formal adjudication using arbitral or judicial proceedings. Similarly, none of the three agreements explicitly contemplates using dispute settlement models based upon traditional laws and practices. While a particular panel might adopt procedures that are sensitive to traditional practices and languages, none of the agreements offers any guidance as to the adoption of such practices. So, in large part, we shall have to wait and see. The single experience to date with the Inuvialuit Agreement suggests that we should be slow to conclude that the parties have adopted dispute resolution mechanisms that are more culturally sensitive than those available from the courts.

Third, the overall impression of the entire basket of dispute resolution proceedings under all three agreements, but especially under the SA and NFA, is one of complexity, especially if one considers not just the arbitration provisions but also the various quasi-judicial boards created by other provisions of the agreements. This complexity seems unnecessary and may itself thwart rather than facilitate the resolution of disputes. There may be lessons here for the design of dispute resolution provisions in future land claims agreements.

This chapter has served as a preliminary inquiry only into the dispute settlement provisions of northern claims agreements. Other questions need to be asked in order to determine more precisely the effectiveness of the dispute resolution procedures that have been adopted for each of these agreements. Relevant questions would include the extent to which there are differences between the parties to the agreements that remain unresolved and the reasons why parties select particular dispute resolution techniques. In addition, we would benefit from a clearer understanding of the role of the implementation committees established under post-IFA land claims agreements, as well as the functional relationship between these committees and arbitration procedures.

Acknowledgments
I would like to thank the following for taking the time to comment on my first draft: Cathy Bell, Geoff Lester, Dougald Brown, John Merritt, Dick Spaulding, Jonnette Watson Hamilton, and Laurie Pelly.

Notes
1 *The Western Arctic Claim: The Inuvialuit Final Agreement* (Ottawa: Indian and Northern Affairs Canada, 1984).
2 *Sahtu Dene and Metis Comprehensive Land Claim Agreement* (Ottawa: Indian and Northern Affairs Canada, 1993). Note as well that the *Sahtu Agreement* generally follows the text of the *Gwich'in Comprehensive Land Claim Agreement* (Ottawa: Indian and Northern Affairs Canada, 1992) and that the terms of the dispute settlement articles are, to all intents and purposes, identical.
3 *Agreement Between the Inuit of the Nunavut Settlement Area and Her Majesty the Queen in Right of Canada* (Ottawa: Under the joint authority of the Tungavik Federation of Nunavut and the Honourable Tom Siddon, Minister of Indian Affairs and Northern Development, 1993).
4 Being schedule B to the Canada Act, 1982 (U.K.), 1982, c.11; as to the degree of protection afforded and for the possibility of justifiable infringements see *Campbell* v. *British Columbia (A.G.)*, [2000] 4 C.N.L.R. 1 (B.C.S.C.), per Williamson J., esp. at paras. 126-28 and 181.
5 *Cree Regional Authority* v. *Canada* (1991), 81 D.L.R. (4th) 659 (F.C.A.) and *Eastmain Band* v. *James Bay and Northern Quebec Agreement (Administrator)* (1992), 99 D.L.R. (4th), esp. 26-27.
6 For a discussion of this point, see *Carcross/Tagish First Nation* v. *Canada*, (2000), 184 FTR 184 (T.D.); the trial judge held that the terms of s.4 of the Yukon First Nations Land Claims Settlement Act, S.C. 1994, c.34, caused a loss of s.87 Indian Act tax exemption for all Yukon First Nation Citizens, not just those party to a Final Agreement. The Court of Appeal reversed [2001] FCA 231 on the grounds that: (1) the courts should not readily interpret Parliament as having repealed a "cherished tax exemption" especially where such was alleged to have occurred as here through a "double incorporation" (i.e., incorporation of the clause of the Umbrella Final Agreement [UFA] into the individual First Nation Final Agreements and thence into the federal ratification legislation), and (2) in any event the federal ratification legislation gave legal effect to the Final Agreements and not to the UFA which was not intended to "have a life of its own."
7 The language of the provisions does vary. The Nunavut Land Claims Agreement Act, S.C. 1993, c.29, s.4(1), states that "the Agreement is hereby ratified, given effect and declared valid." This is followed by two "for greater certainty" provisions which indicate that "the Agreement is binding on all persons and bodies that are not parties to the Agreement" and that "any person or body on which the Agreement confers a right, privilege, benefit or power or imposes a duty or liability may exercise the right, privilege, benefit or power, shall perform the duty or is subject to the liability, to the extent provided for by the Agreement." The Western Arctic (Inuvialuit) Claims Settlement Act, S.C. 1984, c.24, s.3, states more straightforwardly that "the Agreement is hereby approved, given effect and declared valid" but goes on to state that "on the extinguishment of the native claims ... the beneficiaries under the Agreement shall have the rights, privileges and benefits set out in the Agreement." The Inuvialuit Final Agreement statute does not explicitly deal with the effect of the agreement on third parties, as to which see, generally, Thompson, "Land Claim Settlements in Northern Canada: Third Party Rights and Obligations" (1991) 55 Saskatchewan Law Review 127. Finally, the Sahtu Dene and Metis Land Claim Settlement Act, S.C. 1994, c.27, s.4, provides that "the Agreement is hereby approved, given effect

and declared valid" followed by a "for greater certainty" provision modelled on the Nunavut Land Claims Agreement s.4(3) and one designed to ensure vesting of title in designated Sahtu organizations as provided for in the agreement.

8   On the jurisdiction of the superior courts to deal with the constitutional issues that may underpin land claims agreement litigation see *Hydro-Quebec* v. *Canada (A.G.) and Coon Come*, [1991] 3 C.N.L.R. 40 (Que. C.A.).

9   Federal Court Act, R.S.C. 1985, c.F-7. See *Cree Regional Authority* v. *Canada*, note 6.

10 Presumably the Federal Court Trial Division, even though s.5.3.1 of the Nunavut Final Agreement explicitly mentions the grounds referred to in s.28 of the Federal Court Act. *Canada (Attorney General)* v. *Inuvialuit Regional Corp.*, [1994] F.C.J. 1615 (F.C.A.) is distinguishable on this point, see discussion *infra*, note 75. See also Nunavut Final Agreement, s.6.6.1 jurisdiction to review decisions of Surface Rights Tribunal in relation to wildlife compensation matters explicitly accorded to Federal Court of Appeal.

11 Sahtu Agreement s.6.1.2 (and see also Sahtu Agreement s.4.5.1 providing for an appeal as of right from a decision of the Enrolment Board to the NWT Supreme Court) and see *First Nation of Nacho Nyak Dun* v. *Furniss* (1997), 10 C.P.C. (4th) 45 (Y.T.S.C.) interpreting a similar provision in the Nacho Nyak Dun Final Agreement (one of the Yukon Final Agreements) and concluding that the territorial superior court had concurrent jurisdiction under this provision to rule on the validity of a federal Crown lease even though ordinarily this was a matter that would have fallen within the exclusive jurisdiction of the Federal Court. Justice Vickers observed that:

> I conclude it was the intention of the parties to the Final Agreement that the construction and interpretation of the document be fair, large and liberal. The parties designed the document intending that all future disputes be resolved by this court because of the presence of the Court throughout the Territory and for the purposes of continuity.
>
> Article 2.11.9 refers to any action or proceeding arising out of the Final Agreement. The interpretation of these words must be remedial as best ensures that the intention of the parties is fulfilled. The words "arising out of" are not restricted to the narrow meaning "arising under." In addition, they mean "connected with" or "related to." The validity of the lease is a matter directly connected with or related to the Final Agreement and accordingly, a matter within the jurisdiction of this court.

See also *Tr'ondek Hwechin* v. *Canada*, [2002] YJ 75. This case involved an attempt by a Yukon First Nation to obtain declaratory relief from the Yukon Supreme Court in relation to the management of certain mining claims. It is apparent from the decision that the petitioners had first proceeded in the Federal Court trial division seeking to question a decision that had been made by the Chief of Mining, Land Use and Reclamation under the terms of the Yukon Quartz Mining Act, RSC 1985, c. Y-4. The petitioners had elected to discontinue that action for undisclosed reasons.

12 And see the discussion of *Inuvialuit Regional Corp.* in the text to *infra*, note 75.

13 *Accord*, Justice Vickers in *Furniss*, esp. at para. 29.

14 Thus, s.38.3.17 of the Nunavut Final Agreement provides that: "Except in respect of disputes arbitrated under these provisions, nothing in these provisions affects the jurisdiction of any court." See also s.18.1.7 of the Sahtu Agreement dealing with wildlife compensation. On the availability of a stay see s.10 of the Arbitration Act, R.S.N.W.T. 1988, c.A-5.

15 While both parties have continuing obligations under the agreements, the Crown bears the brunt of these obligations. While the parties may make some effort to stipulate what happens in the event of non-performance (see, for example, part 10.10 of the Nunavut Final Agreement indicating what happens in the event that government fails to pass implementation legislation), in general, the parties have left these questions to be resolved in accordance with generally applicable laws including the law of remedies.

16 The list is not as extensive because the arbitration panel is accorded a broader jurisdiction under the Sahtu Agreement. For example, wildlife compensation disputes under the Sahtu Agreement may be referred to arbitration, s.18.1.4.

17 Nunavut Final Agreement, ss.40.4.10 and 40.5.9.

18 *Ibid.*, s.26.6. In the case of the Inuvialuit Final Agreement, a dispute of this character would simply be referred to the standing panel, Inuvialuit Final Agreement s.18.8.

19 Sahtu Agreement s.16.2.3 referring to each party submitting "its own plan" and the minister making a decision with written reasons. *Quaere* whether the minister is confined to choosing as between the two plans? The Nunavut Final Agreement s.8.4.5 is a little more nuanced and refers to the appointment of a conciliator who submits a report to the minister for consideration and decision.

20 See Nunavut Final Agreement ss.5.3.16-5.3.23; and Sahtu Agreement ss.13.8.24-13.8.30.

21 *Guidelines: Comprehensive Land Claims Implementation Plans* (Ottawa: Department of Indian and Northern Affairs, 1989); see esp. at 1, noting that Canada had been criticized by both the Auditor General and others for its failure to properly carry out and implement the James Bay and Northern Quebec Agreement and the Inuvialuit Final Agreement.

22 See, for example, *A Contract Relating to the Implementation of the Nunavut Final Agreement* (Ottawa: Minister of Supply and Services Canada, 1993).

23 See Nunavut Final Agreement s.37.2.5; and Sahtu Agreement s.29.1.1.

24 In the Nunavut Final Agreement (s.37.3.3(e)), this is expressed to be without prejudice to article 38 arbitration or any other legal remedies that might be available. The Sahtu Agreement is more prescriptive and states (s.29.2.3(d)) that "unresolved implementation disputes shall be resolved pursuant to arbitration under chapter 6." *Quaere* whether this latter provision expands the scope of the compulsory jurisdiction provisions of article 6 (see *infra,* text to notes 43 *et seq.*)? This seems to be a far-fetched interpretation, given the care with which the parties circumscribed the jurisdiction of the panel.

25 The parties selected Brian Crane, Q.C. Crane is a senior partner in the law firm Gowlings. He was principal legal advisor to the Gwich'in throughout the negotiation of their land claims agreement (Gwich'in Agreement). Crane's report was delivered to the parties 19 October 2000: "Nunavut Waters and Nunavut Surface Rights Tribunal Bill, Report on Outstanding Issues," submitted to Nunavut Tunngavik Inc., Department of Indian Affairs and Northern Development and Government of Nunavut, 19 October 2000, mimeo, n.p. Crane's experience would include direct involvement in a similar exercise for the Gwich'in (*viz* the negotiation of the text of the Mackenzie Valley Resource Management Act, SC 1998, c.25, which, *inter alia*, gives effect to provisions of the Sahtu and Gwich'in claims).

26 The issues included: (1) the use of a non-derogation clause, (2) the inclusion of a description of Inuit rights in the Bill, (3) water licence applications that do not conform with plans, (4) payment of user fees, and (5) difficulties with the French text of the bill, *ibid.*

27 The terms of reference for the exercise identified three objectives: (1) to clear up any misunderstandings as to the basis and substance of the parties' positions to date, (2) to facilitate representatives of the parties in finding acceptable outcomes, and (3) where acceptable outcomes were not apparent, to express his or her recommendations as to the best way to resolve any remaining differences. Any recommendations were to be non-binding and expressly stated not to constitute a formal legal opinion. The procedure contemplated: (1) review of reference materials and the written positions of the parties, (2) review of written refutations to written positions, (3) convening of a workshop, and (4) submission of a report describing the work and any outcomes and recommendations. The cost of the exercise was borne by DIAND, *ibid.*

28 Crane commented adversely on this in his report, *ibid.*, and, given the "legal" nature of many of the issues under consideration, his comments are well taken. Surely it is essential in any non-binding ADR procedure such as this that government takes steps to ensure the representation and participation of all government interests that might be affected.

29 Meetings are typically attended by the deputy minister for DIAND, the secretary to Cabinet of the Nunavut government, and the executive director of Nunavut Tunngavik Inc. Other officials may also attend.

30 Initially, therefore, the meetings were also attended by the Nunavut Implementation Commission, the statutory body responsible under the Nunavut Act, S.C. 1993, c.28, for overseeing the transition to the new territory.

31 For example, negotiations on the Nunavut Final Agreement ran from 1980-93 and might be said to have commenced even earlier. I have compared article 38 of the Nunavut Final

Agreement with article 41 of the Nunavut Settlement Area, Agreement in Principle (1990). While some changes were made to the arbitration article, there was no reallocation of responsibilities as between, for example, the surface rights tribunal and the arbitration panel.

32 N. Louise Vertes, et al., "Five Year Review 1993-1998, Implementation of the Nunavut Land Claims Agreement" (not published but available at <http://www.ainc-inac.gc.ca/nu/nunavut/imp/5yrnun_e.pdf>), October 1999, 2-118. The five-year review was called for by s.37.3.3(b) and s.23.7.1 (specific to the Inuit employment plans of the agreement) of the Nunavut Final Agreement.

33 Nunavut Tunngavik Inc. is the main Inuit organization responsible for the administration of the claim and the guardian of Inuit rights and benefits under the claim. Nunavut Tunngavik Inc. is the Inuit organization responsible for signifying Inuit approval to any nominations to the arbitration panel.

34 Vertes, "Five Year Review," 5-32.

35 The rules on bias for tripartite panels in commercial arbitrations stipulate that even though each party has the opportunity to appoint a member to the panel, there is the same expectation of impartiality as there is of a sole arbitrator. "The nominees are not to adjudicate as representatives of the parties who nominated them notwithstanding the fact that there may be a professional ongoing relationship between the nominators and the nominees": *Revenue Properties Co.* v. *Victoria University* (1993), 62 O.A.C. 35 esp. at 40-41. See also *Szilard* v. *Szasz*, [1955] S.C.R. 3. Even in the case of a tripartite "rights" arbitration in the labour field, the prevailing view is that while one may expect an appointed member to be partial, the parties "are entitled to independence of mind" and "the appearance of independence of mind" and hence the courts have ruled, *inter alia,* that an employee of one of the parties cannot sit as a nominated arbitrator: *Re Bethany Care Centre and United Nurses of Alberta, Local No. 91 et al.* (1983), 5 D.L.R. (4th) 54 (Alta. C.A.), leave to appeal to S.C.C. refused 2 February 1984. I am not as familiar with the membership of the Inuvialuit panel in this context but note that one of the Inuvialuit appointees to the panel hearing the DEW Line Site arbitration *infra,* note 42, was Peter Cumming, now a justice of the Ontario High Court. Before the arbitration, Cumming had considerable prior involvement as a legal advisor to the Inuvialuit during the negotiation of the Inuvialuit Final Agreement. I am not fully aware of what his continuing involvement might have been after the claim was finalized.

36 The Sahtu Agreement also contains a clause (s.6.1.7) specifically reserving the right of the parties to refer a dispute to other ADR mechanisms including mediation or arbitration pursuant to the Arbitration Act, R.S.N.W.T. 1988, c.A-5.

37 *Ibid.*

38 The Nunavut Final Agreement has some special provisions declaring that, in some circumstances, the Designated Inuit Organization shall not be liable.

39 The federal appointments shall include the chair and vice-chair with the caveat that these appointments shall "be acceptable" (Inuvialuit Final Agreement s.18(4)) to both the Inuvialuit and industry and, failing that, the chief justice of either territory may make the appointment.

40 While this model may work for arbitrations commenced under Inuvialuit Final Agreement s.18.32 (see below), it may be harder to box all arbitrations under s.18.35 into either a s.18.12 arbitration or a s.18.13 arbitration.

41 *Inuvialuit Regional Corporation and Inuvialuit Land Corporation* v. *R in Right of Canada as represented by the Minister of National Defence and the Minister of Indian Affairs and Northern Development,* Award No. 1 and 2, both dated 17 February 1994, hereafter *IRC 001-94* and *IRC 002-94,* at 4-5. It is fairly easy to think of situations where the jurisdictional problems would be harder to resolve, such as where an environmental concern in Yukon Territory had effects in both the Northwest Territories and Yukon Territory. How should the panel be struck in such a case?

42 The clauses use slightly different formulations. Section 38.2.1(a) of the Nunavut Final Agreement provides that the board's optional jurisdiction shall comprise "any matter concerning the interpretation, application or implementation of the Agreement *where the DIO and Government* agree to be bound by the decision." "DIO" (Designated Inuit

Organization) and "Government" are both defined terms. The Sahtu Agreement (s.6. 1.5(b)) does not include the phrase "implementation" and uses the lowercase term "*party*." This latter is not a defined term. The parties to the agreement are the Crown in right of Canada and certain named Dene and Metis communities "as represented by the Sahtu Tribal Council" (see the title page of the Sahtu Agreement). It is not completely clear that the term "party" as used in paragraph (b) should have this confined usage, since we know that compulsory arbitration may, under certain circumstances, be triggered by another person (see s.6.3.2 and the discussion under "Arbitration under the Inuvialuit Agreement," this chapter, p. 315-19).

43   While this is the broadest of the three, it is still narrower than the language typically used in commercial agreements which would generally confer jurisdiction as to "all matters in difference between the parties," Anthony Walton, *Russell on Arbitration*, 18th ed. (London: Stevens and Sons, 1970), 68. The main point here is that anything short of a very general conferral of jurisdiction will invite disputes as to whether a particular submission falls within the scope of the compulsory arbitration provisions.

44   "Industry" is defined twice in this section of the Inuvialuit Final Agreement, once for the purposes of ss.18.4 and 18.5 and once for the purposes of ss.18.12-18.15. It is not expressly defined for the purposes of s.18.32.

45   Section 18.35 of the Inuvialuit Final Agreement creates a list but it is in effect a summary of other provisions in the Inuvialuit Final Agreement which themselves confer jurisdiction on the board. While there is nothing inherently objectionable about such a repetition (and in fact it is much more useful to the reader than the more cryptic references in the Sahtu Agreement and Nunavut Final Agreement), it does raise the problem of what happens when the language of the list in s.18.35 does not quite track the more substantive provision in the body of the balance of the Inuvialuit Final Agreement. For examples see, in particular, paragraphs (c) and (f) of s.18.35 and the corresponding cross-referenced provisions.

46   *Quaere* how a panel should be structured for such a case since it does not obviously fall within either of the categories stipulated by ss.18.12 or 18.13 of the Inuvialuit Final Agreement. This is an unusual provision. The general rule is that the northern land claim agreements do not afford beneficiaries or potential beneficiaries any access to the dispute settlement provisions of the agreements. The premise is that such persons must commence an action in whichever court they believe may have jurisdiction: see *Charlie* v. *Vuntut Gwichin Development Corporation, Her Majesty the Queen and Vuntut Gwichin First Nation*, [2002] FCT 344; and see also *Scheffen* v. *Barber*, [2002] YJ 10, esp. at para. 19 dealing with the interpretation of Tr'ondek Hwechin Self-Government Agreement (SGA) and Justice Veale noting that the Tr'ondek constitution did not provide a mechanism for enforcing decisions of the General Assembly "except by way of court applications."

47   The point is not completely clear, for how is last offer arbitration under s.7.63 of the Inuvialuit Final Agreement relevant to need and to alternative sources of land, and why are issues other than compensation referred to in paragraph (f) of s.18.35 and not paragraph (b)?

48   This is a remarkably broad provision. There is perhaps an analogy here to compulsory unitization provisions of modern oil and gas legislation (see, for example, Canada Oil and Gas Operations Act, R.S.C. 1985, c.O-7, ss.37 *et seq.*, but *quaere* whether there is sufficient guidance offered to the arbitrators to make it workable).

49   *IRC 002-94*.

50   In fact it seems preferable to conceptualize s.18.35 of the Inuvialuit Final Agreement as a "for greater certainty" provision. However, this approach seems implicitly to have been rejected by the panel because it is inconsistent with the idea seemingly accepted by the panel when it held that s.18.35 confers an *additional* source of jurisdiction.

51   *IRC 001-94, 9*.

52   The distinction here seems to be that the more subjective and perhaps political issues are to be sent to arbitration, whereas the more technical issues go the surface rights board.

53   A defined term in the agreement; the term extends to a variety of agencies and successors including the Canadian Museum of Civilization and the Canadian Parks Service.

54   The context suggests that this is limited to the situations in which use and occupation is

required to deliver and manage government programs and services, to carry out inspections pursuant to law, and to enforce law (see s.21.3.1 of the Sahtu Agreement), but the point is not completely clear.

55 There is also a reference to the interim jurisdiction of the arbitration panel in s.25.5.2 of the Sahtu Agreement pending establishment of the Land and Water Board. Given that this jurisdiction is related to "rights of access," it is not clear whether this is a jurisdiction that is subject to a double contingency, i.e., no SRT and no LWB.

56 The U.K. Act is reproduced in Walton, *Russell on Arbitration,* 427. The new U.K. Act (Arbitration Act, 1996 (1996, c.23, s.48) is even more explicit as to the availability of a full range of remedies in the absence of agreement between the parties.

57 See Walton, *Russell on Arbitration,* 186 (according to law); 72 (example of a arbitrator being confined to interpreting the agreement with no jurisdiction to award damages); and 288 (further noting that the jurisdiction to award specific performance is implied by virtue of s.15 of the U.K. Act).

58 Sahtu Agreement s.6.3.9, and Nunavut Final Agreement s.38.3.13, and Arbitration Act, R.S.N.W.T. 1988, c.11, s.25.

59 This is not the place to detail all those rules. Suffice it for present purposes to mention a few examples. Section 7.60 of the Inuvialuit Final Agreement provides that in valuing land the board shall bear in mind the intrinsic value of land for wildlife, while the Sahtu Agreement and Nunavut Final Agreement (s.21.9.9) both contemplate that the panels should have regard to the cultural attachment of the beneficiaries to land and the special and peculiar value of land to the beneficiaries. The only references to traditional laws and customs in dispute settlement provisions of the agreement are found in the enrolment provisions of the respective agreements (see Nunavut Final Agreement s.25.3.1 and Inuvialuit Final Agreement s.5.2(b)).

60 Arbitration Act; the procedure contemplated is very formal and includes application of the Evidence Act, examination of witnesses under oath, and compellability of witnesses and documents, as well as provision relating to the taxation of costs.

61 On s.18 of the Inuvialuit Final Agreement as a complete code, see the discussion under "Arbitration under the Inuvialuit Agreement," this chapter, p. 315-19.

62 Inuvialuit Final Agreement s.13.20; compensation for interference with wildlife harvesting activities contemplates mediation (by mutual consent) between a beneficiary claimant and a developer before a dispute is referred to arbitration.

63 The Sahtu and Nunavut Panels have established rules for the commencement of an arbitration: Sahtu Dene and Metis Arbitration Panel, *Arbitration Rules,* adopted 1 August 1996; Nunavut Arbitration Board, *Rules,* n.d. The Sahtu Rules confine themselves to the bare essentials required to initiate an arbitration (i.e., contents of a submission to arbitration and reply and the responsibilities of the administrative secretary), leaving it to the particular panel to adopt further rules for a specific dispute. The Nunavut Rules are more broadly based and deal, for example, with choice of language (English, French, or Inuktitut, rule 2(3)), and evidence (providing, *inter alia,* that the panel "shall give due weight to Inuit knowledge and customs and social, economic and cultural factors of significance to Inuit, rule 11(1)).

64 There are no reported decisions (or decisions on the QL database) relating to the ILA other than the judicial review cases noted in this article (*infra,* notes 75 and 76), a case argued at the time the Gwich'in Agreement was to presented to parliament for ratification (*Inuvialuit Regional Corporation* v. *Canada* [1992], 53 F.T.R. 1 and one case in which the IRC is a defendant: *Inuvialuit [Regional Corporation]* v. *Canadian Reindeer [1978] Ltd.,* [1993] N.W.T.J. 45 [N.W.T.S.C.]); the plaintiff Inuvialuit corporation in that case alleged trespass against the defendant (a non-government party) for continuing to graze reindeer on lands now owned by the Inuvialuit. Clearly, this latter dispute did not fall within the scope of even the wide arbitration provisions included in the Inuvialuit Final Agreement. Obviously, there may be other cases that have been commenced but which were settled or withdrawn.

65 *Nunavut Tunngavik Inc.* v. *Canada (Minister of Fisheries and Oceans)* (1998), 162 D.L.R. (4th) 625 (F.C.A.); *Nunavut Tunngavik Inc.* v. *Canada (Minister of Fisheries and Oceans),* [2000] 3 CNLR 136 (FCTD), aff'd (2000), 262 NR 219, and leave to appeal to SCC refused [2000] SCCA

616; and *Kadlak v. Nunavut (Minister of Sustainable Development)*, [2001] Nu. J. 1. In addition
to these decided cases, Nunavut Tunngavik Inc. has also commenced a judicial review application in the territorial superior court contesting the validity of the new Firearms Act on
the grounds that it is inconsistent with the wildlife provisions of the Nunavut Final Agreement. I have reviewed the Turbot cases more extensively in "Implementing the Fisheries
Provisions of the Nunavut Claim: Re-Capturing the Resource?" (2003), 12 JELP 141-204.

66 See also *Qikiqtani Inuit Association* v. *AG Canada as representative of The Minister of Indian
Affairs and Northern Development and Nanisvik Mines Ltd.*, [1999] 3 C.N.L.R. 213 (F.C.T.D.);
judicial review application of the first licensing decision of the Nunavut Water Board.
Although the applicant adduced standard judicial review grounds for their application,
they also alleged breach of the terms of s.13 of the Nunavut Final Agreement. As such, the
dispute might have been amenable to voluntary arbitration although clearly not compulsory arbitration. For litigation on overlap claims commenced by First Nations in
Saskatchewan which equally could not be the subject of arbitration see *Fond du Lac Band*
v. *Canada (Minister of Indian and Northern Affairs)*, [1993] 1 F.C. 195, and Manitoba, *North-
land Band of Indians* v. *Canada (Minister of IAND)* (1996), 5 C.P.C. (4th) 1 (F.C.T.D.); examination of witness on discovery.

67 *Sahtu Secretariat Inc.* v. *Canada*, [1999] F.C.J. 121 (T.D.) rev'd, on consent, following a settlement between the parties [2002] FCA 315. I commented on the trial decision at some
length in Bankes and Quesnel, "Recent Judicial Developments of Interest to Oil and Gas
Lawyers" (2000) 38 Alberta Law Review 294 at 361-63.

68 One of the interesting features of this case was the plaintiff's successful application under
rule 475 for a determination that the term "royalty" as used in the Sahtu Agreement was
not ambiguous: *Sahtu Secretariat Inc.* v. *Canada*, [1997] F.C.J. 897 (T.D.).

69 *Ibid.* One of the reviewers of my first draft asked whether part of the problem was a lack
of understanding as to the arbitration procedures and raised the question of whether the
respective panels had a duty to educate the parties. My answer in both cases is no. As
to the first, where there is a dispute that is close to submission to the courts, lawyers will
be involved and can be taken to be weighing all the dispute resolution options available.
This really answers the second question as well. However, the one panel whose practice
I am familiar with (the Sahtu Panel) has prepared a brochure precisely for this purpose.
The brochure describes the panel's jurisdiction and panel members. The panel has also
prepared a translation of its rules, *Arbitration Rules*, into North Slavey (both a written form
and an oral transcript are available).

70 The Inuvialuit Settlement Region refers to the entire area of traditional use and occu-
pancy; it is not confined to Inuvialuit title lands.

71 R.S.C. 1985, c.C-34.6. *Quaere* whether the territorial Arbitration Act applies (and note
that, given the geography, it may be that of Yukon or the Northwest Territories) or
whether it is implicitly excluded?

72 *IRC 001-94* and *IRC 002-94*, 6.

73 IFA, *supra*, note 1, s.1(b).

74 *IRC 001-94*, 26.

75 *IRC 001-94*, 31 and 42; *IRC 002-94*, 32 and 41.

76 It may also have been the case (see discussion *supra* in the text to notes 56 and 57) that
the panel had doubts as to its jurisdiction to award specific relief, but the only doubt that
the panel expressed was the more general doubt as to the availability of specific performance against the Crown, *ibid.*, *IRC 001-94*, 36.

77 *IRC 002-94*, 28.

78 *IRC 001-94*, 39; *IRC 002-94*, 38.

79 *IRC 001-94*, 40; *IRC 002-94*, 39.

80 *Canada (Attorney General)* v. *Inuvialuit Regional Corp.*, [1994] F.C.J. 1615 (F.C.A.). The court
applied a purposive interpretation of the agreement (see esp. para. 10) and confirmed that
the statutory approval of the Inuvialuit Final Agreement was sufficient to act as a source
of jurisdiction for the Federal Court of Appeal notwithstanding the failure to include the
Arbitration Board in the list in s.28(1) of the Federal Court Act of those federal boards,
commissions, and other tribunals the jurisdiction over which was statutorily conferred
on the Federal Court of Appeal by that act.

81 *Canada (Attorney General)* v. *Inuvialuit Regional Corp.*, [1995] F.C.J. 958 and 960 (F.C.A.).

82 *Nowegijick* v. *R.*, [1983] 1 S.C.R. 29, and *R.* v. *Horseman*, [1990] 1 S.C.R. 901; both decisions are cited as authority for the proposition that treaties and statutes relating to Aboriginal peoples must be liberally and generously construed. Note that both the Nunavut Final Agreement and Sahtu Agreement contain provisions to the effect that there shall be no presumption that doubtful expressions in the agreement be resolved in favour of either party (Nunavut Final Agreement, s.2.9.3, Sahtu Agreement, s.3.1.20).

83 See at 23 of *IRC 001-94*, "The Arbitration Panel is of the view that the purpose and intent of sub-section 16(8) is to provide a fair and reasonable opportunity to the Inuvialuit to benefit from the economic activity being undertaken by Canada in the ISR and the Western Arctic."

84 See further the comment above in note 73 perhaps explaining the reticence of the panel on this point.

85 To the same effect see Vertes, "Five Year Review," 2-119, making the following observations as to the reasons for no referral to arbitration under the Nunavut Final Agreement: "The Parties to the NLCA and the Implementation Committee cannot say why, but have offered the following observations: Referral to the Arbitration Board requires the agreement of the involved Parties; and decisions by the Arbitration Board are binding." Later in the report the panel itself made further comments, 5-33.

86 Contrast c.19 of the Nisga'a Final Agreement, Canada, British Columbia, and the Nisga'a Nation (4 August 1998, reprinted December 1998) and its accompanying Appendices M-1 to M-6. The appendix contemplates: (1) collaborative negotiations, (2) mediation, (3) use of a technical advisory panel, (4) neutral evaluation, (5) Elders Advisory Council, and (6) arbitration. The provisions are far too long and complex (covering over thirty pages of text) to analyze in detail here.

18
Commentary: Intercultural Dispute Resolution Initiatives across Canada
Andrew Pirie

> The exchange of treaty offers on December 11, 2000 between
> the Nuu-chah-nulth Tribal Council (NTC) and the Governments
> of Canada and British Columbia moved the parties closer to
> finalizing an agreement-in-principle. The key elements of the
> governments' offer to the NTC include a land base of 339.8
> square kilometres, a cash component of $203.8 million ... The
> key elements of the NTC offer to Canada and B.C. were a
> land base of 3,336 square kilometres, a cash component of
> $950,000,000.
>
> – Federal Treaty Negotiation Office, *Treaty News,* 2001

In Canadian society, it is difficult to imagine disputes that are simultaneously more complex, pressing, profound, and troublesome than the disputes
presently existing between Aboriginal and non-Aboriginal governments.
The enormous chasm between the above treaty offers echoes these concerns. This is not to say that controversies over matters such as free trade,
the environment, Charter rights, racism, and the like are not important
and challenging. Even neighbour disputes can reach tragic proportions.
But none of these disputes fully compares to the problems of a country
attempting to come to grips with hundreds of years of colonial history and
reconciling itself with the First Nations who suffered, and continue to suffer, enormous injustices. The ways in which these long-standing disputes
are resolved are sure not only to shape the course of many people's lives
but also to define the future identity of a nation and its citizens. Accordingly, the examinations by Bell, Lowe and Davidson, and Bankes in the
preceding three chapters of various initiatives in Canada that address
these significant disputes merit close attention.

In this brief commentary, I would first like to review Bell, Lowe and
Davidson, and Bankes's work on intercultural dispute resolution initiatives across Canada to determine if any common threads bind their
thoughts together. I would then like to offer some of my own observations
on their work that might assist our collective understanding of how best
to proceed.

Intercultural Dispute Resolution Initiatives across Canada

In her chapter "Indigenous Dispute Resolution Systems within Non-Indigenous Frameworks," Catherine Bell seeks "to review indigenous community-based dispute resolution processes negotiated within the broad parameters of the ADR movement."[1] She begins this review by considering the challenges involved in incorporating traditional values or indigenous traditions into contemporary systems of justice because "identifying core community values and strengthening community traditions are essential for the success of indigenous justice initiatives."[2] Bell notes some successes – the respect for community consultations and consensus that preceded the signing of the Alberta Metis Settlements Accord; the specific roles of elders in the work of the Metis Settlements Appeal Tribunal; the consensus-based approach of the Elders Advisory Council under the Nisga'a Treaty; the embedding of Inuit values in the decision-making processes and structure of the Nunavut government; and the tribunals established under land claims agreements (such as those created under the Yukon Umbrella Land Claim Agreement) that incorporate indigenous values and processes.

Bell recognizes the influence alternative dispute resolution, or ADR,[3] has had on these developments because, as she states, the goals of ADR "to create a process that is meaningful to the parties and improves relationship, participation, responsibility, and satisfaction" are also goals shared "by many traditional and contemporary indigenous dispute resolution mechanisms."[4] A clear example is the Nisga'a Treaty. The rationales for resolving disputes among Nisga'a, provincial, and federal governments are articulated in the treaty as a common desire:

1   to cooperate with each other to develop harmonious working relationships
2   to prevent, or, alternatively minimize disagreements
3   to identify disagreements quickly and resolve them in the most expeditious and cost-effective manner possible, and
4   to resolve disagreement in a non-adversarial, collaborative, and informal atmosphere.

The treaty goes on to establish a three-phase process (collaborative negotiations, facilitated processes, and adjudication) to be followed if disputes over treaty terms cannot be resolved through informal discussions. Indeed, the details in the treaty of how the collaborative negotiations are to take place read like a page out of *Getting to Yes,* Roger Fisher and William Ury's well-travelled primer for ADR enthusiasts on principled or interest-based negotiation.[5]

The mission statement of the Metis Settlements Appeal Tribunal also combines traditional Metis dispute resolution values and ADR rationales in stating that "alternative dispute resolution (ADR) mechanisms are incorporated into tribunal processes so that disputes are settled in an effective and timely way, with the least possible disruption to Metis life and relationships."[6]

Despite these positive messages, Bell is clear to make the point that problems exist. She mentions the process of indigenization (incremental modifications to conventional processes before Canadian courts and administrative tribunals) as potentially a Band-Aid solution that does not address the root causes of conflict in Aboriginal communities. The dispute resolution reforms simply fail to address the impact of colonization. In addition, Bell notes that if only those parts of indigenous knowledge, values, and processes that do not conflict with Western values and laws are adopted, the internalized oppression experienced by some Aboriginal peoples is reinforced and further cultural assimilation is promoted. Bell posits that "it is only when Aboriginal jurisdiction and dispute resolution systems are equal in authority and legitimacy to ... non-indigenous governments and processes that true Aboriginal justice can be obtained."[7]

Diane Lowe and Jonathan Davidson, in "What's Old Is New Again: Aboriginal Dispute Resolution and the Civil Justice System," examine the potential for incorporating Aboriginal dispute resolution into the civil justice system in Canada. Lowe and Davidson refuse the temptation to superficially equate acronyms, since they note that "the system of Aboriginal Dispute Resolution is fundamentally different from the system of Alternative Dispute Resolution."[8] Referring to the traditional custom of publicly acknowledging dispute resolution success at a potlatch or other ceremonial gathering, Lowe and Davidson state, "contemporary ADR has no equivalent to these processes."[9] Instead Lowe and Davidson acknowledge "the Aboriginal peoples of Canada employ a wide variety of traditional dispute resolution techniques" but "all ... share a basic emphasis and reliance on kinship and community and the desire to maintain (or restore) harmony in the community."[10]

Lowe and Davidson then consider some examples of traditional Aboriginal dispute resolution techniques being fused with the contemporary justice system. They reference sentencing circles for Native offenders, the operation of consensus building in the Metis Settlements Appeal Tribunal, and the successful mediation of a custody dispute before the courts by a council of elders. Lowe and Davidson also mention the recommendation from the Canadian Bar Association Task Force on Systems of Civil Justice[11] for a multi-option dispute resolution system that would enable the contemporary legal system to recognize, incorporate, and defer to culturally appropriate dispute resolution. As examples, Lowe and Davidson note the mandatory and court-annexed mediation projects in Alberta, British Columbia, Ontario, and Saskatchewan and conclude that it is certainly possible for mediations to be conducted in ways that are "more relevant, valuable, and effective to Aboriginal parties."[12]

In "The Dispute Resolution Provisions of Three Northern Land Claims Agreements," Nigel Bankes surveys the dispute settlement provisions of the Inuvialuit Final Agreement, 1984; the Sahtu Dene and Metis Comprehensive Land Claim Agreement, 1993; and the Agreement Between the Inuit of the Nunavut Settlement Area and Her Majesty the Queen in Right of Canada, 1993. Each of these agreements contains techniques adopted to deal with the settlement of future disputes. While lacking consistency across agreements, the techniques include resort to the courts when necessary, administrative tribunals with co-management and regulatory jurisdiction, arbitration boards, ministerial power to make the final decision in some cases, and implementation committees responsible for overseeing transitional matters and resolving disputes regarding implementation. Concluding there is "surprisingly little consistency" in this "bewildering potpourri of dispute settlement provisions,"[13] Bankes sees these dispute settlement provisions characterized by formality, use of quasi-judicial procedures (subpoena, cross-examination, binding decisions), and, ultimately, winners and losers. Absent from the agreements are regular references to mediation or a general requirement for collaborative negotiations.

Accordingly, Bankes analyzes the arbitration provisions of the three northern agreements, specifically the terms around the appointment of arbitrator panels, the jurisdictional complexity (the scope of the issues that may be referred to arbitration), the available remedies or types of awards that a panel may give (subject to judicial supervision on jurisdictional grounds), the parties, and special procedural rules. Bankes also considers the experience to date with the use of the courts and arbitration and discovers that "the parties have not made extensive use of the arbitration provisions."[14] In the limited experience to date with arbitration, Bankes chronicles some of the usual legal manoeuvring that can take place in these quasi-judicial hearings but does note the proactive nature of one panel in its efforts to provide guidance to the parties in order to "avoid arbitrations in the future."[15]

Bankes concludes with several insights on the design of these dispute resolution provisions. He finds the entire basket of dispute resolution procedures under all three agreements imbued with an unnecessary degree of complexity that may "thwart rather than facilitate the resolution of disputes."[16] He concludes that "the parties have certainly not lavished on the subject of dispute settlement the sort of attention accorded to the subject by some more recent agreements, such as the Nisga'a agreement."[17]

Common Threads

Bell, Lowe and Davidson, and Bankes's works convey many important and unique messages respecting intercultural dispute resolution. However, several common threads run through their work.

First, the clash of cultures that can occur in disputes between Aboriginal and non-Aboriginal parties is most evident. Whether the disputes involve land claims, criminal cases, civil claims, treaty terms, or myriad other matters, a cultural conflict appears almost always present. This raises imposing questions for an already challenging task: How can all these problems be resolved in satisfactory ways when such a gaping cultural divide separates the parties? How can the disputants heed the encouragement of the courts to resolve their differences by negotiation when indigenous and Eurocentric (or Western) perspectives on both the process and the problems make seeing eye-to-eye a complicated task?[18] How can justice be done when the there is no agreement on what justice means?

When addressing these cultural complexities, Bell, Lowe and Davidson, and Bankes focus mostly on process design, hoping that culturally responsive dispute resolution mechanisms will be able to cope best with the complex substantive issues. Indeed, the guarded optimism that emerges from their work seems predicated on the successful designs of dispute resolution systems that minimize or eliminate cultural incompatibilities by making these systems more sensitive to and reflective of Aboriginal values. The prescription seems to be to add more Aboriginal input, representation, traditions, and values with a corresponding reduction in the complexity, formality, and rigidity of existing justice systems.

A second common thread is the authors' analysis of ADR's contributions to successful intercultural dispute resolution. While the full history of alternative dispute resolution is dealt with elsewhere,[19] the ADR movement has had, and continues to have, an unquestioned influence on disputing developments around Aboriginal issues. Bell and Lowe and Davidson direct much of their attention to those parts of ADR that stress collaboration, community, and consensus as useful and guiding principles. Similarly, Bankes notices the absence of ADR features such as mediation, collaborative negotiations, and other consensual measures in the design of the initiatives he explores. This particular ADR focus is explained, although not without some trepidation, by reason of the apparent fit between these ADR characteristics and the traditional values and approaches taken by Aboriginal peoples to resolving conflict. As well as providing creativity in dispute systems design (DSD) for these complicated matters, this side of ADR also has obvious implications for the cultural challenges discussed above.[20]

A final thread is not nearly as visible but still imbues each of the authors' works. Although none of these authors uses the term extensively, power plays a leading role. For Bell, it is the worry that incremental change in reforming existing justice institutions may be confused with the "end goal" and that "even if existing reforms are sufficient to meet the concern of some First Nation communities, shifts in public opinion could have a significant impact on how discretion within the existing system is exercised at a future date."[21] Lowe and Davidson also address power. While acknowledging there are "opportunities ... to enable the incorporation of traditional Aboriginal dispute resolution into our civil justice systems,"[22] they point out that the Task Force on Systems of Civil Justice "did not specifically address concerns of Aboriginal persons."[23] Their description of sentencing circles as "the best-known adaptation of a traditional Aboriginal dispute resolution technique being used within the contemporary justice system"[24] needs to be understood in light of Chief Justice McEachern's remarks in *R.* v. *Johns* that "the public must also be made to understand that the court retains both authority and jurisdiction to impose whatever sentence the judge, rather than the circle, decides or recommends in any particular case ... the judge and the judge alone must decide what sentence should be imposed."[25] Bankes acknowledges "the inequality in bargaining power between the parties to the agreements."[26] He examines and hints at where the balance of power lies when complicated questions arise – in the federal and superior courts through their significant supervisory jurisdiction or, in some cases, in the government's right to make the final decision.

Reflections on the Common Threads
In considering the future evolution of intercultural dispute resolution in Aboriginal contexts in Canada, much can be gleaned from a full appreciation of the specific roles that culture, ADR, and power will have in that evolution. Unravelling these specific threads, seeing their interrelationships, and imagining new ways in which these strands can be integral parts of the whole fabric will be immensely important to the overall project. Bell, Lowe and Davidson, and Bankes's works contribute important information and analysis.

However, the works of Bell, Lowe and Davidson, and Bankes can prompt another perspective or two. One perspective is broad and theoretic. The other point of view is more close-up and personal. Taken together, both perspectives shed more light on the picture.

First, I have argued elsewhere that the ADR movement is, at its essential foundation, ideology.[27] In all ADR's modern popularity with its multidisciplinary trappings, diverse forms, and global appeal, alternative dispute resolution is really telling us what is natural, normal, and essential about disputing behaviours and institutions, about what is good in dispute resolution and what is not, about what is common sense, and about how the world is and how the world should be vis-à-vis disputes. While ADR emerged out of popular dissatisfaction with the formal administration of justice in the United States during the 1970s, the modern movement is no longer solely about being better than courts or confined to mediation activities. Many court-connected initiatives, such as the mandatory mediation programs referred to by Lowe and Davidson; private judging, such as the arbitration developments mentioned by Bankes; and administrative arrangements, such as the Metis Settlements Appeal Tribunal considered by Bell now fit comfortably under the ADR umbrella. ADR figures prominently in commercial affairs, public policy discords, disagreements on trade, and on and on. The scope of ADR has expanded far beyond its early attention to neighbourhood justice or families in crisis. As a field of study, what ADR now does is hold up the broadest ranges of disputing practices, behaviours, and institutions for critical scrutiny and then provides impetus for reforms in the ways in which we go about disputing.

However, just as we know there are differing ideologies or fundamental understandings of important subjects such as economics, politics, equality, the family, and the like, there also are, not surprisingly, different understandings of the ADR movement. On the one hand, ADR can provide alternative images of disputing that more accurately mirror people's diverse experiences, that overcome barriers to bringing disputes forward, that reduce dependence on professionals, that empower those who traditionally have been excluded from having their important struggles aired, and that take a more holistic view of the dispute. On the other hand, ADR may mirror much of what was there before, and, for example, obscure or hide ADR's quest for economic efficiencies, preservation of the status quo, tightening of social control, encouragement of a regressive reaction to legal rights, or continued oppression of the least powerful in society.[28] While there can be a sense that ADR primarily stands for empowerment, respect, collaboration, and consensus, there are clearly examples of disputing scenarios where some or all of these defining elements are neither present nor perhaps could they be. One can imagine the unscrupulous partner attempting to avoid responsibilities, the commercial enterprise interested only in the bottom line when it comes to the environment, or high-ranking officials evading war crimes tribunals. Empowerment, respect, collaboration, and consensus may be fine and dandy in one context but be completely inappropriate or unachievable in another. So ADR's ideological shape is still forming. The ideology of ADR depends on what is constructed as natural, normal, and essential in disputing and on who does this constructing.

Understanding ADR as developing ideology about the disputing world can open up further inquiry, particularly critical inquiry. Careful attention can be paid to the longer-term consequences of embracing a movement that promises so much hope but that may actually exacerbate existing inequalities either inadvertently or intentionally. Also, because of the indeterminate nature of most disputes, particularly disputes around Aboriginal issues, we know that process matters. The course a dispute takes and its eventual outcome will be greatly influenced by the disputing options employed. For example, the enormous energy and resources used to produce the Supreme Court of Canada's decision in *Delgamuukw* and other landmark court cases will result in much different futures than if this litigation had not occurred because ADR as ideology frowned on such confrontation.

Thinking of ADR as ideology also easily encourages us to question the assumptions we might make about approaches to intercultural dispute resolution in Aboriginal contexts. Is going to court to get pronouncements on legal rights which are sui generis counter-cultural or a wise strategy for peoples who experience serious and systemic economic, political, and social inequalities? Will concepts of consensus, collaboration, and cooperation as the required norm in dispute resolution really help when the ultimate solution seems to require such a fundamental redistribution of wealth? Do attempts to balance power by making systems sensitive actually play into the hands of the most powerful in society? When ADR is appreciated as an ideological construct, there are more opportunities to fully unravel its meaning, goals, consequences, and costs rather than mutely accepting its teachings as simply common sense.

From a second and closer perspective, alternative dispute resolution, whatever its ideology, has certainly raised awareness about disputing detail. We now more readily realize, among other things, that there are various conflict styles, boulwareism (take-it-or-leave-it) is a specific negotiating tactic, and reframing can help parties move away from entrenched positions. In intercultural dispute resolution, ADR has paid attention to fine behavioural differences between individualists and collectivists, from the disrespect crossed legs may show in a business negotiation in Thailand to the inferences drawn when no eye contact is made with the judge by an Aboriginal person.

However, one disputing detail has been particularly stressed. That detail is the distinction between integrative and distributive bargaining. Sometimes this distinction is characterized as the difference between win-win and win-lose strategies, interest-based bargaining versus positional bargaining, problem solving and adversarial tactics, or collaboration and competition. Riskin and Westbrook explain this distinction as follows:

> The adversarial orientation usually is grounded upon the assumption that there is a limited resource – such as money, golf balls, or lima beans – and the parties must decide whether and how to divide it. In such a situation,

the parties' interests conflict; what one gains, the other must lose. An adversarial orientation naturally fosters strategies designed to uncover as much as possible about the other side's situation and simultaneously mislead the other side as to your own situation. Until recently, the adversarial orientation has been the basis for most of the writing about negotiation by lawyers, as well as most of the popular writing about negotiation.

The problem-solving orientation is quite different. It seeks to meet the underlying needs of all parties to the dispute or transaction, and, accordingly, tends to produce strategies designed to promote the disclosure and relevance of these underlying needs. The recommended techniques include those intended to increase the number of issues for bargaining or to "expand the pie" before dividing it.[29]

ADR has, by and large and as a part of its dominant ideology, strongly favoured the integrative, interest-based, problem-solving collaborative, win-win approach. And why not? Who would argue against processes that encourage parties to work collaboratively together, to identify their underlying interests, and to develop creative win-win solutions? The alternative is often presented as a nasty, long, and costly fight that would only harm long-term relationships, result in winners and losers, and produce agreements or court judgments that would not be lasting.

There is no question that the ADR emphasis on this dichotomy has resulted in many positive changes as disputants, their lawyers, and others connected to disputing practices have learned about and consciously chosen to take an integrative approach to problems. Indeed, many of the specific successes that Bell, Lowe and Davidson, and Bankes describe are evidence of just such a choice.

The problem is not that disputes between Aboriginal and non-Aboriginal peoples will not benefit from "expanding the pie" and carefully considering how important interests can be accommodated. Indeed, in a recent thoughtful piece, Professor John Borrows locates the discourse on Aboriginal claims, particularly commentary from the Supreme Court of Canada, in citizenship theory.[30] If the problem is framed as "resolving the place of Aboriginal citizens in Canadian society" or "the resolution of those issues that tear at the heart of our common humanity,"[31] integrative bargaining can be seen as a powerful tool to enhance these citizenship relationships.

The problem is that justice between Aboriginal and non-Aboriginal governments will eventually require an enormous distribution of resources. The parties can collaborate, cooperate, and be creative, but, at the end of the day, land, money, and other tangible goods must change hands. Many, although not all, of the disputes are essentially distributive in nature. Positions have to be taken. The offer of 339.8 kilometres of land and $203.8

million is met with a counter-offer of 3,336 square kilometres and $950 million.[32] Bridging such a gap might be helped by reframing interests or paying attention to objective criteria, but not likely. The emphasis on integrative bargaining can take attention away from recognizing the enormity of the distributions that will be necessary to do justice. Getting to yes ideas may not work well in these types of cases.[33] Reaching just settlements, which are so structural in nature, seems more likely to depend on progressive political processes and action, coherent and courageous judicial involvement, and probably more respectful signals of our collective social responsibility than on negotiators finely trained in the art of principled negotiation.

Conclusion

The work of Bell, Lowe and Davidson, and Bankes makes important contributions to our understanding of how disputes between Aboriginal and non-Aboriginal peoples in Canada can be processed. Their spinnings on the common threads of culture, ADR, and power are certainly crucial. These threads can be essential parts of a rich and vibrant fabric that can be shown with pride. But there is a danger. When the parade finally passes, we may have simply witnessed the emperor's new clothes.

Notes

1 Catherine Bell, "Indigenous Dispute Resolution Systems within Non-Indigenous Frameworks: Intercultural Dispute Resolution Initiatives in Canada," Chapter 15, this volume, p. 244.
2 *Ibid.*, p. 253.
3 Bell suggests that it is no longer appropriate to use the term "alternative dispute resolution" because the expression suggests that these processes are peripheral and inferior to judicial processes when in fact they may be more "appropriate," and because "alternative" has become a misnomer as ADR has become more mainstream. I prefer the term ADR over BDR (better dispute resolution), IDR (innovative dispute resolution) and, for convenience, "appropriate dispute resolution," and explain my reasons in Andrew Pirie, *Alternative Dispute Resolution: Skills, Science and the Law* (Toronto: Irwin Law, 2000); <www.quicklaw.com>.
4 Bell, "Indigenous Dispute Resolution Systems," p. 257.
5 Roger Fisher and William Ury, *Getting to Yes: Negotiating Agreement without Giving In* (Boston: Houghton Mifflin, 1981).
6 Bell, "Indigenous Dispute Resolution Systems," p. 261.
7 *Ibid.*, p. 244.
8 Lowe and Davidson, "What's Old Is New Again: Aboriginal Dispute Resolution and the Civil Justice System," Chapter 16, this volume, p. 280, quoting Mark Dockstator.
9 *Ibid.*, p. 281.
10 *Ibid.*, p. 282.
11 Canadian Bar Association Task Force on Systems of Civil Justice, *Report of the Task Force on Systems of Civil Justice* (Ottawa: Canadian Bar Association, 1996).
12 Lowe and Davidson, "What's Old Is New Again," p. 292.
13 Bankes, "The Dispute Resolution Provisions of Three Northern Land Claims Agreements," Chapter 17, this volume, p. 303.
14 *Ibid.*, p. 314.

15 *Ibid.*, p. 318.
16 *Ibid.*, p. 320.
17 *Ibid.*, p. 320.
18 See, for example, *Delgamuukw* v. *British Columbia,* [1997] 3 S.C.R. 1010 at 1134, where the Court emphasized "that the best approach in these types of cases is a process of negotiation and reconciliation that properly considers the complex and competing interests at stake."
19 As a start, see Pirie, *Alternative Dispute Resolution,* 6-14.
20 For a window into dispute system design, see *ibid.,* 272-74.
21 Bell, "Indigenous Dispute Resolution Systems," p. 275.
22 Lowe and Davidson, "What's Old Is New Again," p. 280.
23 *Ibid.*, p. 288.
24 *Ibid.*, p. 283.
25 *R.* v. *Johns,* [1996] 1 C.N.L.R. 172 at 181 (Y.T.C.A.).
26 Bankes, "Dispute Resolution Provisions," p. 302.
27 Pirie, "Alternative Dispute Resolution," 29-32.
28 For an introduction to the critiques of ADR, see Pirie, "Alternative Dispute Resolution," 11-14.
29 Leonard Riskin and James Westbrook, *Dispute Resolution and Lawyers* (St. Paul, MN: West Publishing, 1987), 116.
30 John Borrows, "Uncertain Citizens: Aboriginal Peoples and the Supreme Court" (2001) 80 Canadian Bar Review 15.
31 *Ibid.*, 39.
32 Indian and Northern Affairs Canada, "Treaty News" (Winter 2001), Federal Treaty Negotiation Office; <www.ainc-inac.gc.ca>.
33 See James White, "The Pros and Cons of 'Getting to Yes'" (1984) 34 Journal of Legal Education 115.

Conclusion

19
A Separate Peace: Strengthening Shared Justice

John Borrows

As the concluding chapter of this volume, I take up Jeremy Webber's sharp observation as a starting point: "That indigenous dispute settlement should operate, in many ways, ... through its own hybrid procedures, with only partial regard for non-indigenous legal institutions and authority."[1] I take this approach to more forcefully insert the significance of indigenous values into this book's discussion of intercultural dispute resolution. As such, in these remarks I "argue for mechanisms of adjudication and adjustment that take fundamental account of indigenous methods of social ordering" as *the* best means to facilitate the insights contained in the foregoing chapters.[2] Integral to my position is that intercultural dispute resolution in an indigenous context would best thrive through the recognition of separate indigenous justice systems. The independence of indigenous legal systems is, in fact, necessary for healthy intercultural relations. The existence of vibrant, innovative indigenous systems would generate greater contrasts and comparisons concerning appropriate paths to justice. As such, the promotion of multiple indigenous orders would build healthier interactive intercultural regimes.

Without the existence of separate indigenous dispute settlement systems, the range of what is considered "intercultural" in dispute resolution would be severely narrowed. If each group in an intercultural relationship did not have the space to define, interpret, and apply its own culturally appropriate dispute resolution principles, the intercultural aspects of its association would eventually disappear. This would have disastrous consequences for both indigenous peoples and those around them. Indigenous peoples would lose sustained access to normative standards that nourished their societies for generations.[3] Non-indigenous peoples would lose insights held by indigenous dispute resolution systems that could benefit non-indigenous justice systems.[4] Together, both parties would forfeit significant opportunities to build relationships that restrain domination and disrespect. You cannot talk of intercultural dispute resolution without also talking about systems that should exist outside of the shared space.

Indigenous peoples have long possessed normative values to guide their response to disputes. These norms, and the structures they can generate, have not received sufficient protection and preeminence in alternative dispute resolution discussions. Many chapters in this book help to remedy this defect, though the necessity of separate indigenous dispute resolution authority needs to be reinforced. Andrew Pirie reminds us the ADR movement is saturated with ideology that strongly favours integration between peoples.[5] There is nothing wrong with this pursuit, as long as integration does not lead to forced assimilation. Care should be taken that intercultural dispute resolution does not become colonialism's leading edge, erasing cultural difference in the guise of sharing. As Julie Macfarlane observed: "If there were no alternatives to assimilation, or the swallowing up of one culture by the other, there would be no purpose to the intellectual and practical energies that prompted this book."[6]

Separate dispute settlement regimes are necessary to resist assimilative cultural pressures in the world today. Imagine dispute resolution within Canada, and between Canada and the United States, if Canada did not have a separate justice system. Canada would have much less to draw upon in counter-balancing the influence of US culture. The United States would set the stage in processing conflict even more strongly than it does now. Canadian culture and distinctiveness would further wane, if both domestic and intercultural dispute resolution regimes were mere extensions of US institutions. A separate system gives Canada a great advantage in dealing with US-generated cultural conflicts. Canada's alternative dispute resolution system, relative to that of the United States, is necessary for the country's continued cultural development. Indigenous peoples must also be able to implement their own norms within their own systems to resist countervailing cultural influences in intercultural dispute resolution. As Canada's relationship with the United States demonstrates, while a separate system alone does not guarantee cultural survival, its presence can help confine powerful assimilative tides.

To advocate for separate indigenous justice systems, however, is not to deny the vital importance of intercultural dispute resolution. In fact, the existence of separate systems could actually strengthen bonds between cultures.[7] It could also, paradoxically, enhance our own self-understandings. Natalie Oman makes this point in her chapter.[8] She claims that when groups *actively* engage with others who have different cultural orientations, both can experience a "sharing of horizons." This sharing occurs when parties generate a "'language of perspicuous contrast' that develops out of the discourse of members of the participant cultural groups." Drawing on the work of Charles Taylor, she states that such engagements develop a "language in which we could formulate both their way of life and ours as alternative possibilities in relation to some human constants at work."[9] Her thesis is that forced consensus between groups can be reduced if diverse cultures do not casually disregard differences. When domination by one system over the other is reduced, both parties' freedom to follow their cultural practices can be increased. Long-term peace is not assured if one party constantly overwhelms the other because of an absence of formally recognized dispute settlement systems. Forced consensus (which really amounts to duress and coercion) is exacerbated without independent spheres.

The call for separate justice systems, therefore, does not take place at the expense of developing appropriate intercultural dispute resolution. Both activities must proceed together, and can be mutually reinforcing.

Critiques of Separate Indigenous Justice Systems

Unfortunately, there are those who regard the existence of independent indigenous systems as corrosive. They worry about weakening of community ties within nation states if indigenous difference is too strongly promoted. They argue that separate systems could unravel intercultural community connections. Alan Cairns and Thomas Flanagan, in their own ways, have both expressed concern about indigenous difference in relation to civic peace in the larger community.[10] Bryan Schwartz has also argued that separate justice systems have many drawbacks.[11] Despite the force of these arguments, they can be overstated. "It is clearly unhelpful to talk as if there is a zero-sum relationship between minority rights and citizenship; as if every gain in the direction of accommodating diversity comes at the expense of promoting citizenship," as Will Kymlicka and Wayne Norman have written.[12] In fact, "refusal to grant recognition and autonomy to such groups [as Aboriginal peoples] is often likely to provoke even more resentment and hostility from members of national minorities, alienating them further from their identity as citizens of the larger state."[13]

Dual citizenship is not an unknown concept in the world. Indigenous peoples can be citizens of their nation states and not have to relinquish their indigenous citizenship. Yet those who cast doubt on the wisdom of such claims simply see it a different way. The remainder of this chapter examines six objections to separate dispute settlement systems. Schwartz advanced them in an important submission to the Manitoba Justice Inquiry a decade ago.[14] His work, published in the *Manitoba Law Review*, remains one of the clearest statements in the literature cautioning against separate spheres. The issues he raised continue to resonate with those opposed to such systems.[15] Responding to his points provides an excellent opportunity to demonstrate the practice of intercultural dispute resolution. Strong "perspicuous contrast" can be developed because his ideas differ so strongly from those I have heard in indigenous communities. In the

remaining space, alternative readings of Schwartz's arguments will be generated to illustrate that measured separatism need not be detrimental to
this book's call for intercultural harmony. I thus write *both* to persuade
readers of the need for such systems *and* to exemplify an application of
intercultural engagement encouraged in this book.

Concern One: Separatism Leads to Indifference from the Larger Community Instead of Supportive Intervention

Schwartz argued that separatism leads to indifference from the larger community instead of supportive intervention. He wrote, "if Aboriginal justice
systems are detached from the larger network, the consequences will not
be a benign, 'no-strings-attached' support. It will likely be increasing indifference and neglect. Why should voters and politicians care about communities that are not strongly connected to their own?"[16]

Schwartz is correct to note that indigenous separatism can lead to indifference if the parties do not simultaneously cultivate mutual involvement
and concern. His observation deserves serious consideration. Discussions
of separation should not proceed without dialogue also attentive to intercultural structures for dispute resolution. Peace, friendship, and respect
would not be advanced if indigenous peoples became completely detached from those living on their traditional territories in contemporary
nation states.

Yet, despite the force of Schwartz's observation, it has to be asked
whether separatism would, in itself, be *the* reason for indifference and
neglect if Aboriginal peoples revitalized more exclusive systems. As Schwartz
himself wrote: "the interweaving of Aboriginal communities with the
larger community of a province and the nation can be poorly done."[17] In
fact, the interweaving of these communities has been very poorly done. Indigenous peoples have suffered immeasurably because of this failure. The
drive to completely assimilate indigenous peoples has led to indifference
and neglect. Assimilation has been even more damaging than Schwartz's
predictions regarding separate justice systems. Supportive intervention from
the larger community does not always flow from shared systems. One has
to be careful not to equate incorporation with benign assistance. Yet his
point remains: supportive relations are also not likely to automatically
flow from separate dispute settlement systems. They have to be cultivated.

How can deep cultural difference be cultivated while encouraging intercultural negotiation? In the past, commentators often framed this question's answer as an either-or proposition: as if separatism precluded space
for intercultural integration. While the establishment of indigenous systems of dispute resolution could lead away from intercultural sharing, this
does not have to be the case. In this vein, Judge Turpel-Lafond's advice of
a few years ago seems particularly appropriate:

We spent several years in a distracting debate over whether justice reform involves separate justice systems or reforming the mainstream system. This is a false dichotomy and fruitless distinction because it is not an either/or choice. The impetus for change can be better described as getting away from the colonialism and domination of the Canadian criminal justice system. Resisting colonialism means a reclaiming by Aboriginal people of control over the resolution of disputes and jurisdiction over justice, but it is not as simple or as quick as that sounds. Moving in this direction will involve many linkages with the existing criminal justice system and perhaps phased jurisdiction. For example, is there a community with the capacity to take on cases of individuals who have been charged with first-degree murder and are considered criminally insane and violent? These are not problems that Aboriginal people dealt with traditionally and it will take some time before offenders can be streamed into an Aboriginal system (if ever). Communities may not want to or may not be ready to take on these kinds of issues.[18]

While Judge Turpel-Lafond focuses her comments on the criminal justice context, her insight could be applied more generally. Thus, to take her point and answer Schwartz's concern: it does not necessarily follow that the facilitation of exclusive spheres of indigenous dispute resolution leads to indifference and neglect.

Having both separate and shared approaches to dispute resolution can overcome entrenched power dynamics that disadvantage indigenous peoples in the colonial state. As David Kahane wrote earlier in this book, we should "connect justice in the resolution of disputes with resistance to entrenched power dynamics between cultures. This, in turn, requires that we identify asymmetries of power that characterize relations between parties to a dispute, and recognize the extent to which the cultural terms of dispute have previously been shaped by these power relations."[19] Judge Turpel-Lafond's counsel, to get beyond false dichotomies, appropriately focuses our attention on how best to rebalance asymmetrical power. Indigenous peoples can develop intercultural alliances to enjoy the benefits Schwartz cites, while simultaneously deepening their distinctive cultural forms. Such steps can be mutually reinforcing. They can play an important part in overcoming power imbalances indigenous peoples encounter in contemporary dispute resolution processes. If implemented effectively, separatism does not preclude supportive intervention and mutual concern.

Concern Two: Separatism Can Limit the Real and Perceived Right to Participate Fully in the Politics of the Larger Community

Schwartz's second criticism of separatism in indigenous dispute resolution relates to its potential political participatory limits. He states that "Most

Canadians ... want Aboriginal people to be full and accepted participants in the national political system."[20] He observes, "we want Aboriginals to be able to serve as members of Parliament, to be judges in the provincial and federal courts, and to occupy other high positions in the general political system."[21]

In making the above statement Schwartz focuses too narrowly on rigid conceptions of nationalism. Indigenous peoples are not prevented from serving as prime minister or as chief justice on the Supreme Court of Canada just because there are also aspects of their political-legal participation exclusive to their First Nation citizenship.[22] Participation in larger political communities does not have to suffer because indigenous peoples belong to some groups to which others are not a part. For example, people from Quebec are not prevented from participating in Canada because their dispute resolution procedures are based on the Civil Code, while the rest of the country is based on the common law. Navajo people in the United States can run for high political office in that country even though the tribe has its own justice system.

The point I wish to stress is that being an indigenous person (with a political identity, legal entitlements, and normative responsibilities) does not prevent one from possessing other formal identities, entitlements, and responsibilities. Indigenous peoples do not have to relinquish their participation in wider national and international communities just because they have separate dispute resolution systems. Indigenous peoples are traditional, modern, and postmodern. This reality should be reflected in their varied dispute resolution processes. The larger community should recognize this too. Tradition is present within indigenous communities because ancient values inform how they see the world today. It infuses their feasts, songs, ceremonies, stories, and other community events; tradition is manifest in family relations, personal motivations, and material representations. Tradition influences a great deal of indigenous thought and action. It influences conceptions of nationalism. Furthermore, "traditions can change and the potential for growth ... should not be underestimated," as Val Napoleon observes in her chapter.[23] The challenge indigenous peoples face in light of their unfolding traditions (when considering dispute resolution) is in dealing with the strong modernist and postmodernist trends that also permeate their lives.

Schwartz's caution about separate indigenous justice systems fails to take account of these vibrant strands of thought. It is framed in overly modernist terms. He seems to believe that people would only accredit dispute resolution systems that correspond with modernist political organization. Modernism has been the prevailing philosophy in the world, at least for the past one hundred years. People must account for its presence in framing dispute settlement systems. Wars have been fought over its principles. Modernism's drive to create categories and spaces that separate peoples, nations, and so-called "races" from one another has been pervasive. Modernism promotes bright lines and borders. It prefers precise boundaries, crisp margins, and sharp edges to distinguish one group of people from another. Indigenous peoples have not been immune from modernism's influence. In fact, they partially invoke this language whenever they call for separate or exclusive spaces to work out their affairs, as I have done in this chapter. At such junctures indigenous traditions interact with modernism to assert a right to separation and exclusivity.

Drawing on the language of modernism to argue for separate indigenous justice systems is not a problem if one recognizes its limits, and its interface with other ideas. If taken to its extreme, however, modernism can mutate into single-minded nationalism; this would be a problem. Indigenous peoples can fall into this trap. They can try to recreate their worlds in a modernist image, placing primacy on tribal affiliation and identity to the exclusion of traditional and postmodern identities. Of course, indigenous peoples are not the only ones who can fall victim to rigid modernist thinking. Schwartz may have fallen into this trap when he expresses concern about Aboriginal peoples' wider political participation if they establish their own systems. In so stating, he may have overly determined a narrower vision of Canadian nationalism in his discussion. The problem with such a view is that claims to authenticity, purity, or truth often implicit in modernist identities can work to exclude many people. Such line drawing can inappropriately erase people's differences. This problem exists whether one's focus is on indigenous nationalism or Canadian nationalism. Nationalism can harm those who do not fit the space modernism has carved out for them. This can occur in indigenous systems too. However, when modernism is blended with traditional values, its worst features can be moderated, and Schwartz's caution can be affirmed and placed in its proper perspective.

While tradition and modernism exert their pull on indigenous peoples' discussions of dispute resolution, postmodernism also makes its presence felt. The postmodern idea is hard to escape: that everything is subject to overlap, with everyone experiencing layered identities. Postmodernism, in the context of dispute resolution, could therefore insinuate that there is no need for separation, since everything is fluid and can change. Why bother with separate justice systems, the postmodern critic may ask, when any dispute resolution process will partake of intersubjective indeterminacy and flux? Such focus would assert that it would be more productive to focus on intercultural dispute resolution, in recognition of people's overlapping communities and identities.

In response to the postmodern-centred vision of the world, it should first be noted that there is truth to the statement that indigenous peoples are postmodern. Indigenous communities are inflected with influences from a thousand different sources. Individuals are suffused with a wide array of allegiances and identities: indigenous peoples may simultaneously be Anishnabek, Haudenosaunee, English, French, White, Brown, Christian, Jewish, professor, student, employer, employee, Canadian, American, and so on (or any combination thereof). These identities can shift and re-form depending on a person's context.[24] Taken to the extreme, everything could be labelled intercultural within indigenous dispute resolution. Yet misapplication of postmodern influences could lead to arguments for integrated systems of dispute settlement that eschew separation. Taking postmodernism in this way would not accurately reflect indigenous experience and aspirations. Indigenous traditions and modernism moderate the most radical elements of postmodernism's indeterminacy. While it would be wrong to say that tradition and modernism anchor postmodern diffusion, it is true that postmodernism jostles with traditionalism and modernism to form indigenous peoples' approaches to their world.

The blending of these three approaches is significant in answering Schwartz's concern about separatism placing limits on indigenous participation in the wider political community. Remembering the role traditionalism plays in communities allows indigenous dispute resolution to be more attentive to underlying, longstanding normative values. Invoking the influence of modernism in both indigenous and non-indigenous communities would support the real and felt needs for exclusive or separate dispute resolution structures. Acknowledging the insight of postmodern thought would suggest the need to pay greater attention to intercultural engagement in dispute resolution structures. When each factor is accepted as an influence on dispute resolution, Schwartz's second concern, about the potential limits on wider indigenous political participation, can be placed in its proper context. Indigenous peoples are not prevented from participating in the intercultural politics of the larger community, even if they possess separate conflict resolution systems. Separate systems become a barrier to wider participation only if we narrowly focus on modernist conceptions of political ordering and ignore traditional and postmodern influences in our respective societies.

Concern Three: Separatism Does Not Allow for the "Checks and Balances" Effect of Having Different Orders of Government

Schwartz's third concern about separate indigenous justice systems relates to its effectiveness as a governmental choice. His point is that indigenous communities might not be well served if separatism implied unrestrained decision making. He believes that Aboriginal justice systems will work better if they are subject to larger forces of review. He expresses this concern as follows: "Provinces check abuses at the local level; national governments can stem overbearing provincial governments. Conversely, local autonomy helps prevent central governments from being arrogant and insensitive. If Aboriginal communities participate in the life of a larger federation of Aboriginal communities, then some of the necessary, mutually correcting interaction of local and larger government can occur. Still, even a federation of Aboriginal communities in Manitoba would be a 'small world.'"[25]

Schwartz properly identifies checks and balances as an essential concern in indigenous dispute resolution. Experience has shown that people will abuse their authority if they are not accountable to others. Indigenous people are no exception. Effective checks and balances can constrain abuse through mutual oversight and countervailing power. In most contexts this means that one level or branch of government can curtail the other unless they cooperatively work together to cultivate their mutual interests. The idea is that such systems will curb oppression and tyranny because of the veto-like power one branch or level of government has over the other. Given this theory of checks and balances, one should ask whether the existence of separate indigenous justice systems would frustrate or facilitate effective, appropriate checks and balances.

Schwartz argues that exclusive indigenous justice systems might frustrate effective checks and balances because they could become detached from provincial or federal judicial and legislative oversight. One solution to this concern would be to encourage indigenous peoples to design their own system of checks and balances. They could generate culturally appropriate constraints for those exercising dispute settlement authority. For example, indigenous communities could create something akin to a legislative override if decisions of their justice system required review. Canada has taken this route through the inclusion of s.33 in the Canadian Charter of Rights and Freedoms.[26] Centuries earlier, the Haudenosaunee trod a similar path by creating a system of override through adherence to their Great Law of Peace.[27] In fact, there are some who say that the Iroquois system of checks and balances was an inspiration to those who framed the US Constitution, with its system of mutual oversight and review.[28]

Indigenous peoples could also separate their branches of government, if that was their choice. They could allow their councils, chiefs, and dispute resolution bodies to act in tension with each other. They could require joint action by different bodies before certain decisions were taken. Councils could be constrained from acting unless their decisions received approval from their chiefs. Chiefs could be required to obtain the legislative support of councils before they acted. Dispute resolution bodies could be constrained by both chiefs and councils; substantive and procedural limits could be placed on their review-making powers.

The point is that indigenous peoples could facilitate checks and balances through innovation and experimentation when setting up their own justice systems. They could do this in a manner that most appropriately matches their cultural norms. "Conflict resolution systems should be tailored to the needs, capacities, and sensibilities of those they serve, rather than being designed as one-size-fits-all depots," as Michelle LeBaron points out in her chapter.[29] In fact, the introduction of separate justice systems could introduce much needed reform, at least in Canada under the Indian Act. This act created a structure that placed too much power in the hands of the band council – a single government body. A separate dispute settlement system could dissipate the potential for abuse that exists in the Indian Act system. It could do this by spreading decision-making authority more evenly through communities. This conclusion, that a separate justice system could facilitate checks and balances, is somewhat ironic given Schwartz's caution that such systems could frustrate this objective. Yet the fact remains that separate justice systems could check the univocal power of chief and council and create a much higher degree of accountability than the disguised ministerial oversight found in the First Nations Governance Act.

Indigenous peoples could also facilitate checks and balances in their dispute resolution processes by setting up a review system that takes advantage of larger cultural groupings. For example, individual bands might choose to instigate dispute resolution initiatives at the local level, and then institute a wider panel, elders council, or court to consider appeals. Such steps would balance against local authority. This is the route the Metis Settlements followed in creating the Metis Settlements Appeal Tribunal, as Catherine Bell describes in her chapter.[30] It is also the course the Navajo have chosen in their justice system, as Chief Justice Robert Yazzie outlines in his chapter.[31] These few examples demonstrate that indigenous peoples can take appropriate steps to ensure their dispute resolution bodies do not abuse their authority.

However, while such initiatives might partially answer Schwartz's concerns, they do not address how indigenous dispute resolution bodies would interact with provincial or federal structures. His argument stresses benefits to indigenous systems being subject to larger Canadian sources of review. Schwartz is concerned that indigenous peoples will be oppressed if dispute settlement is not subject to these wider forces. In addressing this concern, the foregoing intercultural focus in this book can come into play. Indigenous peoples should not be forced into a subservient position when resolving broader intersocietal conflicts. This insight counsels that the theory underlying checks and balances be taken seriously. For example, *if* indigenous peoples are going to be constrained by provincial or federal governments in their dispute resolution structures, it *also* stands to reason that provincial or federal decision-making structures should be constrained by indigenous systems in order for the checks and balances circle to be complete.

To fully embrace the force of Schwartz's point, intercultural dispute resolution should be designed to give indigenous peoples appropriate checks and balances over the exercise of federal and provincial authority. This power should extend to constrain Cabinet, legislative, or court decisions that adversely affect indigenous peoples. It would be interesting to see Canadian structures restrained by and have to grapple with the Cree concept of *Weche*, as outlined in Elmer Ghostkeeper's chapter.[32] The idea behind *Weche*, with its notion of "a partnership between different belief systems," would be a powerful antidote to the pervasiveness of non-indigenous authority. Adherence to this concept would provide much needed balance if it was institutionally wrapped around the very core of governance in Canada. Intercultural exchange would be rigorous if federal or provincial governments could not act until they took account of this teaching. Intercultural engagement of this type would be consistent with Dale Dewhurst's observation that "Aboriginal justice systems must be designed as authoritative and parallel models of justice."[33] If indigenous peoples possessed real reciprocal authority, they might be less concerned that the Canadian government could check their authority in appropriate circumstances. Anything less in structuring a system of checks and balances would be "prone to fail."[34] Indigenous peoples must have the ability to limit federal or provincial authority for intercultural dispute resolution to succeed. Concepts under the guise of intercultural engagement that do not challenge the domination, fabrication, and racism of the colonial state, as Bruce Duthu observes, "in fact serve to perpetuate them."[35]

Concern Four: The Proper Administration of Justice Requires a Level of Impartiality That Can Be Difficult to Achieve in Small Communities

The fourth concern Schwartz raises in cautioning against separate systems is that, "in a small community, it is fairly easy for one faction to take over, to dominate all aspects of life, to favour its own and discriminate against others."[36] This can be a problem, he says, because "the proper administration of justice requires a level of impartiality that can be difficult to achieve in small communities."[37] It is true that there can be grave dangers concerning real or apprehended bias if dispute resolution is not attentive to problems of nepotism; personalized preferential treatment can be a challenge at any time or place. As Schwartz observes: "If justice is solely administered by the inhabitants of small communities, all of whom know each other, the possibility for personal favouritism and discrimination is high."[38]

It is possible to take account of Schwartz's criticism, however, and still advocate for the separate settlement of disputes, even in small communities. First, it is important to note that partiality and bias can exist even when administering justice in an impersonal, large community. The Supreme Court of Canada has observed that many indigenous people have experienced discrimination and bias even within the large, impersonalized system it administers. In *R. v. Gladue* the court highlighted the justice system's shocking breakdown relative to indigenous peoples in Canada by citing numerous reports and quoting troubling statistics.[39] In this regard Justices Cory and Iacobucci wrote for a majority of the court:

> *The figures are stark and reflect what may fairly be termed a crisis in the Canadian criminal justice system.* The *drastic over representation* of Aboriginal peoples within both the Canadian prison population and the criminal justice system *reveals a sad and pressing social problem* ... The unbalanced ratio of imprisonment for Aboriginal offenders flows from a number of sources, including poverty, substance abuse, lack of education, and the lack of employment opportunities for Aboriginal people. It arises also from bias against Aboriginal people and from an unfortunate institutional approach that is more inclined to refuse bail and to impose more and longer prison terms for Aboriginal offenders.[40]

The court's statement demonstrates that one should not expect bias and discrimination to automatically dissipate just because dispute resolution is administered in larger communities.

Of course, pervasive bias in the larger system should not prevent one from addressing the possibility of discrimination occurring when smaller communities engage in dispute resolution. Yet at one level this is a more difficult task than it immediately appears. The challenge flows from the fact that each culture may have unique procedures for constraining prejudice and unhealthy predisposition. Impersonalized distance and disengaged decision makers may not actually serve all communities very well. Acknowledging this dimension of indigenous dispute resolution raises deeper issues about the nature of fact-finding and judgment that lie behind Schwartz's concern about impartiality. Each small community that administers justice will need to reflect on whether their modes of dispute resolution inappropriately favour certain groups at the expense of others: for example, men over women, elderly over the young, large over smaller families, the politically well connected over the disenfranchised and those on the margins, the powerful over the powerless (or any combination thereof). This is not an idle or unfounded concern. Some initiatives have been discredited because issues of personal advantage or institutional abuse have come to light.[41]

In one respect, the issues addressed in the last section help address this concern. Checks and balances can be designed within indigenous communities to diffuse power and reduce bias. Furthermore, checks and balances can be created between indigenous communities and surrounding nation states to ensure that local factionalism does not create injustice. Engaging these insights is more likely to overcome the challenge of justice in small communities than an over reliance on technocratic, third-party decision makers. In fact, Larissa Behrendt highlights the special problem of mediation models relying on so-called neutral third parties in indigenous communities. She writes: "Getting over the hurdle of giving a stranger, an outsider, the power to facilitate the dispute resolution is not something addressed within the mediation model."[42] The use of people known to the parties is an important part of many indigenous dispute settlement systems. As many administrative law regimes demonstrate, there are great advantages in having people with specialized knowledge and experience administer settlements. Justice Yazzie makes a similar point when discussing the qualification and appointment in Navajo communities.[43] Despite the challenges this vision of justice presents to dominant systems, indigenous peoples can practice dispute resolution in small communities while acting on Schwartz's more general point. Dispute resolution can be successful in small groups if the chosen method "fits" with their cultural norms, protects vulnerable people and groups, and provides effective checks and balances.

Concern Five: A Separate System of Aboriginal Justice Would Too Greatly Depart from the Principle of Equality for All Canadians

Schwartz's fifth concern about indigenous peoples operating separate justice systems raises equality issues. He rightly observes that many in the larger state worry that the creation of a separate indigenous system would be too great a departure from the principle of nationwide equality. One might counter, however, that every Western nation's dispute resolution system currently departs from the principle of equality for all its citizens. For example, in the Canadian context, the Supreme Court of Canada observed: "By 1997, Aboriginal peoples constituted closer to 3 percent of the population of Canada and amounted to 12 percent of all federal inmates. The situation continues to be particularly worrisome ... in Saskatchewan, where they made up 72 percent of [provincial correctional] admissions."[44]

A study reviewing admissions to Saskatchewan's correctional system in 1976-77 appropriately titled *Locking Up Indians in Saskatchewan*, contains findings that should shock the conscience of everyone in Canada. In comparison to male non-natives, male treaty Indians were 25 times more likely to be admitted to a provincial correctional centre while non-status Indians or Metis were 8 times more likely to be admitted. If only the population over fifteen years of age is considered (the population eligible to be admitted to provincial correctional centres in Saskatchewan), then male treaty Indians were 37 times more likely to be admitted, while male non-status Indians were 12 times more likely to be admitted. For women the figures are even more extreme: a treaty Indian woman was 131 times more likely to be admitted and a non-status or Metis woman 28 times more likely than a non-native.

The Saskatchewan study brings home the implications of its findings by indicating that a treaty Indian boy turning 16 in 1976 had a 70% chance of at least one stay in prison by the age of 25 (that age range being the one with the highest risk of imprisonment). The corresponding figure for non-status or Metis was 34%. For a non-native Saskatchewan boy the figure was 8%. *Put another way, this means that in Saskatchewan, prison has become for young native men, the promise of a just society which high school and college represent for the rest of us. Placed in an historical context, the prison has become for many young native people the contemporary equivalent of what the Indian residential school represented for their parents.* [Emphasis added by the court.][45]

The argument that separate indigenous settlement systems would depart from the principle of equality for all is somewhat disingenuous when one considers the facts on the ground. There is already a shocking departure from the principle of equality in the way indigenous peoples are represented in current systems. Sad statistics, and the reality they represent, do not reveal a high level of intercultural engagement under the guise of equality in Canada. Yet this response, while dispositive of Schwartz's concern at a pragmatic level, does not address his deeper philosophical objections. To capture his normative argument, Schwartz writes: "Perhaps Canadians rightly expect that a reasonable measure of political and legal equality is maintained among citizens. When the stakes are high, as when for example a serious criminal offence is alleged, the ideal should be that an accused will not be treated any more harshly or leniently on account of his ethnic origin. Nor should the group affiliation of the victim or the place where the offence occurred diminish the demands of equal justice."[46]

"There must be one law for all" is an important principle for many in Western legal systems.[47] Critics of separate Indigenous systems worry that the recognition and affirmation of difference departs from this standard.[48] They raise questions about legal consistency and uniformity in the country under such systems. The idea that indigenous peoples could receive differential treatment in their legal dealings is regarded as inimical to proper government. Such feelings are often motivated by concerns relating to race-based entitlements,[49] fairness,[50] certainty,[51] political stability,[52] cost,[53] citizenship,[54] and the territorial integrity and sovereignty of the country.[55] The theme underlying these sentiments is that the application of different standards by or for indigenous peoples is contrary to fundamental principles of political and legal order. A.V. Dicey, an English constitutional lawyer, is frequently cited in support of this view: "We mean ... when we speak of the rule of law ... that every man, whatever his rank or condition, is subject to the ordinary law of the realm and amendable to the jurisdiction of ordinary tribunals."[56]

However, implementing separate justice systems does not necessarily imply a departure from the principle of one law for all. Despite many historic failures in applying differential treatment to people (indigenous, Black, Chinese, Japanese, French Canadian, women, and so on), courts have held that the affirmation of difference does not necessarily lead to inequality and unfairness. People should not be made unequal by applying "the same" standards to them in every case. The classic example of this danger arises when the application of so-called equal standards prejudices the ability of members of a group to participate because of their personal characteristics. For example, subjecting all police officers to an employment requirement that they be over a certain height, when that criteria is set by taking the average height of a man, may be discriminatory when applied to women who tend on average to be shorter.

The recognition of difference can be necessary to achieve equality. In the Canadian case of *Law* v. *Canada (Minister of Employment and Immigration)*,[57] Justice Iacobucci observed: "True equality does not necessarily result from identical treatment. Formal distinctions in treatment will be necessary in some contexts in order to accommodate the differences between individuals and thus to produce equal treatment in a substantive sense. Correspondingly, a law which applies uniformly to all may still violate a claimant's equality rights."[58] Just because a person is subject to differential treatment does not always mean he or she has been denied equal benefit and protection of the law. As Justice Iacobucci observed, the fairness of differential treatment will always be a contextualized determination that depends on the right at issue, the person's socioeconomic status, and that of comparative groups. Applying these principles to the implementation of separate justice systems, one could also argue that differential treatment of indigenous and non-indigenous peoples does not always raise concerns about inequality, fairness, certainty, and so forth.

In further considering critiques that separate justice systems depart from the standard of one law, we should take into account the fact that Canada, Australia, and the United States are federal systems. Many different legal standards apply with these countries as a result. In Canada, for instance, there are ten provinces, three territories, and one central government that create and enforce a variety of different legal rules. Some of these laws even contradict one another. For example, some provinces permit state-funded denominational schools, while others prohibit them. Some provinces are obligated to fund religious schools through constitutional obligation, while others have no such constraint. That Canada has different, sometimes contradictory, laws passed by diverse legal regimes does not bring the legal system into disrepute. In fact, the respect the system enjoys is heightened because the passage of different laws demonstrates a much needed ability to respond to local circumstances. It is usually applauded that provincial governments can each pass different regulations under identical federal law (when given the responsibility to administer such statutes), because it allows legislators to be sensitive to matters of a purely local nature.

Few would suggest that provincial, state, or regional variation is a departure from the principle of one law for all. Indeed, the multiplicity of legal responses within federal legal systems is unified by the fact that each must be consistent with the Constitution to be valid. When one remembers that indigenous difference in Canada finds its recognition in the same constitutional regime that supports this federal structure, one appreciates that separate justice systems would be no more a departure from principles of fairness and equality than the implementation of other laws in Canada's federation.[59]

Finally, one might even consider that, aside from pre-existing indigenous laws, some countries have laws operating on their soil that do not emanate from central, state, or provincial governments. For example, Canada gives effect to many different legal regimes within its territory that do not originate in their territory.[60] For instance, there are extra-territorial applications of criminal law. Many countries have statutes that allow them to prosecute their citizens for crimes committed in another country.[61] Canada has accepted this principle.[62] Canada also recognizes the principle that tax obligations can be incurred to another country, even if one is working in Canada, depending on the laws of one's country of citizenship.[63] In addition, diplomats possess immunity from the operation of domestic law, and the idea that countries can enjoy sovereign immunity is not an unfamiliar concept. Similarly, admiralty law and military law each contemplate extra-territorial application for their effective operation.[64]

The point of these examples is to show that the idea that Canadians live under one law is an overly simplistic view of how legal regimes interact within the country. The argument that there should be one law for all does not communicate the multiplicity of laws necessary to the functioning of any society. While it is appropriate to uphold the idea that a country's laws should be harmonized, balanced, integrated, and unified, it is inappropriate to hold that law should be undifferentiated. In this light it would be wrong to argue that exactly the same legal principles should apply to everyone in the same way. The existence of local, regional, provincial, and indigenous regimes are better explained and protected by the realization that differential treatment might be the best mechanism for everyone living together under one law.[65] Separate indigenous dispute settlement regimes can exist in a country and not depart from the principles of equality for all.

Concern Six: Separate or Privileged Treatment for Aboriginal Offenders Would Make Less Visible a Symptom of Underlying Social and Political Disorder Rather than Dealing with Its Causes

In a final point disputing the creation of separate dispute settlement systems, Schwartz argues that "separate or privileged treatment for Aboriginal offenders would make less visible a symptom of underlying social and political disorder rather than dealing with its causes."[66] In this vein, he writes: "The number of Aboriginal persons accused of crimes and incarcerated in the system is an expense and an embarrassment to the larger system. Hiving off Aboriginal people in a special system might reduce the 'public relations' embarrassment to the general community and ease consciences, but it would do little to address the underlying social and political causes. By making the problem less visible and expensive or by creating an impression that 'something has been done,' it might even discourage responsible conduct by politicians."[67]

Schwartz wants his readers to address the underlying causes of social and political disorder in designing dispute resolution systems. Yet it is difficult to discern how he would distinguish symptoms of disorder from their causes. The answer to this question requires judgments about human nature; it involves conclusions about how society can best organize to facilitate human flourishing. Who knows the difference between a cause and a symptom in remedying socio-political problems? Unfortunately, there are no neutral third-party perspectives from which to answer this question. Some theoreticians, ideologues, or empiricists act as if they have such answers, but their claims are subject to cross-cutting debate and disagreement. "What is the good life?" and "How is it achieved?" are issues that have occupied and divided people from earliest times.

Classical liberal responses dealing with underlying socio-political issues would emphasize freedom of individual choice, property rights, free trade, and the enjoyment of civil and political liberties against governmental intervention. Great faith is placed in these approaches in Canada, Australia, New Zealand, and the United States, countries studied in this book. Strong arguments can be made to support these suppositions; there is much wisdom in such remedies. Alternatively, communitarians would place greater emphasis on societal responsibility in overcoming social breakdown and disorder. Those favouring this approach would justify governmental intervention in various ways. Social assistance, affirmative action, redistribution of wealth, and the creation of socioeconomic rights may be within the catalogue of approaches taken by communitarians. One could also find a great measure of wisdom within these prescriptions. And this would not end the debate. Numerous other theories and approaches could be multiplied in trying to distinguish causes from symptoms of societal disorder.

It is not easy to know how to proceed when faced with differing theories about the causes of societal disorder. One could attempt to justify following this or that particular theory based on one's own research, view, or knowledge of the world – and then try to impose such views on others. This would not be helpful. Forced compliance is the cause of much disorder in the world. Alternatively, one could attempt to convince others of the wisdom of a particular point of view. This approach is messier and also contributes to disorder, but is much more respectful of human agency and choice. Because we are not likely to find widespread consensus on how to best resolve disputes over questions of underlying socioeconomic progress, we need intercultural negotiation and dispute resolution. Intersocietal persuasion fosters individual dignity and social tolerance; it is at the heart of civil societies. To avoid imposing one vision of society on indigenous peoples over another, intercultural dispute resolution provides a better path forward. While indigenous peoples should have the primary right and responsibility to respond to questions about the causes of disorder within their own communities, they cannot avoid engagement with others in this world (especially when others may be part of the problem and solution). Enabling indigenous peoples to examine fundamental questions both within their own normative frameworks *and* in shared intercultural spaces would keep visible indigenous issues in various societies. It would draw more people into problem solving than do centralized systems currently in operation. The creation of separate regimes, if employed in the way described in this chapter, would not conceal indigenous problems, as Schwartz fears. Rather, it could heighten people's engagement with indigenous issues.

Conclusion

Anishnabek philosopher Dale Turner observed that "if Aboriginal peoples are to gain recognition of their rights in their most robust form, we must generate explanations that make sense to people who possess power to enforce them, but we must do so guided by our own intellectual traditions."[68] This chapter has argued that intercultural dispute resolution is best facilitated through separate systems because they most strongly promote answers to questions guided by indigenous traditions. I have tried to show how this approach has advantages for indigenous peoples and for those with whom they interact, despite numerous objections. I have also tried to demonstrate how a sharing of horizons can generate alternatives to the "human constants at work" in relationships. If indigenous peoples are to avoid being swallowed up in their intercultural interactions, they must set aside intellectual space to interpret and apply their own normative values. Strengthening a commitment to shared justice is best advanced through indigenous and non-indigenous peoples creating a separate peace.

Notes

1 Jeremy Webber, "Commentary: Indigenous Dispute Settlement, Self-Governance, and the Second Generation of Indigenous Rights," Chapter 9, this volume, p. 153.
2 *Ibid.*
3 In this volume Dale Turner speaks of the necessity of indigenous intellectuals sustaining contemporary understandings of traditional normative orders; see Dale Turner, "Perceiving the World Differently," Chapter 3, this volume.
4 For a discussion of lessons that have been learned from indigenous peoples by the wider system, see Diane Lowe and Jonathan Davidson, "What's Old Is New Again: Aboriginal Justice Dispute Resolution and the Civil Justice System," Chapter 16, this volume.
5 Andrew Pirie, "Commentary: Intercultural Dispute Resolution Initiatives Across Canada," Chapter 18, this volume, p. 335.
6 Julie Macfarlane, "Commentary: When Cultures Collide," Chapter 5, this volume, p. 99.
7 John Borrows, "Uncertain Citizens: The Supreme Court and Aboriginal Peoples" (2001) 80 Canadian Bar Review 15.
8 Natalie Oman, "Paths to Intercultural Understanding: Feasting, Shared Horizons, and Unforced Consensus," Chapter 4, this volume, p. 81.
9 *Ibid.*, citing Charles Taylor, "Understanding and Ethnocentricity," in *Philosophy and the Human Sciences*, vol. 2 of *Philosophical Papers* (Cambridge, UK: Cambridge University Press, 1985), 125.
10 Thomas Flanagan, *First Nations, Second Thoughts?* (Montreal: McGill-Queen's University Press, 2000); Alan Cairns, *Citizens Plus* (Vancouver: UBC Press, 2000).
11 Bryan Schwartz, *First Principles, Second Thoughts: Aboriginal Peoples, Constitutional Reform and Canadian Statecraft* (Montreal: Institute for Research on Public Policy, 1986); Bryan Schwartz, "A Separate Aboriginal Justice System?" (1990) 28 Manitoba Law Journal 77-91.
12 Will Kymlicka and Wayne Norman, eds., *Citizenship in Diverse Societies* (New York: Oxford University Press, 2000), 39.
13 *Ibid.*, 40.
14 The Manitoba Justice Inquiry remains one of the most comprehensive reports concerning the operation of the courts and the Canadian "justice" system in the lives of indigenous peoples in Canada.
15 The editorial pages of the *National Post* newspaper in Canada frequently repeat similar objections.
16 Schwartz, "A Separate Aboriginal Justice System?," 79.
17 *Ibid.*, 78.
18 Mary Ellen Turpel, "Reflections on Thinking about Criminal Justice Reform" in Richard Gosse, James Youngblood Henderson, and Roger Carter, eds., *Continuing Poundmaker and Riel's Quest* (Saskatoon, SK: Purich Publishing, 1994). See also James (Sakej) Youngblood Henderson, "Implementing Treaty Order," *Continuing Poundmaker and Riel's Quest*; Matthias Leonardy, *First Nations Criminal Jurisdiction in Canada* (Saskatoon, SK: Native Law Centre, 1998); Bruce Wildsmith, "Treaty Responsibilities: A Co-Relational Model" (1992) University of British Columbia Law Review (Special Edition, Aboriginal Justice); Leonard Mandamin, Dennis Callihoo, Albert Angus, Marion Buller, "The Criminal Code and Aboriginal People" (1992) University of British Columbia Law Review (Special Edition, Aboriginal Justice).

19 David Kahane, "What Is Culture? Generalizing about Aboriginal and Newcomer Perspectives," Chapter 2, this volume, p. 38.
20 Schwartz, "A Separate Aboriginal Justice System?," 79.
21 *Ibid.*
22 John Borrows, *Recovering Canada: The Resurgence of Indigenous Law* (Toronto: University of Toronto Press, 2002).
23 Val Napoleon, "Who Gets to Say What Happened? Reconciliation Issues for the Gitxsan," Chapter 11, this volume, p. 190.
24 In fact, Schwartz recognizes the influence of overlapping identities in indigenous communities when he observes: "another fact that should not be overlooked is that an extremely high proportion of persons born on reserves end up living in the cities. Part of the preparation for that life should be contact with the legal and political systems that are exclusively in place in the rest of Canada." Schwartz, "A Separate Aboriginal Justice System?," 79.
25 Schwartz, "A Separate Aboriginal Justice System?," 79-80.
26 Section 33(1) of the *Canadian Charter of Rights and Freedoms* reads: "Parliament or the legislature of a province may expressly declare in an Act of Parliament or of the legislature, as the case may be, that the Act or a provision thereof shall operate notwithstanding a provision included in section 2 or sections 7 to 15 of this *Charter.*"
27 Francis Jennings, *The Ambiguous Iroquois Empire* (New York: W.W. Norton, 1990).
28 Donald A. Grinde Jr., and Bruce E. Johansen, *Exemplar of Liberty: Native America and the Evolution of Democracy* (Los Angeles: American Indian Studies Centre, 1991).
29 Michelle LeBaron, "Learning New Dances: Finding Effective Ways to Address Intercultural Disputes," Chapter 1, this volume, p. 20.
30 Catherine Bell, "Indigenous Dispute Resolution Systems within Non-Indigenous Frameworks: Intercultural Dispute Resolution Initiatives in Canada," Chapter 15, this volume.
31 Robert Yazzie, "Navajo Peacemaking and Intercultural Dispute Resolution," Chapter 6, this volume.
32 Elmer Ghostkeeper, "*Weche* Teachings: Aboriginal Wisdom and Dispute Resolution," Chapter 10, this volume, p. 162.
33 Dale Dewhurst, "Parallel Justice Systems, or a Tale of Two Spiders," Chapter 13, this volume, p. 213.
34 *Ibid.*, p. 213.
35 N. Bruce Duthu, "Commentary: Reconciling Our Memories in Order to Re-Envision Our Future," Chapter 14, this volume, p. 235, quoting Taiaiake Alfred.
36 Schwartz, "A Separate Aboriginal Justice System?," 79.
37 *Ibid.*, 80.
38 *Ibid.*
39 *R. v. Gladue,* [1999] 1 S.C.R. 688.
40 *Ibid.*, paras. 64 and 65, emphasis added.
41 Emma LaRoque, "Re-Examining Culturally Appropriate Models in Criminal Justice Applications," in Michael Asch, ed., *Aboriginal and Treaty Rights in Canada* (Vancouver: UBC Press, 1997), 75.
42 Larissa Behrendt, "Cultural Conflict in Colonial Legal Systems: An Australian Perspective," Chapter 7, this volume, p. 125.
43 Robert Yazzie, "Navajo Peacemaking."
44 Solicitor General of Canada, Consolidated Report, *Towards a Just, Peaceful and Safe Society: The Corrections and Conditional Release Act – Five Years Later* (1998), 142-55.
45 *Gladue,* 58 and 60.
46 Schwartz, "A Separate Aboriginal Justice System?," 80.
47 *R. v. Curley,* [1984] 4 C.N.L.R. 72 at 74 (N.W.T.C.A.). The judge in *Curley* rejected the idea that the Inuit should be judged by their own standards.
48 Melvin Smith, *Our Home and Native Land: What Governments' Aboriginal Policy is Doing to Canada* (Toronto: Stoddart, 1996), 151-52; for a refutation of this argument see *Campbell v. B.C. (A.G.),* [2000] 4 C.N.L.R. 1 (B.C.S.C.).

49 Tom Flanagan, *First Nations? Second Thoughts* (Montreal and Kingston: McGill-Queen's University Press, 2000), 194: "It would establish Aboriginal nations as privileged political communities with membership defined by race and passed on by descent. It would redefine Canada as an association of racial communities rather than a polity of individual human beings."
50 Bryan Schwartz, "A Separate Aboriginal Justice System?," 77-91.
51 Flanagan, *First Nations? Second Thoughts.*
52 Owen Lippert, ed., *Beyond The Nass Valley – National Implications of the Supreme Court's Delgamuukw Decision* (Vancouver: Fraser Institute, 2000).
53 Roslyn Kunin, ed., *Prospering Together: The Economic Impact of Aboriginal Title Settlements in BC*, 2nd ed. (Vancouver: Laurier Institute, 2001).
54 Gordon Gibson, "Comments on the Draft Nisga'a Treaty" (1998-99) 120 BC Studies 55 at 62-69.
55 Geoff Hall, "The Quest for Native Self-Government: The Challenge of Territorial Sovereignty" (1992) 50 University of Toronto Faculty of Law Review 39.
56 A.V. Dicey, *Introduction to the Study of the Law of the Constitution,* 10th ed. (London: Macmillan, 1959), 193.
57 *Law v. Canada (Minister of Employment and Immigration)* [1999] 1 S.C.R. 497.
58 *Ibid.,* 25.
59 Sakej Henderson, "Empowering Treaty Federalism" (1994) Saskatchewan Law Review 251.
60 Geoff Hall, "The Quest for Native Self-Government: The Challenge of Territorial Sovereignty" (1992) University of Toronto Faculty of Law Review 39.
61 *Ibid.,* 45-48.
62 *Libman v. R.,* [1985] 2 S.C.R. 179.
63 Hall, "Quest for Native Self-Government," 48-49.
64 *Ibid.,* 55-60.
65 Patrick Macklem, *Aboriginal Difference and the Constitution* (Toronto: University of Toronto Press, 2001).
66 Schwartz, "A Separate Aboriginal Justice System?," 80.
67 *Ibid.*
68 Turner, "Perceiving the World Differently," Chapter 3, this volume, p. 64.

Contributors

Nigel Bankes
Nigel Bankes is a Professor of Law at the University of Calgary, where he has taught a variety of subjects including property law, natural resources law, oil and gas law, energy law and Aboriginal law.

Larissa Behrendt
Dr. Larissa Behrendt is a member of the Evalayai Nation. She is Professor of Law and Indigenous Studies and Director of the Jumbunna Indigenous House of Learning at the University of Technology, Sydney. She is admitted to practice as a barrister. Her book, *Dispute Resolution in Aboriginal Communities* (1995), was published by The Federation Press.

Catherine Bell
Catherine Bell is a Professor of Law at the University of Alberta specializing in Aboriginal legal issues, property law, community-based legal research, and dispute resolution. She has published widely on First Nation and Metis rights issues and is the author of *Alberta's Metis Settlements Legislation: An Overview of Ownership and Management of Settlement Lands* (Canadian Plains Research Center, 1994) and *Contemporary Metis Justice: The Settlement Way* (Native Law Centre, University of Saskatchewan, 1999). Current research includes a collaborative project with First Nations in British Columbia and Alberta on protection and repatriation of First Nation Cultural Heritage.

John Borrows
Dr. Borrows is Anishnabe, and a member of the Chippewa of the Nawash First Nation. He is Professor and Law Foundation Chair of Aboriginal Justice at the Faculty of Law, University of Victoria, in British Columbia, Canada. His publications include *Recovering Canada: The Resurgence of Indigenous Law* (University of Toronto Press, 2002), and he is co-editor of *Aboriginal Legal Issues: Cases, Materials and Commentary* (Butterworth's, 1998). Professor Borrows is the 2003 recipient of a National Aboriginal Achievement Award in the area of Law and Justice.

Jonathan H. Davidson

Jonathan H. Davidson is originally from Halifax, Nova Scotia. He completed undergraduate degrees in Business and Law at Dalhousie University and received his master's degree in Library and Information Studies from the University of Alberta. He is currently Reference Archivist at the Provincial Archives of Alberta.

Dale Dewhurst

Dale Dewhurst is an academic, mediator, and lawyer. He is currently the Academic Coordinator of Legal Studies at Athabasca University. In addition, he is completing his PhD in Philosophy at the University of Alberta. His research interests include philosophy of law, access to justice, alternative dispute resolution, and the ethics of empowerment and fulfilment.

N. Bruce Duthu

N. Bruce Duthu, a member of the Houma tribe of Louisiana, is an internationally recognized scholar on Native American issues, including tribal sovereignty and federal recognition of First Nations. The courses he has taught at Vermont Law School include Criminal Law, Federal Indian Law, Products Liability, Torts, and Comparative Law of Indigenous Peoples.

Elmer Ghostkeeper

Elmer is an elder of the Paddle Prairie Metis Settlement. He is the past president of the Federation of Metis Settlements and has participated in constitutional and land claims negotiations on behalf of the Metis settlements. He has a master's degree in Anthropology from the University of Alberta and is the author of *Spirit Gifting: The Concept of Spiritual Exchange* (The Arctic Institute of North America, 1996). He is currently the Director of Tripartite Negotiations for the Metis settlements.

David Kahane

David Kahane is an Associate Professor of Philosophy at the University of Alberta, specializing in multiculturalism and democratic deliberation. He has published work in *Canadian Journal of Political Science*, *Journal of Political Philosophy*, *Negotiation Journal*, and *Social Theory and Practice*.

Michelle LeBaron

Michelle LeBaron is Professor of Law and Director of the Program on Dispute Resolution at the University of British Columbia. She teaches and writes about conflict as it relates to culture, personal, and organizational change, spirituality, and creativity. Michelle's most recent books are *Bridging Troubled Waters: Conflict Resolution from the Heart* (Jossey Bass, 2002) and *Bridging Cultural Conflicts: A New Approach for a Changing World* (Jossey Bass, 2003).

Diana Lowe

Diana Lowe is the Executive Director of the Canadian Forum on Civil Justice. The forum is a non-profit, independent organization dedicated to bringing

together the public, the courts, the legal profession, and government to promote a civil justice system that is accessible, effective, fair, and efficient. The
forum was created on the recommendation of the Canadian Bar Association Task
Force on the Systems of Civil Justice to fill the gap in civil justice information
that exists in Canada, and is located at the Faculty of Law, University of
Alberta. More information about the forum can be found at <www.cfcj-fcjc.org>.

Morris Te Whiti Love

Morris Te Whiti Love is the Director of the Waitangi Tribunal in Wellington
New Zealand. The Waitangi Tribunal hears claims from Maori against breaches
of the principles of the Treaty of Waitangi as a result of acts or omissions of the
Crown since 1840. Morris is of the Te Atiawa tribe of Taranaki, Wellington, and
the Queen Charlotte Sounds. He has been a policy manager in the Ministry for
the Environment and worked on the reform of the resource management law
in New Zealand. Morris was also involved in issues related to indigenous rights
in relation to fisheries, geothermal energy, and indigenous forests, to name a
few. Morris has had a particular focus on dispute resolution generally but especially the use of mediation and negotiation in disputes involving indigenous
people.

Julie Macfarlane

Dr. Julie Macfarlane is a tenured half-time Full Professor at the Faculty of Law,
University of Windsor, and Visiting Professor at Osgoode Hall Law School. She
devotes the other half of her time to her consulting practice, which offers
conflict resolution service, training, facilitation, and systems design for a range
of public and private sector clients. Her two most recent books are *Rethinking
Disputes: the Mediation Alternative,* an edited collection of essays on mediation
practice published by Emond Montgomery, Canada, and Cavendish Publishing, UK (1997) and *Dispute Resolution: Readings and Case Studies,* also published
by Emond Montgomery (2nd ed., 2002).

Val Napoleon

Val Napoleon is from northeastern British Columbia and is of Cree-Saulteaux-
Dunne Zah heritage. She is also an adopted member of the Gitanyow (Gitxsan)
house of Luuxhon, Ganeda (Frog) clan. She worked as a community activist
and consultant in northwestern British Columbia for over twenty years, specializing in health, education, and justice issues, and she has served on a number of provincial, regional, and local boards. Val received her LL.B. from the
Faculty of Law, University of Victoria, in April 2001 and completed her articles
with the Victoria law firm Arvay Finlay in October 2002. Val is currently practising law part time and completing interdisciplinary graduate work in law and
history. She began her doctorate in the spring of 2003.

Natalie Oman

Natalie Oman has a doctorate in philosophy from McGill University and conducted research on intercultural negotiation and First Nations self-government
as a postdoctoral fellow at the University of British Columbia's Faculty of Law.
She is currently an adjunct professor and doctoral candidate at Osgoode Hall
Law School.

Richard Overstall

Richard Overstall has a past life as a mining geologist, a sawmill worker, a farm labourer, and a land- and river-use activist. For the past twenty years, he has worked as a lands and resources researcher for Aboriginal peoples in north-western British Columbia, principally the Gitxsan and Wet'suwet'en. For and with them, he has coordinated the non-Aboriginal expert evidence for the trial of the Delgamuukw Aboriginal title case, advised on treaty and consultation negotiations, managed wildlife surveys, produced and researched documentary films, and designed justice and education programs. Richard graduated from the University of Victoria Law School in 2000 and currently practises law in northern British Columbia.

Andrew Pirie

Andrew Pirie is a Professor of Law at the University of Victoria, British Columbia. He was the director of the University of Victoria Institute for Dispute Resolution from 1989 to 1996 and has held leadership positions in other national conflict resolution organizations. Professor Pirie teaches courses on ADR, mediation and negotiation theories and practices, and civil procedure. Andrew is the author of *Alternative Dispute Resolution: Skills, Science, and the Law* (Irwin Law) and several shorter works on ADR.

Dale Turner

Dale Turner is a Teme-Augama Anishnabe from northern Ontario. He is an Assistant Professor of Native American Studies and of Government at Dartmouth College in Hanover, New Hampshire, and publishes on indigenous sovereignty issues and indigenous intellectualism.

Jeremy Webber

Since August 2002, Jeremy Webber has been Professor of Law and holder of the Canada Research Chair in Law and Society at the University of Victoria. He is also Visiting Professor of Law at the University of New South Wales. From 1998 to 2002, he was Professor and Dean of Law at the University of Sydney. He has published extensively on indigenous rights, constitutional law, and legal theory. His work is comparative, with special attention to Australia and Canada. His principal work is *Reimagining Canada: Language, Culture, Community, and the Canadian Constitution* (McGill-Queen's University Press, 1994).

Robert Yazzie

The Honorable Robert Yazzie is the Chief Justice of the Navajo Nation. He is a graduate of Oberlin College of Ohio, and he received the degree of Juris Doctor from the University of New Mexico School of Law in 1982. He presided as a district judge of the Navajo Nation from 1985 through 1992, when he became Chief Justice. He is noted as a leading Indian nation jurist, and for his promotion of traditional Indian law and traditional Navajo justice methods.

Index

272-73; authenticity requirement, 18-19; conflict resolution and, 12, 161; cultural assumptions, 16-17; mechanisms, 44

conflict resolution. *See* alternative dispute resolution; indigenous dispute resolution; intercultural dispute resolution

Constitution Act, 1982, viii-ix, 57, 172, 196

Cornell, Stephen, 235

Cory, Peter, 354

creativity as core competency, 18

Cree sentencing circles, 284-85

Crocker, David A., 186

cultural difference: concepts of governance, 198-99; generalizations institutionalized in dispute resolution, 29, 48-52; intercultural (mis)understandings in ADR, 41-42, 96-99, 333; irreducibility of difference, 80-82, 97-98; liberalism and cultural difference, 29-32, 97; race as identifier, 36-37; relationship to land, 4, 58, 62-63, 64-65; understandings and dispute resolution, 33, 45-47. *See also* indigenous dispute resolution (separate system); intercultural understanding

culture and identity: changing role in ADR, 33-34; "co-formation of cultures," 37; collectivistic approach of First Nations, 15; component of conflict resolution, 13-15, 16, 33-34, 161, 235, 255-56; cultural memberships, 37, 134-35, 171-72, 191; cultural reassertion and self-determination, 152; generalizations and institutionalization, 29, 48-52; "generic multiculturalism," 35-36; multiple cultural group memberships, 34-35; "politics of cultural generalization," 29, 38-40, 44, 46; power and the shaping of cultures, 36-37; variable in dispute resolution, 13-15, 16, 33-34, 161, 235, 255-56; Western understanding of "culture," 164, 173. *See also* indigenous dispute resolution; intercultural dispute resolution

Delgamuukw v. *British Columbia:* impact, 58, 59-60; implementation barriers, 177-78; irreconcilable use limit, 200-1, 211n31; reconciliation process of Gitxsan, 176-78; source of Aboriginal title, 196, 203, 205; Supreme Court conditions, 59-60, 196-97; title test and Nisga'a Final Agreement, 197-98

Dene dispute resolution, 281. *See also*

Sahtu Dene and Metis Comprehensive Land Claim Agreement (SA)

Desjarlais, Lawrence, 172

Devlin, Richard, 78

DEW (distant early warning) sites, 315-19

doctrine of extinguishment, 63, 69n18

dominant culture: determination of Aboriginal rights, 57-58, 60-61, 198-99, 210n17; efficiency and cost-effectiveness valued, 16, 22; neutral adjudication model, 29, 30-31, 33-34, 44, 52, 97-98; privileged in conflict resolution, 33-34, 44, 52, 72, 95, 97-98, 333-34

Draft Declaration of the Rights of Indigenous Peoples 1993 (United Nations), 133

Durie, E., 135

empathy as core competency, 19-20

Erasmus, George, Chief, 61

Erb, Marsha, 251

family group conferencing, 18

Federation of Metis Settlements, 167, 170, 248

First Nations. *See entries beginning with* Aboriginal; *names of specific nations*

Fisheries and Oceans Canada, 207-8

Flanagan, Thomas, 169-70, 345, 363n49

Foster, Sarah J., 108

Frankenberg, Ruth, 36

Fuller, Lon, 199

gatekeepers, 113, 263-64, 265

"generic multiculturalism," 35-36

Getting to Yes (Fisher, Ury, Patton, 1991), 22, 33

Ghostkeeper, Elmer, 39-40

Gibson, Virginia, 14

Gitxsan First Nation: Canadian Statement of Reconciliation (1998), 185; *Delgamuukw* decision, 58, 59-60, 176-78, 196-97, 200-1, 205; difficulties with reconciliation process, 177-78, 192; external reconciliation, 186-87, 196-99; feasting, role of, 82-84, 85, 91nn36-37; Gitxsan Unlocking Aboriginal Justice (UAJ), 190; intercultural understanding model, 74, 82-84, 84-86; internal reconciliation, 188-91; Kitsegukla incident, 70-72; nation-building vs. nation-diminishing, 190-91; Reconciliation Agreement (1998), 177; reconciliation recommendations to government, 191-92;

Norman, Wayne, 345
Noskey, Ken, 50, 248
Nunavut Arbitration Panel, 306
Nunavut Final Agreement (NFA):
appointment of arbitration panel,
301-2, 304-5, 324n35; courts'
involvement, 299-300, 314-15; implementation committee, 302-3, 323n24;
vs. Inuvialuit Agreement, 319-20;
jurisdiction of arbitration panel, 307,
309-11, 312; legal standing of
decisions, 311-12; procedural rules,
312-13; quasi-judicial tribunals, 300-1;
territorial and federal officials' meetings, 303, 323n29
Nunavut justice system, 252-53. *See also*
Nunavut Final Agreement (NFA)

O'Donnel, Judge, 285-86
Oman, Natalie, 46
One Nation Party (Australia), 118
Ontario: mandatory mediation, 290
Overstall, Richard, 43, 180-81

Pearce, Barnett, 101-2
Perdue, William, 199
"perspicuous representation," 73, 75
Picard, Madam Justice, 269
Pocklington, Sarah, 199-200
Pocklington, Tom, 199-200
Poitras, Richard, 172
"politics of cultural generalization," 29,
38-40, 44, 46
Potts, Jim, 233-34

R. v. *Gladue*, 354
R. v. *Hill*, 76
R. v. *Moses*, 283-84
Racial Discrimination Act (Australia,
1975), 119-21
Rawls, John, 73
reconciliation: Aboriginal vs. European
social structure, 180-81; Aboriginal
kinship system, 181, 188-89, 191,
199-200, 282; Australian Council for
Aboriginal Reconciliation, 36-37,
81-84, 185; Canadian Statement of
Reconciliation (1998), 185; definition,
178; different concepts of governance,
198-99; difficulties for Gitxsan (BC),
177-78, 192; external, 186-87, 196-99,
234; future-use, 197, 200-2, 204, 205-6,
212n52; internal issues, 188-91, 197,
199-200; irreconcilable land use limit,
200-2, 204, 211n31; nation-building vs.
nation-diminishing, 190-91; recommendations of Gitxsan to government,

191-92; restorative justive, 179-80; trust
as reconciliation device, 181, 196, 201-7,
234-35. *See also Delgamuukw* v. *British
Columbia*
respect and empathy, 19
Riel, Louis, 170
Rosen, Lawrence, 77
Ross, Rupert, 17-18
Royal Commission on Aboriginal Peoples
(RCAP), ix, 241

Sahtu Dene and Metis Comprehensive
Land Claim Agreement (SA): appointment of arbitration panel, 301-2, 304-5,
324n35; courts' involvement, 299-300,
314-15, 322n11; implementation
committee, 302-3, 323n24; vs.
Inuvialuit Agreement, 319-20; jurisdiction of arbitration panel, 307, 310-
11, 312; legal standing of decisions,
311-12; procedural rules, 312-13;
quasi-judicial tribunals, 300-1
Saskatchewan and mandatory mediation,
290-91
Schwartz, Bryan, 345-60
sentencing circles: in contemporary
system, 283-85, 295n14, 331;
gatekeepers, 113; representation of
women's interests, 20-21, 95, 156;
view of wrongdoing, 18
Simpson, Audra, 65
Sioux Nations, 236
Smith, Susan Tuhiwai, 65
Sorry Day (Australia), 116, 182
South Island Landless Natives Act (New
Zealand, 1906), 130
Spirit Gifting (Ghostkeeper, 1996), 167-68
Stewart, Jane, 185
Stuart, Barry, 283-84
Sugunasiri, Shalin M., 77
Supreme Court of Canada: on fiduciary
power of government, 202. *See also
Delgamuukw* v. *British Columbia*
Sveen, Cathy, 262
symmetrical reciprocity, 78-80
Systems of Civil Justice, Canadian Bar
Association Task Force, 280, 288-89,
292-93, 331-32

Taylor, Charles, 74, 80-82, 83-84, 86, 87
Te Ture Whenua Maori Act (New
Zealand, 1993), 138, 142
terra nullius, 118-21
third parties: core competencies, 17-20;
cultural frames of reference, 13, 22,
24; cultural representation, 47, 126;
cultural sensitivity, 45-47; in Islamic

Printed and bound in Canada by Friesens

Set in Stone by Brenda and Neil West, BN Typographics West

Copy editor: Judy Phillips

Proofreader: Susan Safyan

Indexer: Patricia Buchanan